The Alexander Medvedkin Reader

CINEMA AND MODERNITY

Edited by Tom Gunning

The Alexander Medvedkin Reader

Compiled by Alexander Medvedkin, Jay Leyda, and Nikita Lary

TRANSLATED AND EDITED BY NIKITA LARY AND JAY LEYDA

THE UNIVERSITY OF CHICAGO PRESS
CHICAGO AND LONDON

The University of Chicago Press, Chicago 60637
The University of Chicago Press, Ltd., London

Printed in the United States of America

25 24 23 22 21 20 19 18 17 16   1 2 3 4 5

ISBN-13: 978-0-226-29613-5 (cloth)
ISBN-13: 978-0-226-29627-2 (paper)
ISBN-13: 978-0-226-29630-2 (e-book)
DOI: 10.7208/chicago/9780226296302.001.0001

Library of Congress Cataloging-in-Publication Data

Names: Medvedkin, Alexander, author. | Leyda, Jay, 1910–1988, author, translator. | Lary, N. M., author.
Title: The Alexander Medvedkin reader / compiled by Alexander Medvedkin, Jay Leyda, and Nikita Lary ; translated and edited by Nikita Lary and Jay Leyda.
Other titles: Cinema and modernity.
Description: Chicago ; London : The University of Chicago Press, 2016. | Series: Cinema and modernity
Identifiers: LCCN 2016012020 | ISBN 9780226296135 (cloth : alk. paper) | ISBN 9780226296272 (pbk. : alk. paper) | ISBN 9780226296302 (e-book)
Subjects: LCSH: Medvedkin, Alexander. | Motion pictures—Soviet Union.
Classification: LCC PN1998.3.M433 A44 2016 | DDC 791.4302/33092—dc23 LC record available at http://lccn.loc.gov/2016012020

♾ This paper meets the requirements of ANSI/NISO Z39.48-1992 (Permanence of Paper).

CONTENTS

CVs and Addenda

Remembrance and Revival

PREFACE

"I am a very unusual artist. My whole life was devoted to doing what I alone could do."[1] In this statement Alexander Medvedkin summed up his life's work and struggles. He was a contemporary of the acknowledged pioneering Soviet filmmakers—Eisenstein, Pudovkin, Dovzhenko, Vertov, Esfir Shub, Kuleshov. Born in 1900, he was just two years younger than the youngest of them, Eisenstein. He outlived them all, dying in 1989, before the final collapse of Soviet Communism, in which he retained his fervent belief to the end. In his artistic legacy, he was a victim both of his originality and unorthodoxies and of the authorities in charge of film production and distribution. Much of his contribution to film was lost, suppressed, prevented, and ignored or forgotten. In the writings collected for this book, we see the support given to Medvedkin by Eisenstein and Dovzhenko and the writer Maxim Gorky, and later by the French filmmaker Chris Marker. In an article posthumously published (and transcripts of lectures to students), Eisenstein ("Medvedkin's Chaplinesque Genius" [18])[2] enthusiastically testifies to Medvedkin's originality and importance. When the evidence is considered, Medvedkin takes his rightful place alongside the major Soviet film directors of the first post-Revolutionary generation.

Medvedkin had an outstanding comic talent. The film *Happiness* (1934) is the principal surviving testimony to this talent. Eisenstein compared it to Chaplin's (while specifying the Bolshevik director's distinctive socialistic treatment of his comic hero). He was also an experimentalist interested in transforming the practice of filmmaking. The most notable of his experiments was associated with his Kino-Train project in 1932, during the First Five-Year Plan. With it he took the production of film away from, and outside, the film studios, moving it into a mobile, traveling laboratory, projection room, and living quarters set up in three train cars, ready to be hitched onto a locomotive and moved to locations selected for their critical role in the country's economy in this time of rapid collectivization and industrialization. The film screenings of the Kino-Train took place outside the established distribution networks, with the films being shown, in the first instance, on location to audiences who had participated in their making. These audiences' viewing experience was no ordinary one; there were public discussions after each screening in order to uncover the film's bearing on the viewers' own roles in the workplace and in society, and, correspondingly, the actions they could take to remove production obstacles and deadlocks. These viewers were engaged as participants and agents before, during, and after the making of the film. With regard to an earlier film, *On Patrol* (1927), Medvedkin said that "the viewer was on an equal footing with the author" inasmuch as the viewer was invited to propose solutions to problems of military strategy presented in the film. This was an interactive training exercise. In the Kino-Train project, filmmaking and viewing now had even more direct practical consequences: "The screenings would turn into production meetings." The films found further use in other locations where industrial workers, collective farmers, and miners faced analogous problems.

Medvedkin's revolutionary practice in film went beyond that of his major contemporaries. Although they were transforming the subject matter and the language of film, they were still working in studios or out of studios in major centers, and screening their films in movie theaters, workers clubs, and whatever facilities existed in villages. True, the studios were also undergoing transformations to ensure that they met the needs of the emerging Communist society; they were no longer private or joint-stock companies, and new internal committees and bureaucracies and overseeing bodies participated in artistic decisions and spoke for government policy. Challengingly, Medvedkin's Kino-Train was a demonstration that filmmaking could be transformed from outside the dominant structures, as opposed to within them. His filmmaking practice was "unusual," and even subversive.

There had been precedents for some aspects of filmmaking in the Kino-Train. The agit-trains in the immediate post-Revolutionary years brought films, plays, pamphlets, and posters from the towns to soldiers engaged in the Civil War and to civilians, in order to educate them about the new, post-October world and its challenges. Some of the agit-trains gathered documentary film material, which was brought back and edited in the studios (Vertov's Kino-Eye films). But Medvedkin was concerned to stress the difference between his Kino-Train and the agit-trains: "The agit-trains had music—a gramophone, a singer, and folk instruments; they had a ready-made program, and were not concerned with local life." In contrast, Medvedkin's Kino-Train films were concerned with critical problems of local life—in factories and mines and on newly collectivized farms. There was another partial precedent for his practice in the small, temporary film studios set up to record work on some of the country's major projects. These were removed from the major studios, but they were not mobile in the way the Kino-Train was, nor was their primary audience the workers involved in the projects and in the making of the films. In Medvedkin's summation, "Nobody had mastered film as deeply and productively as our Kino-Train." The contrast with Dziga Vertov's films is instructive. Vertov's Kino-Eye offers a director's revolutionary way of seeing and visually constructing a world in transformation. In the first instance this revolutionary seeing is confined to the screen; its transformative effect on the world remains contingent. Medvedkin invented a distinctive form of engagé investigative documentary cinema, with its own place in the history of world film.

Medvedkin found his way to film from his experiences in the hard-fought Civil War that followed the October Revolution. He had been a fighter in the 1st Cavalry Army commanded by Semen Budenny, and there he also engaged in theatrical work aimed at bolstering the morale of his comrades-in-arms. His theatrical pieces helped the cavalrymen to laugh at the hardships of their everyday life, and at the same time educated them about the goals they were fighting for. Medvedkin was sensitive to the need to adapt this educational work to the men's "wishes and interests."[3] He soon found that satire offered a productive way of combining his twin purposes of entertainment and education. His frontline theater proved to be both "an invaluable laboratory of comic art" and a great preparation for his subsequent work in film.

Medvedkin was a militant believer in the Communist, Bolshevik revolution. He carried his militancy with him from the frontlines of the Civil War to those of the First Five-Year Plan. In his trips or "sorties" on his Kino-Train in 1932 to the battlefields of industrialization, mine-works, and collectivization, he had a new weapon of attack—filmmaking, or rather filmmaking revolutionized and, moreover, taken to the limits of what was technically and humanly possible, so that in the space of three days he and his team would research a situation and write a script based on it; shoot, process, and edit a film; and last, screen it and hold public discussions of it. "The Kino-Train: 294 Days on Wheels" [2] is a firsthand account of this experiment. In terms of speed, what Medvedkin did is comparable to what is now readily done with digital cameras and computer editing. One great advantage he had was that he had an assured audience in a way that a filmmaker working outside the principal distribution systems and venues today cannot often hope to have, and what is more, an audience of actively involved viewers and "actors."

Acknowledgment of Medvedkin's role in the history of Soviet film was long withheld. In part, this was precisely because he was working outside the established system and norms of Soviet film production. Authorities were suspicious of the Kino-Train films, which could not be vetted before and after production.[4] As these films were, in the first instance, specific and local in use and intent, they could also easily escape notice and disappear. Jay Leyda, who was in Moscow in 1933–36, saw a few of these films (as well as the just-made satirical comedy *Happiness*), and referred to them in his history of Soviet film, *Kino*. But it is only in recent years that a number of the Kino-Train films have been rediscovered.[5]

Another reason that Medvedkin's place in Soviet film was marginalized had to do with his "unusual" preferred genre, satire. He found it an effective tool for educating his audiences and ridiculing abuses, corruption, and ignorance. What he could not prevent was that, even in the hands of a true believer, satire was prone to ambiguity. It was subversive. In our conversations about this book, Medvedkin said that the film *Happiness* "drives a stake into the peasant's dream of attaining a kulak's prosperity. That is a solution for just 1 percent. The kulak dream is mocked." It is satirized. But for many viewers the central character of this film, Khmyr, who fails in his attempt to lead a rich peasant's life, is more plausible as an incompetent and a misfit in any social order than as the reliable member of a collective farm he is meant to become. For authorities in the thirties, Khmyr and his precursors in the Kino-Train films were a troubling reminder of the widespread reluctance of peasants to hand over their livestock and landholdings, however meager, to collective farms. Poor peasants were not the stereotypical class enemy. And not all workers were suited for a collectively organized workforce.

In discussions with Stalin in 1934, Boris Shumiatsky, the man with major responsibility for the Soviet film industry, said that filmmakers were afraid of the comic genre because of the possibility of satire in it.[6] Shumiatsky was no doubt including himself among the fearful and distrustful film workers. It is a fact that Medvedkin's major completed satiric film, *Happiness*, saw limited distribution following its release in 1935, and was suppressed in 1937. The original negative disappeared, as did the positive copies with a color sequence (see the note "The Suppression of *Happiness*" [24]). The film did not surface again until its screening at the Moscow Film Festival in 1959.[7] In the early sixties it was seen by Chris Marker at the Brussels Cinemathèque; struck by its originality, he did what he could to assure its recognition as a major cinematic achievement.[8]

Medvedkin's exploration of comic satire met with an untimely end. His major project, the film to which he wished to devote himself after *Happi-*

ness, was "The Unholy Force" [12]. Its scope was ambitious—an exploration of the unhappy lot of the Russian peasantry. It was a satirical attack on the old, pre-Revolutionary social order and on the still-potent forces of religion, but it also suggested that the Russian peasant might always be, by nature, a rebel, for whom there could be no ideal society. The film was stopped by Shumiatsky himself in 1935, on the eve of the day shooting was set to begin. Medvedkin's creative efforts for many years after this were largely devoted to multiple revisions of the script in a continuing attempt to get approval to make the film.

During the years devoted to "The Unholy Force," Medvedkin made other films—two comedies in particular, *The Miracle Worker* (1936) and *New Moscow* (1938), and many documentaries. But he speaks dismissively of much of this other work, or passes over it. He had a "passion for satire"; ordinary film comedies were "fundamentally alien to me."[9] He does give special attention to one experimental documentary project he undertook during World War II ("Soldiers Shooting Films" [3]). Medvedkin's "Second 'Autobiography'" [22] suggests that he turned to his other documentary work after 1949 as a substitute for the work he really wanted to do, while the fairly descriptive summaries he gives of the films—on topics such as colonialism, the arms race, militarism, and ecological crises—indicate that for him the films were a continuing contribution to the building of socialism. They also tantalizingly suggest that these films challenge mainstream "Western" perspectives on these topics. Nonetheless, throughout this period, the unmade film "The Unholy Force" remained his major preoccupation, and, with his continued work on the script, this literary work was a major outlet for his creativity.

Medvedkin's literary talent was indeed considerable. In it he was much influenced by the Russian satirical writer Saltykov-Shchedrin. His ear was attuned to the pithy, graphic sayings of the people. He liked to quote them and also to develop them as metaphors informing his plots. He knew well, too, the chants of the Russian Orthodox church services,[10] and remembered the beauty and power of their language, and was not afraid to draw on this vocal and choral tradition, even though he mocked the dogmas underlying it. In "The Unholy Force," with its epic struggle waged by peasants against the forces of Heaven and Hell, he was also influenced by fairy tales, folk legends, and the graphic art of traditional woodblock cartoons. Stylistically. the film might have been a major development of the distinctive caricatural realism he developed in *Happiness*.

There is a fundamental paradox in Medvedkin's satirical position. Satire was, as he ruefully remembered, "a double-edged sword." He sought to limit its implications and to remain faithful to Communist ideals. It was easy to attack narrow-minded blockheads and officials who abused their positions. But he did not wish to generalize the attack and, in so doing, imply that certain power structures invited abuse or, alternatively, that human nature was impervious to social engineering. Possibly he was even blind to the suggestions and implications of his satires, maybe deliberately blind. He had been a revolutionary fighting for Bolshevik Communism, and he never allowed himself to question what Communism became. It is strange that his outings on the Kino-Train took him to places, such as eastern Ukraine, where mass starvation was resulting from the drive to collectivize agriculture, and yet the evidence of hunger never enters into his field of vision (not all of his peasants are sound and robust, but the emaciation of a Khmyr in *Happiness* is no more than an aspect of his characterization).

Other silences appear in his writings. The picture of the Civil War that Medvedkin gives in "Cavalry Days" [1] comes from the perspective of a strong, healthy young man who enjoyed the rigors and comradeship of army life. It is centered on his discovery of himself as an artist and on the role art could play in the life of the Revolutionary army. Little in this account points to the ruthlessness and brutality of the war that are so striking in the *Red Army* tales of Isaak Babel, who, interestingly, fought in the same 1st Cavalry Army as Medvedkin. A particularly glaring omission in the writings has to be any mention of the Terror. A side effect, such as the years of low film production, warrants a mention in his "Second 'Autobiography'" [22], but not the Terror as such. Medvedkin was of course aware of it, and he did barely allude to it in filmed interviews with Marina Goldovskaia [23] made in the last months of his life. As for Stalin himself, it is possible that Medvedkin accepted that Stalin was or had to be above and beyond human criteria and judgment, as Nikolai Izvolov suggests in his reading of the treatment of the supreme, all-powerful leader in his appearance at the end of the film *The Miracle Worker* (see "Alexander Medvedkin and the Traditions of Russian Film" [20]).

Medvedkin's autobiographical writings indicate that he was happier to attribute his difficulties in film to wreckers and opportunistic bureaucrats than to a system and leader that had a restrictive view of the kind of art that was necessary and appropriate. The opportunists and intriguers certainly existed, but it is also true that Socialist Realism had become entrenched in film by the time he was seeking approval to shoot the satirical "Unholy Force," with its ambiguities and defiance of now-entrenched conventions.

Stylistically his explorations had taken him very far away from the naturalistic realism that lay at the base of Socialist Realism. He had a great gift for visually and dramatically caricaturing social types; and often they even have the freedom of movement of characters in cartoons. In 1933 Medvedkin wrote that "hyperbole" was his basic method of transforming material in *Happiness*: "In taking material from folklore, the film turns it into a realistic conception by means of hyperbole."[11] In effect, he was advocating a form of "hyperbolic realism."

There are, not surprisingly, parallels and precedents for Medvedkin's comic turns and imagination—in the film work of Mack Sennett, Charlie Chaplin, Fatty Arbuckle, and others. But Medvedkin was a highly original artist, in the perhaps perverse sense that he sometimes had to make his own discoveries for himself, alone or in collaboration with his actors. Medvedkin did not necessarily need the example of American (Canadian, English) directors and actors to come to his own findings; moreover, his comic turns and theirs often had a common source in older forms of popular entertainment, such as burlesque clowning, variety shows, and the circus. In the context of Russian cultural politics, however, there is a significant connection to be made between the use Medvedkin made of the lesser, popular theatrical forms and the use made of them by the great theatrical director Meyerhold. Medvedkin's Civil War plays for cavalrymen and his later film work drew on the circus, fairground attractions, street theater, mime, and masks in his quest to cross the barrier between the stage and the audience in order to engage the imagination of his viewers. These lesser theatrical forms were also major sources of inspiration for Meyerhold in his radically revolutionary stagings of Russian classics (and of plays by his contemporary, Maiakovsky). Running through Medvedkin's writings on his cavalry days and on the Kino-Train [1, 2] is a quiet subtext acknowledging his affinity for the inspiration and strivings of the great leftist director. Meyerhold's free vision and ambitions led to his execution; Medvedkin survived, while enduring a slow artistic death, which he likened to a drawn-out "Golgotha," with its implications of a way of sorrows and a crucifixion.

The idea for a book collecting Medvedkin's film writings originated with Jay Leyda. The book would bear witness to a life in film that had been forgotten, suppressed, marginalized, and truncated. Medvedkin was naturally excited by this prospect. The material for the book existed in his archive of scripts and autobiographical and critical writings written over the years. He actively cooperated in assembling the material for the book. In its final form, the Medvedkin book does not correspond in all respects to the book agreed upon by Leyda and Medvedkin; certain omissions and changes were necessary for reasons given below, in the "History of *The Alexander Medvedkin Reader*" [28]. Despite the omissions, this book provides rich testimony, direct and indirect, to the talent and inventiveness of a great and revolutionary filmmaker.

Nikita Lary

NOTE ON TRANSLITERATION

The Modified Library of Congress system is used for transliteration in the text, with simplifications (the general elimination of the soft sign in proper names) and variations (the use of accepted English spellings for certain names—e.g., Alexander, Eisenstein, Meyerhold). The *-ii* ending of first names has been changed to *-i*; the *-ii* or *-yi* ending of surnames has been changed to *-y*.

On the Front Lines of War and Revolution

I Cavalry Days[1]

I set out on the fatal road of satire as far back as 1920, not suspecting that this was my direct road to Golgotha.

I've taken many knocks over the past fifty years! Critics and authorities beat me unsparingly and drove me to tears. I would shrug, while cursing the fatal inclination taking me down untrodden paths. At times I swore to lead a normal life, such as all my clever comrades led . . .

And then . . . Everything would start up again, until the day of my next dressing-down!

Fifty years of this! I kept on attacking rows of windmills with the fortitude of a Don Quixote, exciting the merriment and sometimes the derision of many of my contemporaries.

My foolishness was something they could not comprehend. In terms of everyday thinking, it was much easier—above all, more advantageous—to remain uninvolved. But something kept me on my path of thorns. I believed—still believe—that my persistence did not have to do with the romanticism of untrodden ways, but rather with an all-absorbing problem, which I have been tackling all these years, at the same time as I exacerbated my bruises. My important problem was simply this: to create satirical genres for film, the old "art of illusion." Even today I believe that these satirical genres provide the best kind of political cinema. I want to speak about my long, difficult explorations in this area.

I'll begin with 1920, during the Civil War, when I was still in the Red Army, because it was then that I discovered my steadfast interest in satirical works. And so—to the unforgettable spring of 1920. Denikin's White Army had just been finished off in the foothills of the Caucasus. The divisions of the 1st Cavalry Army had been given less than a week to recover. The ranks of our cavalrymen were dispatched thousands of versts westward to confront the Polish White Guards of Pilsudski in the west.

Look at a map: from the Cossack villages in the mountains beyond Krasnodar our road led to Rostov-Donbas-Ekaterinoslav-Rovno-Lvov . . . Seventeen hundred versts on horseback! And all around the spring was running wild. Drunk with victory, we rode through the Ukrainian spring to the accompaniment of singing larks, above which rose our brass bands and Cossack songs from the steppes:

> Rap-tap-tap, on your window,
> Come, sweetheart, come,
> My horse is thirsty,
> My horse is panting!

I was twenty years old. My breeches were cut from a piece of red velvet with yellow flowers on it (curtains were often used at that time!). I proudly jingled my spurs and enjoyed the wonderful, happy, carefree spring.

Oh, that spring of 1920! . . . I can remember nothing more beautiful. And if it wasn't for the tiresome problems because of which I am writing this piece, I could write a whole book in one fit of inspiration, without lifting pen from paper. But what cannot be, cannot be. I will begin by speaking about satire.

Day by day our horsemen moved west. During this unending march we tried to create a theater of sorts for the soldiers of our 31st Cavalry Regiment. The idea of improvising theatrical performances probably sprang from the discomforts of life on the march. The best framework for such a show proved to be the adventures of an officer and his batman. In amateur theaters all over Russia dozens of vaudeville shows with this theme were playing with success at this time; they had titles such as "Batman Shelmenko" or "The Batman's Tricks" or "His Excellency's Wife." In them the scoundrelly orderly typically puts the officer into a ridiculous situation, perturbing his complacency.

Somehow our instincts had led us to a genre close to clowning, and as we went along we invented comic turns and repartees. Fearlessly, without concern for the strictures of censorship, we dug up for our improvisations some highly risqué dialogues and situations from the salacious folklore of soldiers. In consequence, my partner, Pavlo Bezchastny, and I got summoned to the stern Regimental Commander after every show. He would shout at us and pound the table with his fist, and then upon remembering one particularly funny episode, he would start laughing till tears came to his eyes, and throw us out.

Pavlo Bezchastny, the regiment's clerk, turned out to be a terrific, born comedian. Long-limbed, tow-haired, with a button nose and colorless eyes peering out between pale lashes reminiscent of a pig's, he spoke with a woman's high-pitched voice. Without even trying, he could stir up Homeric peals of laughter. To step onto the stage with such a partner and to invent comic scenes with him was an enthralling experience for a raw youth like me.

Pavlo opened up for me the immeasurable, boundless power of laughter and harnessed me to its chariot for life. It was as if he was helping me to find the motor spring of a vast, unknown art form and to discover its own particular laws.

As I was feeling my way, I discovered the "automatism" of laughter: if you rouse a spectator from a state of rest by means of a good repartee and get a burst of laughter from him, and then before he has composed himself you direct a cascading series of comic effects at him, you can get him to laugh without stopping. There comes a point when, almost without effort, you get the spectator to laugh.

Pavlo had mastered this art to perfection! He would wait imperturbably until the spectator had had his laugh; then, at the critical moment (not too soon, not too late) he'd toss in a couple of words or a mere gesture or an unexpected stunt, and the laughter would roar without stopping. "To get more laughter from laughter! That's the trick," said dear Pavlo. It was only much later that I understood that this was the way Mack Sennett, Max Linder, Lloyd Harold, and the great Charlie Chaplin worked in the movies.

Our farcical improvisations suddenly produced a quite unexpected response thanks to an apparently trifling circumstance. The Batman Pavlo and I, always in the role of the Officer, both of us imperturbable, started weaving into our performances some very free ad-libbing on topical issues. For instance, we might bring up for no particular reason our quartermaster, who had been caught pilfering the day before, or the unlucky gunner who had been slapped in the face by an unruly hussy in front of the whole regiment. Or we might suddenly start making fun of the rough-and-ready elegance of the regiment: with the help of a hussar's cloak from a theater in Rostov, Pavlo would demonstrate a series of new fashions on successive days, decorating the officer's boots with cockades and tassels, or with the antique spurs worn by knights.

When we introduced these new characters into our sketches, they met with such wild success that our ardor for acting out the soldiers' ordinary anecdotes cooled. Instead we directed all our inventive, nervous energy to the troubles of regimental life.

The Commander now felt emboldened to suggest topics. "You should act out the exploits of the 5th Squadron with the nuns!" he said, laughing in anticipation of the amusing spectacle. The exploits with the nuns! When the long march to the west had totally exhausted both the men and the horses, the regiments stopped for a break. The 5th Squadron was lucky: it was quartered in a former convent.

Two days later the regiment was up and ready to resume marching when the Commander stopped at a little bridge across a river and ordered a sudden search of the army convoy. From the carts, which were covered like gypsy caravans (we called them "booths"), the soldiers drove out four embarrassed postulants, who were eloping with our lads. In the fifth place came a portly nun who was the treasurer or communion-bread baker and had been seduced by the Squadron leader himself . . .

Well, that was a laughing matter throughout the Division! We included some buffoonery about this incident in the play about the Batman and the Officer, and its effect was enormous. Pavlo and I got caught up in the general fit of laughing. Out of honesty we had to interrupt the performance so that we could laugh without inhibition together with our audience and enjoy the comedy of the situation we had enacted. And then, having laughed our fill, we resumed the performance as though nothing unusual had happened.

Here, in clowning, was born my tragic passion for satire as a particularly effective weapon of revolutionary art. I understood then that my days for dreaming about being a mechanical engineer after the war were over. That was not what mattered! Now it seemed the most worthwhile thing in life would be to be devote myself to comedy and satire. In their various forms these genres could make people laugh till they cried, and in so doing, they could destroy the enemy of the people and burn up the remnants of the cursed past.

The march through the Ukraine seemed unending. But the day came when its western limit appeared. Cannons were rumbling beyond the town of Uman. Soon the 6th Division was sent into the legendary raid on the rear ranks of the White Poles.

Later, in the approach to Lvov, Pavlo Bezchastny was severely shell-shocked by the first aerial bombardment. A sense of the enormity of this loss has stayed with me for my whole life. When I remember him today, I ask myself if my whole artistic life might have taken a different shape if I hadn't lost him.

War does not leave time for bitter reflections. There are marches. Battles. The soldiers' grueling labor . . . Many truthful and talented books have been written about this, and it is not my present task to write another, although it might well be not one of the worst . . .

Our division was embroiled in heavy fighting near Zamostie, when, like an evil genie from a bottle, Wrangel burst out of Crimea and attacked us in the rear. And again we were thrown into a thousand-verst-long march on horseback, this time to the east, in order to fight the Black Baron.

We fought in the dry steppes of Taurida near Agaiman. We crossed the Sivash lagoons. We fought on the Chongar strait. We broke through to the spreading Crimean steppes. We were traveling in two columns: parallel to us galloped the horsemen of Makhno,[2] who had persuaded us to take him as an ally in the fight against Wrangel.

Together with "Father" Makhno and his bands we rushed to Simferopol. Then we spent the next six months pursuing the "Father" all over the territory of Ekaterinoslav.

It was a bad time for theater. We lived on horseback. During our infrequent rests, men were falling off their feet. But the last flare-ups of the Civil War were being extinguished.

All this time I had been attached to the Regimental Commander as aide-de-camp in charge of operations. But now the "Father" had been flushed out of the Ekaterinoslav region. For the first time the regiment settled down for a long rest in a Ukrainian village. My entire military role was at an end.

The Commander urged me to resurrect the theater for soldiers. But I had to choose an occupation for the long term! I still had dreams of completing my technical education, which had been interrupted by the war, and becoming an engineer. The technical institute, which I left in 1918 when I went to the front, was appealing to me with tremendous power. Maybe, too, some of the factors weighing on me were my exhaustion after the difficult life at the front and a bout of typhus that almost cut short my life. I had to choose! And it was hard to choose because I had been thoroughly infected by the magic of comedy . . .

The cunning Commander resorted to duplicity. He swore that he would release me in a year's time so that I could study, and that he would personally help me to realize my dream of becoming an engineer . . .

And so in 1921 I became the director of the Club of the 31st Cavalry Regiment of the 6th Chongar Caucasian Division. My lot was cast; it determined the whole course of my life. A year went by, and another, then forty years, and a half century; and I never went back to my dream of being an engineer . . . Maybe this all came about because a fascinating field for artistic investigations was opening up before me. After just one year, I would have thought it frivolous to give it up for anything else!

And yet already at this time an abundance of knocks were landing on my head because of satire. The Commissar of the Division[3] gave me three days in the guardhouse because of a catchphrase I'd hung up in the club:

> Learn how to shoot straight.
> Don't forget, the Entente[4] is a . . .

In place of the last word was a well-drawn picture of a half-undressed prostitute.[5] Next day I was summoned to the club for a meeting with somebody in the Political Section! He shouted and stormed! And ran to the Regimental Commander: "Even if the phrase is right, it's not for publication. If you let this free thinker have his way, he'll cover the walls with words that will get us all into trouble!"

The Commander, an old hand from the Putilovo factories, had his wits about him: "I don't see any harm in the phrase!" he retorted. "The phrase is very relevant. This is a cavalry regiment, not a finishing school for daughters of the nobility!" Then the worker from the Political Section brought in the Commander of the 6th Chongar Division. He issued a summary order: "Confine the author of the unpublishable phrase to the guardhouse for three days." The whole Division laughed. I was hurt and in a state of restless agitation. In the evening I went of my own accord to the lockup in the regimental headquarters. But less than an hour later, the Division Commander entered, followed by the Regimental Commander.

The Regimental Commander embraced me and burst out laughing. "Is this fair?" I asked, almost in tears. "You are very bad!" said the Divisional Commander. "You wrote a wonderful slogan, but it's one that really cannot be displayed! It's been taken down, and not many people have read it. This was done at my command. But now there's a bigger buzz about you and your slogan in the Division than before. They're not laughing at you, but at the point you made! . . . Both you and I are political workers, and political education is a complicated matter! I lift your punishment, and I really should thank you, but I cannot!"

From my very first steps I should have understood that the path of satire would be fraught with unpleasantness and trouble. I did not interpret the signals correctly and continued to invent new forms of political work involving satire. And in the course of my work I nearly drowned a pig in a bog. The pig belonged to a clamorous Cossack woman, who demanded that I pay her 750 million rubles by way of compensation. Here is the whole story in brief.

In the spring of 1923, the head of the British government began to speak to the Soviet government in the crude language of ultimatums. The whole Soviet people were angry about this. Our 6th Chongar Division was no exception, and our spring maneuvers that year turned into a demonstration of military might.

In connection with this I managed to borrow a sow from a dour Cossack woman. We painted the pig with black and white glue-paint, and fastened a bourgeois top hat to her head. We drove a stout stake of ash wood into the ground in a puddle of water and attached the unfortunate sow to it. Above her we suspended a poster saying:

> We have chased this gentleman,
> Named Curzon, into a quagmire,
> For his barefaced insolence![6]

The whole Division marched past. The effect was terrific.

I was so excited with my success that I forgot about the pig and her surly owner! And that was my failing! A sudden downpour turned the puddle into a lake, and the sow was drowning as the squadrons marched past, laughing and hallooing. Then she managed to jerk the stake free, and dragging it behind her, the frightened pig in a top hat ran down the street giving heart-rending squeals. Her strident mistress chased after her in pursuit . . .

A costly retribution awaited me!

The Cossack woman had a loud voice. She sought out the Regimental Commander and demanded a sum of 750 million rubles in compensation. In those years 750 million rubles wasn't a big sum, but they could have only come from my own pocket, the resources of which amounted to mere kopeks. Fortunately, everything ended well. The pig was caught and washed. The woman calmed down after we told her what a nasty piece of work this Lord Curzon was and how splendid her own sow had looked in its incarnation as a bloodthirsty imperialist.

The search for unexplored ways of agitation and propaganda has proved to be my lifetime "hobby." To this day I have not cured myself of this dangerous pursuit . . .

Now that I was free from military duties, nothing prevented me from immersing myself in the creation of my own special theater. It was soon known in the Division for its unusualness. It produced only its very own plays, cartoon dramatizations (*lubki*[7]), clowning routines, and operettas, with irreverent inventions and surprising genre innovations.

One day, we posted announcements on fences in the village where our regiment was stationed, Nikolaevskaia stanitsa:[8]

OPEN MEETING OF HORSES IN THE
CLUBHOUSE OF THE 31st CAVALRY REGIMENT

The clubhouse was cramped, with low ceilings, and stuffy. Kerosene lamps of various sizes provided the lighting. I was a master lampman—that profession still existed at that time, and it was particularly important in railroad work. The illumination in the club was 10–15 amps, and I took on the responsibility for it after the melancholy soldier Pantelei Onishchenko, to whom it had been assigned, crushed all the glass we had for the lamps in his enormous hands.

Much today lies deeply buried and beyond recall! I experienced considerable sorrow over the meager resources of the clubhouse, but even for me it is difficult to believe that we had no electricity, no radio, no makeup, and no recorded music. During the whole time I served in the regiment, we did not have a single film screening. About movies we knew only by hearsay. No photographic camera existed in the regiment. In the Division there was not one single car.

We made stage sets out of old issues of a newspaper called *Poverty*. And it was from this newspaper that we gathered most of our information about what was going on in the world. The newspaper said: "The Volkhov Hydroelectic Station—the biggest in Soviet Russia—is under construction . . ." Four years were to go by before its launching. It would have provided adequate lighting for our stage. But in the meantime our dreams were confined to our three powerful, "Lightning-Model" kerosene lanterns.

But we managed. In spite of our limitations the club was jam-packed:

OPEN MEETING OF THE HORSES . . .

The curtain rose.

On stage there was a Presiding Council comprising only horses. The Chairman, the Secretary, the Speaker—all were horses. Instead of a pitcher, there was a water pail for horses. From time to time, the Speaker would lower his head and drink, he was agitated . . .

We had made life-size horse heads from old issues of *Poverty* by pasting together four or five layers of paper and giving them the necessary shape while they were still wet. We colored them with thick applications of chalk, soot, and ochre. We sewed on big eyes, about the size of peaches.

The heads looked funny. A horse's head and a typical cloak from the Caucasus were all it took to make one of our "horses."

And so the curtain rose.

THE HORSE-CHAIRMAN. Comrades, sit closer together please! And don't tap the floor with your hooves. I declare the meeting of military horses open!

The horse-poet of the 4th Squadron, called Predator, takes the floor.

PREDATOR. We've had glorious campaigns.

Like the winds, we've galloped in all directions. We've all shared hunger and hard times . . . Comrade soldiers, tell us who brought you glory.

You often fed us with straw taken from roofs. The wounds you gave us from your spurs have not healed . . . Who was with you when you went on the attack or were scouting? Why don't you take care of us, Comrade soldiers? Soon we'll be galloping with you into mortal combat . . . And yet you have so little care for us! How can this be, Comrades?

He drinks, lowering his head into the horse pail.

THE HORSE-CHAIRMAN. The floor is given to the horse named Whirlwind, my best comrade-in-arms from the cannon squadron.

Whirlwind climbs up to the tribune. His head is bandaged. He addresses the Horse-Chairman.

WHIRLWIND. I cannot speak poetically . . .

THE HORSE-CHAIRMAN. Speak as you know best!

WHIRLWIND. I cannot speak . . . I can only weep! I was beaten on the head and I weep!

THE HORSE-CHAIRMAN. Who did it?

WHIRLWIND. The farrier, Vania Bessonov. He was shoeing me and he hit me with the file.

THE HORSE-CHAIRMAN. Is the 1st Squadron farrier Bessonov here?

VOICE FROM THE AUDITORIUM. He didn't come! . . . He feels ashamed and asks to be excused! . . .

He's been put in the guardhouse.

THE HORSE-CHAIRMAN. Have you anything more to say, Whirlwind?

WHIRLWIND. I was Whirlwind; now I am an invalid. How can I be a warrior when I am aching all over? A horse wants to live. How can a horse fight if you beat him?

Whirlwind goes off. In the auditorium the horse called Raven stands up and goes to the tribune. As he advances he mutters threateningly:

RAVEN. I'll tell everything . . . You've no regard for a horse. I am angry! You won't make me shut up!

THE HORSE-CHAIRMAN. The 3rd Squadron Horse Raven has the floor.

RAVEN (*drinks from the pail*). The platoon commander, my master Godswill, forbade me to come to the meeting. He said, "You are a horse! You are not supposed to discuss things, but you have to take me anywhere I say, in silence!" But I find this unacceptable!

THE HORSE-CHAIRMAN. Please calm yourself, Raven!

RAVEN. I was shell-shocked in the Polish campaign, brought back oozing sores from the campaign against Wrangel, and now my withers have been beaten. But that is not the point!

THE HORSE-CHAIRMAN. What is the point?

RAVEN. The point?

THE HORSE-CHAIRMAN. Yes, what is the main point?

RAVEN. The point is LOVE! . . . (*he sings*).

THE HORSE-CHAIRMAN. Dear Raven! What is this? This is an open meeting, and you are speaking about love?

HORSE-RAVEN. Love is the point, because my platoon commander Godswill furiously spurs me to the other end of the settlement. He spends the whole night with his sweetheart, and I spend the whole night out in the wind and rain . . . This is the point! . . . The main point is LOVE!

THE HORSE-CHAIRMAN. What do you suggest?

RAVEN. Remember all of you:

If your horse Raven
Goes weak in the legs,
Your cavalry will not last.

THE HORSE-CHAIRMAN. What do you say, comrade combatants?

AN OLD SOLDIER (*in the auditorium*). You can't go on in this way, comrade horses! . . . Not all of us are such wretches! We love our horses! Surely we're not all like that!

HORSE FALCON. Not everyone.

THE HORSE-CHAIRMAN. The horse Falcon has the floor!

FALCON. My master neither eats nor sleeps,

Till I am stabled and fed!
I'll not spare my life for him

In the fiercest, most vicious battle!
I have two strong pairs of legs,
And he's got a Budenny saber![9]
We give you our all!
And he's my closest friend!

. . . The open meetings of horses were a regular hit with our audiences. Every time we put them on, we added new facts from the life of the squadrons. An abundance of material came from soldiers and the veterinarian of the regiment.

The wet and nasty fall of 1922. Our regiment was stationed in the upper reaches of the Kuban, in the remote and poor Nikolaevskaia stanitsa. Life for us political workers was hard. All the soldiers and officers were billeted with Cossacks, and were more or less fed by them. It was only in the spring of 1923 that the squadrons were fed from a communal pot.

A difficult autumn! . . . At this time many men from Budenny's army—natural horsemen—were released and sent home. Their place was taken by recruits from the central Russian provinces, many of whom were handling horses for the first time ever. To turn them into cavalrymen was difficult.

I forget how many of them were illiterate, at least 50 percent, and maybe 70 percent. In the regiment these lads had a huge burden to contend with: military drill; political instruction; learning to read and write; caring for their horses . . . It suffices to look at the faces of these youths on old photographs to realize that the Party performed a titanic job in educating the people . . . The eyes peering from these photographs belong to men with an unbelievably impoverished inner life!

If we, the soldiers of the Party, believers in the as-yet-unknown new world of Socialism, were unable to imagine its amazing reality, then what can be said about a peasant's son? His whole world ended at the outskirts of his village, within which the age-old horrors of poverty and ignorance all still ruled. These, nonetheless, were the fellows that the Party turned into the officers who fought in the Great Patriotic War: in 1941 they were thirty-five to thirty-eight years old. They commanded infantry battalions and tank units in the battles for Moscow and Berlin with unparalleled resolve, mastery of military skills, and faithful adherence to the Party of Lenin. Such were the parameters of growth of our recruits from 1922.

They had a difficult beginning in that rainy autumn when we dumped a huge load of study onto them. It wasn't easy for our cavalry horses either. A cavalry requires maintenance, but how could we maintain our stock of horses in that year, when they were being exhausted in our campaigns? To preserve what remained was of the utmost importance. The squadrons made stables from the materials we had to hand. Nobody could give us construction materials. The natural world didn't offer any either. Our only construction materials were rushes and straw for roofs, and brushwood and clay for walls.

Due respect must be paid to the wonderful inventiveness and doggedness of our officers, who created perfectly acceptable stables out of nothing! Here you could see the age-old love of a horseman for a horse. A cavalryman would rather not eat than see his horse go without. Exhausted, and wet to the skin or freezing, he would not think of taking shelter until he had protected his battlefield companion from the elements. His relations with his horse were on the same footing as with another man . . .

The Party Conference of the Division in this very difficult autumn adopted the slogan "In celebration of its 4th anniversary, the 6th Chongar Division aims to become exemplary!" It may readily be conceived how few of the conditions existed for becoming exemplary. This was a huge responsibility for the troops and officers and political staff! The atmosphere of those days was conveyed in our grotesque musical comedy "A Night in the Stables." On stage it was dark. The entrance to the stables; a smoking kerosene lantern; our cardboard "horses" chewing hay. A young orderly was lying on a pile of hay. Homesick, he sang:

I just don't get the point
Of a model regiment.
With all the chores,
And the sweat breaking out,
My head all swollen with worry . . .
One rifle, five regulations,
Political lessons . . . Vaulting onto horses . . .
What a life!
Standing guard, reading maps,
Lining up horses! Cleaning out stables! Cleaning boots!
My hair stands on end! . . .
I just don't get the point
Of an exemplary regiment.
At home they miss me . . .
Auntie writes me letters,
Dear Mommy lights candles for me in church . . .

At home Dunka stands crying for me
All day by the fence—
—Where is my sweetheart?
But your sweetheart is a blockhead,
Shiftless and lazy,
Messing things up in the squadron!
I just don't get the point
Of an exemplary regiment.
Who the devil needs it!
Who'll be to blame
If next month we die?! . . .
I come from Nizhny,
The horse I got is stupid,
I'm ready to cry!
He kicked me in the stomach th'other day,
Both my ears were ringing,
I thought I was kaput!
I just don't get the point
Of an exemplary regiment.
It's quiet all around,
In God's blessed world!
Why chase us like ones possessed?
Maybe the brigade officer
Wants an award.
That's what it's about . . .
And so Dunka must cry,
While th'other day a horse kicked me
In the belly . . .

The whole stable rises up against this orderly, who knows nothing about fighting. The horses demand more humane treatment. A stern sergeant comes running and restores order. The horses demand a replacement for the orderly, and so on.

We had a fondness for cartoonish *lubok* pieces with music, which without any justification we called "operettas." Of course, these were not operettas, but rather an exploration of lesser theatrical forms rooted in clowning and the theater of the grotesque.[10] Besides the horses the participants in our shows included Nicholas the Miracle Worker of Myra, who appeared in the form of an icon but with the real, living face of an actor in makeup; a Clock, which started ticking during a conflict involving a bad sentry at his post and an enormous louse, made out of sacks, which threatened to bring death to the very unclean platoon; and Old Father Chapman, a fairground clown, who would pull out of his magic bag a Bungler, Cholera, Home Brew, and a Village Priest . . .

The subjects were topical and incisive. The Regimental Commander, wise and experienced, would often tell me what to take aim at. One day he summoned me to receive an order:

"Please write an operetta about lice!"

"Well so be it, if it must be."

And so I wrote about lice. Later I wrote a "VD" operetta. These theatrical *lubok* sketches were played on the stages of the Division to constant laughter and were particularly successful.

Now, many years later, these topics have lost their relevance, and no doubt our young people would view them with wondering amusement. And so my artistic conscience requires that I consider whether what we did in the twenties was a profanation of the great art of theater. Isn't an artist who so abased himself rather pathetic? In speaking about my artistic path, wouldn't it be more tactful to pass over these sad pages of my life?

These questions arise because our historians of the arts are often embarrassed about this unrepeatable phase of our history and hide their contempt for it behind conventional, sometimes insincere praise for "Blue Blouse" spectacles.[11] I feel no shame, however, that in my theater we sang and shouted about lice, hunger, venereal disease, rudeness, and loutish behavior.

It may sound outlandish now, but in those years lice were indeed a governmental problem. "Either lice or Socialism" was the way Vladimir Lenin formulated the problem. In a speech at the 7th All-Russian Congress of Soviets, Lenin said: "A third scourge is descending on us—lice and typhus, which are mowing down our troops . . . Comrades it is impossible to describe here the horror of those places struck by typhus, where the population is weakened and powerless, and there are no material resources, and all life and communal structures disappear . . . We say here: 'Comrades! We must direct our attention to this question. Either lice will defeat Socialism, or Socialism will defeat lice!' "

Our enemies mocked the Bolsheviks and our misfortune, for which we were not responsible. The poet Demian Bednyi was driven to write: "Are we to blame if building a new society has meant fighting against lice." It fell to us to sing about lice, because like Maiakovsky, even if only at the level of our regiment, we were called upon "to clean up tubercular gobs of spit using the caustic language of posters for instrument." Recruits coming from indigent villages were bringing lice with them. Every kind of instrument had to be thrown into the battle against this evil.

And so we sang in accordance with the commands of military commanders.

LICE

On stage two clowns made a terrible racket as they fought against lice having the form of big firecrackers. One clown beat them with a huge paddle, the other with the butt end of a giant ax. They sang:

FIRST CLOWN. Lice will be the death of me!
It's two weeks now they're biting me!
SECOND CLOWN. Lice, little lice, little lice!
Taking one little bite at a time!
TOGETHER. They're all over my shirt,
Devil take them!
Devil get them!
Who'll exterminate them?
They bite here, they bite there!
It's more than I can take!
I wish they'd croak!

A Third Man appears—a clean, neat, "exemplary" soldier. He mocks the lice. He plays with the ax and the paddle, and then sings the verses that end the humorous lesson:

To rid yourselves of filth
(And this you must know!)
Go to the steam bath more often.
Steam and wash yourselves there.
And wash your underwear!
Once it's white and clean—
The battle's done!
Then press it with a hot iron!
Bullets and daggers
Cannot fight lice!
Everyone knows
Boiling water's your tool!

Don't get filthy again! Stay clean, men!
Go to the bathhouse!
Steam and wash yourselves!
That's all.

Cleanliness and neatness were the subject of several of our stage performances. We made fun of slovenly and untidy individuals, and named them. We targeted them in *lubok* sketches, humorous verses, songs, and in our poster newssheet *Turpentine*.

One of these songs I still hum to myself when I am by myself and in a good mood. We sang it on stage. A neat and nimble lad in a helmet would polish his already-shining boots with a brush. In front of him stood a tall, lanky person in inordinately large and absolutely filthy boots. To make him even funnier, we put the boots on platforms, and gave the man red hair and pockmarks. The clean lad enacted a comic scene with him and sang his song:

I clean, clean my boots!
And make their tops shine,
Same as a mirror shines!
Hey, ho, it's good to be alive.

I don't care, lads,
If my pants are covered with patches!
That's no big deal,
I can spend a year mending them!

As for you, Comrade Loser,
You'll soon lose your head!
Your helmet you've already lost!
You are not a comrade but a pig!

You fool, you are sloppy and slovenly!
You should be beaten!
You're not worth a penny!
You're a danger to the Republic!

Poverty was stifling us. We had no makeup. We used charred cork, and rouge that we stole or begged from the wives of officers. There were no materials to make beards and mustaches. We tried to use our poverty as a basis for satiric interludes. I would go out onto the forestage with a pair of large scissors:

"We need a beard for Nicholas II! . . . Who has a coat made of red fur?"

"Over here! Pass the scissors!" someone in the audience would merrily respond.

"We also need some dark hair for a brunette, gray hair for God-the-Father and red hair for the Archistrategos[12] Michael."

"Here! We've got it! Some sheep skin for the brunette!"

To the accompaniment of laughter and spontaneous jokes I would descend with my scissors into the noisy auditorium, and cut out the necessary hair from the sheepskin coats . . .

"Couldn't you try a little harder? So that we laugh till we cry?"

"We're doing our best."

We had no glue to use in sticking on mustaches and beards. We made a paste out of flour and water. Sometimes a beard would come off during a performance; the audience greeted these mishaps with friendly laughter. After the performances the mustaches and beards had to be soaked off with hot water.

The officers' wives left "our group" in protest during the first rehearsal of the "VD operetta." Maybe that was just as well. Having men play women's parts strengthened the grotesque conventions forming the basis of our theater. We transformed the lanky clerk Ivan Zakharych Kandyba into a tender-hearted blonde. We improved his figure with hairpieces and a specially cut dress. On his head we tied a coquettish handkerchief, under which hung jaunty curls cut from our audience's sheepskins . . .

Our poetic stanzas were often rough. Not everything would have withstood censorship. But the censors were far away. And the editors were still farther away. And the Military Commander fully trusted our scrupulousness regarding the Party.

Usually our performances were prefaced by a speech by the Military Commander or by the Regimental Commander or by a veterinarian. We would simply give form to their ideas in theatrical representations, and the spectators, who filled the hall to overflowing, would listen to the speaker and wonder: "Well, what are the mavericks from the regiment going to show us today?"

Our "Miatiukha and Pantiukha" rapid-fire, satirical verses were especially popular in the regiment. We regularly featured them at the big club evenings, and if for some reason we did not, people from the auditorium would call out: "Miatiukha! Give us Miatiukha!" The verses openly named people who had committed various infractions. The success of the satirical verses was a direct function of their highly topical nature. It fell to me to be the author of the operettas, plays, and verses; the chief performer; accompanist; wardrobe assistant; the makeup artist; and also to play the part of the matchless Miatiukha. We observed the fifth anniversary of the October Revolution by mounting a satirical play, *The Judgment of God*, the text of which I still remember. We pasted together old newspapers and painted them to make a set giving a satirical representation of the kingdom of heaven. We drew exaggeratedly elongated saints and holy men. Winged angels fluttered above in the air. In the center was the throne of the Almighty. On the throne sat the Lord God of Sabaoth. Into the drawings of figures, we introduced the actual faces of actors from our troop, as is allowed for in *lubok* prints. An antiquated Servant of God held the forestage.

CHOIR. Holy, holy, holy! . . . Holy Lord of Sabaoth!
Heaven and earth are filled with thy glory!
SERVANT. Tsar of tsars and commander of the world!
May thy glory shine in the ages of ages!
There are people awaiting judgment,
They've arrived from some kind of planet.
One calls himself tsar,
He says he is God's anointed . . .
How so? His face is all swollen,
An alcoholic perhaps? God knows!
He is trembling, and picking his nose.
GOD OF SABAOTH. Let the martyr pass to the head of the queue!
CHOIR. Holy, holy, holy! . . . Holy Lord of Sabaoth!
Heaven and earth are filled with thy glory!

Nicholas II is led in. He has been badly shaken up by the Revolution.

NICHOLAS II. I stand before your icon, Lord!
We, Nicholas II, by the grace of God,
Tsar of Poland and Grand Duke of Finland,
Tsar whom the workers did not love,
Etc., etc., etc., etc. . . .
(*crying*) Almighty, we have left our office,
Or in short, we were discarded . . .
"We have no wish for a tsar! they said.
"We cannot afford one."

GOD OF SABAOTH. Answer me, Nikolai: To whom did you give Rahssia away?

NICHOLAS II. (*Snivels.*) I gave Rahssia to Kerensky.[13]
But he could not hold onto it and ran away.
It was a real scandal! (*he wails*).

GOD OF SABAOTH. Subscribe Nikolai to all forms
Of pleasures of paradise!
All 24 of them!
A pail of vodka a day!
As much herring as he wants for snacks!
Angels! Flap your wings to blow away the flies!
Issue him with two changes of linen a day!

CHOIR. Holy, holy, holy! . . . Lord God of Sabaoth!
Heaven and earth are filled with thy glory!

. . . .

SERVANT. Kolchak[14] has arrived, most merciful God!
Without head, hands, or legs!
And without his golden galloons!
Also without kidneys! . . .

GOD OF SABAOTH. Add him to the army of saints,
And tie up his body in a bundle!

CHOIR. Holy, holy, holy . . .

The angels carry a bundle containing the remains of Kolchak across the stage. A leg with a spur and a hand with a huge whip are sticking out of the bundle.

. . . .

SERVANT (*leading Wrangel, mutilated and on crutches*). Baron Wrangel has arrived, Lord!
All covered in dust!

GOD OF SABAOTH. Add him to the army of saints!
Issue him golden crutches!

CHOIR. Holy, holy, holy! Holy Lord of Sabaoth!
Heaven and earth are filled with thy glory!

. . . .

A stretcher is carried in. On it lies the suffering Makhno.

SERVANT. Makhno, Lord! Ah me!
In terrible shape!

MAKHNO (*raising himself on the stretcher and threatening God with his fist*).

I've a grudge against you!
If you are God—
Then why-y-y didn't you help me?
You couldn't? Then it's time
You joined the ranks of the invalids!

GOD OF SABAOTH (*furious*).

The little monster is still bickering!
Sign him up for hell!
Not another word from him there!
Let the motherfucker shut up about his leg.
Stop this unseemly assault.
Shut the gates for some stocktaking!
Expel the defeated generals!
Double-fuck their mothers!

The Servant covers his ears in horror. The Choir sings to drown out God's swearwords.

CHOIR. Glory to thee, Lord, glory to thee! . . .

Our little theater was an invaluable laboratory of comic art for me. Things I thought of and wrote in the morning, I would often try out before an audience the same day in the evening. Really funny things got an enthusiastic response from the spectators, and we would develop them in subsequent performances. Anything forced and exaggerated would be met with silent indifference, and we would eliminate it without regrets.

Later, when I discovered the existence of films, my laboratory training stood me in very good stead. The rain was pouring down, one day, two days, and finally the whole week long. The Cossack settlement, which was uninteresting even in the absence of rain, looked so ugly and unprepossessing that memories of its impassable streets still evoke feelings of bitter depression. The dull, gray days were somewhat tolerable. They were taken up with more heavy labor than we soldiers could complete. But when evening came and the village was plunged into darkness, there was nothing to do.

In the Cossack houses dim wick lamps burning sheep tallow would be lit. Night seemed unending. It didn't take much effort to get soldiers and officers to drop in each evening at the club, coming from different squadrons and all parts of the settlement. In their presence we rehearsed our clowning pieces, and we pasted together and painted the horses' heads, the sets, the icons for the cartoonish *lubok* pieces . . . And almost every evening, in the presence of the men, we were busy writing our satirical newssheet *Turpentine*.

We completely renounced any thought of publishing long, wearisome articles in *Turpentine*. I am convinced from my experience that articles like this never get read in poster newssheets. Whatever fine words and profound patriotic feelings are put into them, their efficacy is close to zero, even if their outward appearance is magnificent . . . We had made this sad discovery earlier with the *Red Cavalryman*, a regular, proper newspaper. We therefore boldly rebelled against established models. The basic format of *Turpentine* was an acerbic, satirical quatrain and a note of 8–10 lines, along with a caricature. The result was that people always congregated in front of *Turpentine*; they would laugh, and have long arguments.

I still have a remnant of one issue of *Red Cavalryman*, the newspaper of the 1st Cavalry. The other parts of the paper had been used to roll cigarettes (no cigarettes or cigarette paper was available). In what is left, a whole column is devoted to *Turpentine*. I am quoting from this page in the *Red Cavalryman*:

> Well, you merry men of Chongar,
> Come on, brothers! Be merry!
>
> The Belorechensk *TURPENTINE*! You don't know what it is? The Belorechensk men have it hanging on a wall in their club. It's a poster newssheet. But what a newssheet! Every word's a joke. And nobody knows whom the paper will chew up next. *Turpentine* is a deadly thing! You won't quickly forget how it delivers its doses.
>
> Who needs it? And what for?
> Listen to the men of Belorechensk.
> If a fire's coming your way,
> *Turpentine* will tell you: Beware.
> A womanizer you:
> *Turpentine* exposes you!
> A churchgoer—Pshaw!
> Dirt-black like an Arab—Pshaw!
> A bungler—Pshaw!
> Lazy and a poor soldier—Pshaw!
> As for the proud cock who is too good

For the military and his studies,
A good splash from a pail
Will clear the brains
Of this mommy's darling,
. . . .

A caricature shows one of Budenny's cavalrymen in a helmet getting married in church. The text:

Alleluia, alleluia, alleluia!
Lord bless the young couple.
Alleluia, alleluia, alleluia!
Comrade Alleluev is getting married . . .
Reverend Father, I kiss your hand!
I am a Servant of God, member of the
Russian ComParty.
In God's temple all are as one!
I left my Party card in the squadron!
I used to persecute God,
But now my path leads to his temple!

Alleluia, alleluia, alleluia!
The groom and his bride
Circle round the icon!
Count on *Turpentine* to kick them
In the right place for stupidity.

Turpentine was written in the evenings round a large table. Everyone who wanted participated. There were bursts of laughter and merry exchanges with the victims and their defenders.

We were the first to be informed of anything that happened in the squadrons, and we were never short of material. We were truly happy when we learned that the command of the 1st Cavalry Army knew about *Turpentine*. One day some officers returning from the district headquarters told us that upon analyzing some slipshod work by officers during maneuvers, Kliment Voroshilov[15] exclaimed to them: "Your work deserves to be exposed in the Belorechensk *Turpentine*."

We had so much material for the paper that we could process only a tenth of what we received. And so the squadrons started putting out their own "affiliated" newssheets—*Pepper, Hedgehog, Red Satirikon, Splinter, At Random, A Smack on the Withers*, and others.

Soon I was transferred to the Political Section of the Division, with the task of disseminating my experience to all the regiments. To start with, I selected factory lads for each club, knowing they would have the guts to resist established powers and routines.

I've kept a photo of the Chongar club heads. In the background is a display of our jovial satirical papers. Today I remember my unforgettable friends, whose best attribute was an inexhaustible invention of new and effective modes of agitation and propaganda. We were an idiosyncratic "club of mavericks," as we were called in the Division. In my long life it was the most interesting collective of like-minded men with whom it was my good fortune to solve some very difficult problems.

We rebelled against institutionalized political work, and looked instead for dynamic, absorbing methods and structures of education in the Red Army. We squeezed out the dispiriting political gobbledygook, replacing it with specific, gripping presentations, based on the requests and interests of the young soldiers of the Division.

But all this was far from easy! We didn't have many friends like the old political commissar who said to me: "It doesn't matter if the soldiers go to the club just for some company! There's no need to keep driving splendid truths into their heads, when they have long since absorbed them. You could end up with the opposite effect. Keep a sense of proportion!" Today, half a century later, in similar situations, we speak of a "surplus of information." I am afraid that this "surplus" is the root of many faults in our political agitation and propaganda. Even though we were accused of all kinds of mortal sins, the fact remains that we succeeded in making our clubs real, noisy, lively, creative centers of social life.

When the political work of our Division was examined by the Political Directorate of the Western Front, the results were a surprise to me. The inspectors gave a high appraisal to the originality of style and the distinctiveness of our clubs and recommended my promotion to the position of instructor of the Political Directorate of the Western Front so that I could disseminate the experience I had acquired in the Division.

Before I had finished even a year's work in the Political Directorate, I was summoned to serve as senior instructor of GLAVPURKKA, the Main Political Directorate of the RKKA (the Workers and Peasants Red Army) in Moscow. But the higher I rose in the ranks, the more detached I became from direct mass instructional work, and I soon realized that a big part of my pioneering endeavors would prove useless. This caused me a great deal of distress!

For two years I did interesting work in GLAVPURKKA, and as a senior instructor I was one of the leaders of extramural propaganda for the Red Army. In this work it was my good luck to become acquainted with the production of films in the Gosvoenkino (State Military Film) Studio.

Now I knew what I would do!

In the beginning, my requests to be transferred to civilian life were categorically and repeatedly denied. But in filmmaking I could see such an exciting path for my life's work that administrative office work lost all interest for me, and I became a poor official. And so the authorities were obliged to let me move into filmmaking. In May 1927 I became a film worker.

2 The Kino-Train

294 Days on Wheels

(The Kino-Train of the First Five-Year Plan)
(1972, rev. 1984)

Nineteen thirty-one. The first steps along the road of Socialism had initiated amazing, momentous events throughout the land. It was difficult to remain on the sidelines and work on petty, meaningless assignments . . .

There, in this situation, I got the idea to engage film in the fierce battle against the host of malicious opponents striving to block the unprecedented construction of a new era. The villains were many: remnants of the White Guards; kulaks[1] and saboteurs; bureaucrats; loafers; bunglers; mere fools—one and all of them, miserable specimens of mankind.

A term to identify them came into the language at the beginning of the thirties—"real agents of evil"[2]—so that the people, acting in concert and using all available means, should counter their wicked deeds and destroy the enemy in a battle to death, for which new, special strategies were continually required. Punishment was visited on the enemy in ruthless purges of government organs. They were driven back in raids conducted in "light-cavalry actions" by the Komsomol youth,[3] and through control measures of the RKI [the Workers and Peasants Inspectorate] and denunciations in frontline newspapers published at new project sites. Later the Party unleashed on them the powers of the PolitSections attached to machine-and-tractor stations, sovkhozes,[4] and railways. This was the vast front line of class war leading to the socialistic transformation of the country that was being discovered under the quite remarkable First Five-Year Plan.[5]

The idea that enticed us was to enlist the stubborn "art of illusion "[6] in this sacred battle and to equip Soviet movie screens with "weapons" in the guise of genres of incisive political film. This was the origin of the mobile kino-factory, the Kino-Train with an extraordinary program:

—Today we shoot. Tomorrow we screen!

No ordinary, pacific documentaries and newsreels, but rather, merciless exposures of scandalous situations and the causes of stoppages. Display the *real agents of evil* on the movie screen and confront them there with documented evidence for the charges. No retreating till the work sector was reorganized and villains were neutralized![7]

Fig. 1. The logo of the Kino-Train, used on notepads, in letterheads, and in the masthead of the Kino-Train newspaper, *Tempo*. Here the Kino-Train is called the Factory Train, operating under the banner of Soiuzkino, the central organization for film production.

Fig. 2. The three Kino-Train cars, hitched to a locomotive.

The idea was enticing! But in the meantime *no wheels* could be had!

The year was 1931. A catastrophically small number of train cars remained in the land; all of them were old. The manufacture of new ones had not yet begun. The Five-Year Plan had generated a flow of passengers flooding all the railway lines. Old people—people of my generation—can never forget the battles at ticket windows in train stations, the fights to obtain train tickets.

Our idea met with enthusiastic sympathy, but yielded no train cars. We kept knocking on all doors for seven months, and then, at last, one of the happiest days of my life arrived. Three old, ailing cars were assigned to us.[8] We rushed them to the Voitovich factory, where before our eyes the regular train-car innards were ripped out, and space was made for the studios of a never-seen traveling kino-factory on wheels.

One car was reserved for the crew's living quarters, while in the other two we assembled (with what difficulty!) all the technical components for film production. Half a car was set aside for the main workshop—the film laboratory. The remarkable lab head, Grisha Sheviakov, a Kino-Train enthusiast, guaranteed he would raise the processing norm to 2,000 meters of film a day. This meant that our main principle—"Today we shoot, tomorrow we screen!"—was becoming a definite reality.

Don't forget that this was forty years ago. Even wild dreamers did not foresee the marvels of television and would have mocked a prophet who said that there would be television reports broadcast live from Red Square! Films were in no hurry; they were still silent. Nobody in the world was hustling film along and making it preempt the techniques of its fast-paced TV successors.

Everything was simpler and quieter, but also poorer. Seeking to shatter ordinary rhythms and norms, we naturally looked with hope and anxiety to Grisha Sheviakov, who had guarantied us 2,000 meters of film a day, to be processed under all conditions, even if the train was in motion . . .

Half a car was set aside for the roomiest workshop, dedicated to montage, with six editing platforms. The scriptwriters and film directors also had to work at these stations. There was, simply put, no other space for them anywhere in the train, as subsequent experience confirmed.

Next to the montage shop we laid out a fairly effective animation studio with three workstations. Two of them were used specifically to make an animated comic series "The Adventures of the Camel." The Camel was a happy invention of the poet Aleksandr Bezymensky for the construction site of the Stalingrad Tractor Plant. The infamous Camel, made of plywood, symbolized lagging. He appeared at the entrances to workshops and offices that were falling behind or failing. The only way of getting rid of this symbol of disgrace was to decisively raise your sector out of its stagnancy . . .

This remarkable hero served us very well! The animation artists drew short escapades involving the Camel on transparent celluloid. A simple filming technique was used to make the comedies. For instance, we made a photograph of the unbelievable litter on the station platform at Dolginskaia, while images of the Camel were made with the image multiplier. A keeper led the Camel onto the station platform, pumped him up with a hose, and the Camel hovered like a balloon over the door of the stationmaster's office.

The Camel stalked through the courtyards of factory workshops when they were lagging, spat at drunks and idlers, floated above the gates of MTSes (machine-and-tractor stations) when they were holding up the harvesting of the crop, ran after trains, popped up behind the Presidium at meetings, slept next to unrepaired tractors, and so on.

The third bench in the animation workshop was set aside for film titles. Films were still silent, and many intertitles were used in them. Cardboard characters in various fonts were made for us in Moscow.

We set up a production screening room next to the montage shop. It was two meters long (the size of an ordinary train compartment). A very basic projector was set up in the projection booth (one square meter!) This is where the production cycle ended.

There were five or six film crews on the train. Each one had a cameraman and a director who more often than not served as the production coordinator as well.

Despite our very cramped space, we gave up one half of a train car for a garage. Forty years ago you could not rely on local organizations to provide motorized transportation, but without a car we could have done nothing. Sergo Ordzhonikidze, a warm supporter of our project, gave us a new one-and-a-half-ton truck from the first consignment from the new Gorky automobile factory. Lowering the rear platform of the train car, we could roll the truck down on special runners.

When we stopped, we would use the vacated garage space to set up a printing press and an editor's desk for the Kino-Train's newspaper, *Tempo*, which proved an important linkage in our work of political mobilization.

Space was very tight! The electric power generator, the storage closets, the lighting storehouse, the five projectors—all this required space, which was measured out in square centimeters. At every step our lack of space was the bane of our existence. We did have one consolation: people did so much in even-more-cramped submarines!

We had thirty-two sleeping berths for a very congenial crew of enthusiasts. There would have been no room for a thirty-third enthusiast, even though the volume of work called for double the number of staff. Screening out lackluster people, we faithfully opted for stalwart romantics of unbounded boldness:

—One square meter of living space (the norm in a four-seat compartment) for one year;

—No restrictions on working hours;

—Obligatory deckhand chores at any time of day or night, such as filling laboratory tanks, making film intertitles, loading or unloading the truck, driving out for food, cleaning the quarters, and so on.

—Obligatory professional competence in several fields, including skilled film editing (everyone had to pass an exam for this) and film projection (another exam!), and as lighting man, composer of titles, and handyman. Experience led to later corrections in this idealistic scheme. But though editing girls and projectionists joined the train, the deckhand chores remained.

The head of production, B. N. Shumov, was merciless, and he managed the business splendidly, even if it meant squeezing the romantics dry. He

Fig. 3. Medvedkin and part of the Kino-Train crew in Moscow in 1932. On the back of the photograph Medvedkin wrote: "The start of the relay race that ended forty years later," with specific reference to Chris Marker's taking up of the work of the Kino-Train in France.

assigned duties liberally, for all hours of the day and night, without sparing even scriptwriters or directors from the performance of the dirtiest chores. We quietly consigned "to shore" those who were not strong enough to endure the tyranny. Man, we felt, was rather like metal, which is good for spaceships if it is strong, and otherwise—for making saucepans and soldiers' buttons . . .

My archives contain a number of interesting documents from those restless times. With their help I will tell the story of one of our expeditions. We were just leaving Dnepropetrovsk for Moscow when, suddenly, our departure was countermanded by a telegram. On the advice of People's Commissar for Heavy Industry Sergo Ordzhonikidze, we were being urgently dispatched to the Krivoi Rog Iron-Ore Basin.[9] The 17th Party Conference[10] had just ended. Its resolutions provided for a radical, unprecedented shattering of the whole fabric of the vast country. With 518 new plants scheduled to be built under the First Five-Year Plan, scaffolds for the first giant projects were already rising, Magnitka, Dneprostroi, Uralmash,[11] and the first tractor factories.

Bread! Metal! Coal! The pace of construction, the fate of mechanization and rearmament in a backward agricultural economy, the whole life of the country—all were bound up with these burning problems.

Fig. 4. Twenty-five carts loaded with iron ore waiting for the tracks to be cleared.

The metallurgical factories in the south were incapable of smelting the required amount of steel. Construction projects were on starvation rations. The iron ore of Krivoi Rog was in fact the "grain crop" of the metallurgical industry of the Five-Year Plan. But the problem of shipping ore from Krivoi Rog had reached a critical pass and had given serious worries to the delegates at the 17th Conference.

Take this interesting photograph I found in my archives: twenty-five wagon-pushers, their wagons loaded with ore, stand waiting for someone to clear away a wagon overturned in an accident. This characteristic picture of the times is an eloquent testimony to the quality of management, the state of the technical equipment, the weak leadership, and the lack of education and training. At the same time it bears witness to those heroic times, when the Party got the entire Soviet people's attention focused on one enormous problem—to produce 9 (NINE!) million tons of steel in 1932—leaving aside the fact that for the huge country rallied under the Five-Year Plan 20 million tons would have been too small an amount! Today when we look at a report of the Central Statistical Bureau in a newspaper, our eyes indifferently pass over the figure 109 (ONE HUNDRED AND NINE!) million tons of steel produced in 1968. [*marginal note in Medvedkin's hand*: In 1973—171 million tons!] This old, accidentally surviving photograph ignites a flame of unexpectedly powerful feelings from a boring statistic!

Our metallurgists had a difficult start. Run-down blast-furnace operations, transportation, coal supplies—all were letting them down. The ore from Krivoi Rog, in particular, was a problem. The operation of the mines was terrible. Millions of tons of ore were piling up at depots, while loading and shipping it to the DonBas [steel mills] was an acute problem.[12]

Our Kino-Train was put on a siding at the station at Vechernii Kut. Right from the start of our Krivoi Rog expediton we understood that we would find no lack of urgent subjects. They were obvious, ready to hit one in the eye, begging to be put up on the screen.

Many of the messy situations could not be explained by the objective difficulties[13] of the grim thirties. At many mines the shortages of manpower and the disastrous turnover of cadres were directly connected with a total lack of concern for human resources. Urgent questions of food, housing, and development were left to sort themselves out. Remnants of the battered kulak class compounded the problems at every site.

One of the best films from this sortie was *How Goes It, Comrade Miner?* Its director, Nikolai Karmazinsky [*insert in Medvedkin's hand*: and the cameraman A. Bogorov, both experienced newsreel makers], struck the right human chords in a "conversation" about the living conditions of the Krivoi Rog miners.

[*typewritten insert by Medvedkin*: They lived in antiquated "bedrooms"—dormitories with curtains separating families from bachelors; queued for bread; and cooked on primus—or kerosene stoves in filth and darkness, because the Union Mining Committee was dysfunctional. This was contrasted with the Comrade Shvarts Mine, where a street of small, new houses for the miners was named after the president of the Mining Committee and where the dormitory for bachelors was run by a demobilized officer, who ensured a smooth organization of living conditions, along with general order and cleanliness. Women brought freshly baked bread, already cut up into pieces, from the bakery straight to the dormitory, and they would place the bread on bedside tables in clean baskets covered with a napkin. A kettle was always on the boil, so that anyone could drink as much tea as he wanted after work. The canteen of the mine was shown in *Film Letter to the First Krivoi Rog Kitchen Factory from the Canteen of the Comrade Shvarts Mine*. In this one-reel film the director openly attacked the communal food services of the October Mine Administration.]

The huge kitchen factory was feeding the miners so badly that they had stopped going to it. The cooking was bad; thieving was rife; the staff were rude. The clever, dodgy operators running this enterprise juggled figures to convince the management that the whole problem had to do with a lack of provisions.

On-screen, Karmazinsky contrasted this ugly setup with the splendidly running canteen at the Shvarts Ore Mine. In an old and humble building two hearty Ukrainian cooks ran things, pouring an immeasurable love for work into their food. Their Ukrainian borschts, cheese pancakes, and dumplings were famous far beyond the boundaries of the mine, and the overflowing canteen always hummed with the happy voices of contented patrons. Karmazinsky's story was a demonstration that perfectly decent communal food services could be arranged at any mine.

Pursuing the heated discussion, the director made *A Film-Letter* (one reel). The target here was the disorderly administrators, drunks, and other disturbers of the peace in some of the dormitories of the mines. Again, contrasting examples showed the excellent life led in the clean, well-regulated dormitories of progressive mines.

The Kino-Train grasped the principle of conflict from the first films made in Krivoi Rog, applying this principle wherever it could. This—the on-screen collision of sharply criticized abuses with bright, positive examples showing how people can create order—was a weapon for fighting the many tricks sluggish leaders used to resist any radical restructuring of work. People quickly and unthinkingly get used to disorder, seeing it as the norm, and live with the sincere conviction that there is nothing to be done! This outlook grows especially strong when there are shortages of manpower, and supplies are meager, and people all round continue to work as in the old days ("Don't worry, everything will be fine"). The terrible strength of inertia! We got a tighter and tighter grasp of its laws with each new sortie and tirelessly directed all our efforts against it.

We very quickly understood that our films were not going to have a practical effect if they were screened in clubs, after work, to the accompaniment of music . . . We had to find our own form of screening. As a rule a film was shown without music, as if it was a challenging lecturer at a workers' general meeting or a production conference. "What are you doing, dear comrades?" was the question our screen usually, relentlessly posed. Plus: "Look how well your neighbor deals with similar difficulties!"

To see your friends on-screen, your own workplace, your own street, is incredibly interesting for anybody! And we did not just show your workplace and friends—no! We usually showed an unjustifiable, intolerable failure in your workplace, your life, and the lives of people close to you.

We exploited this attribute of film to the utmost, and our calculations were correct: the reaction in the audience was wonderfully keen. Party and Komsomol activists were quick to take up our criticisms. Immediately after the screening there would be heated arguments, a practical plan for restructuring would be designed, someone would be designated to take charge, resolutions made to remove incompetents and patent adventurers, or even to bring them before the courts.

In this way, the food services of the kitchen factory at the October Mine Center were restructured, the unscrupulous operators were put in prison and the incompetent cooks fired, the supply of produce was improved and supplementary farming along the lines followed by neighbors was introduced, and so on.

We produced three to five copies of these films. Mass agitators with portable projectors traveled with the films from mine to mine. Everywhere the Party activists and the mine managers seized on our suggestions and criticisms. Thus *How Goes It, Comrade Miner?* and *A Film-Letter* really did help to improve the life of the miners. In the conditions of 1932, that very difficult year, this was of decisive importance in the fight against failure at Krivoi Rog. In subsequent Kino-Train sorties these two films were unfailingly helpful to us in interventions into the crucial problems of those grim years—food, living conditions, physical and emotional well-being . . .

Forty years have gone by. [*marginal note*: And now fifty-two years!] It might be easy enough to make things up, without my intending to do so, as often happens in memoirs. But here in front of me is a yellowing sheet from the Kino-Train newspaper, *Tempo*, dated 7 [3?] December 1932. Take the first column of this paper. Read carefully the text of this selection. Six months after the release of the two above-named films, they were doing excellent "work" among the DonBas miners. Cooks from the Donetsk mines were speaking about their undertakings in the paper. An initiative of the best director of supplies was noted; the best supplementary farming project was written up; undisciplined administrators in dormitories were criticized.—The Kino-Train intervenes everywhere as the arbiter of competitions, as judge, as inspector; it announces the pending verification of pledges given at screenings.

But let's return to Krivoi Rog. The successful eruption of our first films into the life of the Basin heartened our collective. We understood that making a sharply critical film was only half of the job. The main thing was to make good use of it as a weapon in generalizing the experience of leading workers and in mercilessly criticizing and reorganizing broken-down sectors. Luckily, the task of tackling these very difficult problems was taken on by my deputy, M. A. Starovoitov, a talented "mass agitator"[14]

КОЛХОЗ „ЗАПОВИТ ИЛЬИЧА" ЧЕРЕЗ КИНОФИЛЬМ ЗОВЕТ ВАШ КОЛХОЗ ПОСЛЕДОВАТЬ ЕГО ПРИМЕРУ!

Пролетарии всех стран, соединяйтесь!

Темп

Декабря 3-1932 г. № 4 Сталино

Орган Кинопоезда и техпропа НКТП СССР.

Приходите смотреть фильмы кинопоезда

В ФИЛЬМЕ „ПИСЬМО КОЛХОЗНИКАМ" УВИДИТЕ, КАК ОДИН ИЗ КРУПНЫХ КОЛХОЗОВ СТАЛИНЩИНЫ „ДОНБАСС" ДОПУСТИЛ В СВОИ РЯДЫ КЛАССОВОГО ВРАГА, ДОВЕРИВ РУКОВОДСТВО НЕДОБИТОМУ КУЛАЧЕСТВУ.

ЭТОТ ФИЛЬМ ПОДРОБНО РАССКАЖЕТ ВАМ, К ЧЕМУ ПРИВЕЛА НЕДОСТАТОЧНАЯ БДИТЕЛЬНОСТЬ КОЛХОЗНИКОВ.

ЛУЧШИЙ КОЛХОЗ СТАЛИНЩИНЫ „ЗАПОВИТ ИЛЬИЧА„ РАПОРТУЕТ В ЭТОМ ФИЛЬМЕ О СВОИХ ДОСТИЖЕНИЯХ И БРОСАЕТ СОЦИАЛИСТИЧЕСКИЙ ВЫЗОВ ВСЕМ КОЛХОЗНИКАМ ДОНБАССА.

Колхозники! Вы должны поделовому принять этот вызов передового колхоза!

ПОЗОР ОТСТАЮЩИМ! А некоторые отсталые колхозники под влиянием кулацкой агитации всячески пытаются еще задержать выполнение своих обязательств перед государством. Хлеб разбазаривается, продается спекулянтам, а план не выполняется.

Колхозник Горобец орган. крас. обозов.

НУЖНО ОРГАНИЗОВАТЬ ХЛЕБОЗАГОТОВКИ! Организуя хлебоздачу, необходимо, чтобы каждый колхозник знал, что чем скорее будет выполнен план хлебозаготовок, тем быстрее можно будет приступить к распределению доходов.

Полным выполнением хлебозаготовок нанесем решительный удар кулачеству и его агентуре—оппортунистам.

НИ ОДНОГО ДНЯ ПРОМЕДЛЕНИЯ!

Дорогие товарищи колхозники!

В ожесточенных классовых схватках идет сейчас борьба за хлеб. Но наш колхоз „Заповит Ильича" Григорьевского сельсовета № 2, Сталинского района (Донбасс), в этой борьбе вышел передовым.

Мы свой годовой план в1703 центера полностью выполнили еще 12 сентября 1932 года.

После выполнения плана мы тщательно подсчитали свои ресурсы и еще дополнительно сдали государству 149 цетнеров. План свой мы выполнили благодаря правильной организации хлебозаготовок. В момент организации красных обозов, кулацкая агентура пыталась сорвать вывоз хлеба. Но этим вылазкам кулачества была быстро противопоставлена широкая массовая работа.

Каждая малейшая попытка врага, у нас получает должный отпор. В напряженной, повседневной борьбе мы укрепляем свой колхоз для дальнейших побед.

В этом году за своевременную хлебоздачу наш колхоз получил 1200 руб. деньгами, швейную машину и промтоваров на 4500 р.

Выполнив долг перед государством и полностью окончив озимовый сев, мы приступили к распределению своих доходов и боевой подготовке к будущей весне.

Рассказывая о своих успехах, мы вызываем все колхозы Донбасса последовать нашему примеру.

По поручению колхозников:

Предколхоза: ЗАМЕТА

Секретарь партячейки ГОНЗЕНКА

Предсельсовета МАНОСТЫРНЫЙ

Колхозники ударники: ГОРОБЕЦ РЫПАЛОВ С. ВЕЛЬБАЕНКО Ф.

Fig. 5. An issue of the Kino-Train newspaper. The banner headline reads: "'Lenin's Legacy' Kolkhoz Is Using Film to Challenge Your Kolkhoz to Follow Its Example." The headline inside the box reads: "Come and See the Films of the Kino-Train." The text is a call for action to overcome delays, lack of organization, and the power of the kulaks.

and an excellent organizer. As an indication of his aptitude for the business two facts will suffice: in order to join the Kino-Train he left the post of secretary of a large Party organization at a brake factory in Moscow; and after leaving the train he worked during the war years as secretary of the Kuibyshev Oblast Party Committee.

Mobilizing Party activists; checking on corrective measures; recruiting local-press organs, and also engineers and technicians from the intelligentsia; putting various kinds of pressure on official leaders (who usually resisted restructuring!)—all this huge body of questions of organizational and political work, Starovoitov could accurately, resolutely, and effectively resolve.

For reasons of space I will not give a detailed account of the political mass mobilization work of the Kino-Train, although we made many important and interesting discoveries. I will dwell only on controls over implementation. At the screenings a reorganization plan was usually adopted in an amicable spirit, without any special pressure. On the very next day, however, a mountain of prosaic obstacles would arise before the executors. Inertia and sluggishness would dampen the enthusiasm; the best intentions would too easily turn into phony promises. Accordingly the Kino-Train especially insisted on controls over implementation in all its sorties (I am speaking about the first year of work). We always took on the duties of arbiters of competitions and strict inspectors. A cameraman would be assigned to a mine, a kolkhoz,[15] or a failing construction project; his camera was as great an object of fear for the *real agents of evil* as a cannon. In truth we seldom did any filming for the purpose of inspection. But the mere fact that a cameraman would be coming back with his imposing tripod (we didn't have a single handheld camera!) was of enormous significance.

I have dwelt in specific detail on the first two films of the Krivoi Rog sortie because in our search for methods of mobilization and of organizing work, these proved to be the most productive of results. It was much more difficult to sink our teeth into the problems of production breakdowns. We had arrived in Krivoi Rog at a time when the question of delivering ore extracted from the Basin was at a critical juncture. The worst stranglehold was at the dispatching platforms, where the ore was loaded onto freight cars. As a rule, it was loaded BY HAND. The heavy lumps of ore (50–60 percent iron!) were loaded by shovel into antediluvian carts. There were never enough men to do the work. The organization of work was so bad as to be beneath criticism. The loading plans were not being fulfilled. Behind Sergo Ordzhonikidze's stern telegrams we could sense the anxiousness of the DonBas metallurgical factories.

We did everything we could to help the miners in restructuring the work of the dispatching platforms. We released two trenchant critical films, *For the Brigade* and *No Avoidance of Personal Responsibility*. They contrasted the mess at a number of mines with the Red Guard Mine, which did an excellent job with the loading of ore in identically difficult conditions.

Our mass agitators took these films and our projectors to unsuccessful dispatching platforms, and co-opted the best brigade leaders, foremen, and shock-workers from the Red Guard Mine to accompany them. It often turned out that their contributions at workplace screenings were as useful as our hastily made films.

The struggles with absenteeism, drunkenness, and disorder were treated on-screen in our *Kino Gazette* series. The first five films, which had been released during the first sortie, had for the most part been informational. Newspapers in Krivoi Rog were critical of the problems. But to capture certain *real agents of evil* on film was difficult.

I will always remember one case in particular: the train's most productive cameraman, Viktor Maslenikov, wished to make a film about a mine manager who was a hopeless drunkard. The manager would stagger off to work in the morning along the street of the mining settlement, and—staggering—he would return home. For several days Viktor tracked the man with a cumbersome Debrie camera, without luck. Sensing that something was wrong, the "hero of the story" had begun to leave home before daylight and to return only late at night. Once when he suddenly appeared at the normal time there was nothing to shoot: the "hero" was in a hopelessly sober state. Maslenikov lifted his blockade and then suddenly, ten days later, came charging back and succeeded in capturing the drunkard on film. The man was soon fired from his job.

Our films "with the thrust of a dagger" were proving to have great power. Sometimes the wives of alcoholics caught on film came to see us on the Kino-Train—and so did calmed-down debauchees and repentant disrupters of production—in order to ask us to remove sequences in which they were shamed. We couldn't oblige, but in some instances we promised to shoot them again on film if they reformed themselves.

Another trenchant story that I recall from our *Kino-Gazette* series is *The Camel at Dolginskaia Station*. We had been struck by the exceptionally filthy station with garbage strewn all over the platform, broken windowpanes, and unshaven, drowsy railroad workers. We shot all this; then we put an enlarged photograph of the station in an image multiplier, superimposed on it the image of a thin camel walking down the platform, with a guide (another cartoon) who led the camel to the door of the stationmaster and inflated the camel with air from a hose. The camel floated up like a balloon tied to the door to serve as a symbol of distress.

Of course, our *Kino-Gazette* films contained a number of ordinary or mediocre or simply bad pieces—a consequence of the difficulties of dealing with unfamiliar subject matter and the insufficient experience of the very young artistic workers on the train.

The Krivoi Rog sortie took place at a time when the technical reconstruction of the Basin was at a critical juncture. Major disasters threatened the metallurgical industry owing to the use of manual labor for the extraction and loading of ore. And yet even the simplest percussion drills (jackhammers) were hardly manufactured here in those difficult years.

The prehistorical pick still remained in general use in the mines. Heavy jackhammers were imported from England for hard currency (of which there was little enough at the time!). The scrapers were the pinnacle of mechanization in the Basin—primitive scoops with a motor and winch to haul ore, substituting where possible for a man with a shovel. But even these very, very simple devices required an army of technically literate workmen, which did not exist! Engines were burning out; winches and compressors were breaking; jackhammers were breaking down. Maintenance services were needed, and they too did not exist. And so the broken mechanical equipment was often sent to the dump; and the foremen, beside themselves, would go back to the pick, shovel, and wheelbarrow . . .

Meanwhile, DonBas was sending increasingly alarming telegrams. Metal was the "bread" of the Five-Year Plan. The holdups with the ore disrupted the running of the furnaces. The Basin administrators and Party organizations were conducting an intense battle in the area of mechanization. They suggested to the Kino-Train a number of urgent questions that had to be addressed.

The *Kino-Gazette* series included several pointed critical pieces stigmatizing wrong attitudes toward technology, with six one-reel films devoted to crucial questions of mechanization, including

The Key Reconstruction Sector in KrivBas[16]
The Need for a Mastery of Machinery!
A Socialist Assessment of the All-Ukrainian Ore-Mining Conference
Join the Battle for Technology!
The Jackhammer

We believed the best help we could offer to the miners was in the education of cadres. And indeed in this area we did achieve a fair amount.

Young Misha Lifshits, just beginning as a cameraman, made a film of the excellently organized courses for the scraper operators of the Red Guard Ore Mine. Courses in the prescribed format had been set up throughout the Basin, but for the most part they existed only on paper, and those that actually existed were hopelessly bad. In a nine-minute film, Lifshits compared the Red Guard Mine with one in which instruction had completely broken down. The school had broken windowpanes; the scanty course materials were dumped in a heap; a piece of paper had been torn from a class list to make a cigar. The unshaven, unkempt course director was filmed running away from the camera. The film was released under the title *A Summons to Socialistic Competition*—from the top students of the Red Guard Mine to the students and youth of the DonBas. The film called for the introduction of order into courses of instruction, schools, and technical study groups. Our mass mobilizers used this film at workplace screenings to conduct the huge organizational work required for a radical restructuring of the education of cadres.

I remember Misha Lifshits's work because something funny happened to him later on. Some time after the screenings, we sent the film's author (and cameraman) on a circuit for control purposes to film how people had restructured things. Misha returned from the trip confused, and reported that at the first ore mine he visited nothing had been done. The door to the school was locked. One window was not fastened. Inside nothing had been cleaned up. Misha had hardly finished filming all this when a commotion began. He was taken off to the office of the mine director, where he faced all sorts of pleas for a few more days. Finally, Misha agreed to wait on the condition that the coordinator be replaced by a serious fellow, and the courses fully staffed and regularly offered. The mine director undertook to answer for this.

"And you agreed?" we asked the cameraman.

"They begged me so hard I did."

"Well, you did the right thing! Keep after them until they shape up."

Until the end of our Krivoi Rog expedition, Lifshits was assigned to the subject of technical instruction. He was feared at mines where the instruction was shaky. He was welcomed when he was filming a noticeable improvement. This nineteen-year-old youth, who was not a Party member and was handling a movie camera for the first time, suddenly acquired a taste for political and organizational work and plunged into it. Cranking his camera in different mines, he became a specialist in methods of technical instruction, intervened in the organization of this matter, passed on the best experience, and boldly introduced order where there was none.

Not surprisingly he acquired an authority that, as I remember, at first baffled us.

The need for mass training of the cadres of Krivoi Rog mechanics that year is something I spoke of above. The moral satisfaction the novice cameraman got from knowing the direct usefulness of his work may be readily conceived. But Lifshits was not the only one about whom this was true. The whole collective of the train swiftly grasped the importance of the problems we were called upon to solve in Krivoi Rog.

One of the most memorable films of this expedition was just 184 meters long. Its title was *A Socialist Calling to Account: From the Mine 3 Blacksmiths to the Central Krivoi Rog Workshops*. The cameraman Gleb Troianovsky and I came upon the blacksmiths' workshop by chance. More than a dozen new train carts stood before the blacksmiths. Ruthlessly stripping off the new paint, two somber smiths were breaking off the locks that were supposed to safeguard the carts from overturning, and replacing them with ugly (and strong!) hooks. For more than a year the carts produced by the factory for the mines of the Basin had been lemons. Their couplings tended to fly open when the carts were moving; the carts would overturn and spill heavy ore onto the tracks. All movement of the carts would come to a stop. Time would be lost while the cart-pushers removed the overturned cart from the tracks and cleared the rails.

In my photograph collection there is one I include here: twenty-five men with loaded carts, waiting for the way to be cleared after one such accident.

Carts had tumbled off the tracks and were lying on the slopes along the sides; they were overgrown with weeds. Or they were sticking out of quagmires. The entire transportation network of the above-ground workings of the mine had sorry memorials adorning it, and we recorded them on film.

The smiths were angry. Apart from the useless couplings, they had to replace the four iron blocks that held the wheels on each new cart: the factory was installing blocks made of soft, gray iron. They were done for in a few days. And so the smiths replaced them with blocks made of hard iron.

The mine was just twelve kilometers from the factory. The quarrel of the mine administrators with the factory had been going on for many months. One of the blacksmiths got hold of a battered notebook and agitatedly turned its pages with his soiled fingers. He named dates: when letters were written; when the factory was visited; when assurances about corrective measures were given; when spokesmen came and agreements were signed.

The film took the form of a socialistic calling to account of the factory by the blacksmiths. They put their names to it, in addition to those of the film director and the cameraman. The film was made in just twenty-four hours. The session at the factory was stormy. "**What Are You Doing, Dear Comrades**?" the smiths asked from the screen, on which the disgusting history of the carts was unfolding shot by shot. When the light flashed on in the room, it was some time before the heavy silence was broken. "Again!" someone shouted from the back rows. The film was screened again, and then again.

The chief engineer of the factory angrily accused us of slander, threatened to make us answer for it, denied the very fact of a dispute between the mines and the factory, and worked up a real rage as if we had been mistaken. Then one of the somber smiths took the floor. He was not a practiced speaker, and leafed through his greasy notebook, giving the dates of protests, complaints, assurances, indictments, meetings, written responses, and so on. Unexpectedly he turned to the workers in the room: surely they had to know what the mines needed. He, the blacksmith, could see sitting among them some comrades who used to come to the workshop. Why were these comrades silent?

Now the boilermen spoke up. Without niceties of expression, they attacked the factory management and fully supported the claims made in the film. The Party secretary of the Krivoi Rog Municipal Committee, sitting on the tribunal with us, very sternly advised the chief engineer to recognize the error of his first speech, to accept the blacksmiths' calling to account, and to "settle." The engineer did so without much enthusiasm . . .

But the men of Krivoi Rog, warmed up by the disputes, took over the meeting from us. Two workers carried in a heavy machine, the size of a tree trunk, and rusted all over. They deposited it on the tribunal. It had obviously been lying in a dump heap for ages, and was obviously long past being resurrected. The workmen addressed the tribunal:

> Let the angry guests from the mines take a look at their own work. This is a Climax heavy-duty drill recently purchased from England. Its cost was 600 gold roubles. In the mine it was put in the hands of unskilled workmen. When the lubricating oil was used up it was not replaced because the oil cap had been lost and a wooden plug had been driven in flush with the hole. The engine burned out. The tool was thrown onto a slag heap, where it got covered with waste matter. Nobody took the blame. Look about in their slag heaps and their leaky sheds! See how many jackhammers, cables, and engines you find there!

The meeting became noisy again. Maintenance men stood at the tribunal and spoke about the appalling state of the equipment sent from the mines for maintenance and about the disappearance of a large part of the equipment without trace! We asked the meeting to assign to us a brigade of the most scrupulous men to help us to file an on-screen *Counter-Claim: From the Krivoi Rog Workshop Men to the Miners of the October Mine Organization*. This film bore the signatures of men from the workshops. It was even more trenchant. Our mass educators went with it to all the mine centers and, assisted by Party activists and management, conducted a long campaign to introduce order in this crucial sector . . .

And so, the great "art of silent film" became a strict judge of society—perhaps for the first time—when the white rectangular screen would go dark and open precise, well-targeted fire at the nastiest logjams constricting the life of the Basin.

In this role silent film became truly silent for the first time: the piano music that had invariably accompanied it from its birth was a patent interference here. More often than not, this "judge" acted without words, in charged silence, and confronted the "defendants" seated before it with irrefutable, documented accusations.

But the defendants were Soviet people, pioneers of Socialism. They had just set out to build an unprecedented, new world. Much was still unclear to them. And there was much they did not yet know how to do.

Villains, class enemies, philistines, bunglers—were using the situation in order to shove sticks into the spokes of all sorts of wheels. The people could take the toughest criticism from the screen with a pure heart, and join us in confronting the *real agents of evil*. And around the Kino-Train a dynamic group of committed helpers and doers soon organized themselves, with members of the Party and the Komsomol youth regularly taking the lead.

One can readily conceive how our train collective became a cohesive unit in these circumstances. We forgot about normal work hours, days off, everyday hardships, and the tiredness we felt. We did our deckhand chores in concord and with jokes and our own catchphrases, and likewise any extra chores. The sleepless nights were no burden.

. . . The train was standing on the sidings at the station at Vechernii Kut. A grove of oak trees rustled nearby. The Sagsagan River was a hundred meters away. After the sleepless nights all of us would bathe in it together, and then the cook would feed us a meager breakfast. On warm days we would sometimes carry pillows and blankets into the oak grove, and have a delicious slumber there.

Our life was wonderful! But our films were very grim ones. The drunkards, truants, and idlers we had criticized on-screen were not left in peace by their wives. The men would come to us, demanding protection and justice. All kinds of people came knocking on our door—brigade leaders fired for negligence, exposed pilferers, pillagers of the people's wealth awaiting trial, dormitory officers subjected to criticism, technicians who had botched the mechanization of work, bureaucrats, and others—all with complaints and protests, and demands that we cut out certain "unsuccessful" sequences.

The year was 1932. Now, nearly forty years later, I think it was the grimmest year of class war, when the enemy hidden in our ranks were delivering their last, desperate, rearguard attacks. Only close contact with Party activists and with the best organizers of production and engineers helped us to avoid mistakes and to improve the effectiveness of our unusual weapon as we went along.

The grimness of our kind of film nonetheless often bothered me. Maybe this is why I resolved that in addition we had to make comedies on the train. This was going to be difficult. We were already working fifteen to eighteen hours a day. Somehow I managed to write a script at night. And soon we shot a two-reel comedy, *About Love*.[17] We began screening it toward the end of our sortie, and it was always well received. Our mass educators were pleased to notice that our grim sessions changed for the better. Our uninvited interference in social conflicts looked quite different when the evening ended in friendly laughter. Plaintiffs, defendants suffering from criticism, their judges—all joined in laughter.

"The serious business of laughter!" Laughter restored the unity of the collective of viewers, reasserting their common aims and the excitement of their difficult life. The script of *About Love* survives (and it is published here). God knows, it was no great work of art, but I remember how the actor Maslatsov aroused the unstinting laughter of people in this "eccentric" comedy,[18] when he depicted the extraordinary adventures of a somewhat simpleminded miner as he, against all odds, mastered the skills of a scoop operator, with which the audience were familiar.

We spent two months in Krivoi Rog. And we made twenty-one films—in all, twenty-four reels, amounting to 6,320 meters of usable footage.

Our work was highly valued. The local organizations rewarded the Kino-Train with a Banner of Honor, and youth brigades of miners all over the Don Basin competed for the right to call themselves "Brigade of the Kino-Train."

The Ore Trust management, on its own initiative—and to our surprise—paid all our expenses for the sortie and acquired the entire stock of films made in the Basin. The Trust could have avoided these expenses: the train figured in the Soiuzkino budget, and we had had no thought of payment, but Zorin, an Old Bolshevik, who headed the Trust, said: "I cannot understand why we should use your work without compensation when it has been of such value for the Basin. And as for the fact that you exist on a budget line, well, maybe you will enjoy giving up your situation of dependency."

Of course we enjoyed it! When we arrived with our train back in Moscow, we casually let drop in our conversation with the officials, sticking up our noses as if we were mere boys—"Oh, by the way, the Trust management has paid for the Krivoi Rog journey, although managers are usually tight-fisted and we had no idea of asking them!" This was the more apposite as the film officials had not believed in our experiment, had interfered with us in every possible way, and would have been happy to close us down as unviable.

The two tiresome months on a railway siding came to an end. We had forgotten that we had wheels under us rather than a brick foundation: every morning the same too-familiar landscape would open up before our windows, with the oak grove, the smooth strip of river, and the gray-white slag heaps on the horizon. Suddenly one night, when everyone was asleep, a locomotive gave our home a big jolt. Rocking and thumping along the track joints, we went sailing off into the dark, reminded that we were on wheels!

What kind of a sleep could we have? Even the most phlegmatic and dour comrades jumped out of their compartments into the corridor, shouting like children outdoors.

We were hitched only to freight trains, which in the thirties would crawl along at a turtle's pace, and stand for hours on dead-end sidings and at small stations. Savoring the bliss of doing nothing, we rejoiced at the inconveniences like children. All worry and stress would instantly fall away, and a strange and somewhat uncomfortable peace suddenly descend on us! People became kind, talkative, and noisy. I tried to make up for the many nights without sleep, but how do you fall asleep when wheels are bumping underneath you and peals of laughter come from the corridor, while in the sitting room someone sits at the piano, which during the feverish work of the sortie had been left unopened for weeks. Now, from afar, through the door of the train car, it was wonderful to hear a melodious aria from *Rose Marie*.[19] Of course this was Slon (Elephant), our nickname for Viktor Slonimsky, giving a rendition of his crowning piece.

On traveling days the deputy housekeeper, Dima Khamarito, found a way to surpass herself. The food on the table in the campaign cabin was sumptuous: suckling pig or lamb, turkey or goose. God knows from what stores Dima, a powerhouse, even managed to produce a sturgeon for supper. But "the wine they drank 'as water.'" Strange as it may seem, that first contingent of Kino-Train romantics were nondrinkers, who did not feel particularly oppressed because of the high moral and spiritual discipline required of everyone at work and especially during their hours of rest.

Sometimes somebody would dissent from this unwritten code of our jolly ship. He would be warned once, twice, and then—"put ashore." As I have said, this was done amicably and decisively.

Now, on rereading this, I am sorry to find an unnecessary stress on the personal pronouns "I" and "me." In actual fact the burden of the formidable problems of the train rested on the shoulders of a remarkable collective of thirty-two enthusiasts. Just eight of us are still living. Some of us died of old age; most gave their lives for the Fatherland, defending it rifle in hand from the Fascist invaders. They live in our memories as vibrant, interesting people.

All of them had to be stalwart inventors in order to squeeze a whole kino-factory into the incredibly tight space of the train cars, in defiance of all accepted norms, and to get this factory to issue without fail, day and night, our "film missiles" attacking the old world. When I say everybody had to be an inventor, this really was the case.

Two inseparable friends, the two Vasias—Krylov and Matiushin—lived somewhat aloof, in the third car, in a tiny compartment squeezed between the film laboratory and the electric generator. In terms of their responsibilities, one was a driver, the other an electrician. Actually, they were a remarkable team of master engineers. Their four hands cheerfully and unfailingly solved any technical puzzle. They turned the garage into a printing shop, although this difficulty had seemed simply insoluble. They got water for the laboratory when this seemed a wild dream in the particular conditions at one railway station. They brought an electric power line to the train, improved the cook's stove top, invented super-efficient shelving, repaired film projectors, remade doors, and so on and so forth.

And they were always cheerful! They were bound by a tender friendship, which a roughness of manner hid from the eyes of others. "Well, this is an epidemic," Vasili Iakovlevich Krylov would grumble to his friend. "You've taken the pliers again."

"Here they are. They're staring at you! Tell me if you're going blind so I can get you a pair of glasses."

"Phooey! An epidemic!" Krylov put a thousand quite contradictory meanings into this word. It served as a swear word and also as a sign of enthusiasm over the boundless cleverness of his friend Matiushin. It served for manly disappointment when something did not work out and for childish joy when his anxious wife sent an unexpected parcel from Moscow. "Well . . . an epidemic."

At night, making my way to the laboratory through the dark cars, I liked to turn into their compartment, which was tight as a clothes cupboard. We would drink very strong tea to drive sleep away and have a leisurely talk on general topics. A piston was tapping; behind the partition the Debrie-Matipo film printer rattled, and the drum used to dry film squeaked. Slowly we would slake our thirst for tea and conversation.

The two friends' voices still sound in my memory, but they are no longer alive . . .

In the kino-laboratory behind the partition were the two young lab assistants, Kolia Zviagin and Zhora Davydov. They worked for the lab head, Sheviakov. One evening the two youths asked me to look in and throw out their boss, who, more than many of us, knew no limits in matters of work. He did not sleep for many nights at a time, and I often had to intervene.

I sent Sheviakov to bed, and then on one pretext or another the kids kept me in the workshop and ambushed me with quite unexpected questions: "Will there be war? Is it true that the Kino-Train will be sent to Tashkent? How many years will our train travel about Russia?"

These two romantics were young and very hardworking. I cannot remember a single instance when they were responsible for the lab's delaying a film or wasting material. But the pair—Kolia Zviagin and Zhora Davydov—were saucy fellows and liked to scatter dust in the eyes of local beauties! They had hung a mirror fragment in the drier, and, yes, they just had to look at themselves: a forelock to smooth down or a profile to check (a snub nose or not a snub nose?). They had clean shirts, caps, and elegant leather outfits—indeed our whole detachment wore leather jackets, trousers, and shoes. The young swells were not afraid of me. I remember Kolia Zviagin saying once when we met: "We went to the theater yesterday, took our seats, all dressed in leather—not bad, eh? All around people were whispering, 'Film people! The Kino-Train!' And we pretended we heard nothing. We just sat and looked at the stage! Not bad, eh?"

Wonderful romantics! They went off to defend the Fatherland in 1941 and did not return. Zhora Davydov ran in to see me the day he left for the front. Unable to find words in his state of agitation, he asked me with childlike sincerity to get together the right people and quickly make a film of Tolstoi's *War and Peace*: "This novel arouses patriotic feelings. I cannot express my thoughts in words but I feel it in my heart—this film has to be made as quickly as possible!"

He did not come back. Neither did Doda Karetny, the cameraman of the animation workshop of the train, nor Sasha Glukhovsky, the lighting man, nor Grisha Ashkinazi, whose one person comprised the entire administrative department of our enterprise: bookkeeper, train commander, office director, dispatcher, and head of personnel.

No, it was not a simple task for one man to carry out the administrative functions required for a studio that produced seventy-two films in six sorties! Nobody made any concessions for the originality of the enterprise: we had our own official seal, a checking account in a bank, an approved factory insignia (of course a boldly onrushing train!), and no license for any liberties with the financial abracadabra, complicated accounting forms, and official correspondence.

But he did it! All by himself! And fearlessly! Without once crying: "Double my staff! I'm getting in a muddle!"

Sometimes I was worried when Grisha turned up when I was shooting:

"Grisha, is something wrong?"

"Nothing!"

"Well, why did you leave the train?"

"Sasha, the paperwork was driving me crazy! Is one allowed to breathe fresh air during production work?"

"Yes. Do breathe! Or rather run to the office! Get the brigade leader here in a hurry for the shooting; we've been waiting for him!"

"Aye, aye! The brigade leader! Quickly!"

He went to the front in the first days of the war and did not come back. But how can one forget a remarkable man who could discover the poetry of creation in the intractable material of office work?

The unusual nature of the enterprise gave everyone surprising possibilities for invention and creative experimentation. While Ashkinazi was a "one-person band for management and bookkeeping," Boris Shumov was a "one-man orchestra." As my first production deputy, Shumov contrived in *all* touring conditions (meaning *crises*) to coordinate and harmonize the work of all our shops and shooting crews and to release film after film without holdups despite the technical difficulties and shortages.

Boris did not have an abundance of people. Our allocation of personnel and output to each team was done roughly, at a glance, with naive omissions and inevitable mistakes. This stubborn man suffered much to get our whole machine working: at first dead; then creaking at every joint; and once it was in operation, in need of constant tuning in accord with exact rhythms. Bottlenecks could appear at every stage. For example, a large amount of running water was needed to process the film. Where could it be found, and how delivered to Sheviakov? What if the water was too hard or contained harmful chemical impurities?

Boris and I were friends for more than forty years, and I cannot remember him ever shouting at people, although any crisis was usually his to deal with. Always even-tempered and gentle, he spoke laconically, with an amazing ability to rally capable men round him, and thanks to some special key he possessed, he alone was able to release enormous creative energy from them.

When I remember Boris Shumov, I sometimes wonder why it was that people always liked him. For as long as I knew him, he had a "dog" of a job, in which an administrator's "squeeze" could crush a man. I think he was loved because he never oppressed or humiliated a subordinate; he had a specific understanding of another man's difficulties, valued him and his work, and would help him, while modestly remaining in the shadows.

In the Kino-Train he had dictatorial powers to summon any worker to do deckhand chores—such as pouring water into tanks, shooting intertitles, editing or projecting a film. At two or three o'clock in the morning he might knock at a compartment:

"Sibiriak! Go and shoot some titles!"

Nikolai Vasilievich Sibiriak was an actor and director, who had come to us from Vsevolod Meyerhold's theater.[20] An old, respected man, he would silently dress and hasten to the workshop to shoot some titles.

"Don't you have anybody younger?" I'd ask Boris, annoyed.

"Why? Of course I do, but Sibiriak himself told me to allow him no exemptions or privileges."

Sibiriak was a staunch romantic. He had come to us for a term from the theater and eagerly experimented with new satirical genres with me. On top of that, he unfailingly carried out the heavy deckhand chores, shoveled coal, did kitchen duty with everybody else, and served as odd-jobs man at the shooting locations.

Everyone understood that we could not do without the deckhand chores, yet some remained unreconciled to them. Some of them argued, "scrimshanked," refused. Boris would come to me in the editing lab at night: "What shall we do with R.? Once again he has refused to help Sheviakov in the lab. He's rebelling, says he can't sleep, feels tired, won't come."

Nikolai R., an administrator, had been fired up with enthusiasm for our train and talked us into receiving him into our family. We took him. The enthusiasm soon dissipated. His work was neither good nor bad. One day he was drunk and raucous, another he'd find it difficult to get up for deck-hand chores. Shumov spoke to him in a friendly manner, then Starovoitov did, and then I . . . Now, he didn't want to help! I came to a decision: "We will sign him off the train."

"When?"

"Three days for him to get ready. You can order a ticket."

No shouts, no arguments. An accounting was given to R. along with a ticket to Moscow. It was all done quietly and without a row: he did not have to do chores, but the same as on a ship we could not manage without chores. At lunch in the saloon, I asked the romantics to give their open support to Shumov in conflicts of this kind.

Besides his responsibilities for the workshops, Boris Shumov was swamped with the organizational hassles of the "shooting crews" (if that is the name for a basic "motor unit" having just two components: a film director and a cameraman). Often the film director carried the film cases and reels, assisted the lights-man, and carried out the functions of crew director or administrator.

The truly unique crew director on the train was Viktor Slonimsky.

"Slon! . . . Slon, fetch it! . . . Slon, get them to agree! . . . Drop this off at the mine! . . . Take the scythe back to the kolkhoz! . . . Slon, we are waiting! . . . Slon, don't be late!"

Figaro here, Figaro there . . . I had my own Figaro, my slow, sleepy friend Viktor, who looked like an old and respectable elephant [*slon*]. And the more we hurried him, the more quietly he would move, for one way or another everything would sort itself out, and anyway he did not have five pairs of hands!

And somehow he did do everything in time, and the train people loved him. Moreover, Slon was an excellent piano player. I remember him at the piano in the saloon in the evening. As I worked in the editing room in the next car, I loved hearing the distant melody from the operetta *Rose Marie*: "The flower from the fragrant prairies!"

Music!—The wonderful, strange power of music is something I felt most strongly on the Kino-Train. At times we were tired to death because of inordinate work and because dead-ends and disappointments outweighed our joyful achievements, but luminous melodies and sounds could instantly captivate us. It is hard to explain what happened to me in those minutes; it was as if some wonderful drug propelled me from my compartment into the editing lab.

As for Slon, you can still meet him at the Mosfilm Studio. His bulk has increased; he has become imposing, and even slower, as befits an elephant, and our meetings are always an occasion for special rejoicing.

Our Daily Bread

We were still recovering from Krivoi Rog when we were summoned by the comrades who decided our fates:

"Will you go to the grain harvests?"

"Where?"

"Crimea and the Ukraine."

Another car, to produce *The Peasant Newspaper*, was attached to the train, and in the twinkling of an eye we were dispatched south from a freight station. Another rail journey! Young birch woods in the Moscow environs, railway sheds, sidings, sailed past the windows. The farther south we advanced, the fewer the woods, while great expanses of wheat were already turning yellow.

Hot June days. Gathering in the harvest in Crimea and South Ukraine begins in the first days of July. We were running late! Mowing grain is like a battle: when it begins the manpower and equipment must be ready, and gaps in the organization of the brigades must have been filled. All the manpower is thrown into the battle without an hour's delay, whatever the state of the fighters and the commanders.

This time our Kino-Train was scarcely delayed at intermediary stations, and was quickly sent through to the south, to the front zone of the harvest. Today I am reminded of this "dedicated" route when I see convoys of trucks with the sign "Harvest Truck! Yield Right of Way!"

Convoys of tanks and war supplies were pushed through to the front in like fashion . . . Needless to say this (unexpected) privilege made our collective of romantics coalesce, filling us with reverential trepidation and building in each of us a readiness for combat. Expanses of fully ripened wheat were sailing past the train windows, and we were worrying: "How and what to film? With the grain crops, too, would we find active forms of direct intervention and methods in the Party's intensive struggle for the Five-Year Plan?" Everything would be easy if we confined ourselves to shooting formulaic documentary reports along the lines of "A rich crop has ripened in South Ukraine. The members of the Rising Sun Kolkhoz Association are hard at work in the fields. Shock-worker Ivan Protsenko delivers a double quota," and so on . . . But no, *that* was not the task for which the Kino-Train was needed. We had to engage in the fight for the harvest as organizers. How to do so was as yet unknown. And that is why we were nervous as we looked out of the window at the unbounded yellow sea of the enormous crop.

Bread—a grand subject! The Party's battle for bread was filled with gripping drama and unmatched epic feats. Hunger's scrawny hand had held us by the throat (for many years now!) and threatened to strangle the Revolution.

All these things existed: workers who got an eighth of a loaf a day (fifty grams!); starving children in towns; ration cards giving no food supplies; the Red Army fighting without food; shameless speculators and cruel bagmen who left hungry men threadbare; kulaks with piles of grain rotting in pits who used starvation as a means of attacking Soviet power; the inhuman blockade of the Soviet government by the Christian world greedily awaiting the time when hungry men would sell the achievements of the Revolution to it, all for the sake of a piece of bread.—All these things have now been forgotten with a strange lack of thought. Nowadays you can enter a bakery where a wonderful fragrance of bread greets you! And an angry old woman will piercingly cry: "You've got no Orlov loaves again! When will this outrage stop?" Do not judge her! This old woman has known very hard times, and now that the Party has overcome the most difficult problem of all—the supply of bread—she is right to make strict demands of the careless bakers. It is not for us to defend them. . . . In that year the battle for bread was far from over. The class enemy had not surrendered any of their positions; in some places they were even on the attack. Half a year after our bread expedition, the Party Central Committee gave this description of the situation in the country:

> The successful solution of our difficulties encounters fierce resistance from anti-Soviet elements in the villages. The kulaks have not conclusively lost their influence even though their economic base has been smashed; former White Army officers, former priests and their sons, former village policemen, and other anti-Soviet elements settled in the villages try in every way they can to break up the kolkhozes and to undermine the initiatives of the Party and the government in the area of agriculture. . . . Anti-Soviet elements penetrate the kolkhozes in the

guise of storekeepers, brigade leaders, etc., and even as executives in the administrative bodies of kolkhozes. They wreck machines; sow the fields patchily; pillage kolkhoz property; organize the pilfering of seeds; sabotage the preparations for the grain crop. Sometimes they even succeed in destroying kolkhozes.

(Resolution of the Joint Plenum of the Central Committee and of the Central Control Commission of the Communist Party of Bolsheviks, 11 January 1933)

The Party opposed this hostile force with a new, flexible form of struggle involving the PolitSections of MTSes (machine-and-tractor stations) and sovkhozes.[21] Their style and methods of work turned out to be close to the practice of the Kino-Train, so that later we readily became their active helpers everywhere. [*marginal note in Medvedkin's hand*: This sentence does not clearly express my thought. Make changes, for instance: "The style and methods of work of the Kino-Train corresponded to the resolution passed by the Plenum."] It was not, however, until one year after our first expedition that the PolitSections were set up, and when the Kino-Train set off for Crimea, and "tied up" at the sidings at Dzhanka, the organization of the PolitSections was still a half year away.

In Crimea everybody was out in the fields. The sound of intense work reverberated from the vast steppe day and night. Nothing was the same as it is today! Horses did the mowing, carting, and threshing. The outcome of the battle for the harvest depended on the manual labor of thousands who had not yet learned to work in collectives. The pinnacle of mechanization was a horse-drawn reaper—or "raker"—out in the steppe, apart from an antediluvian steam engine on the threshing floor, which consumed mountains of hay in order to power an antiquated thresher.

Suddenly mowing time had arrived across a broad front, and changes in the use of people and machinery were going to be difficult to make. We decided that the main task of the Kino-Train should be to show onscreen the experience and skill of the best brigades and individual kolkhoz workers, and to contrast their feats with the weak labor organization and indiscipline that infected all young kolkhozes during the first years of their existence.

The Oblast Party Committee advised us to get the train over to the station at Biiuk Onlar. Here in just three days we shot a film about the excellent Lithuanian kolkhoz[22] called Veitlus. The key to its remarkable achievements was its president—a huge, blue-eyed hero and a natural organizer. Somehow everything he did came out simply and rationally: everybody had a task; there was no fuss; the horses were strong; the threshing machine ran steadily all round the clock and kept adding to the flow of golden grain. Our film was about this man's simple secrets.

By the fifth day of our arrival in Crimea, the train's projectionists were traveling with the film all over the steppe, talking in the evenings with brigades and on threshing floors about the intelligent and simple ways that existed to organize the mowing, avoid fuss, get rid of unneeded idlers in the harvesting operations, keep the horses in sound health, and so on.

Our mass agitators were short of specific knowledge. Many questions left them at a loss. We established a rule—never lie and honestly acknowledge our ignorance about agronomy to people who drank in our every word. For the mass agitators this was scarcely an obstacle in the evenings on threshing floors and with brigades in the fields when, with the help of the dimly lit screens, they led big discussions about the essential point: where the obstructions were located, and what could be learned from a neighbor and put to immediate use.

The District Party Committee suggested that we dispatch the train to Evpatoriia, where the harvesting was a matter of special concern. For our work in Evpatoriia we now had both experience and ready-made films. Besides the film about the "Veitlus" Kolkhoz, we had two short episodes of our *Kino-Gazette* series shot for the locals, giving a direct, unpleasant juxtaposition of the Veitlus situation with the facts jeopardizing the harvest in laggardly brigades.

In those days the laboratory and the editing station of the train worked round the clock. Sheviakov turned dry and green with fatigue. He wouldn't leave the developing room, and was falling asleep as he worked. At times I forced him to come away to his compartment, from which he would quickly slip away as soon as I relaxed my control. In this way he would get edit-ready positive film onto the montage table in a matter of hours after it had been shot. He further contrived to print four or five copies of each film and gazette. Starovoitov would grab them from him and rush away into the steppe.

Sheviakov wasn't the only one to suffer. Everyone felt the heat! Everyone was working at full-out intensity, performing miracles of initiative, persistence, and inventiveness. Somehow our relations with one another on the train worked out smoothly. I cannot remember that I, as the director of the train, ever had to shout, punish, or waste time with tedious investigations by Party members into accidents and fights. Maybe this is why during the forty-five hot days of this (most intense!) sortie our three groups—or rather three directors and three cameramen—shot eleven films with 3,659 meters of total usable film, and Sheviakov, moreover, managed to print them in the quantity needed for the work of mass mobilization.

While acting as leader of these wonderful people, I contrived to be one of the three directors and "surfaced" with exactly one-third of the usable footage. In so doing I did not forsake my passion for satire. For instance, in the *Kino-Gazette* No. 16, I and Gleb Troianovsky, the cameraman, filmed a rather funny story mocking the hopeless organization of work in one of the field camps. Gleb (a mommy's boy!), famous in our family for his feminine gentleness, grew tired of following me about with the heavy camera and the huge, old tripod, while I was carrying the horrible chest with the lenses and the film container without knowing what to shoot! Of course people were working, mowing, carting the wheat, feeding the horses—but it was pointless to shoot "just that." In the field camp the tired cameraman collapsed in the shade under a cart and condemned me with an excruciating look. I was gloomily wandering about among the cooks and assorted idle people when I stumbled upon a topic about do-nothings during the harvest.

Four corpulent cooks were pressing around a fire, getting in one another's way. It was crowded for them around the one pot, in which they were boiling dumplings, when in fact one of them could have done it all by herself! A half-asleep carter had been hanging about next to an empty cart, wearing himself out with boredom, stroking one bare leg with the other; he was yawning and in danger of dislocating his jaw. I counted eighteen souls in the field camp, more than half of whom were clearly superfluous.

Over two days Gleb and I excitedly filmed a highly relevant story about the bunch of do-nothings, furnished it with satirical touches, then provided nasty, mocking titles for it and included it in a *Kino-Gazette* exhorting the kolkhoz members to look around more often—to check whether there were any spare hands, because they might be very necessary in a nearby field during this hot battle for the harvest.

At every step yesterday's individual peasant farmers showed their organizational naïveté and their inability to make peasant farming the endeavor of a united collective. But this was collective farming during its bright youth, a time filled with remarkable discoveries, when the eyes of simple, scarcely literate peasants were just beginning to open to the exciting horizons of Socialism. It is not surprising that the grain losses in the harvest were sometimes of catastrophic dimensions. Because of this Gleb and I were driven to make a sharply critical kino-pamphlet called *The Hole*.

The comic motif of the film had the actor Volodia Maslatsov playing a simpleminded water carrier, who does not notice it when a bullock knocks a plug out of his cask. He arrives in the steppe with an empty cask. And here he is in big trouble! Everybody vents their anger on the carrier: the brigade leader, the cooks, comrades, Komsomol members, Pioneers,[23] plus his wife and the newspaper. The point of the comic motif was "Everyone can see the little hole, but no one sees the big one." And we followed this with a documentary account of the big hole into which the kolkhoz harvest was pouring.

The horse-drawn reaper was an imperfect machine. It battered the husks and scattered the grain. The horses trod on the husks. Many trodden-on husks with a lot of grain remained in the stubble. A threshing machine in need of adjustment scattered more grain from the floor. More grain was lost along the road by the carters. The journey of the crop from the husks growing in the steppe to the barn was a terrible one.

Here we included another comic fable in the film: Maslatsov is walking in a field, bent over under the weight of a huge bag of wheat. The bag has dozens of holes. As he carries the bag to the barn, the grain runs off in continuous streams, the bag is half-emptied. Our actor, no longer bending but dancing, happily pours the pitiful remains of the harvest into the bin in the barn. And everyone else is happy! They all congratulate him: the brigade leader, comrades, Komsomol members, and his wife and the newspaper.

In the film we included a documentary episode about the fight of the kolkhoz members in the Balandino district against the losses of grain. To the reaper they attached the simplest of grain catchers. We showed its design and operation, and showed the huge pile of grain that this simple device saved in one day of harvesting.

In the "Ilich" kolkhoz, nearby, the losses were especially great. When the Ilich people were shown this film by our mass mobilizers they rushed to make the simple catching device. But only two days were left till the reaping was at an end, and the sad kolkhoz workers could only scratch the back of their necks and lift their hands—in which positions we took the opportunity to film them!

The harvest in Crimea ended as any battle does. The last reaping machines were still rattling somewhere. Bullock carts were conveying wheat to the threshing grounds. In the evening songs sounded in the steppe and on the threshing floors.

A telegram from Moscow instructed us to go straight to Ukraine, where the harvest was just beginning. We enjoyed catching up on some sleep in our narrow compartments while the locomotive carried us north.

The kolkhoz carts were already raising dust on the byroads of the steppe, and here and there harvesting machines were rattling.

In Elizavetgrad (now Kirovograd) we went to the Oblast Party Committee, which suggested that we make Adzhamka station our base and assured us that everything would be the same as in Crimea: the disturbingly tight deadlines for the harvest, the lack of draft cattle, and in general the same organizational disorders and difficulties with machinery. But our train came to Adzhamka with valuable experience from Crimea, and above all with films.

Starovoitov hurried off with the films into the fields. The District Party Committee assembled a group of mass agitation workers for him, including agitators from the District Committee, agronomists, and Communists mobilized from the factories. One day later our projectors were at work with the entire output of films from the Crimean sortie. The cameramen went out to shoot stories for the *Kino-Gazette*, and we quickly prepared scripts for one-reel films.

Here, too, in the Ukraine, we discovered excellent organizers, whose experience suggested to us the subject of a film, *Let's Organize Production Links*. Looking back at the events of those years, it is striking to see the unprecedented scope of the search undertaken by the people to find the best organizational forms of collective work. There were many mistakes, naive experiments, and delusions when individual peasant farmers were first becoming part of a collective brigade! Confusion and irresponsibility were the inevitable result of mass work without an experienced command staff or agronomists (and with the kulak intrigues!). The "Link"—an idea thought up by the people—amounted to a flexible, primary work cell in which everyone knew what to do and how to do it, so that any idlers and do-nothings were apparent. This concept played a huge role in the victories of the kolkhoz system. But all this became clear much later. The idea had to be fought for at the time of our sortie.

Let's Organize Production Links gave vivid examples of the muddles that existed in brigades working as unorganized groups during the harvest, contrasted with the experience of excellently organized links. The film, which was shot in a feverish rush, was of course not a distinguished cinematic achievement, but it was a useful tool in the hands of mass agitators, who could supplement it with examples from the actual practice of viewers.

The film director, Garri Piotrovsky, a taciturn and pedantic man, was famous on our train for his intolerance of all disorganization. This was his obsession. I could say many kind words about this marvelous man. He used to come into the saloon and spend half an hour gathering up the chessmen scattered over the table.

"Want to play, Garri?"

"No, I've no time to spare."

"Well, why are you going after the chessmen?"

"There's something about disorder that bothers me!"

"But you work in the editing shop, so why should this bother you?"

"I don't know, but something about it bothers me."

He was sparing with his words. Sometimes he wouldn't break his silence. But I recall how he sang with us in the evenings. His voice was excellent. He would be transfigured and unrecognizable, and we unconsciously yielded to him and began singing more softly. Later he fought in the Northern Fleet, where his health was undermined; he suffered in silence and died in silence.

That sultry summer Garri would come back from the fields, thin and black with dust. The two of us would take a walk to escape the commotion on the train. With difficulty I would extract from him a sparing account of what he had shot, how he had shot it, and I would toss out numerous facts, addresses, and names that might be useful for the difficult subject of his film.

Our mass agitators, starting with Starovoitov, told us what fired up the harvesters on the broad front line. More often than not, Starovoitov returned late at night, thoroughly tired, after the discussions at the camps in the fields. He would pull me outdoors from the editing room so that we could have a quiet conversation about what to shoot for our *Kino-Gazette*, and where.

In Adzhamka we shot and released three numbers of our *Kino-Gazette*, and they proved to be our most effective intervention into the life of the steppe. Short critical pieces we could shoot quickly, without wasting effort on script work and an intricate development of a story. Most of the *Kino-Gazette* issues during the sortie were made by N. N. Karmazinsky. As an experienced newsreel maker and a born journalist, Karmazinsky went about the business with assurance, giving me no trouble. In consequence I was able to write the script for an eccentric comedy, *Tit*,[24] in the space of a few nights and immediately set about filming it. And Karmazinsky made a very necessary film, *Wheat Sheaving*.

The harvest yield that year was excellent. Wheat was piling up in the steppe and the out-of-date threshing devices worked round the clock. But the threshing progressed haltingly, with gear wheels breaking, straps tearing, and machines breaking down. In most cases, spare parts had been unavailable from time immemorial, and there was a lack of educated mechanics. Hours were spent digging into broken threshers, while people wore themselves out from inaction on the threshing floor.

I recall the hot steppe, the unbearable heat and the stupefying stillness on the threshing floors when no one could revive the dead machinery . . .

Meanwhile, the mown wheat was waiting for the workers' hands. With one week of rain, the losses would have been immeasurable. And so the Regional Party Committee was exhorting men and women: "You have to sheave the wheat!" All free hands, all draft animals, all carts had to be thrown into the fight to save the harvest from the danger of rain. N. N. Karmazinsky made his very necessary film about this in the space of a few days.

Our youngest cameraman, Misha Lifshits, had an outstanding idea during this sortie. He collected a large detachment of Pioneers and schoolboys and led them to the empty steppe when the last stacks had been removed. For three days the Pioneers worked, gathering the remaining ears of wheat, the ones that had been ruthlessly abandoned during the harvesting and transportation, and had been trampled into the ground by people, horses, and machines. There was an abundance of them on the field roads. The Pioneers piled up a huge mountain of them . . .

The film—one reel, 285 meters long—was called *Pioneers, Hurry to the Fields!* The titles proclaimed: "A socialistic film-challenge from the Pioneers and schoolchildren of Adzhamka region to the Pioneers and schoolchildren of Ukraine." The Pioneers' names appeared next to the director's and the cameraman's. Sheviakov quickly made some six to eight copies of this film. After screening this "red-hot" film, our agit-workers were unanimous in speaking about the excited response of kolkhoz children and how, on the morning after a screening, the deserted steppe would come to life again.

Misha Lifshits!—a very young lad, not a Party member. The circumstances turned him from a cameraman with a narrow trade into a political worker. First he appeared as a technical agitator for the miners of Krivoi Rog, and then he was transformed into an organizer of the children's struggle against harvest losses, and later in the Don Basin he emerged as a prosecutor, recording in a short film the sabotage and wreckage of a kolkhoz done by kulaks. Nowadays I sometimes meet the now gray-haired Misha in Moscow. He is about sixty years old, but his eyes are as young as before:

"How is life, Misha?"

"All right. I'm working hard!"

In the feverish intensity of the journey our cameramen could not confine themselves to just "shooting" film. Their eyes were opened to the most critical conflicts in the battle for Socialism; they met interesting people; they were direct witnesses of intolerable disruptions and foul-ups. Thus many of the stories and subjects of the Kino-Train were suggested by cameramen, although more often than not they modestly remained in the background.

In this connection I want to say a few words about the cameraman Viktor Maslenikov. He occupied a special place in the fortunes of the Kino-Train. During the first year he made twelve films and perhaps twenty-five pieces for the *Kino-Gazette*. Bear in mind that he did this with the unbelievably heavy "Debrie-L" camera, fastened to a cumbersome tripod. With this assemblage Maslenikov ran about the fields during the harvesting and during military maneuvers, and he also managed to film in the tight cage-like offices of superintendents at construction sites. Restless and penetrating, Viktor was not very talkative, and in this regard resembled Garri Piotrovsky, with whom he often worked in the course of all the sorties of the Kino-Train. With his great spiritual charm, Viktor enjoyed the general sympathy of our "romantics," who gave him the friendly nickname Kotausi [Kitty]. This is what I still call him today.

Now, forty years later, I often think, "What happiness it was to lay out new paths at the great centers of construction of the new world and to work with a collective of such bright, interesting enthusiasts!" A whole book could be written about them. I cannot do this here; my task is a different one. It hurts me, but I won't stop to say even a couple of warm words about many of my comrades.

About two close friends I have to say something. They shared a compartment for a year, and shot picture after picture. That year, soon as evening fell, they stuck their noses into a chess game and forgot about everything on earth. The whole time Nikolai Nikolaevich Karmazinsky would continually draw on his stinking pipe, stuffed with such an impossibly filthy tobacco that his friend and roommate, the cameraman Zhenia Bogorov—a nonsmoker—reeked of nicotine even more than he.

As a rule, smoking was strictly forbidden in the compartments and workshops of the Kino-Train. The one exception was for Karmazinsky, who had made the right to smoke in his compartment a condition of his working on the train. And he smoked without interruption and seldom aired the compartment. Forty years later I remember with strange vividness the sour blast that hit my nose whenever I opened the door leading to these noble friends.

They were connected by a truly creative friendship and a valuable gift for extracting gems of sharp, clear generalization from the intractable material of perfectly ordinary news. Half a word sufficed for them to understand each other. Sometimes, however, the Leningrader Zhenia Bogorov liked to show off and boast of the unparalleled rigor and culture of the Leningrad school of film. We would forgive him his presumptuous arguments, for we knew in our hearts that, for all that, the Muscovites were better. Still everyone loved Zhenia, and the Karmazinsky-Bogorov artistic duo were extremely valuable: they were the most experienced newsmen, and the young people always found it interesting to study with them.

. . . But let us return to the hot Ukrainian steppes of 1932, where the reaping continued in the sultry haze. In those years, for the first time in the history of agriculture, the peasants were discovering the amazing joy of collective work. A storm of hitherto unknown sensations, feelings, endeavors, and accomplishments swept into peasant life. With great difficulty the petty property holder was being fired up and driven from one extreme to a new one in which everything found its place! Many things were incomprehensible; how to do many things remained unclear. The strength of the kolkhoz system was not immediately discovered, and the kolkhoz was not immediately able to put an end to the age-old poverty of the muzhiks.[25] And so there were many skeptics, whose tormenting doubts were carefully fomented by the kulak remnants. Maybe this is also why there were quite a few idlers, indifferent men, and deceivers. The principle they lived by was to do as little as they could and get as much as they could. The distribution of income according to the number of eaters rather than according to the work done suited them perfectly. They were the first to run with empty sacks to the barn to receive their share.

In our satirical comedy *Tit* we showed the idler Tit and his huge family, fourteen eaters in all, kicking up a cloud of dust as they rushed with their empty sacks down a village street, for fear of being late. I remember the strong response of the spectators, who knew the psychology of neighbors like Tit.

I have kept a still from this comedy in which a horse is pulling Tit to work with a rope. A cable attached to the cart traces is looped round Tit's neck, and drags him along. He has dug in his heels. "Tit is in no great hurry to get to work," said the intertitle. With its eccentric episodes the comedy was a retelling of the Russian proverb

"Tit! Time to do some threshing!"
—"I've got the stomachache!"
"Tit! Time to eat kasha!"
—"Where is my big spoon?"

When Tit is sent to feed wheat into the thresher, his pants fall down, and he has to work with only one hand. He disturbs people as he looks about for a length of rope to substitute for his lost belt. But the rope end with which he ties up his pants turns out to be a loose end attached to a harrow, and the horses pulling it drag him together with a pile of wet hay to the top of an enormous stack.

One day Tit is sent to town to sell geese, and he displays all sorts of laziness and evasions, until eventually he decides to go for a swim. To keep the tormented geese from running away, he ties them to his clothes. While he is bathing, the geese carry off his clothes into a thick cluster of sunflowers. Unable to find them, he has to return to the kolkhoz without geese or clothes, dressed as a *bayadère* dancer, with two sunflowers on his chest, and a band of sunflowers in place of pants. A photo survives of this sensational shot, which always drew Homeric laughter from the viewers.

Tit was probably V. A. Maslatsov's best role. Here, as nowhere else, he fully revealed his outstanding talent as an "eccentric" actor, possessed of an art close to a clown's.[26] As I remember, later, after leaving the train, Volodia worked for a while with great success as a circus clown.

As always, the script of *Tit* was written in the train late at night, when the workshops were relatively quiet, and organizational and editorial questions scarcely disturbed me. We shot this comedy in two parts in literally a few days, and it did excellent service for us on all the later sorties.

I regarded *Tit* as my greatest success in comedy.

Our mass agitators said that in any field camp, people would laugh till they cried when it was shown, and then when the discussion began after the screening, they would look for their own Tits and produce the names of idlers and kulak-types, whom they summoned before the "Gromada" [Political Assembly]. And here, in a way that was not always friendly or democratic, the latter would be made to undertake self-criticism.

Almost always after the serious discussions about work arising from issues dealt with in our critical films, someone from the public would cry out: "*Tit*! We want *Tit* again!" And everyone would cry "*Tit*!" And none of the exhortations of the brigade leader ("Members of the Gromada, we need to start harvesting at dawn") could extinguish the wish to laugh one more time at Tit and his voracious family, running to the barn with empty sacks for an advance of grain.

In the forty-five days of the kolkhoz sortie the Kino-Train shot and screened eleven films (twelve reels), totaling 3,659 usable meters. We were beginning to enjoy things after finding our place in the struggle for bread, and we had started work on new films when a telegram arrived from Moscow directing us to immediately move the train to Vinnitsa for some Red Army maneuvers. I do not remember the journey over to Vinnitsa, but in our annual reports two dates survive:

End of the wheat sortie—August 19
Start of the military sortie—August 22

Just four days were spent in moving the train and switching our collective to the solution of new problems!

Four days! Nowadays this figure is by no means sensational. But in 1932 the film art of "illusion" was an unbelievably slow-paced and intractable medium in terms of technical capabilities and political responsiveness. And so our four-day exercise, in which we completely transformed the production of a fairly complex company, gave us as much satisfaction as the successful sortie we had just completed. There was a particular, profound reason for this—namely, we had special expectations of the Kino-Train's military sortie because in fact our organization had first been conceived as an experiment to find forms and methods of filmmaking suited to the needs of the Red Army in the grim wars ahead.

I have kept the very first rough draft of my memorandum to Soiuzkino and PUR [the Political Directorate of the Workers and Peasants Red Army] about the need for a mobile kino-factory set up on a train for work in wartime conditions. I wrote it in August 1930 together with my now-deceased friend, the cameraman M. E. Gindin. We expressed our great concern, because filmmaking was not prepared for work in wartime conditions, which would require a quick—and difficult—reorganization. In those years it was of course difficult to imagine either the nature of the future war or our methods of work in the army. Twenty-five years after the Great Patriotic War I want to quote word for word from the Kino-Train project that we had sketched out eleven years before the war began:

1. The kino-base of the PUARM [Political Directorate of the Army] will be a miniature kino-factory on wheels (like the publishing office of

an itinerant newspaper), adapted to the independent production of film shorts and specially compiled programs.

2. As an organic cell of the PUARM, the kino-base shall be entirely devoted to agitprop work arising from both the general political tasks of the army and immediate military ones.
3. Accordingly the kino-base will produce

    a. newsreels (about our victories, prizes, heroes, etc.);
    b. military-instructional and informational films about the strategic inventions and new weapons of the enemy and about means of combating them;
    c. posters (for example, "Mobilize for the Attack!," announcements to civilians, etc.);
    d. caricatures, cartoons, comic broadsheets (for instance, about the struggle against looters and deserters, the struggle for discipline, etc.);
    e. watchwords (about the treatment of prisoners, etc.);
    f. animation films.

4. The basic principles of work will be topicality; speed; accuracy of contents; clear political solutions for mass-agitational topics.

    In these respects the kino-base shall generally operate according to the principles of work of an army newspaper . . .

    . . . Our aim must be to project agitational film shorts onto army screens every single day in order to generate enthusiasm, explain new watchwords, and show heroes and conquests, the enemy's bestial cruelty, and so on . . .

Our appeal was heard. The train was created in spite of all difficulties and, above all, in spite of the material difficulties in the country, which was just beginning to industrialize. The magnitude of these difficulties is destined to be forgotten, but we remember what was involved in giving us train cars, equipment, and generous material support for an experiment with a quite unclear outcome.

Our Meeting with the Red Army

At Vinnitsa we were as usual put on a siding at the station. When our romantics stepped off the train, they knew that they had come to examine the state of military preparedness for war. Here the experience of our previous sorties could be of little use. The Red Army with its well-defined military and political organization would not accept our critical style of tracking down shortcomings. And because of the rules governing military maneuvers, the lack of targets for sharp criticism, and the very different connection with viewers, we had to reexamine the forms, methods, and genres of our film work.

The commanding staff and the political organs gave us a friendly welcome and helped us unstintingly, in every way, until the end of our mission. Knowledgeable advisers were assigned to us as consultants; we were dressed in military uniforms, given maps of the military operations, and, most importantly, provided with transportation. The Kino-Train was connected with the army staff by field phone, and at any time we knew what was happening and where—with regard to both the "Reds" and the "Blues." This unexpected service allowed us to do an unusual experiment for those times—to project a film digest of operations in the first and second stages of the maneuvers.

On the animation tables we made "live" military maps, changing according to the course of events. On these maps, with the help of our consultants, we marked the military units' marches, forced river crossings, military engagements, flank thrusts, and so on. The three animation tables on the train worked round the clock.

All eight cameramen were assigned to the "front line." They returned to the train, usually after nightfall, tired and dusty, bringing the day's stock. Or, more commonly, it would be delivered by cavalry orderlies. A positive screening print was completed during the night. Next morning the film chronicle of the maneuvers was edited and combined with the animated maps. And in the evening the film was screened for the participants in the maneuvers.

The live animated map connected the scattered episodes of the newsreel, making sense of the actions of regiments, companies, and platoons, and visually displaying the meaning of the events to the participants of the maneuvers. The films bore titles such as these:

Second Stage of the Voronovitsa Maneuvers
Operations Film Digest, No. 4
17 August 1932

These films—made in an unbelievable rush, the product of round-the-clock work—had no claim to high cinematic quality. There was no sound, but instead intertitles. Often the outdoor shooting was not done in key places, and sometimes it was not comprehensible. But nonetheless the commanding staff and the political cadres and the linesmen took a keen interest in our film digests because they projected maps showing the movements and battles of the "enemy," and because the events they recorded gave viewers the opportunity to interpret the intentions of the "Reds" and the "Blues" and allowed them to see themselves during a battle or a forced river crossing.

Today, when I watch the latest news on television, with direct broadcasts from Sverdlovsk and then from Riga and Simferopol, I remember our antediluvian expedients to shave time off literally every single hour in order to get important information to the viewer as quickly as possible. Sometimes a cameraman would give a can of film to the cavalry orderly assigned to him, who would then gallop to the Kino-Train, where Sheviakov was waiting for him so that deep in the night he could hand-develop it without losing a minute. And the film director was waiting for Sheviakov so that he could look at the barely dry positive and edit it at once. The title man was waiting for the director, and so on.

I remember the merry excitement with which we looked for and eliminated any "empty minutes," as we worked out a maximally compressed technological process with no pauses between shooting and screening. One of the enthusiastic promoters of this absorbing experiment was the excellent production organizer Boris Nikolaevich Shumov. He had read a story in some magazine about the way film stories were made in America. A cameraman would shoot a sensational story about a fire, an explosion, or a big accident, and then rush in a car to the studios, processing the film as he went. His wife or his son was at the wheel, and the father performed his magic with the developer in a closed container.

Apart from the four film digests of operations at the Voronovitsa maneuvers, we shot eight films, amounting to twenty parts or 5,385 usable meters. In view of the special character of frontline work, we had got an agreement from Moscow to have reinforcements for the train. The directors Bubrik and Morgenshtern came, and the cameramen Makaseev, Krichevsky, Simonenko, and Florenko joined in the work.

Just nine years after this trip our cameramen were thrown to the front to make a film chronicle about the Great Patriotic War. Everything now was different than we had assumed in the Voronovitsa maneuvers. In the space of nine years the Red Army had changed beyond recognition, and I find it interesting to view the scope of these changes in relation to our films back them. Thus the Kino-Train film *Combat Fire of a Platoon* reflects the weak firepower of the infantry in the thirties. Their armaments included neither submachine guns nor mortars, just a few hand-loaded cannons. The tried and tested weapon was the Russian 7.6 mm rifle and the hand grenade. *The Hundred-Kilometer March* shows the infantry—the "Queen of the Fields"—which for the time being totally lacked all the blessings of motorized vehicles and mechanization. The commanding officers instructed us in the key challenges that an army on the march at that time faced: maneuverability, overcoming obstacles and obstructions, maintaining discipline, setting up outposts, physical endurance, and so on. *Engaging in Battle* was made in strict accordance with the established norms and strategic principles of the military theoreticians of those times.

Today I find it unbelievable that there were no tanks, that the artillery was not the god of war, and that the role of aviation was secondary. The shape of that far-distant Red Army revives in my memory. I compare the picture of the Voronovitsa maneuvers with what we saw in the great battle against Fascism! The two prewar Five-Year Plans formed an extraordinary springboard for our victory, changing an industrially backward country into the invincible arsenal of the Red Army! Then, in those years, in the wastelands and on the outskirts of old towns, giant metallurgical plants, aircraft factories, and car and military-machine plants were rising up, and were ready just in time for the fatal encounter with Hitlerism.

I recall the slogan born of the people—"Complete the Five-Year Plan in Four!" It released a previously unseen energy in the country. And indeed the First Five-Year Plan, which seemed unreal to the whole world, was fulfilled in four years,[27] and thus the unheard-of pace of the Second Five-Year Plan was set. The weapons placed in the hands of the Red Army were of a power such as we could not have dreamt of during the Voronovitsa maneuvers, in which our old Mother Infantry and her antediluvian rifles raised a cloud of dust while the commanding staff struggled to discern the shape of the terrible future battles. Our film *Engaging in Battle* is a record of that distinctive transitional time. A big part in it was played by an "animated" map, on which large military units moved, drew near, and joined in battle.

"Problem films" were a challenging test of the soldiers' wits. In the Gosvoenkino Studio back in 1927 we had made a film called *On Patrol*, with four absorbing tactical problems.[28] I have a leaflet explaining how to make use of this film with an unusual structure. At the outset titles advised the viewer:

Study the Movements of the Patrol!
Note Their Mistakes!
Decide Quickly How You Would Act
in Their Place!

When We Stop the Film,
Discuss This!

Following the discussion, we would display one example of a correct solution on the screen.

One of the absorbing mind-benders in this film went like this:

Problem No. 3
Messing Up!

On the screen an infantry squad is engaged in a patrol. A suspicious type is caught. He is searched, and a piece of a military map with pencil markings is found.—A spy!

What Do You Do Next?

The squad officer sends the spy off to the staff headquarters in the company of a not-very-bright soldier, to whom he entrusts a report he writes on the spot, before continuing his patrol. The escort conducts the arrested man but is suddenly alarmed when a cavalry patrol appears in the distance. On seeing the escort and the man under arrest, the cavalry detachment gallops up to intercept them.

What Do You Do Now?

The escort panics, and pushing his charge, he tries to make him run. Then, understanding that it is futile to run, the escort makes him lie down in a field of rye. The escort pulls the report out of his cap, and decides that it should not fall into enemy hands. He stuffs it into his mouth, chews it, and swallows it. The men on horseback surround the escort: "Stop! Hands up!" The escort raises his hands, and is appalled: "But we're on the same side!" The riders laugh. The escort's confusion increases: "But I've swallowed the report! What can I do now?" The escort scratches his head.

What Mistakes Did
the Squad Officer and the Escort Make?
What Must He Do Now? Discuss!

The screening was interrupted; and the viewers heatedly discussed the events. Many mistakes had been made. The officer should have read the report to the escort. The escort should not have destroyed the report without checking whether the men before him were enemies. The escort had one way out: to get the spy to headquarters and report everything. I recall the bubbling passions at the screenings we held in the Moscow garrison barracks. Officers often "joined battle," quoting from the regulations and recalling instances from the Civil War. With difficulty we separated the sides in order to project on the screen an example of a correct solution: this is where the patrol were going; this is where they got the spy . . .

But now the viewers were armed with a critical point of view on everything. It is obvious how useful this was for the military training of young soldiers of the Red Army.

The "problem film" we made during the Voronovitsa maneuvers was a repetition of our earlier Gosvoenkino experiment. But I do not recollect whether we got to use it in our work with military units. Probably not! We were hampered by the dispiriting lack of time, just as we were by the inescapable lack of space on our train cars. With enormous labor we would familiarize ourselves with new subjects, and then, just when we were getting a feel for the most important problems and finding creative solutions for them, the train would go clickety-clacking down the track, carrying us on new outings, with unfamiliar problems.

During the maneuvers I made a two-reel military comedy, *Pitfalls*. "There are no hopeless situations!" we proclaimed on the screen (the script of the comedy survives). Maslatsov, an artillery overseer, is sitting on a roof and adjusting how his guns are firing when the courtyard is suddenly filled with enemy uhlans. The only thing the lad can do is hide in the stovepipe. But then a fire is lit, and Maslatsov, covered with soot and looking a fright, is forced to climb out onto the roof. An uhlan notices him, and to escape his curiosity Maslatsov plunges headfirst down the pipe, from which thick smoke is now pouring. Looking like a devil, Maslatsov tumbles out of the stove into the hut and frightens the fat cook almost to death. The nasty uhlan takes aim at him. This is the end!—except that the gun in the hands of the frightened uhlan is shaking, and Maslatsov safely escapes thanks to the awful panic he has caused.

Take Advantage of Any Slip Up
by the Enemy.
But Don't Make Any Yourself!

Maslatsov hides in some rushes, tidies himself up, and peeks out at the road, where he sees a ragged old man making futile efforts to drag a cart out of a swamp. Maslatsov helps the old man, who in return hides Maslatsov under some hay in the cart. The old man drives him to the village but behaves strangely, stopping the horse beside an enemy sentry, a doltish fellow, to whom he tries to explain in gestures that there is a Red Army man hiding in the cart. The simpleminded sentry is busy making a whistle out of a reed, and the old man's efforts are in vain. Furious, the old man pulls the hay off Maslatsov—but the sentry has just got the whistle to work, and he won't be stopped for joy.

Spitting at the fool, the old Judas drives on with Maslatsov. He wants to lock up the prisoner in a storehouse, but Maslatsov, sensing danger, refuses to go along and crawls inside an upright barrel. The old man casts off his robe (he is a priest), sets his fat wife on top of the barrel, and gives her strict instructions to guard the captive and not come off the barrel, while he runs to headquarters. Maslatsov tries to overturn the barrel with the priest's wife on top, but the heavy woman is on the alert, and the captive cannot overwhelm her. After some comic episodes in his struggle, Maslatsov inches the barrel toward a ditch.

Meanwhile the priest has reached headquarters.

Maslatsov slowly moves the barrel over the ditch and escapes through the gap. The priest comes running up at the head of a detachment of soldiers. The wife on top of the barrel signals to indicate "He's here! Take him!" But on turning the barrel over, all they find is an empty space.

I am relating here just a few of the artilleryman's wild adventures after my rereading of the script in my archives. The men involved in the maneuvers gave the film an excellent reception. Just like the Kino-Train's previous comedies, *Pitfalls* found great success in all the succeeding sorties. Our train left Vinnitsa. Quite worn out, we understood that overall we had passed our military test with honors. The flattering comments about our company by the leaders of the maneuvers were one confirmation of this; the proof we gave of our technical proficiency during the experience was another one. "No matter what—we'll manage!" our enthusiasts would repeat with satisfaction as they rested during the journey, after cheerfully completing the communal deckhand chores.

Nine years later, in the first days of the Great Patriotic War, I went together with Vsevolod Pudovkin and Mikhail Romm to a meeting with the Minister of Film[29] in order to propose that a 'kino-automobile-train' be quickly provided for the front line, with a simplified design adapted to the radically new conditions of war. The reason I did not go alone was that my relations with the Minister were in a hopeless mess. Pudovkin and Romm spoke about the value of our first Kino-Train and the obvious usefulness of my proposal. The Minister listened to my proposal with great understanding and interest, and asked me to wait a few days so that he could get advice.

My second meeting with the Minister was distressing. Some old film masters had demonstrated to him the uselessness of my project and convinced him that the first Kino-Train had been but a rash and futile enterprise. The Minister's words were dry; he was obviously piqued at having nearly been the victim of a mad scheme. But the vast majority of film artists, including Sergei Eisenstein, Alexander Dovzhenko, Mikhail Romm, and Eduard Tisse, and a series of military-news filmmakers were true friends of the Kino-Train. They were not simply observers on the sidelines, but interested participants in our difficult exploration, who had joined us in the critical examination of the results of each sortie. And almost all the main body of news-filmmakers from Moscow had taken up the work of the train and regularly found artistic satisfaction in it, going on sorties, shooting combat films, and finding out that they could productively work on the front lines of the Five-Year Plans.

The Kino-Train had more friends than enemies and opponents, but the latter were more active. They enjoyed great influence in the Ministry offices and acted on the sly. Moreover, no moral principles restrained them. Thus they easily put us at odds with the film authorities and very easily discredited the proposal to organize a kino-automobile-train in 1941. For my part, I have never lacked "friends" of this sort, and, besides sorrow, I found and continue to find profound moral satisfaction in this.

The Launching of the Dneprostroi Project

Three days after leaving Vinnitsa, the Kino-Train stood on the high banks of the Dnepr next to a dam. Before the windows of the train rose an unforgettable, shining vision, the Dnepr Hydro-Electric Station. Born of the First Five-Year Plan, the Dnerpr GES was its greatest accomplishment. The whole country built it at the cost of immense efforts. The entire Soviet people were awaiting its start-up.

We arrived at the Dnepr five days before the solemn moment and, without losing an hour, we began work on the only film of this sortie. The most experienced cameraman, Nikolai Karmazinsky, was assigned to the task of shooting and editing a film with all the titles in just four days, leaving room only for some shooting of the eventful celebratory meeting and the popular festivities on the day of the launching. We were strongly drawn to the idea of showing the film that same evening during the large official banquet.

Everything worked out. Without losing time five cameramen filmed everything in which the builders took pride. In editing the film, Karmazinsky included sequences showing the initial construction on the empty banks of the Dnepr, edited for us in the film archives in Moscow. As if time were accelerating, the film showed the extraordinary, shining new giant plant rising before the viewer's eyes, along with the bright little town for the builders. Today our eyes have become accustomed to new, bright towns and huge industrial enterprises. But back then, in 1932, the first film sequence to show a street of eight bright buildings (a whole street!) seemed a marvelous vision of the future! This is why these very simple shots brought tears of joy to the eyes of Soviet men and women.

So, a four-hundred-meter film was practically ready for the celebration of the start-up of the Dneprostroi Project. October 10 arrived. With great agitation we filmed the "meeting" of thousands and the festive processions of builders and guests. We filmed:

Kalinin giving his speech
Sergo Ordzhonikidze giving his speech[30]
The builders and shock-workers of Dneprostroi giving their speeches

The can of film was immediately sent by courier to the train and handed over to Sheviakov's laboratory. By noon Sheviakov had delivered the first positive to the editing table. In the evening there was a large official banquet with guests from the Republics of the Soviet Union and with Soviet and foreign journalists. In the large hall the lights suddenly dimmed, and the first title burst forth on the screen:

THE LAUNCHING OF DNEPROSTROI
10 OCTOBER 1932

The film was a sensation. None of the guests had ever seen a newsreel shot just a few hours before depicting the very people sitting here now, at the height of the celebrations, and who were looking in amazement at themselves on the screen. Now we see nothing surprising in this, but this was in 1932!

A car from Dnepropetrovsk was waiting beside the train. At 8:00 p.m. Sheviakov loaded a second copy of the film into the car. At 11:00 p.m. the film was delivered to the Petrovsii Metallurgical Factory, the largest in the land. A huge screen had been hung in the courtyard. The film was shown to a meeting of thousands of metallurgical workers. It drew forth tears of joy. A second screening was demanded. During this screening the blast-furnace men, the steel smelters, the rollers, sang the hymn of the proletariat, "The Internationale":

> We will build our own new world.
> He who was nothing will be everything!

The battles against White Army generals, against hunger and typhus, poverty and destruction, had not been in vain. The self-sacrifices had not been for nothing now that the first stones of the new world were being laid. The new world was not yet a reality in the consciousness of millions, and now, suddenly: the Dneprostroi Project! A real, shining giant plant—the first one, pointing the way to the peaks of Socialism . . .

The film might have been better or worse. Its success was independent of its makers. It was not their art, but rather the tremendous achievement of the people that produced the universal cry of joy. For the first time the people were seeing their own future projected in the simple, actual shots of the Dneprostroi newsreel. Special trains overcame transportation difficulties in order to have the film delivered to Moscow and Kiev the day following the launching of the hydroelectric station. It was screened in these cities with the same success.

We left Dneprostroi two days after the celebrations, having devoted just seven days to this sortie. And yet we longed to stay! The train was standing next to the dam. Down below the waters of the tamed Dnepr were churning. The autumn sun was shining. And the builders were walking on the dam as if they were on holiday now that the terrible time had come when there was nothing left to do.

NOTHING TO DO! An unlikely, somewhat unsettling pleasure. In the train we acutely experienced this strange state of affairs together with the concrete pourers, the armature fitters, the crane operators. Our workshops were empty. The train seemed desolate. Everyone was on the dam, with the people. Boris Shumov quietly laughed.

"Boria, why so jolly?"

"We are loafers!" said Shumov. "Isn't it wonderful when there's nothing to do!"

I understand why he experienced this strange state with such intensity. In the feverish activity of the expeditions he was the one who slept least of all.

Down by the water beneath the dam Vasia Krylov and Vasia Matiushin caught a huge carp on a spinner.

"An epidemic!" exclaimed Krylov with delight.

"A whole dinner. Wait till you see what there will be at dawn tomorrow!"

. . . Tomorrow. Before sunrise, a shunting engine had hitched onto us and was pulling us off into the darkness, somewhere into the steppes. Our factory—our home—swayed almost reluctantly, rattled over joints and switches, and as usual suddenly reminded us that our enterprise lacked a foundation binding it to mother earth. We had everything—workshops, living quarters, a bookkeeping office, and a garage, but no foundations! We had wheels, which were steadily rolling our train along kilometer after kilometer, toward the front line of the unprecedented battle for Socialism . . .

. . . Ahead lay DonBas.

It appeared in our windows through a screen of autumn rain, striking us with the power of its industrial landscape. Swimming past us in the smoke and mist came metallurgical factories, blast furnaces, stockpiles of ore, smoking piles of slag, cone-shaped slag heaps around dark mine shafts, noisy railway junctions. We rolled through the confusion of station tracks; shunter locomotives whistled and blew steam at us through the train windows.

Yes, this dark kingdom of coal and metal was noisy and uncomfortable! About its life we knew almost nothing—and yet we were going to grapple with the breakdowns here, the interconnected hold-ups, the bottlenecks. We were going to nudge the laggards, put those who were bureaucratic and conservative on trial, and expose the spoilers of the Plan . . .

The Front Line

We were placed next to a factory on the outskirts of old Iuzovka, which still preserved awful traces of pre-Revolutionary misery and squalor. A cheerless place, a joyless time! A wet autumn, gray days, mists. Because of the coal dust and the ashes from the factories, black filth lay all about us. What were we going to film here?

But the DonBas was the key to the First Five-Year Plan, a magic feeder. The services of the DonBas in the transformation of our Motherland are incalculable. Perhaps this is why I want to take the opportunity here to share some thoughts that are outside the scope of a history of this sortie. A man imperceptibly ages. Sometimes you look at an old photograph of yourself and see no gray hair or wrinkles. "When did all this happen? On what day?" Age has no such markers. It sneaks into you a drop at a time, changes your face (and soul!) quite imperceptibly, silvers your hair almost reluctantly, as if to protect you from acute distress. A gentle, or almost gentle, "three-point landing"!

It would be good to get back one's youth without noticing the happy changes: suddenly, imperceptibly, bit by bit, the crow's-feet disappear, the hair grows more thickly and fills in the bald patches, and the withered skin of the face disappears somewhere. This is not naive talk about absurd miracles! Our great Motherland is growing young in just this way, as it sheds its awful decrepitude. Without our observing it, the traces of unbelievable deprivations and decrepitude have vanished from her face.

My generation, the men born with the century, the old men born in 1900, see the miracle more clearly than others do. I was fourteen years old in 1914. I remember the Russia of wooden houses and bast shoes,[31] the policeman with the red cord attached to a pistol, the bureaucratic red tape, the poverty on the outskirts of towns, the squalor of isolated Russian villages.

A land of wood! As a boy I would spend hours kicking about near smiths' shops as I looked for tiny fragments of iron, and rummaging in the town dump and digging in the garbage for rusty nails, pieces of horseshoes, and old locks. For old iron a little boy could always get thirty kopecks a pood,[32] because there was no iron in the land of wood.

I have mentioned the figure—110 million tons—for the amount of steel smelted in the Soviet Union in 1969. We have come a long way from 1913, when just over 4 million tons of iron were smelted in the vast Russian land.

4 versus 100!

4 million—when there were wooden houses, wooden plows, and bast shoes.

100 million—when our spaceships storm the universe. Old Rus has been growing unbelievably young, as if it had overthrown the established laws of aging.

110 million tons of steel! The Don Basin has a special place in this victory. In actual fact it was the only "provider" for all the new projects of the First Five-Year Plan and also the progenitor of the new, huge metallurgical combines. If thirty-six new blast furnaces were established from 1928 to 1936, then the metal for them usually came from the smelters at the old factories of Makeevka and Iuzovka. Later the powerful, newly launched factories of KuzBas, Magnitka, AzovStal, and Zaporozhie came to the help of Old Man DonBas. At the time when our train was shunted onto the Iuzovka sidings, KuzBas and Magnitka were still being built, and they were

the strongest "consumers" of the metal smelted at the old blast furnaces of the south. Imagine the energy that was driving the metallurgists and miners of the DonBas at the time we arrived.

The Kino-Train had finally procured its own printing press, which was put in the garage, and was publishing its own paper, *Tempo*. The editor, "Ian" Krasutsky, a young, bristling journalist, quickly mastered the direct, critical style of our work, and filled the pages of his militant paper with sharp, terse material looking at the experience of the best shock-workers and other leading workers and contrasting it with instances of laggardness and failures for which there was no justification. In conjunction with the film lectures, the paper proved to be an invaluable aid in the train's mass-instructional work.

When our mass agitators addressed the blast-furnace workers at a backward factory, they would screen a film showing the methods of an outstanding worker, Pushkin, and distribute a special issue of *Tempo* to the spectators. Our militant newssheet spoke loudly about the causes of the poor work of the participants in the "film session." The facts were stated: figures, names, and the dates of damaging technological lapses or appalling work in the express-laboratory. Analyses were given of timetable disruptions and of problems with the supply of fluxes, scoops, and iron. Drunkenness, truancy, the "couldn't-care-less" attitude of administrators, and so on were exposed.

Thanks to the newspaper the productivity of our "film prosecutions" increased threefold. I have a half-disintegrating set of *Tempo* in front of me. Our militant paper documented the manifold efforts of the Kino-Train to assist in the heroic battle that the DonBas miners and metallurgists were waging for the Five-Year Plan, and accordingly it can help me to tell the story of this sortie.

I always think of the editor of *Tempo*, Ivan Kondratievich Krasutsky, with gratitutde. Together with a restless energy, he had the ability to take ugly but seemingly small facts from life in the DonBas, grasp the essential points in them, and make penetrating generalizations.

Ivan Krasustsky, persistent, and sticky as a burdock leaf, was a man after all our hearts. In fondness, we immediately baptized him "Jan Pilsudski."[33] I remember Ian's tearful anger and his demands that "this rudeness" be stopped. "Tell them I won't stand it! Why do you call me Pilsudski?!" "But Jan, we say it because we like you."

He was a great inventor, and I will speak below about the miracles he performed with photographs displayed on stands, which were used along with the films.

In the DonBas our tried and tested method—contrasting failures and sloppy work with models of excellence and outstanding achievement—proved its worth. A blast-furnace master worker who was famous at the time, M. P. Pushkin, helped us considerably in our meetings with the Donetsk blast-furnace workers. Our film *Pushkin's Secret* told about the causes of his sensational successes. He had come in second in a national blast-furnace-workers contest, and his name had resounded throughout the land, so that the DonBas blast-furnace workers were eager to see our film. On-screen we showed a series of common faults and disruptions in the blasting process that M. P. Pushkin had managed to overcome. "Our furnace was stuck on a blacklist," he said in *Tempo*, no. 11 (August 1933). "The shifts were beginning to get used to the complaints, and this made it difficult to change things. The loaders, iron-men, and gas-men seemed to be sleepwalking. The worst thing is when men don't care how the furnace operates. Then all at once everybody is agitated and comes running when, as a result of carelessness, the furnace has been overloaded and the flames begin striking the skips. Ore needs to be poured in, but there are no scoops, as the dispatcher has sent them all to the open-hearth furnaces. Or pig iron is tapped, and the taphole needs to be stuffed, but the clay is not ready! Men lazily scratching themselves take a whole hour to change the air pipe, or don't deliver the coke in time. Or there is not enough ore."

"The furnace was sick every hour of the day" said Pushkin. "Only 15 percent of the June program was completed, while in the first thirteen days of July the furnace, operating at low capacity, yielded 20 percent."

Pushkin's main secret was that he could get the people of his shift to direct furious anger against anyone who disrupted the technological process and against any deviation from it . . . The dispatchers got it if they did not deliver scoops on time. So did the brigade from the supplies yard if the materials they provided were not clean. Anyone who held up the smelting was grabbed by the throat—the repairmen, the transporters, the crane operators . . . And most significantly, once they had shaken off their sleepy torpor, they would start moving of their own accord, giving no quarter to friends or colleagues or to the shift boss.

It is difficult to break the inertia of indifference and apathy! Pushkin's secret was that he and his shift smashed this inertia (no quick achievement!). The furnace responded with a flow of metal. One day, two days . . . and after one week the furnace was yielding 225 tons a shift. "Ahead lies 300 tons!" proclaimed Pushkin. Three months went by, and the shift was getting 300 tons from the furnace, exceeding all plan quotas. Now even the half-dead skeptics were on the run in the brigade. Changing an air pipe no longer took fifty minutes with cigarette breaks but rather five minutes without cigarette breaks. Ore, coke, stone—everything was delivered on time and in the prescribed amount.

Pushkin did not forgive any failure, even the most trivial one. "Better not to get involved with that devil," muttered the dispatchers, transporters, and ore-, coke-, and flux-men. Soon his name was famous throughout the DonBas, and then Sergo Ordzhonikidze sent his brigade a telegram congratulating them for winning the All-Union contest!

All this we tried to show in the film *Pushkin's Secret*. Straightaway all the DonBas metallurgists adopted it as a weapon. Party organizations, in friendly cooperation with our mass agitators, incited the furnace workers to battle to introduce Pushkin's experience. Dozens of production meetings began with the screening of this film-lecture, in order to prepare the master metallurgists for a focused criticism of problems. Hundreds of practical suggestions to improve the work of blast furnaces were acted on after these meetings.

One evening some steel smelters paid us a visit. We took them through our workshops, spoke about how we made films, and screened some comedies from our previous sorties. They laughed, praised our project, and hesitatingly admitted that they had come to criticize us for overlooking the steel smelters. At first they spoke politely, choosing their words so as not to offend us too much. Then they lost their temper, their voices growing stronger and angrier. "Steel is steel. Without steel the Five-Year Plan would not be the Five-Year Plan. You make films about blast-furnace workers and about miners, while we steelworkers seem to be strangers to you. And yet we have more sore spots and scandals than the blast-furnace workers."

The Donetsk steel smelters helped us to find the biggest and most critical problems in the operation of Martin furnaces. In front of me I have the issue of *Tempo* from 17 January 1933, which accompanied the film *The Problem of Holes*. "Get rid of holes in the Martin furnaces!" *Tempo* demanded. "Today there will be a trial that examines technological issues . . . The Kino-Train film *The Problem of Furnace Holes* will speak out as the first prosecutor." The genre of the film was suggested by life. It was made in the form of an indictment against the steel smelters of the Iuzovka factory. At our imaginary trial there were judges, a jury, witnesses, and social prosecutors.

Materials relating to the verdict were published in *Tempo*, no. 13 (17 January 1933). In brief, the situation was as follows. The new Martin foundry of the Iuzovka factory had fallen short of its annual quota in the Plan by

24 percent. The bane of the steel foundry was holes in the furnaces. The poor organization of work and the lack of technically educated supervisors meant that the bubbling molten steel was eating through the bottom of the Martin furnaces and flowing in a fiery stream underneath them. We filmed evidence of one of these accidents at the fourth Martin furnace, where 4,200 poods [68,800 kilograms] of steel had solidified and bonded with the furnace walls. With accidents like these the furnaces spent a long time out of operation. "Who is to blame?" asked the film. "Each hole is made by people," responded *Tempo*, "the steel smelters and their subordinates, the dispatchers, the gas-men, the transporters."

Taking the accidents in the fourth Martin furnace as a case in point, the film looked for and showed the guilty parties. In the Technical Control Division there were 216 controllers and 59 technicians and engineers. All they did was record the furnace troubles and prepare instructions for contingencies, but they did not help the steel plants! The film showed the unexacting controllers, the liberal, "couldn't-care-less" engineers and master workers. The steelworkers in the witness stand declared to the judges, "A furnace hole means there is a supervisor who winks at things."

The Party activists helped our mass agitators to organize trials at all the DonBas metallurgical factories. "All rise. The trial will begin!" Everybody stood. The judge let the screen "take the floor" and deliver the verdict. It was not so much specific people that were judged as the ineffective organization of work and irresponsible technical leadership. Thus the passionate criticism of the holes in Martin furnaces transcended its narrow subject matter in order to address the question of improving the technical education of workers and, in particular, to deal with the very urgent problem of smelting high-grade steels.

We took up this question in our film *Steel*. At the beginning of 1933, the first year of the Second Five-Year Plan, the demand for steel by the new machine-tool and machine-building factories would greatly increase. For them, steel smelted in the old ways, using an "eye test," was not good enough. The number of complaints was growing. The plans of new factories were going up in smoke. New car factories faced difficulties owing to the lack of thin-rolled steel. The difficult problem of smelting high-grade steels fell onto the metallurgists. What was required was a smelting regime of unprecedented precision, a precise composition of the charge loaded into the furnaces, and cadres with a high technical education to oversee the metalworkers. Finding a solution was not easy!

Pictures of this difficult time stir in my memories: a rainy, gray autumn; smoke pouring day and night from an old, sooty factory; and all around, the blackness, wetness, and bleakness. High-grade precision steel was needed. But the men in the messy materials yards were working just as in the old days, measuring quantities by eye. Ore, coal, fluxes—everything was delivered to the blast furnace in the same way as thirty years before. The men had never done things differently. "What we get from the furnace is no better than a pig in a poke," the steelworkers said bitterly. There were no technically grounded people for the Martin furnaces. Nobody had yet tried to seriously train them.

The old masters, the true elite among the steel smelters, were practical men who found it difficult to learn the more intricate technology. It was difficult for them to adjust a furnace in accordance with analyses from an express-laboratory and to correct the smelting process with an unusual precision. Their whole life they had trusted their eyes, which had never betrayed them. "My eye never misled me," an old master smelter said, shattered, when a flood of telegrams arrived demanding a halt to the delivery of useless grades of steel.

What we could not find for our film was a first-rate Martin furnace, for which all the attendant problems had been overcome. We filmed bits and pieces: an excellent express-laboratory in one factory, a wonderfully organized materials setup in another, a good training program for cadres in a third, and so on. As always, excellent examples of the best metalworkers and brigades were juxtaposed with examples of the worst.

The film *How to Train a Worker* dealt with the difficult problem of instruction of the cadres of young metalworkers. It showed good examples of the tutelage of young people by old workers from blast furnaces and steel smelters and considered how this principle could be more boldly developed. This film was shot at the request of the Komsomol District Committee, which then adopted it as a weapon, adding its activists to our brigades of mass agitators, and maintaining very close working relations with us during our stay in DonBas. . . . In front of me I have a pile of ragged notes, transcripts and reports, old crumbling newspapers, and sketches for scripts. If I try hard, I can switch off our busy space age, turn away from the flickering TV screen, and tuck away the papers with the names of Richard Nixon, Golda Meir, and Franz Josef Strauss. Then once more there rises before me a wet fall day on the outskirts of old Iuzovka, a slushy, dirty street, suffocating factory smoke, and oppressive anxieties, the causes for which I cannot immediately recall!

What was the most difficult thing of all? The grain crops? The last furious battles of kulaks in villages, factories, and construction projects? The relics of age-old penury and backwardness? What was most difficult? Or easy?

For instance, one of the burning problems of the first Five-Year Plans was the workers cadres, although no one seems to remember this now. I think of Andrei, an old miner from whom I rented a room in Iuzovka during our trip. From time immemorial he and his father had dug coal with a pick. "Everything was easy," sighed the old miner. "There was the coal; here was the pick. You hacked away, piled the coal up, collected your pennies! Whereas now they say, 'Stop, old man! You can't go there!' 'Why not?' 'Because there's a machine there, a machine!' It hisses, shakes, roars, howls like a cannon. My ears ring, and my arms ache. The pick is done for, and so is the miner!"

This picture was close to the truth. A jackhammer had been put in the hands of miners, and a coal cutter was lowered into the vein, pulling behind it a conveyor belt, compressors, motors, and kilometers of electric cable . . .

"The pick is done for, and so is the miner!" Our meeting with the Donets miners came at this difficult time of transition. Grandfather Andrei, like tens of thousands of miners, had to choose: whether to get a whole new training and regime of work, or leave his native mine.

On the Kino-Train we understood the value of any help we could give to the leadership and to Party organizations in the mass training and re-education of large occupational cadres, including miners, blast-furnace workers, and steel smelters and operators of metal rollers. Without overestimating our possibilities we stubbornly looked for new forms of films for training. A continuous-loop film was one such invention.

I will give an example. We found that to explain the design and operation of a jackhammer, the best instructional film aid was an animation drawing (A SINGLE SHOT!), showing the interaction of the parts of the mechanism during its operation. The approximately two-meter strip of film of the moving drawing was glued into a loop and was projected for ten minutes or half an hour while the lecturer explained the principle of the mechanism. This was interesting, graphic, and accessible to the understanding of even a man with little education.

We released a series of five continuous-loop films called *The Jackhammer*. The whole length of the series came to twelve meters of film. To accompany it we published (in an edition of a thousand copies) an instruction booklet explaining how to use continuous-loop films, what was depicted in each loop, and what the agitator needed to point out. All this cost mere pennies. Sheviakov printed a very large edition of the film series, but it was barely sufficient for distribution to the mines, which were flooding us with orders for this unusual instructional tool.

The second continuous-loop series was called *The Coal Cutter*. The five loops of moving drawings showed (1) a general view of the machine in operation; (2) the interaction of parts in the driving component as it was being moved into position; (3) the same at working speed; (4) the principles of motion of the cutting component; and (5) the work of the cutting machine in the coal vein.

The Donetsk Mining Institute, with whose help we made these two films, armed itself with them as instructional aids to use in the main departments and courses for the training of coal-cutter operators. The Party District Committee and the leadership of the Ore Administrations took every measure to ensure the use of these films in workshops and courses at mines throughout the Basin.

The blast-furnace workers had persuaded us to make another continuous-loop series, *The Blast Furnace*. We made it; the series included loops with moving drawings showing the blast furnace in operation, the loading of the furnace, the smelting process, the gas regime inside the furnace, and so on. Next came instructional aids for men working as steel smelters and mill rollers.

But now we lacked time to fully utilize the possibilities available to us in this genre. In those days the technical reequipment of the mines of the Donets Basin had assumed an unprecedented scope. Through the mass training and retraining of the many-thousand-strong army of miners, the slow pace of life was moving several decades ahead. Workshops and courses, schools, seminars, and lecture series—all the various forms and methods of technical education and propaganda were mobilized in order to fill without interruptions of work the most glaring shortages in occupational groups and in master workers such as electricians, compressor operators, fitters and repairmen, conveyor men, adjusters . . . All of the bottom ranks and the intermediate commanding ranks in the mines had to be reeducated!

Each mine had a special TechProp department coordinating all this technical instructional and propagandistic work.

I well remember the unbelievable resistance that had to be overcome by the governing bodies and by the Donetsk Party organization in this titanic struggle, the efforts that had to be made to transform the TechProps into effective resources for the mass training of cadres. An epidemic of "hostility to mechanization" spread from mine to mine, hampering and spoiling the planned reconstruction, which had been difficult to get going. To live unthinkingly, in the old way, without disturbance, was so much easier!

More often than not, anything new at a mine would be affected with breakdowns and snags. Machinery broke, and there were no repair facilities; the mine stood still; the output dropped. The foremen and brigade leaders should have intervened at once, but they understood neither the new technology nor the new organization of work. And so the TechProps dragged out a miserable existence: their buildings were locked up, and their teaching resources were underutilized.

At Mine No. 10 of the Petrovskii Ore Administration the money allocated for the TechProp was used to buy horses. TechProps often had bad workers assigned to them as a form of punishment. The TechProp at Mine No. 4-21 turned into the provider of quick fixes and makeshift solutions: helping supply men, taking the place of the mine chief at an unnecessary meeting, and disappearing on assignments to get machine parts.

All this provided me with sharply critical material for a fierce kino-pamphlet, *A Vacant Place*. Here our "eccentric" actor Volodia Maslatsov played the comic part of an untaught lad who had sworn to acquire technical knowledge but had encountered a TechProp and its leaders that were lifeless. "Not a TechProp but a TechTomb!" Volodia wrote in chalk on a blackboard after all of his comic hyperbolic attacks on certain laws carved in stone had run up against routine and bureaucracy, of which my filming at Mine 4-21 gave a reliable documentary record. As always, in showing negative facts on the screen and generalizing them, we juxtaposed them with the excellently organized (and above all, productive) work in the courses and workshops in the TechProp at one of the best DonBas mines—Komsomol Mine No. 15. The Donetsk District Komsomol Committee used this film in order to examine and restructure the work of the TechProps of the Basin. The Komsomol members joined the mass agitators from the Kino-Train in this big work of organization.

. . . The intermediate commanding ranks in the extraction process received increasing attention in the technical reorganization of the mines. If there was a breakdown in a mine, or coal did not get to the surface, the guilty person often could not be found. So-called objective causes and "circumstances beyond our control" often served as covers for an elastic system of irresponsibility (as they still do today!). The pointedly critical film *Circumstances beyond Our Control* spoke about the failure of the extraction plan at one of the most backward mines and specified who was responsible for what in this failure, emphasizing in particular the role of the foreman.

In the film *The "Komsomol" Mine Calls*, the Kino-Train upheld the attempt of a group of progressive young technicians and engineers to introduce a voucher system in the coal seam, allowing for a series of very useful measures for long-range planning of the work of the mine. . . . On 25 December 1932 our newspaper, *Tempo*, came out with an article headlined "A Film about Diky's Method," saying:

> The Kino-Train has come out with a new film called *The Conveyor Belt*, directed by Comrade Kin. The film shows Comrade Diky's method of moving a conveyor belt in a mine. This film together with newspaper articles will help the mass-agitation brigades of the Kino-Train to disseminate the use of this method in the mines of the DonBas.

The young director, Boris Kin, was a graduate of the Film Institute, VGIK, and one of Sergei Eisenstein's students. I remember him as a continually restless, never complacent inquirer, from whose perseverance I often took refuge in Sheviakov's dark workshops. This outwardly modest, taciturn fellow made his best film, *The Conveyor Belt*, in the DonBas. It provided a solid argument calling for a fundamental change of the work regime in the mines. "Why does the mine stop delivering coal for eight hours a day?"—"Because a shift is reserved for 'maintenance,' which has been introduced so that the conveyor transporting the coal can be moved from the site of extraction in the drift." The life of the mine stopped for eight hours every day. And everyone regarded this as justified and inevitable. Only one person, the conveyor-belt man, Andrei Diky, disagreed. The skeptics mocked him, the conservatives hooted, but Andrei Diky abolished the dead shift in his mine, and the mine started working round the clock. *Tempo*, no. 10, published the following testimonial from Alimov, the director of Mine No. 9:

> **The Statistics of Victory**
>
> The whole seventh coal drift formerly produced 2,400 tons a month. When Diky's method for shifting the conveyor was introduced, the yield went up to 3,360 tons. Coal was now being delivered during a work shift at a time when the mine was formerly at a standstill. Now all the drifts yield 960 tons more than before. Thus each month the mine produces 4,800 tons more than before. Annually, this amounts to 57,600 tons of coal.
>
> Com. Alimov, Mine No. 9

In the film Boris clearly and persuasively showed how the conveyer-belt man, Diky, managed to challenge the supposedly fixed procedure and prove that it was no more than an accepted, received routine.

Our mass agitators immediately got hold of the film. A special resolution of the Party District Committee approved Diky's method and called on all Party organizations in the ore administrations and the mines to introduce it in the Basin. Andrei Diky accompanied our mass agitators on several trips to the mines, where his method stirred up furious passions. "We don't deny it's good for Mine No. 9. You are terrific! But we couldn't do it here!"

Every kind of pressure was applied, and the Diky method was earning its right to live in the mines. But I cannot recall a case in which the reorganization was smooth or "enthusiastic," although its advantages were clear. Was this because of inertia and stagnation?—Not only, for behind the stagnation stood the invisible force of the class enemy, the kulaks. Only recently defeated, they stuck sticks in our spokes wherever they could, taking advantage of any of our errors and rubbing salt in the wounds of the people.

We had been rolling through the land for a year, and there was not a single trip in which we did not feel this evil force at our back and did not encounter this masked enemy, who on occasion delivered some fairly big blows to the new Socialist country! After being expelled from the villages, the kulak remnants took on the sabotaging of factories, mines, construction projects, and transportation . . .

But even in the villages the kulak rabble had not been finally smashed. Our paper, *Tempo*, for 3 December 1932 was addressed to the kolkhoz workers in the Don Basin:

DEAR KOLKHOZ WORKER COMRADES!

With the help of a film, the "Lenin's Commandment" Kolkhoz calls on your own kolkhoz to follow its example! In *A Letter to Kolkhoz Workers* you will see how "DonBas," one of the major Stalinist kolkhozes, allowed the class enemy to slip into its ranks. The not-fully-defeated kulaks were put in positons of leadership. The film shows in detail the results of the insufficient vigilance of the kolkhoz workers. In the "DonBas" Kolkhoz the kulaks and petty kulaks pilfered the grain and frittered away property. The kolkhoz did not fulfill the state quotas. A kolkhoz commission discovered stolen kolkhoz grain that had been buried in the ground by a son of kulaks, Vasili Nikolaev. Only 78 of the 184 horses enumerated in

> the kolkhoz remained. Balabanov, the communal stockman, disposed of 8 pigs and 58 lambs. Grain was given away to idlers and to the relatives of kulaks.

Activists from the best kolkhoz in the Donets region, named "Lenin's Commandment," told about all this in the film. They compared the sabotage committed by the kulaks with the experience of their own kolkhoz, which had organized excellent collective farming in short order.

The Kino-Train brigades and the workers from Party Regional and District committees presented the *Letter to Kolkhoz Workers* for discussion at general meetings of kolkhozes. The meetings exposed saboteurs, assessed poor workers, and sent malicious enemies of the kolkhoz system to trial. "The kolkhozes must not repeat the mistakes of the DonBas Cooperative," wrote *Tempo*.

> The Guilty Are Punished
>
> For abuses in the kolkhoz, for disposal of kolkhoz property, and for disruption of the grain supply, Anton Balabanov, president of the DonBas Kolkhoz, is sentenced to ten years in prison, and his deputy is sentenced to be shot. Ilia Chakov, former secretary of the Party collective of the kolkhoz, is sentenced to five years. Petr Afinkin, the accountant, is sentenced to five years. Fedorov, the storesman, is sentenced to five years in strict solitary confinement for embezzlement of grain and potatoes.
>
> *Tempo*, 3.12.32

The people accepted the Kino-Train's authority. Accordingly we were able to raise a number of urgent questions, effectively and without a great expenditure of resources.

The indefatigable Ian Krasutsky was an enthusiastic advocate of photo-newspapers and photo-posters. In Makeevka alone he published five photo-newspapers attacking deficiencies in the production process and in living conditions. After screenings in kolkhozes, our mass agitators left behind posters such as this one:

> OLD WOMEN IN THE KOLKHOZ
> GET OUT OF YOUR HUTS!
> HELP THE KOLKHOZ TO RAISE
> CALVES, PIGS, CHICKENS!
> FIGHT FOR A PROSPEROUS LIFE!

> [On the poster there was a photo of two old women.]
>
> Vasilisa Savelevna Kirkishkina will no longer sit at home all day. Along with her old man, an inspector in charge of quality, old Vasilisa is now going out and contributing her experience to the kolkhoz. She is teaching the workers of the poultry farm how to look after chickens.

. . . In our accounts of our work with the miners one film stands apart from everything else that we contributed to the technical reconstruction of the DonBas. *Pickax Heroes* is about one Nikita Izotov, who in the middle of the technical revolution in the mines, acting like one of the bogatyrs[34] of old, took his grandfather's pickax and made it famous. Like a sorcerer, he dug out mounds of coal at the same pace as the coal-cutting machine during each shift! The basis of his sensational success lay in his ability to "read the seam," understand its structure, and so aim each blow of the hack that the seam seemed to crumble of its own accord. But oh, how the opponents of mechanization rejoiced at this sensational achievement! "See what you can do with a pickax!" the miners cried as they quarreled with us at the screenings. "Your cutting monsters with their electrical innards and combustion engines aren't worth anything! Nikita can surpass your innovations all by himself."

At this, the bogatyr-hero Nikita himself pounced upon them. The handsome, broad-shouldered giant calmly and sensibly corrected his unwanted followers. "You are looking the wrong way, dear comrades," said he, mocking the reactionaries. "You're beguiled by my pick, when the most important thing in my experiment is the coal seam. If you can 'read' the seam and approach it with a machine instead of a pick, you will have real success! Whereas you are like blind men!" My memory will retain forever the image of this enchanting bogatyr, powerful yet gentle, modest yet merciless, armed with a pickax and fighting for the new technology.

I will not forget an amusing event with Karmazinsky and Bogorov, who filmed Nikita Izotov. He could not be filmed at the actual work site because of gas damps in the mine and the tremendous difficulties associated with work on steeply dropping coal seams. Next to the Kino-Train we fenced off a humble set that was an exact replica of Izotov's work site and the coal seam he was supposed to be hacking at. It was January and freezing cold when Bogorov lit up the set and began shooting. Nikita came out with his pick, but there was a scene of confusion: the seam would not yield to him however hard the famous master hacked away! It was worth seeing the dismay of this bogatyr and our own distress until we understood that the problem had to do with the freezing weather and a sly trick of the filmmakers; they had poured water onto the artificially built-up coal seam so that it would freeze solid. After all these years I can still see this shy, smiling, powerful miner with his profound inner charm, a hero of the First Five-Year Plan.

. . . To conclude my story about the Kino-Train films made in the Donets Basin I must mention a one-reel animated-film comedy—*The Camel*, made by the talented animation artist Gin. In this film our "regular" animated camel went on a journey satirizing transport. Nowadays we have buried the memory of the blood that was sweated by metalworkers and miners owing to transportation difficulties! Steel unnecessarily held over in the Martin furnaces (no scoop delivered!); loading docks covered with coal (no freight cars!); idling blast furnaces (no fluxes!)—all this happened, and all this has vanished, along with the heroic times. Our Camel searched out the guilty ones. I remember how his visits were feared by the dispatchers, the heads of transport departments, the drivers and haulers, the sluggish officials at stations at railway junctions! . . . February. The windows of the train's cars were frosted over. With difficulty a shunting locomotive freed our wheels, which were frozen fast to the tracks. They squeaked distressingly as they carried us north.

Farewell, DonBas!

Once again our kino-factory swayed down sidetracks at stations at crowded junctions, past army trains loaded with coal, ore, and metal . . . Now we knew how much of the workers' sweat and self-sacrificing labor went into each loaded freight car! This was the metal and coal that was the "black bread" of the First Five-Year Plan, the foundation on which the powerful industry of Socialism later matured, and led to our victory over Fascism and the wonderful epoch of the conquest of space!

. . . In DonBas we released sixteen films with an actual length totaling 5,230 meters. These films were the focus of hundreds of production meetings, general assemblies of workers, and technical conferences. In this way they brought real assistance to the Donetsk Party organization and to the leaders of the economy in the battle for metal and coal.

The first year of work of the Kino-Train came to an end. During this time seventy films were released (ninety-one parts) with an actual length totaling 24,965 meters.

We had been engaged in the hot spots in key sectors of the great battle for the socialistic transformation of the country. The leadership had put us onto the front lines of the Five-Year Plan that were in greatest danger and at risk of failing. On our own we investigated the deadlocks to find the nastiest, apparently insurmountable obstacles to growth. No doubt, this is why the vast majority of our films were filled with trenchant critical documentary material. On the screens of workers' clubs or on our own itinerant screens they served as stern lecturers or as well-founded indictments by the court of society aimed at any obstruction to the new Socialist reality.

No, we were not delighted with the cinematographic quality of our films. They were a kind of "black bread," with all the characteristic traces of haste and incompletion belonging to a frontline newspaper. We did not exaggerate the significance of our efforts and never assumed we played a decisive role in the success of the sectors into which the leadership dispatched us. But we always got deep moral satisfaction from the energy and understanding with which Party district committees and militant Party activists seized upon our unusual methods of mass organization and used them to bring about a real transformation of broken-down sectors.

All of us romantics of the Kino-Train got great joy from the universal popular support given to all our presentations. The respect for and the recognition of our usefulness did much to bind our collective in friendship. Perhaps the same masculine friendship arises among tank men or submariners when their work as a group is filled with both great stress and joyful victories.

. . . This was my last sortie. I had spent 294 days living on wheels, and in my opinion they are the most interesting part of my life.

I gave the train over to Iakov Bliokh, a Red Army man like myself. The train appropriated the name of the legendary commander of the 1st Cavalry, K. E. Voroshilov. The renewed collective of the train continued its operations in sorties for another two years. It was seen in Sverdlovsk, Tashkent, Baku, on the Kuban, and in the Ukraine. By this time the Party had created frontline organs of political leadership for the construction of Socialism—the political units of the machine-and-tractor stations, the sovkhozes, and the transportation systems. Their methods of organizational political work were very close to those of the Kino-Train, and as a result it became their close assistant. But this is not part of my story.

Very little was written about us. Our sorties kept us busy to the point of exhaustion, and so we attached no importance to this. We understood only many years later that the silence was a cover for the nasty sentiments and intentions of our persistent enemies.

We were remembered forty years later, and the only reason for this was that progressive filmmakers in France and Italy unexpectedly extolled the Kino-Train and drew on its artistic experience in order to develop forms and genres adapted to militant filmmaking by the working class. For the small handful of old men from the Kino-Train who were still alive, this news was a matter for great rejoicing.

The French director Chris Marker, who rescued our long-past adventures from oblivion, is one of the most interesting documentary filmmakers of our time. He is engaged in the fascinating problems of creating a political cinema devoted to the class struggle in the West.

Below I give some of the correspondence received by me from France in 1969–70. Anyone who has read my memoirs about the Kino-Train will readily understand that all the flattering comments on my work and evaluations of it written by the French comrades belong in fairness to all my comrades, whose heroic work makes up the content of my memoirs.

Proofs of an article in French from the journal ICI of the Association of the International Organization of Documentary Filmmakers (ICI)

From Medvedkin to Zavattini

Much was said about Medvedkin in the corridors of the Association of the International Organization of Documentary Filmmakers in Algiers and during one of the sessions of this organization. Zavattini spoke in detail about the Reggio Emilia group's experience in Italy.

All this aroused the greatest interest. We all know who Zavattini is: the man who wrote the scripts of the most significant Italian neo-realist works (*Shoeshine*; *The Bicycle Thief*; *Umberto D*; *Miracle in Milan*; *Resurrection in August*; and others). He is one of the best scriptwriters in Europe today. He was always inspired by the wish to make new discoveries for film, to reflect new social perspectives. Now, with his characteristic meridional ardor, he has immersed himself in experimental cine-journals, which have been spread throughout Italy by the efforts of the Reggio Emilia group.

As for Medvedkin, that is another question! Who, even among cinephiles, knows him? Not many! He is a Soviet filmmaker from 1928–30, still alive today. Chris Marker with the help of Mario Maret—both well known in Algiers—have raised his name today in film circles today by creating various "Medvedkin Committees" and Groups all over France.

In 1928[35] Medvedkin, a Soviet filmmaker, got a train from his government! A train with a special studio car for filming, a laboratory car for developing, and a car for screening. This train traveled throughout the

Soviet Union,[36] stopping in villages and kolkhozes. The filmmaker set up discussions with the peasants and, with their advice, filmed the special features of their situation; then they developed and edited for them pictures of their life. At this time, when film was still silent, Medvedkin traveled with strips of ready-made "commentary." The most common of these flash phrases was "Comrades, things cannot continue this way."

The aim of Chris Marker and Mario Maret in creating the Medvedkin Groups was to push workers to describe by themselves their living conditions and to get them to take their "representation in film" into "their own hands," at first with the help of professional photographers and filmmakers. And next they proposed to create an exchange center for the participants where they would consider what was "possible" and what was "not," and what "could not continue in the same way."

The first Medvedkin Group exists and works at the Rhodiaceta factory in Besançon. And Chris Marker, the new Medvedkin, spends his time in trains (not special ones), so that he may form more such groups in his travels.

Letter from Chris Marker, May 1969
(typed on paper with the Groupe Medvedkine letterhead)

My very dear Alexander Medvedkin!

Look at this sheet of paper very carefully: it bears your name.

Le Groupe Medvedkine—that is what some young workers from a factory in Besançon wanted to call themselves when, after a whole series of adventures (about which my friends will tell you), we jointly decided to organize an official group whose function was to make a real workers' cinema rather than a triumphalist version of a dialogue of the deaf. I told them about the story of the Kino-Train (I also told them about *Happiness*) and they unanimously concluded that nobody but you could so fully symbolize what they wanted to strive for.

I am sending you a few little documents but, of course, I would prefer it if you could see the film, their first film.

. . . I think it would be wonderful if in turn you could send them a letter and a photo. . . . And since I am an egoist, with a certain order in my thoughts, I will take this opportunity to ask whether you have found any documents connected with the train (photos, accounts of discussions, etc.)

. . . I still hope to find out more about your adventures in the Thirties. I think that a good teaching aid for the members of the group in 1969 would be some film materials relating to your adventures at that time.

And so do you have any such materials, and can you entrust then to my friends?

We have spent a strange, not always easy time here . . . May I assure you that in somber minutes I remembered your name in order to preserve my faith?

Yours sincerely,
Chris Marker

As I understand it, the "strange time" mentioned at the end of this letter refers to the events in Czechoslovakia in 1968, when every artist in the West was confronted with the amazingly direct, ultimate question: "Whose side are you on? Theirs or ours?"[37]

I knew Chris Marker from his films as an indisputably progressive and talented man, and his sincere confession that we had in some way helped him at difficult times gave me great happiness. The letters from France reached me during the International Film Festival in 1969. They were handed to me by the French delegates, who wished to meet me. The meeting was exhilarating! I heard many interesting things about the creation of a "militant working-class cinema" in France. The Besançon workers had already shot their first film *À bientôt, j'espère* about the big strike at the Rhodiaceta textile factories in Besançon. For the first time they had filmed workers, trade-union activists, and the progress of the struggle of the strikers. My French friends told me that our old experience had helped them. They asked us to send back with them for the Groupe Medvedkine everything that survived from the work of the train.

The young French director Bernard Paul came to the festival with his art film focusing on a critical view of society, *Le temps de vivre*, which received one of the first prizes. In an interview with a correspondent from the paper *Moskovskaia Pravda* Bernard Paul said:

> I was particularly struck by the meeting with the Soviet director A. Medvedkin. I was excited when I learned that he was among the filmmakers who had set up the "Kino-Train." . . . That was militant, targeted film journalism. The films drew attention to problems and helped in the regularization of production. In France Chris Marker has recently established several such groups; we call them "Medvedkin Groups." I belong to one of them.
>
> *Moskovskaia Pravda*, 24 July 1969

I sent letters to France for Chris Marker and the Besançon workers, thanking them for their high opinion of the work done by Soviet filmmakers in their attempt to create a political cinema, and for their own use of the methods of the Kino-Train in their bold explorations leading to a "militant working-class cinema." I also sent to my comrades-in-arms some sets of photographs portraying life and work on the train, and an extensively annotated list of all the films released by the Kino-Train during the first year of work.

Soon the answers arrived (in French):

> 8.9.69
>
> Dear Medvedkin!
>
> The letters from the Besançon comrades, which I am sending to you, will allow you to understand the joy and excitement with which they read your letter.
>
> . . . Your words and the amazing testimony of the list of films made by the Kino-Train provide an extremely helpful inspiration for them.
>
> Now they will need to "compete" with the Kino-Train. One of them even spoke these splendid words: "Let him come with his train; we will accelerate it!"
>
> I could only wish that you could come here.
>
> . . . I very much hope to receive notes about the Kino-Train (preferably brought by you in person). I would like to publish something here with photographs. The photographs impress and excite everyone who sees them: the train and you yourself are continuing your agitprop work.
>
> . . . We all hope to receive news of your arrival.
>
> Chris Marker

And a letter from Besançon:

> THE MEDVEDKIN GROUP
>
> Dear Comrade!
>
> All the comrades were moved and glad when they received the documents about the story of the Train given to us by Chris Marker.
>
> What can we say to you?
>
> To begin with, we would not have dared to take the name Medvedkin Group if we had been better acquainted with the amazing achievements of the real Medvedkin Group of 1932–35.

But since we did allow ourselves to do this, we are bound to continue in some measure your enterprise in our own times. Although the conditions are different, the aim remains the same: to give the workers an awareness of the necessity of building a truly socialist society, in which everyone will assume responsibility. Thirty-five years later we are waging the same battle.

. . . We would so like to discuss your work and thoughts with you!

Can't you come to Besançon?

We await your answer,

And we give you a fraternal handshake,

On behalf of the group,

Cèbe

. . . To give a detailed account of the big artistic achievements of the Besançon group would go beyond the framework of my notes about the Kino-Train. In brief, however, it should be said that the achievements of my friends are truly splendid. Their second film, *Classe de lutte*, had a commercial run in Parisian theaters. The letters they sent me from Paris and Besançon are filled with joy at their difficult victories and a vision of bold future attempts.

In this I see confirmation that I was right when I decided forty years ago that if I was to go into film it would be only for the sake of a powerful political cinema, which could serve in the first instance as a direct political weapon. The experience of the Kino-Train and the successful revival of its traditions by progressive French filmmakers is proof positive that this is the best position to take in film.

Moscow
(1969–70)

3 Soldiers Shooting Films

September 1943. A new assignment: I am being sent to the Western Front[1] to serve as overseer of film crews.

A telegram arrives as I am about to leave:

> . . . Iartsevo material expedited on the 20th at 6:00 a.m. by airplane STOP Roslavl front being filmed by Berov Iartsevo-Smolensk front by Krylov Dorogobuzh-Smolensk front by Elbert Elin, Smolensk front by Shneiderov Tsesliuk sent to hospital STOP I have no cameramen on four sectors of the front = Guliaev 203 RADIO . . .

Five cameramen to cover an enormous front! A front continually in motion, with the assault on Smolensk now in progress. "Four sectors"—in other words, four armies with no cameramen.

And I know straightaway: it's there that what has to be filmed is taking place! . . .

Five cameramen! . . . One of them is having car trouble, another has problems with his Eyemo camera, the third is hospitalized . . . and meanwhile the army is reconquering Smolensk, and the impatient generals want a film they can project, while Moscow sends you the sort of telegram you prefer not to read! And what can we film with five cameramen? I need fifty cameramen! . . . Fifty fleet-footed, fearless, intelligent young men, like army scouts, with small cameras and a solid grasp of how to film in the most difficult situations!

. . . This difficult year at the front was coming to an end. The battles for Vitebsk, the liberation of Minsk, the street fights in Vilnius—these had all been filmed.

We were very short of people. In difficult moments we would recall the unrealistic dream of fifty cameramen, until, finally, I found how to overcome a mountain of obstacles and set up a brigade of cameramen.

We did it! We created two brigades and got a program of work for them, and they produced sensational newsreels for the screen.

Unfortunately this came only at the tail end of the war!

Right now I am sorting out a pile of yellowing sheets of paper. They preserve a record of the formidable efforts of the group of enthusiasts who tackled problems that were the source of much amusement to men of a skeptical disposition. This was done in 1944. From among the ranks of the sergeants we had to get two teams of fifty men (but who was going to release them?), arm them with movie cameras (which we did not have!), teach them the cameraman's craft in the space of two or three months, and put them to work on the battlefield! . . .

The skeptics were hasty when they laughed. We held a key to the solution of the problems. It turned out that any number of cameras could be obtained. The American Air Cobra planes sent to us under the Lend-Lease program were equipped with 16 mm fuselage cameras. They recorded air battles and the results of the pilots' gunfire.

As it happened, these film recordings did not help the airmen and were especially hated in the air force. Nonetheless, there came a categorical refusal to release the cameras to us, and then a second refusal, and a third one. But we were not so easily shaken off.

We secured the intervention of Alexander S. Shcherbakov, the head of the Main Political Directorate of the Army. He quickly grasped our idea, gave it his warm support, and to the very end helped us in every way he could. If in this tale of unending ordeals I pass over all the refusals we got, with all the firm nos and amazement over a harebrained scheme, and the many appeals to stop making trouble, then I can come to the main point—namely, we did get the cameras.

The Air Cobra cameras had to be adapted for hand use. We located a factory of wooden pulleys in Moscow, which in those years was manufacturing the stocks for PPSh submachine guns. They made fifty special wooden stocks for us in accordance with our designs.

I will never forget the enthusiasm with which the chief engineer of the studio, I. B. Gordeichuk, and the head of the precision-engineering workshop, B. V. Timofeev, adapted the narrow-gauge American cameras for installation on the Russian wooden stocks. They also built a special viewfinder, which bore a close resemblance to the gun sight of a sniper rifle. When it was assembled, the film apparatus looked like a strange and imposing weapon . . . Later, in the byways of the war, the effect of these apparatuses was sensational. Some mischievous lads who had been assigned to us as cameramen took advantage of the secrecy surrounding this new weapon in order to use it as a pretext to obtain additional favors from army suppliers serving all ranks . . .

The problem of supplying current to the motors of our film-cannons was a difficult one. On a fighter aircraft getting a 20-volt current is not a problem. But for a man with a handheld camera on a battlefield? . . .

After more tribulations and fights, which are not worth going into, we persuaded the director of the MosElement Factory to build some special rechargeable batteries for us and to supply them to our crews. Each battery weighed ten kilograms, and they often stopped working—a battery would run down at a critical moment and stop turning the camera motor. And so our filming enthusiasts each carried two batteries with them, weighing a total of twenty kilograms, at the same time as they ran alongside the advancing infantrymen. And run they did! Without lagging or complaining! They shot. With good results! . . .

The idea of giving a movie camera to a soldier in battle was unusual. It involved an overwhelming romanticism. Maybe this is the reason why so many enthusiasts gave our experiments their unfailing support. The generals, the supplies men, the political workers, the pilots—the frontline men in all the branches—were absolutely faithful, committed supporters.

I want to make a special mention of the help given by Lieutenant-General Galitsky, the commander of the First Guards Army. He attached to our enterprise a new order of significance, seeing in it a possibility that we, the authors of the project, had not been able to imagine! His arguments were more or less of this kind: the very presence of a film controller who records the progress of a battle introduces a big change; every stage of the combat and every move of a company "can be documented on film and can later become a basis for an accurate evaluation of the leadership that had been provided . . ." I well understand," said the general, "that we are still far from the implementation of this idea, but the mere fact of the introduction of this kind of controller into the battle leads an officer to expect that his work protocols will be recorded in the course of the battle."

Lieutenant-General Galitsky communicated his enthusiasm for this idea to the generals and the political staff of the First Guards, and demanded that—to start with—they give us the most combat-hardened and talented young men from the ranks of their scouts and their tried-and-tested sergeants.

I will always remember my first meeting with the men on a bare Lithuanian hill. The thirty men didn't yet understand what they would have to do and were wary. They inquired of our drivers, Who were we? and What did we intend to do with them? . . .

Without saying anything to these former soldiers, we showed them a documentary film, *The Routing of the Germans outside Moscow*. The film shook them up. They were even more shaken by my words: "I have orders to make you into cameramen so that you can film military operations. The deadlines are tight. If you study day and night, we'll be able to take you on film shoots in two months' time."

And thus the incomparable romance of filmmaking burst into the lives of these frontline soldiers. You can only imagine the almost childish enthusiasm with which they plunged into this element!

We divided them into two teams. One of them was headed by the cameraman N. A. Lytkin. The other was placed under the cameramen G. A. Golubov and A. M. Zeniakin. Above I spoke about the enthusiasts who made our project a reality. That said, there was nobody who surpassed these three in fervor and dedication. True, I can't say now who was more responsible for the sleepless nights: the instructors or the men they instructed. The fact is that the instruction continued day and night.

A huge burden lay on the shoulders of my comrades. The trainees had no understanding of photography, still less of cinematography. It is no exaggeration to say that their general education was well below average . . . Nonetheless, they were the elite of the frontline scouts, and gifted warriors, whose proficiency and fearlessness had earned them the well-deserved respect of soldiers. They studied without sparing themselves or their mentors. Our troops were already advancing into Germany, the tail end of the war was in sight, and our lads knew they were late.

The equipment we were arming them with was of terrible technical quality. The cameras often chewed up the film negative. The rechargeable batteries (weighing ten kilograms!) kept discharging. Loading the cassettes was particularly troublesome. They were meant to be loaded with the help of a special device, and in order to load them by hand, three fingers of the right hand had to execute three different operations *at the same time!* and what is more, in complete darkness! Everyone endured many aggravations. But our fervent romantics had not left their patrol work in order to come to us for nothing! They soon learned how to load the cassettes, to shoot, and to develop the film, and also how to adjust the camera when it was turning, and to cooperate with a comrade when his camera was spinning out of control, and with another when his gun suddenly discharged . . .

Our forces had surrounded Königsberg[2] when we gave our students strict examinations (without allowances for material deficiencies) and gave them certificates attesting that they were "Sergeant-Cameramen." In a state of happy excitement, they rushed to battle. Feeling more nervous than their charges, the head cameramen in command led their brigades into their baptism by fire. A. Zeniakin and N. Lytkin have left some wonderful accounts of those days . . .

Our novices had been given total freedom of movement, and used it to infiltrate the rear flanks of the enemy and to set up ambushes on roads. One man would throw a hand grenade, and another would film him doing it, and then they would switch roles, and the first one would film the other one taking prisoners.

In the heat of the moment, they would sometimes forget what piece of automatic equipment they were holding and would swing it around as if it was a PPSh submachine gun. And when this happened, an incredibly smeared panning shot would appear on the projection screen.

In my archive I have a letter from G. A. Golubov that conveys the atmosphere and mood of those days. Here is an excerpt from it:

> Dear Alexander Ivanovich!
>
> I make haste to report that from 7/2 to 16/2 my lads shot 705 feet[3] of film on two cameras, and I can answer for its quality. I am extremely pleased that the entire collective has survived. I sent ten men with two working cameras to a forward position to test them under fire. The results were excellent. The general awarded two of the men a medal for their exploits (removing a wounded soldier from the battlefield). Senior Sergeant Tsepelev was wounded in the leg, but he kept on filming. The lads are terrific! I'll lay down my life before I part with a single one of them. If they had real cameras, you can imagine the takes they would be sending to you for the screen! . . .

Before me lies the frontline newspaper *Red Army Pravda* from 5 April 1945 (no. 80 [7285]). An article by Evgeni Vorobev called "Kino-Machine-Gun" is at the bottom of the page. He writes:

> The appearance of this gun is very warlike. It has a submachine gun stock, something like a gun sight, and a trigger . . . Recently fifteen scouts—all valiant ex-soldiers—armed themselves with these "kino-machine-guns" and set off to shoot some film. Their work was a wonderful addition to the films that had been shot by our frontline cameramen. These experienced scouts, equipped with very portable cameras, were in the thick of the battle and were its closest witnesses . . .

For example, the following battlefield episode next to a trench was shot by Georgi Solpukhov and Ivan Vasilenko: a German moves away from one of our soldiers while shooting at him. Our soldier wounds the German soldier in the cheek, and then the soldier finishes the German off by firing at him shot after shot point-blank. Another episode: ten German soldiers advance toward one of our submachine guns. The gunner shoots seven of them in one sweep, and three try to escape but fall down, mown down by gunfire . . .

Aleksei Komarov, who was wounded while shooting film near Königsberg, successfully shot the enemy's counterattack, a duel between a "Ferdinand" [heavy tank destroyer] and an antitank machine gun . . .

Fedor Balashov caught an interesting moment: the retreating Germans blow up a bridge over the Pregel, then our infantrymen force their way over the ice across the river, and our welders immediately begin repairing the bridge . . .

All of these film shoots were done by young cameramen from a group trained and directed by the cameraman Nikolai Lytkin. . . .

The fifteen men trained by Lytkin suffered a total of fourteen heavy injuries and twenty-seven light ones. Between them, with a defensive battle raging, they took fifty-eight prisoners with useful information, and hundreds of other Germans . . . All fifteen received forty-three medals and awards. Guards Sergeant V. Butsko was decorated five times, Guards Private I. Popov three times, and Guards Sergeant G. Sninukhov was awarded the Cavalry Order of Glory, Second Class . . .

And today, at the front, you can run into a military scout with a movie camera that looks like a submachine gun and with a pack on his shoulders containing a battery that feeds the camera motor. This has recently become one of the weapons belonging to the scouts. For self-defense this cameraman has a Nagant revolver and hand grenades.

Evg. Vorobev

The cameramen-sergeants filmed the fighting in the streets of Königsberg. They were led by a soldier, Volodia Krylov, whom we assigned to N. Lytkin at the very beginning, when we were forming the brigade. In the most dangerous part of the street fighting, the cameramen lost their leader. Vladimir [Volodia] Krylov died the death of the brave on the battlefield. On the same day, his brother Anatoli Krylov, a cameraman in our team, was seriously injured . . .

The military work of a frontline cameraman is one of heroic sacrifice. The same holds true for the work of the brigade of cameramen-sergeants.

The thirty military patrolmen who had mastered filming techniques became full-fledged members of our frontline group of cameramen.

April 1945 arrived, and with it came victory. And today, nearly a quarter of a century after those bright days, I still regret that we took so long to put movie cameras in the hands of soldiers!

([*scratched-out date:* 29.05.68])

Scripts

4 A Little Log

(Film Sketch 1, 1930)[1]

A truck with a load of firewood is rolling along, racing through fields, racing down a road.

Suddenly a little, crooked, gnarled log tumbles off. The truck races on, the log stays behind.

The little log is lying in the narrow roadway; it spells trouble . . .

A peasant is traveling through the fields. He is transporting a cartload of fleece, sitting on top of the tall load . . .

The log is lying in the narrow road. It presents an obstacle for the peasant's cart: no cart's wheel could bounce over the gnarly log. And driving round looks risky: the sides of the road slope steeply down.

The peasant stops the cart and spews forth a juicy curse.

He could toss the little log off the road—all for a small effort. But the peasant is evidently too lazy to climb down from the cart; instead he continues his tedious, drawn-out cursing. He carries on with his meaningless cursing for an abnormally long time; then when he is done cursing he starts to drive round the ill-met piece of wood when—suddenly—the carter slides off the tall load, and comes clattering down, flipping head over heels!

Picking himself up from the ground and almost crying tears of pain and rage, the distraught carter runs off in pursuit of his nag.

He is so caught up in his rage and vexation over what has happened that the idea of tossing the pernicious log off the road does not enter his mind.

Twisting round, he looks back at the log in silent reproach, while at the same time he keeps running after the horse in leaps and bounds, and managing to appear quite comical in his misfortune!

The pernicious log lies in the road, lies in wait for its next victim.

A factory. By the entrance a checkpoint. Above the gate is an expensive-looking sign with gold letters:

THE "SHAME" FACTORY
MANUFACTURERS OF BLACKLISTS

In the yard there are some railroad tracks. Workers are lowering a crate from a flatcar down some inclined planks.

All of a sudden the planks slip apart; the crate crashes down; it is smashed to pieces!

A machine from abroad falls out and obstructs the footpath. On it is a foreign label, "Made in the U.S.A."

The American machine is stuck in the footpath. It is bent, and orphaned like the log stranded on the road.

A worker—a painter—is painting a new blacklist in black paint. On one side of the board a new heading glistens:

SHAME

The workman is painting the board.

He strokes with his brush, but it has no paint on it.

He takes the pail and runs off to fetch some paint.

The American machine is lying in the footpath, blocking it.

The workman who is fetching paint runs past it with his pail. A lever trips him up and—oops!—he is lain out on the ground!

With difficulty he gets up, rubbing an injured spot.

He looks long and reproachfully at the machine in condemnation, seeking to shame it as if it was alive, shaking his head and saying: "You devil of an Englishwoman, you!"

And scratching his bald patch, he says distressfully:

"ITS GOT TO BE MOVED."

Limping, the injured painter goes off.

Meanwhile two carters are driving toward each other on the road with the little log.

Seeing the obstacle, they both stop their horses at the same time.

One of them, a snub-nosed man, holds his horse back by the bridle, freezing into position, and expectantly waits.

From his way of looking, you'd think that the other man is removing the log and is about to complete the job, so that the two carters can drive their different ways in peace.

But the other carter, a drowsy fellow! has no intention of stirring from his cart.

He, too, has decided to wait, and to rely on the snub-nosed one.

And so the two carters stay facing one another, and between them lies the log . . .

They stand still and wait! What could be simpler than just tossing the piece of wood off the roadway? But the carters stand their ground and wait like two stubborn goats!

They stand and wait . . . They are waging a silent fight.

Finally, the drowsy fellow can stand it no longer. Pointing his whip at the log, he says to his opponent: "Get down at once! And stop playing the fool!"

"Aha!" yells the snub-nosed one, his face quite contorted. "You think you have lackeys?! boys?!"

And he is seized with a fit of hysterical, bilious cursing.

Thus the trivial question of the log has been raised to the highly sensitive level of principle.

And this threatens to cause a massive holdup! Each stubborn carter is standing his ground.

The two wave their arms,
stamp their feet,
beat their chests with their fists,
threaten,
jeer,
and mock.

—They have begun a desperate battle.

And the subject of their principled quarrels—the little, crooked, gnarled log—lies in front of them, crying out for somebody to do something!

After working himself into a frenzy of insults, the snub-nosed one comes to a decision, and simultaneously placates and threatens his opponent:

"All right then! Keep on waiting! To the devil with you! I'll go round."

He is carefully leading his horse around, and his cart tilts.

The cart is so heavy that the weight of a wheel pries off a row of paving stones. And thus begins the destruction of the road.

The drowsy fellow moves his cart onto the other shoulder, but the slope is steeper here. The cart overturns, and goods roll down the slope, stirring up dust:

Watermelons . . . apples . . . bread rolls . . . a samovar . . . boxes . . .

Of course the triumph of the snub-nosed carter, who has got past the thrice-damned spot, has no bounds.

He does everything he can to mock his defeated opponent: calling him names, preaching to him, pretending to console him, laughing, and viciously chastising him! He drives on, looking back and shouting:

"I TOLD YOU, SON OF A BITCH, TO PICK IT UP!"

And seeing the helpless, comic bewilderment of his defeated enemy, the snub-nosed man bursts into wild laughter, clenching his stomach as he bends right over.

But his rear axle breaks; it had cracked on the slope without his noticing it. A wheel flies off, the cart collapses!

The snub-nose's laughter sticks in his throat. He is frozen in a position for laughter, his hands clenching his stomach.

A rainy shroud hangs over the factory.

In the factory yard the rusty American machine on the footpath is getting drenched.

Evidently this is not the first time it has been rained on.

The letters saying "Made in the U.S.A." and "Paid for in Soviet Gold Rubles" are rusted and covered with hideous splotches.

The rainy shroud hangs over the factory. Four feet away from the machine stands a canopy specially designed for it. Four workers have taken shelter under it.

Among them is the same painter who got a bruise when he tripped on the machine. Looking at the machine and despondently scratching his bald spot, he guiltily shifts from foot to foot and says:

"IT'S GOT TO BE MOVED . . ."

The machine is getting drenched. An administrator with a briefcase comes charging through the empty factory yard at top speed to get out of the rain.

And as he runs past the machine, he trips on the end of the sharp protruding lever and—wham!—falls at full force into a puddle, throwing up a splash of dirty water.

The four somber workers under the canopy raise an excited clamor.

The tripped-up administrator hobbles over and crawls under the canopy like a wet chicken. Interrupting one another, the workers gloomily target the administrator with their clamor:

"THE MACHINE NEEDED TO BE MOVED
A LONG TIME AGO!"

The unfortunate administrator, on the verge of tears of fury, bent double, shaking with rage, implacably points his finger at the workers:

"YOU DIDN'T MOVE IT! YOU ARE GUILTY!
SABOTEURS!"

It is as if he'd thrown a bomb at the workers. All four seethe with indignation. Sticking their forefingers right under the administrator's nose, they all cry out together:

"YOU'RE THE ONE WHO'S RESPONSIBLE . . . !
YOU GAVE NO ORDERS!
YOU'RE A SHAM. YOU'RE, YOU'RE . . . !"

And so the question is brought into the realm of fundamental principles. A fight flares up. And it flashes red-hot.

Choking with astonishment, overwhelmed with incredulity, the administrator shrugs his shoulders and starts furiously jabbing his finger at the workers. They give as good as they get and, by way of answer, would be happy to impale the unfortunate manager.

Out on the road in the fields the cursed log still lies!

But the road here is no road but one great big rut, carved out by frequent detourings and spills. The road surface has been destroyed; the paving stones are buried in sand.

Sticking out of a pothole is a pair of legs belonging to a cyclist who is buried in it.

His bicycle, twisted and maimed, sticks out from another hole.

The cyclist's feet are sticking out, inert, as if the cyclist had been decapitated.

The "Shame" Factory again.

The painter is once again painting a blacklist. Again the paint runs out. And once more the painter runs off with his pail.

The machine in the factory yard again. Of course nobody has tried to move it. Like a true athlete, the running painter has learned how to maneuver quickly and agilely past it on a narrow plank.

Somewhere on the road in the fields a cart is trundling along. The rear axle of the cart is broken. To take the place of a wheel the carter has made use of a crooked piece of wood. Standing alongside the nag, he urges it on, at the same time as he keeps looking back toward the place where the damned log is supposed to be . . .

Ah! He is swearing now! And roundly spitting!

And again: the "Shame" Factory. This time the painter is coming back with some paint. He has trained himself to jump over the machine from the narrow plank. But he miscalculates, stumbles, and spills the paint. His ankle is severely sprained, and he limps.

The road once more. The steep embankment. Flying down the embankment come somebody's cart, somebody's boot, a wheel, a bundle.

The nasty, gnarled log lies half-hidden in the sand.

Rain once more. Again the painter and the administrator stand under the canopy next to the soaked machine.

The painter is leaning on a crutch. He has aged. His beard has grown out—a lot of time has gone by!

The machine is overgrown with grass and weeds, and only half of it remains.

The diffident painter is still bothered. Guiltily scratching his bald patch, he says out of habit, but quite without hope:

"IT'S GOT TO BE MOVED . . ."

Raindrops roll down like tears from the drenched machine.

The painter cannot bear it. Removing his jacket, he hops with the help of his crutch over to the machine in order to cover it.

But the machine is too big, and the painter's little jacket cannot be of use to it.

The situation is absurd!

The help offered by the painter who injured himself on the machine is also absurd because for a long time (while his beard was growing) he kept saying, "It's got to be moved!" without actually doing anything about it . . .

His little jacket looks like a naive attempt with inappropriate means.

But the administrator, the one truly guilty for the death of the machine, is moved to tears by the heroic gesture of the painter.

With great warmth he clasps his hand! What words of thanks he says, while sniffling with enthusiasm!

He wishes to emulate this splendid example. Resolutely, he takes off his new tweed jacket; in businesslike fashion he empties its pockets. And then—

at the very moment he is about to run out to the machine—he has second thoughts.

Second thoughts! He feels the quality of the tweed cloth, and sticking his hand out from the canopy, he tests how wet the rain . . .

But the rain is too wet. And the administrator resolutely puts his jacket back on again.

Once more: the destroyed bit of the road and—the cursed log. And also the cyclist who was knocked half-dead. Now he is limply slumped on the sloping embankment. The mutilated bicycle lies beside him.

A huge cart has stopped at the destroyed stretch of roadway. Not knowing how to get across, the carter shouts to the cyclist:

"HEY, GOOD FELLOW! ARE YOU DEAD OR ALIVE?"

With difficulty the cyclist raises his head in the direction of the shouter. Then, suddenly, seeing something extraordinary, he gives a start; he grabs a cobblestone and shouts to the carter:

"BEAT HIM!"

The carter sees the enemy, throws down his whip and grabs a stone, quickly preparing to give battle.

CALL ALL SABOTEURS TO ACCOUNT!

In this instance the saboteur is a simple Russian speckled hen.

The villainess is scratching about in a professional way on the shoulder of the destroyed road, looking for food, oblivious to all else.

The cyclist and the carter instantly throw themselves on the saboteur. And the chicken flies up.

The injured parties run after her.

CALL ALL SABOTEURS TO ACCOUNT!

A group of people with an extravagantly official air, led by a policeman, march through the factory yard. They are looking for a saboteur.

The American machine abandoned in the yard has been adapted by a sow for her own use.

The pig is rubbing herself against the American machine. Rubbing herself.

The men all of a sudden tie a leash around the pig. They march her along.

They have arrested the pig. The policeman is leading her. The pig resists because she does not believe she is guilty.

The cyclist walks along the road through the fields. He is carrying his mangled bicycle. It is not so much a bicycle as a reminder of a bicycle! And he is pulling the criminal hen behind him on a rope.

The criminal marches briskly, barely keeping up with the cyclist.

MEANWHILE THE POLICEMAN IS MARCHING THE PIG DOWN A NOISY STREET.
THE PIG RESISTS: SHE DOESN'T KNOW WHY SHE IS SUPPOSED TO BE GUILTY.

A knife is being sharpened in readiness for the punishment of the guilty parties . . .

It is being sharpened with methodical, practiced gestures . . .

But suddenly the hand stops sharpening, as if it were having second thoughts, and decisively throws away the knife.

WHO WILL BE HELD TO ACCOUNT?

The painter has finished painting the blacklist with the title **SHAME** blazing down one side.

Onto the board one after the other jump the words:

SHAME ON THE TOOTHLESS, SPINELESS COMPROMISERS
WHO FAIL TO FIGHT DERELICTION IN PRODUCTION!

The painter reads this with surprise, and then strikes his breast, as if to say, "Is this about me?"

And onto the board jump the words:

SHAME ON YOU, PAINTER, BECAUSE OF THE MACHINE!

The painter grows angry, stamps his foot, shouts, grabs his brush, and paints over this unpleasant inscription . . .

An imposing doorway with, overhead, a placard saying, "Purge of Factory Management in Progress."

In a state of terrible agitation, the just-purged administrator flies through the doorway like a strange bomb.

Still warding off imagined opponents, he stands in one spot, reeling. For some reason he takes off his cap. He looks left and starts to walk. But he looks back and thinks a bit (as if it was about something extremely important). Then he goes right . . .

5 *Stop Thief!*

(Film Sketch 2, 1930)

A watermelon field.

Juicy, mouth-watering melons ripening.

"WHAT IS THEFT?"

—asks the sentinel guarding the collective farm's watermelon field. He is like an ancient philosopher. He answers his own question:

"THEFT IS A CRIME!"

Like an ancient Diogenes he is lying in an empty barrel, surrounded by ripe melons, and he is philosophizing . . . As for thieves, there is one nearby!

Taking advantage of the philosopher's state of abstraction, he creeps up to the largest melon, breaks it off at the stem, and carefully rolls it aside.

Then the miserable creature, a vagrant wretch, selects a second melon.

He stuffs his shirt with complimentary cucumbers, grabs hold of the pair of enormous melons, and kicks along another pair of them with his feet.

The sentinel resembling an ancient philosopher continues to philosophize.

Greedily, the petty thief tries to pick up a third melon, but the ones already in his arms slip and make a noise.

At this point the philosopher discovers him. "Aha!" says he, pointing a finger at the thief's chest. "Aha!"

For a moment the two men freeze in a tense standoff: the melon-field sentinel, with his pointing finger and accusatory "Aha!" and the wretch, stiff with fright, holding the melons under his arms.

But this only lasts an instant. The thief drops one of the melons, breaks away, and runs in leaps and bounds out of the melon field and away down the road.

The sluggish melon-field sentinel would like to tear after him, but he is too slow.

The nimble vagrant, still holding one big melon under his arm, rapidly disappears.

And then the melon-field sentinel clenches his fists and lets forth an inhuman roar, the loudest one he can. He roars as if his father and mother had been killed rather than a melon stolen:

"THIEVES!"

A herdsman is tending some cows in a field next to some wheat.

Alerted by the bellow, he sees the fugitive and starts off as fast as he can in order to cut him off, frightening several cows and driving them into the kolkhoz's wheat.

The wretch runs, gathering courage and keeping hold of one melon.

Running from opposite directions, the herdsman and the sentinel of the melon field try to catch him.

The wretch runs, hoping he may yet escape justice.

Stopping, the melon-field sentinel again roars with an inhuman voice:

"HELP! THIEVES!"

A tractor is plowing a fallow field on the kolkhoz.

Hearing the bellow, the driver looks sharply round, sees the fugitive, jumps off the moving tractor without even stopping it, and throws himself into the chase after the fugitive.

The tractor continues straight on all by itself, while the tractor driver goes off right.

Now three men are running after the wretch, running as fast as they can, in order to catch him and punish him.

The abandoned tractor slowly crawls up hills and down into hollows and ditches.

The philosophical field sentinel is holding a stake and running. Stopping, he roars for the third time:

"THIEVES!"

He roars so loudly and desperately that he nearly falls over.

And thirty women working with hoes in the kolkhoz fields hear his call. In response to the roar, they drop their work and holding onto their hoes they rush off in a pack to chase after the wretched soul, raising a cloud of dust.

Half-frightened to death with the supernatural uproar, the petty thief even comes to a stop. In fear he gives up his attempt. "Devil take the melons!" He drops a melon and is tossing out the cucumbers tucked inside his shirt.

Meanwhile, the cows abandoned by the herdsman have been enjoying their unexpected liberty and trampling the kolkhoz wheat . . .

At the same time, the tractor has reached the riverbank. Inevitably, fatally, it crawls toward the water and topples down into it. Bubbles rise.

Stirring up the dust, the raging, menacing crowd rushes along, with the long-legged tractor driver in the lead.

They are gaining on the fugitive. And the wretch is tiring.

Now they are about to catch up with him!

The crowd rushes along, with their leader, the tractor driver, in front.

The wretch gives himself up. He stops, and suddenly lies down in the dusty road, humbly stretched out at full length, like a dead man, his arms crossed over his breast in resignation.

The raging crowd swoop down. They raise the thief from the ground.

They search him and . . . from his shirt they pull out two stray cucumbers.

The two wormy, crooked cucumbers are attached to the arrested man as material evidence, and he is taken away.

Subsequent events unfold at a cinematic speed.

First, the man arrested with the cucumbers is escorted by two militiamen carrying unmuzzled revolvers and terrifying dossiers.

The people's court is in session . . .

The two wormy, crooked cucumbers lie on the prosecutor's table as proof positive of the criminal act committed by the thief.

A solemn, dispassionate judge, wearing a pince-nez with coldly shining lenses, conducts a solemn interrogation of the accused.

The wretch is placed in a prison car and driven away.

The gates of a correctional institution swing open, and the prison car drives in.

In a dark corner of a gloomy prison cell the somber wretch is now sitting.

He is confined . . .

Confined behind bars . . .

Next he is being released at the gate of the correctional institution.

He respectfully takes his leave. And sets off, well disciplined and docile, carrying a grotesque bundle.

He is walking across a steppe.

There is a watermelon in the road.

It frightens him as if it were death itself. The wretch freezes.

A watermelon in the road. But the wretch has been taught not to love watermelons! He has been taught to fear other people's melons.

And so he turns on his heels and goes back, jumps over a ditch to get off the road, and, making a big detour over stubble, walks almost one mile round this dangerous spot.

THERE ARE THIEVES, AND THEN—THERE ARE . . . THIEVES!

ONE SORT MAKES OFF WITH A COUPLE OF CUCUMBERS,

THE OTHER SORT . . .

On a hill out in the fields a dirty, ruined, rusting, orphaned tractor lies abandoned.

One of its wheels has been chucked off to one side.

Its radiator has a hole in it.

Its levers have cords tied round them.

Its steering wheel is wrapped round with wire.

A hideous, three-inch-thick layer of mud has dried on it.

The tractor has never been cleaned or cared for. This abominable treatment has turned it into a caricature of itself.

THERE ARE THIEVES, AND THEN—THERE ARE . . . THIEVES!

The tractor driver of long legs and heroic mien is snoring beside the wrecked machine. His fair-haired head is flung right back, and from his wide-open mouth come wild animal-like snores.

And once more the same things happen, more or less, as in the catching of the cucumber thief. The philosophical old sentinel of the melon fields triumphantly grins and, just as in the beginning of the film, points his forefinger at this other thief and accusatorily says:

"Aha! . . . Aha! . . . Aha! . . ."

But this makes no impression on the swindler. Contemptuously he opens just one eye and with one furious glance repels the attacker, then resumes whistling through his nose.

The accusatory finger of the attacking sentinel of the melon fields is left comically suspended in midair. The finger pointing at the thief is in a very awkward position. The melon-field man subjects it to a silly examination, then raises it as if to scratch his ear.

But he has a sudden fit of rage, and roars and shakes his fists:

"SWINDLER! YOU STOLE THE TRACTOR!"

Sleepy and disheveled, surprised, the tractor driver props himself up on his elbows and, putting on a strange expression like a hooligan's, threateningly spits forth: "Get lost, you!" And drops back down again.

The melon sentinel roars:

"YOU STOLE THE NINETY[1] YOU GOT FOR PLOWING!"

On a road somewhere in the steppes, the cucumber thief coming back from prison hears this. He stops and even sits down.

The melon sentinel is shrieking frenziedly, with all his might, just as when he caught this thief:

"THIEF!"

And just as in the story of the cucumber thief, a herdsman is tending some cows in the field next to the kolkhoz wheat. Alerted by the cry, he grabs a stake—the same one as in the first chase—-and runs as fast as he can to the assistance of the melon-field sentinel.

The "cucumber" miscreant grabs hold of a stout, knobbly staff and also runs to lend a hand.

The field sentinel roars again about thieves.

And again thirty women hoeing rows hear the bellows and drop their work and rush off.

The cucumber thief is running with his huge staff.

He gets to the tractor driver first.

Upon reaching him, he stops in confusion not knowing what to do.

The tractor driver is very surprised by the impetuous attack!

The wretch suddenly panics at his own audacity.

He panics. His spirit sinks into his feet. And so he drops his staff, takes off his cap, respectfully bows, cautiously shuffles off to one side, and beats a hasty retreat.

The enraged herdsman is running with the stake.

The crowd of kolkhoz women bearing hoes run up in a dense herd.

The women see the cucumber thief, over on the right, shuffling and hopping, in quick retreat from the tractor thief. And the raging torrent of women turns in pursuit of the hapless cucumber thief.

By accident the wretch looks back and sees the unexpected chase. He tears away as fast as he can.

The melon-field sentinel sees the mistake of the kolkhoz women, clasps his head, and sways back and forth as if in a daze.

And the tractor driver-thief observes the whole battle like another Napoleon and grins, grandly supporting himself on the shoulder of the sycophantic herdsman holding the stake.

The peasant women are about to catch up with the cucumber man!

And seeing that his end is near, the wretch surrenders, just as he did the first time. He stops and suddenly lies on the ground, playing dead, meekly stretched out at full length, his arms acquiescently crossed over his chest, awaiting his fate.

To bring the peasant women to their senses, the melon-field man roars and waves his arms:

"STOP, YOU DEVILS! STOP!"

The women stop at the roar and try to make out what is the matter. They move back.

The hapless cucumber man is lying and waiting to be hit.

He twists to the right and to the left, wrinkling his brow, and expressively responds to the expected blows.

The tractor driver-thief stands in front of the clamorous kolkhoz women. He laughs and mocks the melon-field sentinel-philosopher, who is shouting at him:

"THIEF!"

Meanwhile the cucumber man is still on the ground . . . He ventures to open one eye—All safe!

He opens the other eye -AND again, All safe!

He begins to get up . . .

HIS WORTHINESS!

Strutting along like a cock, the tractor driver-thief is leading the singing kolkhoz women, who embrace him.

At the rear, the despised wretch shuffles after them like a lonely cur.

RESPECTED!

In an elegant new leather jacket the tractor driver-thief marches down the street.

He is strutting like a cock!

With arching chest!

A tie!

Groomed hair!

A medal and a ribbon!

Kolkhoz men coming his way bow to him.

Even old men bow. The tractor driver! A personage!

An old woman is sitting and weeping, holding her head between her hands. She is the mother of the wretch. She is crying because of the shame and disgrace that have fallen on her gray hairs. The wretch has returned; he huddles next to her with his bundle.

DARLING ONE!

A blooming, luscious girl is embracing the tractor driver-thief.

MY OWN!

And another girl is embracing him.

DEAR LOVE!

A third girl clings to him.

In a pile of straw in a backyard somewhere, the girl loved by the cucumber man hides and cries.

She does not want to see the hateful offender.

The offender is gloomy. He touches his beloved's shoulder, but she kicks him in the stomach as hard as she can. And sends him flying head over heels . . .

DARLING!

The wrecked tractor is a disgusting sight. It looks maimed with its missing wheel, broken radiator, the wires and cords, and the terrible filth.

DEAREST!

The tractor lies abandoned and ruined in a ditch, at the spot where it stopped plowing . . .

That is why the fields remain unplowed.

THE DEAR COMRADE!

A large village meeting is taking place.

Putting on lofty airs (such lofty airs!) the tractor driver-thief sits in the Honorary Presidium.

He sits—worthy, important, chock-full of emotion. He sits like a bishop, too puffed up with importance to breathe!

But suddenly, in violation of all polite norms, the wretched thief comes forward with a stool and sits next to the tractor driver on the Presidium.

He sits down. He assumes the same air of importance. Like a bishop's.

He sits, chock-full of emotion and puffed up with importance, imitating the tractor driver-thief.

Of course, in the presence of this strange audacity, everybody freezes.

But this lasts only a moment.

From the crowd comes laughter, and shouts and mutterings.

The tractor driver, shocked at the proximity of his insignificant colleague, rises from his stool with a look of contempt and is about to grab hold of him by the sleeves in order to destroy him then and there. Enraged, the wretch pounds on the table with his fist.

The table flies to bits.

The cucumber man points his finger at the tractor man and roars:

"IF I AM A THIEF THEN WHAT IS HE?"

Theatrically, like a proper tragedian in the provinces, the wretch takes his own shirt and rips it in two.

Uproar. Confusion. Chaos.

In the pandemonium someone brings down a shaft on the tractor driver-thief's head. The shaft breaks.

In the branch of an aspen tree, with a hemp rope around his neck, sits the cucumber man, who has decided to commit suicide.

With a tragic air he prepares to jump. He thinks. He positions himself and jumps off the branch, intending to swing from it, a cold unbreathing corpse.

But the thick branch unexpectedly breaks, and the cucumber man drops to the ground with the rope around his neck.

The aspen quivers—it is the gallows tree. The aspen leaves quiver . . .

The cucumber man now attaches the rope to a branch so thick and sound that there can be no thought of its breaking. The wretch stands on a tree stump with the rope around his neck, all ready to join his forebears.

He jumps off the stump but . . . the rotten rope breaks.

Seeing that he cannot die in the rope hanging from a tree, the wretch quickly discards it. Just like the first time, when he was in flight, he lies down, stretches out at full length, crosses his arms over his chest, and dejectedly dies . . .

6 *Fruit and Vegetables*

(Film Sketch 3, 1930)

A shunter jumps out between the wheels of a freight train. He has uncoupled some cars carrying a shipment.

The locomotive gives a jolt to bump away the three uncoupled cars. They detach themselves from the train and coast down an empty track in the station yard.

Slowly, as if in their death throes, the three cars shudder to a halt.

They have stopped in a wasteland of station tracks.

POT

is written on one car;

POT

on another; and in thick chalk on the third:

POTATOES

Three carloads of potatoes to supply the workers have arrived.

The cars stand, waiting for what is to be . . .

An enormous queue of human beings stands, waiting in torment for the potatoes.

Four hundred cooperative shareholders stand in an unending, black spiral winding up a steep Golgotha, on the summit of which shines a sign ten yards high that says:

FRUIT AND VEGETABLES

Carrying bags, sacks, boxes, trunks, the people shuffle their feet and lean apathetically on one another; they doze, they brood. They are not shoving those in front. They are not in a hurry to get potatoes.

Fig. 6. Still from *Fruit and Vegetables*. The "Golgotha" with the long, winding queue of people waiting to buy potatoes.

The listless, apathetic queue, inured to everything, are in no hurry to go anywhere. There are no potatoes in the cooperative, and the people are prepared for a long wait.

Three cars with potatoes have been left on a siding, and nobody is prepared to unload them.

Somewhere inside a building a beautiful heavy door bears a beautiful plaque saying:

FRUITS AND VEGETABLES

"Fruits and Vegetables" occupy a spacious office. There are three of them. They are indistinguishable from the ordinary run of clerks in points of fatness, attire, and physiognomy.

"Fruits and Vegetables" have just one strange peculiarity: they have brightly shining copper foreheads held on by screws and bolts.

Giving off cold metallic gleams, the three bureaucrats lean over their tables:

stiff hairs sprout from the copper of "fruit" number one;

a dandy forelock adorns the metallic hemisphere of the second;

the bald pate of the third shines like a bare radiant globe.

Everything is credible and convincing; even the nuts and bolts fastening the copper plates to their skulls cannot arouse any doubts regarding their verisimilitude . . .

"Fruits and Vegetables" are at work. They are administrating.

Meanwhile the three abandoned freight cars with potatoes are standing on the siding . . .

A boat is leaving the shore of a desolate river. A boatman is in it, with a peasant woman, whom he has come to fetch.

But the boat has scarcely moved (at most a yard!) when three travelers appear. They are in a great hurry to get across!

"Wait!" they cry. "Wait! Take us across the river!"

But the boatman, leaning on his oars with a bored expression, turns away, as if nobody was calling him. As if he was deaf! The three men run up; they fret; they are distressed. They have made great haste—their appeals are especially warm.

But . . . there are three signs on the bank, attached to stout oak posts:

#1
IT IS FORBIDDEN TO SHOUT WHILE WAITING

says the first.

#2
WARNING: A SHOUTER DIED HERE

says the second. And:

#3
NO CROSSING WITHOUT A LOAD
BOAT ADMIN.,
(*scrawled signature*)

As he approaches the other shore, the boatman keeps plying his oars. Imperturbable, bureaucratic officialdom is inscribed on his pockmarked face.

This is a brutal fact of life: even an ordinary boatman or a janitor or an ice-cream man can be a bureaucrat.

With a last weary wave of their hands, the three travelers settle down for a long, tedious wait.

And so here they are waiting on the sand.

On the other shore the boat is now fastened to its moorings. The peasant woman ferried across by the boatman has gone off, and the boatman is sitting on the bank with a line and hook, fishing for perch.

Another four travelers come along and join the others.

The boat is fastened to its moorings on the far shore. Nobody is about to send it back for the waiting travelers.

And now they number fifteen. They are waiting as in the lineup for potatoes, without protesting, meekly, prepared to remain sitting till nightfall.

And the boatman, just like a bureaucratic clerk at a desk, is sitting ("on duty!") while he holds a line and hook. And the people who are waiting are no concern of his . . .

The three cars with the potatoes are still standing on the tracks at the station. Nobody is about to unload them.

The apathetic queue of people is still waiting for potatoes, still in torment. It has not moved.

Standing in the queue are serious, manly steelworkers, militiamen, Red Army officers, Komsomol girls, employees of the Soviet council.

Standing in the queue is a former sailor. Men like him made the Revolution! With a man like this, you can face a whole division.

Indeed, there was a time when this sailor single-handedly captured a three-inch cannon from Kolchak's men[1] (we will show this!). He captured it and pulled it along like a baby carriage. When the enemy gave chase, the sailor bravely loaded a shell into the cannon, bravely blasted the opponent—and the explosion of the shell left a heap of enemies scattered like rubbish over a field.

Shoes, heads, feet, and hands were sent flying through the screen of smoke.

Now this sailor is standing quiet and tamed in the queue.

Meanwhile, the potatoes are standing on the station tracks. And "Fruits and Vegetables" are not concerned about unloading them.

Now their copper foreheads are shining on a balcony. As a demonstration of the great importance of provisions for the workers, one of the copper heads spits from the balcony.

The spit hits the sailor in the nape of the neck. The sailor, looking upward with an air of subjugation, meekly wipes the spittle off with his hand and puts on his cap.

An indigent bourgeoise, his neighbor in the queue, politely unfurls over the hero and herself a big, old-fashioned family umbrella . . .

On the empty shore the empty boat is tied to its moorings. Nobody is near the boat.

Some thirty travelers are waiting for the ferry. Evidently, they have been waiting for a long time, and they have accommodated themselves for a long stay on the sand: some of them sleeping; some playing cards for money; some lazily sprawling.

Only one unrepressed youth, losing his temper, shouts as loud as he can for the boat.

But the imperturbable boatman continues to fish, his stupid face expressing no feelings . . .

A dark putrid liquid oozes through the floor of a train car and trickles onto the sand.

The three train cars with potatoes are obdurately stranded on the tracks.

The potatoes are going to waste; they are rotting.

And there is still the same queue, with four hundred souls winding in a spiral up the Golgotha on whose summit, almost as high as the clouds, shines the sign saying:

FRUITS AND VEGETABLES

Because of the long wait, the old women, militiamen, Komsomol girls, and the sailor have been making themselves more comfortable in the queue.

Suddenly the sailor loses patience. Taking hold of a plywood box, he dashes it with all his might against a post, and his finger pointing into the queue, he roars:

"We are the members of a co-op, aren't we? We are masters, aren't we—or else who are we?"

But nobody has any kind of reaction to this cry of rage, and the sailor, adjusting his cap as if for battle, rushes into the store.

In the store hangs a huge placard with a picture of a downward-pointing hand:

CO-OP MEMBERS FIGHT!
FIGHT IRREGULARITIES!
PUT YOUR COMPLAINTS IN THE BOX!

The sailor runs toward this sign with a large stack of complaints.

He wants to shove them into the box. But . . . there is no box! Somebody forgot to put it up.

Next to the cooperative there is another sign:

MAKE COOPERATION WORK!

And here there is a box.

The sailor rushes to the box. He drops his packet in it and comes away satisfied . . .

But since the box has no bottom, the packet drops straight through it and lands on the floor.

A pig appears out of nowhere, gathers the packet in its jaws, and greedily gobbles up the sailor's complaints . . .

The sailor, his duty performed, contentedly goes back to the queue, sits among the waiting crowd, and starts shamelessly "shooting the breeze" about some gigantic pike he once caught. (When he stretches out his hands to show how large the fish was, there will be a pan shot of a pike three meters long from head to tail.)

Meanwhile, on the river, the enraged passengers have prepared a punitive expedition. A lanky youth is sitting in an unsteady washtub, which has been launched onto the water.

An old woman in minor orders, a humble nun, gives the lanky fellow a fearsome oaken staff, weighing some twenty pounds, with nails and a fiendish knob at the end. A thump with this staff would reduce the boatman-bureaucrat to a wet puddle. The lanky fellow puts the staff into the tub and casts off, paddling with his arms instead of oars.

The obstinate boatman is fishing. Something has bitten, and he is all attention as he looks at the bobbing cork.

In the meantime the lanky fellow in the ridiculous tub has sailed to the middle of the river. The furious passengers send along advice about the best way to let the bureaucratic boatman have a drubbing.

All of a sudden the tub fills with water, and in an instant it sinks. The staff is swept away by the current, while the lanky fellow, blowing bubbles, calls for help.

The lanky fellow is splashing about. He is gasping for breath. Finally overcoming his fear, he lets down his feet, and quite unexpectedly finds that the water is scarcely knee-deep, and drowning all but impossible . . .

At last the boatman jerks up his hook and lands the fish.

It is a gudgeon, small rather than large, hardly worth tormenting people for.

The people are still waiting.

And among them the lanky fellow is the biggest yet also the quietest, the strongest yet also the most humbled. As if he hadn't set off on a "punitive expedition" and hadn't proposed to reduce the boatman to a wet puddle.

The three freight cars of potatoes are standing on the tracks. The yardman comes up, reading a note. He holds his nose. The stench from the cars is so unbearably foul that he is driven away.

On Golgotha the suffering queue of people stands, and waits.

And now a ridiculously small, chubby Pioneer[2] steps in front of this queue.

He stops and, like a commander in chief, casts a look of surprise at this huge human queue and, not unlike a child, expresses his puzzlement with his arms.

Shrugging his shoulders, he speaks his disbelief:

"YOU ARE ALL SO BIG AND STRONG . . ."

And indeed, standing in the queue are commanders, a militiaman, Komsomol girls, a steelworker.

Standing in the queue is the sailor who took a cannon away from Kolchak.

And the Pioneer asks, with growing surprise:

"HAVE YOU NAMED A SHOP COMMITTEE? WHERE IS IT?"

One man quickly stuffs his ears with cotton and fills his mouth with water from a jug. He takes so much that his cheeks look ready to burst.

Chock-full of water, he moves toward the Pioneer.

He stands in a row of people as strange as himself. Everyone looks the same.

All have stuffed ears. All have mouths filled with water. All have one bandaged eye. All are on crutches . . .

This troupe of invalids is the shop committee.

It cannot see. It cannot hear, speak, move. It can do nothing.

And the Pioneer asks the queue of human beings:

"IS THIS A SHOP COMMITTEE OR A TROUPE OF INVALIDS?"

The invalid troupe stand with their mouths chock-full of water, unhearing, unseeing. Silent.

And the Pioneer pretends that he too has a mouth full of water, and caricaturing these strange people, he shows with some expressive body movements how to chuck them out of the cooperative.

The three "Fruits and Vegetables" are leaning out from the balcony. Their copper foreheads dazzling in the sun, they gaze down at the queue with indifference and wait for the end of the workday.

The sailor, looking up at them, cannot restrain himself, and jumps up and pronounces:

"ENOUGH!"

And tightening his belt, he orders the invalid troupe to go to the freight cars.

The invalids turn to one another in confusion, bumping their heads, and bustle about without going anywhere. They are not able to walk.

The sailor, the workers, and the Komsomol girls march along the street.

And the chubby boy-Pioneer marches in step with them, trying to keep up.

The three freight cars loaded with potatoes are standing. The potatoes are rotting.

The members of the shop committee with water in their mouths stand in front of the train cars. Since they cannot pronounce indignant speeches, they gesticulate and demonstrate to one another that, no, they do not agree; no, they are opposed; and yes, they will show the bureaucrats what's what.

The beautiful door with the plaque:

FRUITS AND VEGETABLES

The sailor, the worker, the Komsomol girl, and the little Pioneer boy stop in front of the door.

After reading the plaque, the sailor flings open the door and strides into the office.

The activists enter the office, and the door slams shut behind them.

What happens inside is not known. The door slowly dissolves, and a peculiar picture appears.

A man is performing a strange and incomprehensible act. He takes a bag, beats it against a telegraph pole as if he was a man possessed, flings it down on the floor, kicks it, angrily stamps on it, jumps on it, beats it with a stick, and then dropping the stick, takes out a box of matches. Removing a match from the box, he places it next to the box. Then he unties the sack and pulls a rabbit out by the ears . . .

IF YOU BEAT A RABBIT, YOU CAN TEACH IT TO LIGHT A MATCH . . .

And, indeed, the battered rabbit from the sack strikes a match, looking at the spectator in the same way as a circus performer. Tossing away the match, the beat-up rabbit says with his paws in circus fashion: "Voilà!"

Here the furious face of the sailor appears for a moment.

Suddenly the three freight cars with potatoes give a jolt and quickly roll away, leaving behind a puddle.

But the train cars are not being pulled by a locomotive.

The three "Fruit and Vegetables" with shining copper foreheads are pushing the cars at a speed of twenty kilometers an hour, bringing their whole weight to bear on them.

The cars stop just past a switch. The switchman blows a whistle as he throws the switch.

And again the three cars rush, backward this time, pushed by the copper foreheads instead of by a locomotive.

There is a glimpse of a grim face, belonging to the steelworker who shamed himself in the queue.

And the viewer sees a bald copper pate sweating . . .

The bureaucrat's trembling fingers wipe it.

And potatoes are tossed across the screen.

Lots of potatoes!

AS FOR DEADMEN, WHAT'S THE POINT OF BEATING THEM?

The members of the shop committee are still standing where the freight cars were. They stand and apparently did not notice that now there are no freight cars.

THE LIVING MUST REPLACE THE DEAD!

An emaciated limping nag pulls a cart loaded with the shop-committee dummies, all collapsed into a messy pile. Crutches, grotesque feet, hands, and heads stick out from the sides and top. The cart bounces over the ruts and potholes of the desolate road.

7 A Cock and Bull Story

(Film Sketch 4, 1931)

A huge building is under construction.

On the ground floor a shoe factory is already in operation.

A sign with crooked letters advertises:

RUNNING SHOES

A strange-looking shoemaker is at work at a strange machine, turning out strange monstrous shoes.

Suddenly the ceiling collapses onto the machine.

The shoemaker manages to leap out into the street just moments before a devastating crack looking like forked lightning fractures all eight floors of the building.

Tilting back his head, the shoemaker shouts an angry denunciation at the bricklayers above.

The bricklayers do not hear him: they are building; they are enthusiastically laying bricks. On the seventh floor a brick breaks loose and falls.

Wham!—it hits the shoemaker at full force smack on the head.

It disintegrates into a cloud of dust.

The impact of the brick looks deadly. But once the dust scatters, the shoemaker jerks his head about as if everything was fine, and settles it back in position. Then he lifts a piece of the brick from the ground and readily crumbles it, grinding it to dust between his fingers. Addressing the [film] viewer he protests:

"THIS CAN'T BE A BRICK, CAN IT?"

Looking up, the shoemaker considers how soon it will be before this botched building totally crushes him and kills him.

Angry now, he shouts up to the bricklayers:

"HEY, YOU DEVILS! WHAT IS IT YOU ARE BUILDING!?"

Overhead, the bricklayers, standing in a cradle, are racing to complete the last story of the building.

In response to the shoemaker's shout, one bricklayer sticks his head out from the cradle. The two could be twins.

The shoemaker starts to shout insults at the bricklayer.

The bricklayer listens, listens some more, then phlegmatically says:

"OF WHAT CONCERN IS QUALITY TO US?
SHOCK-WORK NORMS ARE WHAT WE'RE AFTER."

And the two identical-looking men start arguing.

But suddenly a balcony twisted askew by the crack comes off in a big chunk and collapses onto the shoemaker, concealing everything in a cloud of dust.

Extricating himself with difficulty from the debris, the shoemaker emerges covered with the dust of construction materials, all hot and angry.

He spreads out a handkerchief, wraps up two bricks in it for material evidence, and shouts:

"I'LL GET THEM!"

Cursing like a man possessed, he takes to his heels:

"I'LL GET THEM! I'LL PUT THE NEWSPAPER ONTO THEM!"

Meanwhile, up above, the bricklayers are enthusiastically racing to complete the top story . . .

The main entrance of a building.

A sign over the entrance says:

THE THRASHER
NEWSPAPER OFFICE

The shoemaker flies into the editorial office like a whirlwind.

He dumps his bundle of bricks right onto the papers on the editor's desk.

The injured shoemaker shouts,
becomes agitated, stamps about . . .

Meanwhile the last brick is being laid at the top of the building.

"HURRAH!"

joyfully cry the bricklayers.

A red banner appears from somewhere.

The bricklayers burst into song.

A celebration is organized.

Fifteen bricklayers go marching along the roof, bearing a placard:

HURRAH! THERE'S NOTHING WE CAN'T DO!

They go marching along the roof, when c-r-a-ck! the roof collapses with a rumble.

The balconies and the overhangs crumble.

The bricklayers and the banner crash down.

Just one young bricklayer, the one who looks like the shoemaker, manages to get hold of a piece of rope.

He is letting himself down the rope when it starts to fray.

The bricklayer is coming down, and the rope is almost frayed through . . .

And the thick, but rotten, rope breaks, and the construction worker plunges down from the fifth floor.

"A-a-ah!"

bursts forth from someone on the edge of the cradle.

A frightened face flashing past.

Somebody crossing himself.

The corpse of the fallen man is buried in dust.

Everybody freezes.

But the corpse rises unperturbed, calmly shakes off the dust, and, pointing to the bit of rope, asks the viewer:

"IS THIS A ROPE, OR NOT A ROPE?"

The bricklayer pounds his chest with his fist:

"I'LL GET THEM! I'LL TELL THE NEWSPAPER ABOUT THEM!"

Waving the bit of rope, the injured construction worker abruptly takes off.

He flies like a comet through the main door with the sign

THE THRASHER
NEWSPAPER OFFICE

In the office the bricklayer shoves the piece of rope under the nose of the editor:

"PEOPLE SHOULD BE SHOT FOR QUALITY LIKE THIS!"

And the injured bricklayer shouts and is agitated and stamps about . . .
A worker from the rope factory sitting on a stool is in torment. In appearance he is terribly like the shoemaker and the bricklayer.
Pushing as hard as he can, he is trying to squeeze his foot into a new, misshapen shoe.
He has already got one grotesque shoe on. The other shoe just won't go on.
He huffs and puffs in such a weird way that a pendulum clock stops in amazement and pauses before it resumes ticking.
But the shoe will not go on. The rope maker shifts onto a table and huffs and puffs even harder—and a portrait of a genial-looking fat man hanging on the wall suddenly whistles out in surprise.
After failing to get the second shoe on, the rope maker attempts to take the first one off.

"WELL, SCOUNDRELS! FINE SHOES YOU'VE MADE!"

He tries again as hard as he can, and says almost in tears:

"THANK YOU, SHOEMAKERS! YOU ARE FRIENDS INDEED!"

Completely losing his temper, the rope maker jumps up, shouting:

"I'LL GET THEM! I'LL TELL THE NEWSPAPER ABOUT THEM!"

The rope maker tears off, hopping as he runs because of his clumsy footwear.
Again the doorway.

THE THRASHER
NEWSPAPER OFFICE

The half-shod, furious rope-maker runs through the doorway.

Inside the editor's office he hurls himself onto the table, lifts up his leg, and displays the appalling shoe, shrieking:

"SAY, WHAT IS THIS? DEAR COMRADES!"

. . . Down a street runs a newspaperman who is selling copies of the paper.

Three people rush up to the newspaperman: the shoemaker, the bricklayer, and the rope maker. They buy a copy and open ***The Thrasher***.

THE CAMPAIGN FOR QUALITY

cries out one page.

STRUGGLE LIKE WILD BEASTS!
STRUGGLE LIKE DEVILS!

it drones on in an even larger typeface.

Another page appeals:

LET'S FIND THE REAL AGENTS OF EVIL![1]

Next come three black blobs, which are supposed to depict the piece of rope, the shoes, and the bricks.

But . . . the blobs are impossible to make out, and the caption underneath them could be a travesty:

PHOTOS OF SHODDY SPECIMENS

Nothing can be seen in these pictures: they are good as illustrations only to the extent that the photos are themselves specimens of shoddy workmanship . . .

A crowd of people comes running down a street. They are trying to catch a fleet-footed lawbreaker:

"STOP HIM!"

As it happens he is our bricklayer!

"STOP HIM!"

The angry crowd are in pursuit. People are shouting:

"STOP HIM!
HE'S ONE OF THE WORKERS FROM THE BUILDING!"

The chase.

The shoemaker is crossing a bridge. He walks without looking underfoot. He is reading *The Thrasher*. Suddenly—woosh!—he slips, then tumbles off the bridge because there is a break in the railing.

As he flies down, his jacket catches on a hook, and he is left suspended in the air at a terrifying height above the town . . .

He curls right up like a puppy, hanging there between heaven and earth, desperately trying to extricate himself from his hopeless situation.

The rope maker is crossing the bridge, hobbling along with his grotesque shoe.

He is reading *The Thrasher* as he walks. Hearing the shouts of the unfortunate shoemaker, he rushes to his help.

He holds out the end of a strap to the victim and pulls him up onto the bridge.

But suddenly he recognizes the rescued man as the shoemaker and inquires:

"AREN'T YOU THE COBBLER WHO MADE THIS SHOE?"

And he raises the shoe that is flopping on his foot up to the shoemaker's nose.

Upon examining the shoe, the shoemaker joyfully smiles: YES! he does indeed recognize his manner of cobbling shoes . . .

"And so you are the craftsman?" asks the rope maker with merciless calm.

"Yes, I am the man!" answers the craftsman.

In a flash the rope maker pushes the rescued bungler off the bridge, and the man flies into the abyss . . .

Choking with anger, the bricklayer is shouting:

"AREN'T YOU THE ROPE MAKER WHO MADE THIS ROPE?"

Upon examining the proffered piece of rotten rope, the rope maker says with pride and satisfaction:

"Yes, I am the man who made this rope!"

"And so you are the craftsman?" inquires the bricklayer with ominous calm.

"Yes, I am the man!" proudly says the rope maker.

And then, in a flash, the bricklayer pushes the hypocritical rope-maker off the bridge. The rope maker is left hanging above the void from the same hook from which not long ago the shoemaker was suspended.

He hangs above the abyss, calling for help.

And a chance passerby, crossing the bridge, hears the cry.

He rushes to offer help. He tosses the end of a rope to the victim:

"HURRY!
HOLD TIGHT!"

But the rope maker takes a look at the rope, gives it a yank, and declines to save himeslf.

"NO! . . . IT'S NOT GOOD ENOUGH!"

The passerby is petrified with astonishment:

"WHY ISN'T IT?"

Throwing back the rope end, the rope maker says:

"I KNOW! . . . I MADE IT MYSELF!"

And so, to this day, this botcher is suspended above the town.

The gigantic seven-story building, with the catastrophic crack fracturing it.

As in the beginning, the shoemaker stands in front of the building. He tilts his head all the way back. He stands, reflecting:

"ALL RIGHT! . . . EVERYTHING WILL BE ALL RIGHT!"

And, as in the beginning, a large brick breaks loose up above.

It hits the shoemaker on the head . . .

And when the dust scatters, the shoemaker reassures himself by saying:

Fig. 7. Still from *Cock and Bull Story*. A crack in a brand-new building in this film about shoddy workmanship.

"SOMEHOW IT'LL ALL WORK OUT!"

Taking a shoe brush out of his pocket, he wipes the powdered cement off his head, with a well-practiced, efficient gesture, just as if it was dust on his shoes . . .

8 Hey Fool, What a Fool You Are!

(1931)

The Fool in front of a factory building under construction.

The Fool is an engineer.

He looks first at a tiny door leading into a completed workshop, and then at an enormous cast-steel machine . . .

from the door

to the machine.

Even a not-very-smart person can immediately see that the workshop has been built without anyone giving a thought to the need to get the machine into it. Everyone had simply forgotten about this!

The Fool—the constructor—is incredulous. He cannot grasp that there has been a major blunder.

As he looks—from the door

to the machine—

he is consumed by doubts. He recalls something, ponders, does some measurements in his mind, making scientific comparisons between the ever-so-tiny door

and the enormous machine . . .

All of a sudden the Fool strikes his forehead with his hand and roars to someone overhead:

"WAIT!"

Upon hearing this frenzied cry, the bricklayers stop working.

And someone up above says: "What's the matter?"

The Fool nervously shakes out his big pockets, his little pockets, his tiniest pockets, in order to get from them what had substituted for his architectural plan: sheets of writing paper, notepads, scraps of paper with scribbles on them . . .

The Fool is desperately trying to retrieve a lost idea . . .

It is quite clear that the grandiose cast-steel machine cannot fit through the little door . . .

Under the stress, the Fool has broken out in a sweat. He says:

"IT SEEMS . . ."

The frayed and crumpled sheets of paper and notepads fall down and are scattered.

In a fit of new misgivings, the Fool falls to his knees and lifts all sorts of different bits of paper to his myopic eyes, but the unfortunate expert is unable to settle his questions . . .

Meanwhile the bricklayers silently wait.

Finally the Fool raises his head and, still rummaging in his pockets, whimpers:

"Oh, it seems the machine won't fit! . . ."

"Oh, we forgot about the machine!"

And a row starts up among the bricklayers: they've been building and building, and worrying and agonizing, and now . . . And they shout all kinds of nasty things at the expert . . .

"Quiet!" officiously barks the Fool, and, pointing at the wall, he bawls:

"SMASH IT!"

The bricklayers submit to the voice of authority, and start demolishing the brick wall they have just built . . .

Breaking the bricks and prying them off with crowbars, they destroy the new building . . .

The Fool has almost finished collecting the strange documentation in his pockets when a technician runs up to him and grabs him by his shirt-sleeves. He looks around with an air of mystery and whispers in his ear:

"DID YOU FORGET THE TOILETS??"

The anxious words are spread out across the screen.

Quite shattered now, the Fool grabs his pockets.

From the frayed pieces of paper, he takes out a crumpled sketch.

He lies down on the ground and smooths out the piece of paper, quietly whispering:

"MAYBE . . ."

Then all of a sudden, he leaps up and runs away with the technician, wailing:

"Oh! Oh! Oh!"

. . . In an office somewhere all hell breaks loose.

Twenty office workers are turning folders inside out, emptying cupboards, searching under tables and chairs . . .

The office is almost waist-deep in piles of paper.

Some of the workers have their heads stuck in the piles of paper, while others, on top of cupboards, are tossing out sheets of paper from folders and creating a snowstorm . . .

"WHAT ARE YOU LOOKING FOR?"

In response to this question from an onlooker, the sweating Division Admin emerges from one of the snowdrifts and breathing heavily, says:

"THE ARCHITECTURAL PLAN AND CALCULATIONS! THAT'S WHAT! . . ."

The sea of papers heaves and rages.

The book cupboards are adrift, and the desks of the bosses and their subordinates are rocking on the waves . . .

The office workers sink and reemerge . . .

The Fool is experiencing a personal calamity . . .

"WELL, DID THE PLAN EVER EXIST?"

asks the Division Admin, suddenly emerging.

The Fool is jolted. He is remembering something:

"MAYBE . . ."

And suddenly horrified, he recalls:

"OH, MAYBE THERE WAS NO PLAN! . . ."

The worn-out office workers give up their search, and climb down from the cupboards . . .

Two announcements appear in a newspaper in the obituaries section, one under the other.

KOLIA INTERRED
DIED IN PEACE.

THE TsKK SUMMONS THE FOOL, IVAN IVANOVICH,
TO ROOM 133.[1]

A Ford stops in front of the grand entrance of the TsKK.
From the car emerges Ivan Ivanovich, the Fool, neither dead nor alive.
He wants to walk, but his legs will not walk.
He advances—he stumbles . . .
The Fool is placed on an uncomfortable, round stool.
On three sides there are gloomy people staring at him: workers, peasants, Red Army soldiers, members of the Komsomol league, and Pioneers . . .

"FOOL, WHAT A FOOL YOU ARE!"

someone over on the right says.

"YOU ARE A DUMB DOLLY KIND OF MAN!"

someone over on the left says.
The Fool keeps turning on his rotating stool! . . . All hell is breaking loose.
Serious people bear down on him:

**"FOOL, FIRST YOU NEEDED PLANS,
AND THEN SOME CALCULATIONS.
AFTERWARD THE CONSTRUCTION."**

The Fool emerges from the grand entrance, neither dead nor alive.
He leans against a lamppost . . .
The driver takes off the Fool's jacket, then his smock.
He bends the Fool over, as if he were a lifeless doll.
And dashes a bucketful of water on his head . . .
Then he places the revived Fool in the car.
He steps on the gas, stirring up a cloud of dust.

. . . In a region with no water, three men are digging a well.
They are exhausted and sweaty. Stripped to the waist. Dying of thirst.
They stop working, and breathe heavily.
One of them says to an emaciated woman who is peering into the hole:

"WELL, IN ONE WEEK THERE WILL BE WATER . . ."

And at the thought of water, the three men spit on their hands and resume their work with renewed energy, tossing up shovelfuls of earth.

A post with a board on it saying:

GOVMENTEXCAVATIONS

The Fool is standing underneath a sign on a post:

THE NEW SUPERVISOR

Frowning and carrying an enormous briefcase, he goes over to the three earth diggers.

The three of them are working. The Fool silently leans over them and suddenly asks:

"WHAT ABOUT THE CALCULATIONS?"

Without stopping his work, the interrogated man shakes his head: "There are no calculations!"

The Fool comes up from the other side:

"AND THE PLANS?"

"What do you mean by plans?" the second worker shrugs him off.

The Fool bursts out:

"AND THE DRAWINGS?"

"Hey, what a pest! There are no drawings."

"Stop!" roars the Fool.

The workers stop working, and—in shock—they freeze. Then coming to their senses they start protesting.

"Quiet!" bellows the Fool.

The workers climb out of the pit and angrily throw down their shovels.

QUICKLY OR NOT, TWO MONTHS WENT BY . . .

The Fool has surrounded the well with a gigantic structure.

He has built a fence around the structure.

And he has built a sentry box.

Through the window of the sentry box one can see that it is stuffed with armed guards.

At a checkpoint another two guards are standing underneath a sign saying:

GOVMENTEXCAVATIONS

A crowd of kolkhoz farmers approach them carrying buckets.

But the guards refuse point-blank to let them through to the structure.

The kolkhoz farmers protest:

"THE KOLKHOZ CATTLE WILL DIE WITHOUT WATER!
LET US SEE THE MAN IN CHARGE!"

But the guards refuse to let them pass.

And the kolkhoz workers shuffle away.

They go round a corner.

They are shuffling off home.

Suddenly one of them calls out, and they stop and see that the fence has not been completed and a well-trodden road goes past the last link of the fence, and that all the security system is for naught!

The kolkhoz farmers take the road without any permission slips.

Meanwhile, fifteen guards are sitting at the ready in the sentry box, and the two implacable sentries pace in front of the well-guarded gates.

They go past a building with a sign saying:

ECONOMIC PLANNING AND ACCOUNTING DEPARTMENT

And past a second building:

DEPARTMENT FOR SPECIAL CIRCUMSTANCES
AND ROUTINE HOLDUPS

Then past a building bearing the sign: **GYNECOLOGICAL CLINIC**.

The kolkhoz workers stop at a building with the sign:

PROJECT MANAGEMENT AND DRAFTING UNIT

There the Fool, Ivan Ivanovich, is digging the kolkhoz well with the aid of a splendid plan.

A complete drawing of his future well covers the floor of this vast, empty room. Five draftsmen are crawling on the floor, marking off details of the plan.

As for the Fool, he is seated on a three-meter-tall three-legged stool, giving instructions with the help of a long pointer.

A kolkhoz delegate with dirty boots stomps into the room:

"HOW MUCH LONGER IS THE KOLKHOZ
GOING TO HAVE TO SUFFER?"

he shouts at the Fool.

In a rage, the Fool answers:

"GO TO HELL!
DON'T YOU THINK I AM SUFFERING TOO?"

The kolkhoz workers continue to stand in front of the strange installation, and when their delegate comes out, they come to a decision and shuffle off home.

. . . And then two kolkhoz workers walk out into the field.

They start taking measurements—two paces in one direction, and two paces in another.

They take off their shirts.

They pick up some shovels.

They spit on their hands.

And they start digging a well . . .

And while the Fool, armed with a theodolite, rods, and chains, is calculating the location of the future well in accordance with all technical prescriptions,

the two men in the open field disappear underground, tossing up a great pile of clay . . .

Meanwhile, two carpenters finish a new frame . . .

A narrow-gauge track has been laid down on the construction site . . .

A steam locomotive puffs as it tows some wagons . . .

. . . In the field the well is ready: it can boast of an oak surround, a new winch, a light-colored roof . . .

There is even a horse etched in tin decorating it!

A group of kolkhoz workers draw up the first bucket of water, and, rejoicing, they lift up the well's builders and swing them back and forth . . .

. . . But at GOVEXCAVATIONS some fundamental work is being done.

Earth is being hauled in receptacles on a special, mechanized conveyor belt. Clever mechanical contrivances transfer the earth into the train wagons . . .

The little, narrow-gauge locomotive gives a whistle, and the train moves off with its load of excavated clay . . .

The Fool struts like a peacock around this well-organized business, and his pompous arrogance, his well-stuffed briefcase, and his enormous tubular holder filled with drawings all attest to his being a truly happy man . . .

Just then the kolkhoz workers come up to him with their pails and tubs . . .

Upon seeing them, the self-satisfied Fool snorts and starts to shout:

"WHY ARE YOU BOTHERING ME, EH?
CAN'T YOU WAIT ANOTHER MONTH?
GET LOST!"

He is met with silent condemnation. Then someone from the crowd calls out:

"YOU CAN CLOSE UP SHOP, OLD MAN!"

The Fool is frightened.

A panicky, bald-headed official sticks his head out of the window of the DEPARTMENT FOR SPECIAL CIRCUMSTANCES . . .

The engineer climbs down from the locomotive . . .

The professional car driver opens up a copy of *Pravda*, and, just like the first time . . .

In the obituaries section, there is an announcement:

THE FRIENDS AND ACQUAINTANCE OF NICHOLAS,
THE CLEVER, ANNOUNCE THAT HE HAS FOUND
PEACE IN DEATH. THE TsKK SUMMONS THE FOOL,
IVAN IVANOVICH, TO ROOM 133.

Just like before a Ford stops in front of the grand entrance.

Ivan Ivanovich, the Fool, emerges from the Ford with piles of drawings, calculations, and supporting documents . . .

He stands—neither dead, nor alive!

He wants to go in—his feet do not obey him.

He starts walking, and stumbles . . .

HEY FOOL! WHAT A FOOL YOU ARE!

The Fool is spinning! . . . Spinning! . . . Spinning!

WHAT HAVE YOU DONE?

The Fool is spinning on the round stool, and all around there are stern judges . . .

"WHAT YOU NEED TO DO, FOOL, IS
SERVE THE MASSES! . . . AND REBUILD THEIR LIVES
ON THE BASIS OF THE NEW PRINCIPLES!"

The driver has prepared a bucket of water . . .
He has a towel ready . . .
The Fool emerges, reeling, from the grand entrance . . .
Neither dead nor alive! He leans again a lamppost.
The driver repeats what he did the first time.
He removes the Fool's smock and wrings out the sweat from it, then he pours cold water over this boss . . .

WHAT WENT ON THERE, NO ONE COULD SAY
WITHOUT HAVING SEEN IT. A COMPLETE MYSTERY!
EXCEPT THAT THE FOOL WAS DIRECTED TO REBUILD
HIS LIFE ACCORDING TO THE NEW PRINCIPLES . . .

Next to a leaning, collapsing shack, stands a Commission headed by the Fool.
The shack is old. It is amazingly dilapidated and squalid.
But people are still living in it. Yes, one could live in it.
And the Fool, saddened, breaks off a fragment of a plank from the roof and tosses it, then strikes a picturesque, sad pose . . .
Here the Fool is struck by a brilliant thought: he summons the secretary and dictates an order to him.
The secretary rushes off to execute it.
A poster is being pasted onto a decrepit fence:

ORDERS

In connection with the ONSET OF SOCIALISM
And the reconstruction of life in accordance

With the new principles,
I HEREBY ORDER:
1
The immediate destruction of all old, single-story buildings.
2
Expelling their inhabitants onto
the town square.
3
The establishment of a Commission for the Development of a Project for a New Socialist Town.

Paradise. Ons. of Soc.—Iv. Fool

Out of the windows of hovels come flying pillows, samovars, and saucepans . . .

A roof is torn off, then the stovepipe is thrown out, and the stove demolished; doors and windows are knocked out . . .

General commotion! . . . Chaos! . . . Dust! . . .

The inhabitants of the hovels barely manage to escape into the town square . . .

The Fool has erected an enormous stand on the square—the project for the new Socialist town, with one building that will house everybody . . .

It is a grotesque many-storied chest with little windows, as in a prison. But seen from a bird's-eye view it has the shape of a hammer and sickle . . .

The homeless set themselves up as best they can under the stand; some even make themselves somewhat comfortable . . .

One shrewd, devout crone makes use of one of the stand's props in order to affix to it a copy of the miraculous icon of the Kazan Mother of God with an ever-burning oil lamp in front of it! . . .

PROCLAMATION

Money is hereby ABOLISHED.
All silver coins to be handed over to
young children to use in the production of toys.[2]

Paradise. Ons. Soc.—Iv. Fool

A crowd of people stands in front of the proclamation, reading it.

A swindler of a village priest sees an opportunity and pulls out a purse from his pocket. With a great show he wipes away a tear ("Indeed, we have lived to see the day of our salvation!"), and shakes out the contents of the purse onto the ground . . .

Bank notes fly down, and coins roll in the dust.

Following the example of the duplicitous priest, simple people throw their little stores of money onto the ground . . .

And the simple people shed tears and are deeply moved! . . .

And then when they go away, the crooked priest rakes up a huge pile of money, a pile so huge he can hardly count his booty.

Once again, the driver opens up the newspaper *Pravda*:

THE FRIENDS OF
NICHOLAS, THE MOST WISE,
ANNOUNCE THAT HE HAS DIED
AT PEACE WITH GOD.

And another announcement:

THE TsKK REQUESTS COMRADE IVAN
IVANOVICH, THE FOOL, TO PAY A VISIT
TO ROOM 133.

And so, just as before, the Ford is parked by the entrance.

Next to the Ford is a bucket filled with water . . . And a towel!

The driver catnaps while waiting for the boss.

"YOU AGAIN, YOU PITIFUL MAN!"

say the members of the TsKK, throwing up their hands. And the Fool spins round . . . And the justices say:

"YOU SHOULDN'T HAVE KNOCKED HOUSES DOWN, FOOL!"

The Fool spins! . . .

"YOU SHOULDN'T HAVE ABOLISHED MONEY!"

The Fool pouts and frowns.

"GO AND WORK!
LEARN SOME BASIC ECONOMICS!
KNOW THE COST OF EVERY STEP YOU TAKE!"

Somewhere—exactly where is not known—there are some enormous gasoline tanks, with "GASOLINE" written on them.

Two workers led by the Fool (evidently he has a new assignment) are rolling iron barrels past one of the gasoline tanks.

The Fool marches into the office of the specialist in charge and demands that some gasoline be issued to him.

"NO GASOLINE WITHOUT A CONTRACT!
WE FOLLOW BASIC ACCOUNTING RULES!"

is the curt, tough response of the specialist.

"LOOK, WE COME FROM THE SAME FACTORY!"

says the Fool in astonishment. And the specialist sticks to his position:

"CAN'T LET YOU HAVE IT! . . . ACCOUNTING
PROCEDURES! . . . LET'S HAVE A CONTRACT!"

The Fool thinks and thinks, and agrees: "All right, then! So be it—a contract!"

He summons a typist. She types up a contract.

She hands it over to the secretary.

The secretary makes a note of it, and hands it over to the office administrator.

The office administrator records it, and hands it to the registrar.

The registrar—to the accountant.

The accountant—to a courier.

The courier—to the office administrator.

The administrator—to the secretary.

The secretary—to the specialist.

The specialist—to the Fool . . .

The Fool is pleased. He shakes the hand of the specialist.

"I THANK YOU FOR THIS LESSON. NOW I, THE
FOOL, WILL NOT GET WRONG THE BASIC PRINCIPLES OF ACCOUNTING! . . ."

Gasoline is poured into the barrels. The Fool rejoices.

. . . Two workers walk past a gasoline tank.

They suddenly notice something, and stop . . .

A pipe from the bottom of the tank rises one meter in the air.

The pipe ends with a valve. And from the valve (which is obviously malfunctioning) there come three powerful, thin streams of gasoline.

The workers exchange worried glances, and one of them goes over to the faulty valve. He examines it, and pulls it a little.

Suddenly—whoosh—the faulty valve gives way, and gasoline starts gushing out in a thick stream . . .

Without thinking long, the worker leans against the stream with his whole body and stops it by sitting on it . . .

Only a few thin little streams now come out from under the worker. He calls out to his comrade:

"GO AND FETCH ANOTHER VALVE!"

The second worker runs as fast as he can.

A glass gauge shows that the level of the gasoline is slowly moving down.

From underneath the seated worker, thin streams of gasoline are spurting upward and to the sides with ever-increasing force.

The second worker runs into some kind of a warehouse space.

He rushes about from right to left, sees a valve and grabs it, and rushes to the exit.

But a warehouseman takes back the valve. The worker starts shouting about an emergency, and almost crying, he begs:

"BUT LOOK, WE COME FROM THE SAME FACTORY!"

The warehouseman looks at him with compassion, and shrugs his shoulders:

"BASIC ACCOUNTING PROCEDURES!"

The worker understands that there is no arguing with the warehouseman, and tears away in search of the person in charge . . .

The glass gauge shows that the gasoline level in the tank is dropping, lower and lower.

Around the worker who is blocking the big gushing stream, thin streams spurt upward and to the sides.

"WAIT A MINUTE!"

shouts the other worker as he runs past.

Now he comes back to the site of the accident in the company of the specialist who gave the Fool a lesson in the principles of accounting.

In dismay at what has occurred, the specialist shouts:

"WAIT A MINUTE! . . ."

and rushes off together with the worker.

. . . A sign on an office door:

DIRECTOR OF THE EQUIPMENT DIVISION
IVAN IVAN., Fool

Interrupting each other in their hurry, the specialist and the worker tell the Fool about the accident. But the Fool shakes his head:

"BASIC ACCOUNTING PRINCIPLES!"

The worker and the specialist grab him by the hands and lead him to the scene of the accident.

Now big streams of combustible fluid are gushing from underneath the worker.

When the Fool is brought here, he understands everything:

"QUICK!"

he shouts, and drags off the specialist.

He does not take him to fetch a valve, but rather into the office to sign a contract:

"ACCOUNTING RULES! LET'S DRAW UP A CONTRACT! QUICK!"

He summons the typist.

Gives an order to the secretary . . .

. . . Meanwhile streams of gasoline are spurting out from underneath the worker, who wants to stop them! . . .

And just like the first time: the typist hands the contract to the secretary.

The secretary—to the office administrator.

The office administrator—to the courier.

The courier—to the Fool.

The Fool—to the accountant.

The accountant—to the registrar.

The registrar—to the specialist.

And the specialist says to the Fool, with a devilish smile:

"YOU SON OF A BITCH! DAMNED BUNGLER!"

Everyone rushes out of the office to the scene of the accident . . .

Streams of gasoline are spurting out from underneath the worker . . .

Three men come running with the valve. They are running as fast as they can.

They run up to the tank.

The worker who has been holding the valve shut strokes his butt as if it had been kicked, and looks with an air of distress at the breach in the pipe.

Panting from his quick run, the Fool says:

"OH! WHAT A PITY!"

At this point, the Fool's driver opens up a newspaper in the usual way, cranks the car's start-up handle, and drives off . . .

In the newspaper there is the usual:

DEAR COMRADE KOLIA MUDRETSOV–
SMEKALKIN HAS HAD A PEACEFUL DEATH.

And as always, next to this:

THE TSKK SUMMONS THE FOOL,
IV. IV., TO ROOM 133.

But this time the driver does not wait for the drubbing in Room 133. He takes off Ivan Ivanovich's shirt.

He takes the familiar bucket filled with water out of the car . . .

The Fool huddles up in expectation of a cold shower.

But the driver unexpectedly pours the water into the ditch, sits behind the wheel, and drives away.

The Fool does not at first understand that this is a catastrophe. Fear shakes his dentures loose. He takes one step, then another, shouts and waves his hands, and runs after the Ford.

(1931)

[*Note added in 1988*]

P.S. And it is fortunate he did not catch up with it.

After the Ford a black Volga drove up.

A huge dossier was handed over to the chauffeur.

A formidably important client of Rm No. 133 got caught in the car door.

He sent the car off, but could not overcome his fear.

And . . . he started running after the Volga.

And it's a good thing he didn't catch up with it!

9 Tit[1]

(1932)

Part 1

1. Tit sleeping, a beetle on his nose.
2. Tit sleeping.

TIT! TIME TO DO SOME THRESHING!

3. Tit's bare stomach suddenly swells up like a balloon.
4. Tit replies:

I'VE GOT THE STOMACHACHE!

5. Tit sleeping . . .

TIT! . . . TIME TO EAT KASHA!

6[–7]. Straightaway Tit starts looking for his big spoon.
He searches . . .
He searches some more . . .
All the while, the spoon is under his foot—

WHERE IS MY BIG SPOON?

8. He finds the spoon. He spits on it, and wipes it on his trousers.
FADE-OUT.
9. Morning.
10. A bell.
11. Neighbors hurrying to work.
12. They are going to the threshing machines.

TIT IS IN NO HURRY TO GET TO WORK

13. Tit ambles along behind all the others.

As he walks, he holds up his pants,

Then he stretches . . .

14. He gets a splinter in his foot. He limps.

He sits down.

15. He works on pulling out the splinter.

16. When he stands up, the big spoon falls onto the road and remains there, unnoticed.

17. At the threshing machine, Tit's absence is noticed.

18. Tit is still on his way. His trousers are falling down. Suddenly noticing that he hasn't got his big spoon, he hurries back to look for it.

19. The work brigade is getting agitated. They dispatch a special horse and rider to look for him.

20. Tit has found his spoon. He rejoices.

The horseback rider rides up at a gallop, and tosses him some leather straps from the harness.

21. Tit grabs hold of them, and lets the horse pull him.

22. But the horse barely moves, since—

23. Tit is stuck; he keeps pulling his pants up.

24. The fellow cracks his whip, and the horse starts galloping, dragging Tit along behind him.

25. The strange, harnessed contraption charges across a field. Tit is barely keeping up with the horse . . .

26. And since the slippers on his feet are huge, they flip-flop on the ground—

27. . . . until one of them falls off . . .

28. The horse gallops across a dusty field, dragging along the half-unshod Tit at a gallop.

And finding that one of his slippers is missing, Tit unfastens himself and flops down . . .

29. He goes back on foot to find the lost slipper.

30. The rider, who is unaware that Tit is now missing, suddenly looks round, then makes a sharp turn back . . .

FADE-OUT.

WHAT MAKES TIT TIT
IS HIS KNACK OF HOLDING THINGS UP

31. The thresher in operation on the threshing floor.

32. The thresher in operation.

33. The thresher in operation.

34. Tit is in charge of weighing. He fills four sacks with grain from the thresher.

35. But Tit's pants are falling down, because there are no buttons on them.

36. Since he is holding onto his pants, Tit is working with just one hand. He handles the sacks clumsily.

37. The thresher is devouring the stalks, as if in a hurry.

38. The rushing thresher throwing out clouds of chaff . . .

39. Tit's pants fall right down . . .

40. And while he turns away and tries to hold his pants together with a straw, busying himself with his unruly clothes,

41. The sacks are filled to overflowing with grain,

42. And grain spills over the top of the sacks onto the ground . . .

43. And around the thresher it is as if there had been a decision to drown Tit in grain

44. And Tit, who is busy with his trousers, cannot see that the thresher has piled up a huge heap of grain

[45. missing]

46. And turning round, Tit is suddenly frightened. He throws himself at the machine, but a grim brigade leader flings him aside and starts handling the grain himself.

[47. missing]

48. Struggling to cope with his unruly pants, Tit sits down on the straw. Here he sees a very necessary rope end. He feels in the straw for the other end. He ties the rope around him, not suspecting that the rope will attach him to a harrow fastened to a chain that drags the straw high up onto the top of a stack.

49. The harrow drags the next pile of straw to the top of the stack.

50. It drags Tit there too.

51. Seeing that he has been carried up into the heavens, Tit is alarmed and gives such a terrible shriek that people stop the thresher.

52. Tit rolls down to the ground, head over heels.

53. People rush to help him—

54. They lift him up. Carry him off to one side.

[55–60. missing]

61. They release Tit from the rope.

62. They bandage Tit's head.

They bandage it so well that all that can be seen is one of his eyes.

63. Tit is laid on a stretcher and carried away.

64. Frightened people carrying the bandaged Tit.

They carry him past the thresher.

65. They carry him to a large pile of straw.

66. And since it is lunchtime, the people sit down here and there in order to eat.

67. The ne'er-do-well with the injury has remained behind the stack of straw, just where—

68. the cook has left some meat in a large bowl, ready for the second course.

[69–70. missing]

71. The bowl with the meat is close at hand. An old mangy dog is sitting next to Tit.

72. With an effort Tit turns his head toward the people eating lunch.

73. The people are eating, without paying attention to Tit.

74. Next Tit moves the bowl with the meat a little closer,

75. He pulls out his big spoon and—

76. deftly parts the bandages covering his mouth and—

77. Tit starts to demolish the meat. He eats. Hurriedly. He forces himself. He shoves pieces of meat into his mouth with his fingers . . .

TIT'S APPETITE WAS A HEFTY ONE

78. The old dog can't resist: ever so politely and apprehensively, licking his chops, the hungry dog begs Tit to spare him at least one little bone . . .

79. But Tit is a furious eater! He throws a stick at the mangy cur with all his might, and continues to gorge himself like a wild animal.

80. Meanwhile, the kolkhoz farmers have finished their borscht

81. And when the cook comes to fetch the second course—

82. . . . Tit is stretched out as if nothing had happened

83. . . . and in the bowl only miserable scraps are left

84. And the dog off to one side is hungrily licking his chops.

85. The cook roars at the top of her voice

86. And the kolkhoz workers come running

87. And since the guilt of the mangy cur is evident to everyone, they all attack it with sticks and stones, frightening it out of its mind.

88. Two charitable men lift up the stretcher with Tit and carry him to the doctor.

89. The kolkhoz farmers are furiously chasing the guiltless dog . . .

90. . . . and the unfortunate, well-stuffed Tit, looking like a dead man, is being lifelessly tossed about on the hard stretcher.

91. And thus he arrives at the surgery, where the doctor starts removing his bandages.

92. He removes forty bandages from the head of the would-be casualty

93. . . . and all he finds on Tit's forehead is a light scratch . . .

OH, YOU SCOUNDREL, TIT!

94. —roar his bearers

95. But Tit with the look of a dying man shakes his head for them and feebly moans—

THE MAIN INJURY IS IN MY STOMACH

96. And when the doctor lays bare Tit's stomach, everyone sees that Tit's belly is all swollen up like that of a dead horse, and, in plain view, big drops of sweat are emerging on this enormous, taut globe . . .

97. Meanwhile the kolkhoz farmers have caught the mangy cur

98. . . . and to teach the scoundrel to stop stealing they have prepared a solid rope for him,

99. While in the surgery the doctor

100. Has placed medicinal cups on Tit's stomach.

Part 2

ONE DAY TIT WAS SENT OFF TO SELL GEESE

101. Tit is walking down a road. He is carrying six geese. Long goose necks are sticking out all over the place—behind his back, from a knapsack, under his arms.

102. Tit is going to the kolkhoz market.

103. And the geese are sticking their long heads out through the holes in the sacks; they cackle, stir, and get agitated in their confined conditions . . .

104. Tit is tired because of his heavy burden.

He is tired, and so he sits down.

105. He releases the birds to peck in the stubble.

106. As for himself, he lies down.

107. The geese are feeding in a flock.

108. Tit is sound asleep. The sun has exhausted him, and he snores with abandonment.

109. The geese go up to the shore of the lake (indeed a goose likes water),

110. And the geese swim away from the shore.

111. Tit opens his eyes.

He looks—it's as if the geese had never existed . . .

112. Tit starts by looking for the geese inside the sacks:

113. He turns them inside out,

He pats them over.

He shakes them out . . .

114. But . . . there are no geese in the sacks! Even Tit understands this

115. And Tit goes around the field looking for the geese . . .

116. But the geese are in the lake. The geese are swimming.

117. Running up to the lake, Tit casts off his clothes, and swims after the geese

[118–19, repetition of 117, partly crossed out]

120. A goose is a nervous and cunning bird.

The geese adroitly maneuver—like battleships . . .

121. Tit dives under, and swims . . . Then dives again . . .

122. While Tit is diving in the lake—

[123. missing]

124. a tramp makes off with his clothes . . .

125. At last Tit drives the birds onto shore

126. And discovers that he has been left naked!

127. He bewails his situation . . . and bewails it some more . . .

128. Then he stuffs the geese into the remaining sacks,

129. And naked as he was born, he continues walking to the kolkhoz market.

130. Tit is crossing a field.

131. Toward him comes a girl sitting on top of a load of hay in a cart . . .

132. Tit's appearance is definitely strange and unusual:

He is naked, barely covered by sacks, from which stick out the coiling necks of geese . . .

133. Not surprisingly, the girl exclaims, "Oh, my!" The horses are frightened, and gallop about the field.

134. The naked Tit throws down the sacks with the geese and runs across the field into a patch of sunflowers.

135. The horses, frightened out of their wits, are galloping over hummocks, and the hay cart is jumping over ruts,

136. The cart jumps over a ditch, and a wheel flies off. The cart is overturned, and the girl rolls head over heels onto the road

137. And now Tit emerges from the patch of sunflowers.

138. But he is no longer naked.

138a. He is dressed in an amazing fashion, as if he were a ballerina: two sunflowers decorate his breast

And a garland of small flowers girds his loins.

138b. And in this fashion he chases after the one remaining goose . . .

FADE-OUT.

139. A general meeting of the happy collective is under way.

The order of the day is the harvest.

AT THE MEETING TIT IS SILENT AS A DEADMAN

140. Tit has stuffed his mouth with bread. He chews it out of gluttony rather than hunger. He bites off a piece, and places the crust next to him.

141. Some mischievous boys put a shell rock in place of the crust.

142. Tit puts it in his mouth—he can't chew off a piece.

143. Tit moves the rock aside. The boys immediately substitute half a brick for the rock.

144. An impassioned youth is addressing the meeting.

145. Tit listens to his words, He has not noticed the substitution and puts the brick in his mouth . . . No! There's no way he can bite into it!

[145.] The orator—

THE QUESTION NOW IS HOW TO DIVIDE THE HARVEST:
ACCORDING TO THE NUMBER OF EATERS
OR THE NUMBER OF DAYS WORKED?

146. Here it is as if some people were speaking for Tit:

THE EATERS! EATERS! EATERS!

147. Passions are inflamed:

THE DAYS WORKED!

148. Tit rushes out into the street in order to be on time.

149. He is running, faster and faster,

150. He is running fast as an airplane . . .

GOD HAS BLESSED TIT

WITH QUITE A LITTLE FAMILY

151. A cloud of dust rises up behind Tit.
152. In the dust Tit's family is galloping,
153. Twenty-seven mouths in a hurry not to be late.
154. Each one has an empty sack ready

THE EATERS! . . .

155. They are running, yelling, rushing past one another.

Two three-year-olds are left behind.

156. With difficulty they are hauling an enormous empty sack in the dust:

157. Too late!

158. At the barn eighteen sacks of wheat from the collective harvest have been poured for Ivan Ivanovich Ivanov.

IVAN HAS A TOTAL OF 324 WORKED DAYS

159. Ivan hauls away one sack after another . . .

TIT HAS A TOTAL OF 38 WORKED DAYS

160. Tit's numerous children sadly fold away the unnecessary sacks.

In a fit of temper Tit throws down his big spoon.

161. One of Tit's smallest descendants returns it to his father . . .

162. Tit angrily stamps on his Big Spoon with his foot.

Splinters fly from it . . .

AFTERWORD TO THE COMEDY *TIT* [undated]

The Kino-Train developed harsh, merciless film genres. We remained faithful to our goal of SATIRE AS AN ASSAILANT'S WEAPON! Our faithfulness to it was dictated to us by the Heroic, extraordinarily difficult times.

When I look back to the time of the First Five-Year Plan,[2] I feel I can rightly assert that first *Tit* and later *Khmyr* [i.e., *Happiness*] acted from the screen with wonderful effect on the vanguard of the advancing armies of the young Socialist society.

FOREWORD TO THE COMEDY *TIT* [undated]

In their first years, the newness of the kolkhozes resulted in a significant number of naive mistakes. People worked en masse. In the fields and on the threshing floors many unnecessary and idle people shuffled about.

At first people could not decide how to divide the harvest—in proportion to the number of "eaters" or "workdays." An idler with a large family could receive more than an honest worker. An idler was the first to run with his sacks to get his share and often received more than the others. This did not last for long. A material incentive was soon found. But for a long time idlers continued to trip up the enthusiastic believers in collective work, who had felt the incalculable superiority of the new life. These were our reasons for devoting two weeks to the making of the comic film short *Tit*.

10 *Look What Love Did!*

(1932)

1. Maslatsov[1] is struggling to push a wagon loaded with ore. The ore is heavy as iron. Volodia is barely moving the wagon.

VOLODIA WAS WORKING AS A WAGON PUSHER

2. Suddenly the wagon comes to a standstill: it goes off the rails and tips over.

3. As if he is used to it, Volodia pulls out a book from inside his shirt, and settles down for a long, quiet read.

4. But then a little white dog, Belka, runs up to him.

5. The dog raises her front legs. She is bringing a message.

6. Volodia feels behind her collar and finds the message:

NOT COMING. NO TIME.
LOOK FOR NOTE UNDER OUR ROCK.

7. Casting all other thoughts aside, Volodia hurries to the special rock.

8. He runs to the rock.

9. But lying on the rock, there is a big, nasty dog.

10. Volodia goes to one side, then the other—

11. The dog bares its teeth.

12. Volodia tries this and that—

13. . . . he whistles and dances—

14. The dog barks, and threatens to attack the lad.

15. Volodia looks for a way of distracting the dog: he tries showing him a trick, then kneels down.

16. The dog is fed up with him, and stands up and barks threateningly.

17. Volodia goes away from the rock with nothing.

18. He is in despair,

19. He has a sudden realization: Belka can help him.

20. Volodia takes her under his arm and goes with her to the rock.

21. But the nasty dog bares its teeth and barks from afar.

22. Volodia, however, has thought up something else.

23. He wants to dress up Belka with a ribbon . . .

24. Where to get one? Volodia rips his shirt

25. and gets a strip of fabric from it. He makes a bow for Belochka. He arranges it attractively on her little neck, and bravely advances toward the rock.

26. The huge, nasty dog has closed his eyes and is slumbering.

27. Suddenly he opens his eyes. He raises his head in surprise at seeing—

28. . . . an irresistible, flirtatious dog with a bow on her neck standing on her rear legs in front of the rock.

29. Look what happens to the villain:

30. He friendlily wags his tail.

31. Then he stands on his feet.

32. In response Belka also wags her tale.

33. Belka bursts away and starts playing.

34. The dog runs after her.

35. It's a truly human situation: they forget about everything on earth and run off.

36. Volodia gives them a friendly wave of the hand.

37. He moves the rock and—

38. . . . gets the note. He reads it.

I'LL BE WAITING FOR YOU AT THE SCHOOL.
THEY WANT TO EXPEL YOU
FOR NONATTENDANCE. COME!

39. Volodia runs. He trips and falls. He runs.

40. The SCHOOL ENTRANCE. A sign—

COURSES IN MECHANICS
FOR SCRAPER-LOADERS

41. The students arrive. Last of all comes our lass. She looks around anxiously. She is the author of the note.

42. WILL Volodia appear? . . . No, he hasn't come. The caretaker gets the girl to hurry up. He closes the door behind her.

43. And now Volodia appears. The caretaker speaks with him through a window, saying:

YOU HAVE BEEN EXPELLED AS AN IDLER!

44. Volodia begs the caretaker to open the door. The caretaker refuses.
45. The lesson is in progress.
46. Motor parts are lying on a table.
47. Drawings are pinned up on the wall.
48. The students listen to the instructor.
49. Volodia sticks his head through an open window.
50. All it takes is for the instructor to turn his back for an instant—
51. and quick as lightning Volodia dives through the window.
52. He seats himself next to his girlfriend.
53. The lesson continues.
54. Volodia writes a note to her:

1 + 1 = 2?

55. The girl is angry and answers with another note:

2 − 1 = 0!

56. Volodia writes:

AM I 0?

57. The lass confirms this in a note:

YOU ARE A ZERO!
A ZERO AND A BLOCKHEAD!

58. Volodia is upset:

I'LL DO ANYTHING YOU WANT!
BUT PLEASE FORGIVE ME!

59. The lass has decided to punish the lad:

YOU MUST EAT THESE NOTES!
AND NOT MISS ANY CLASSES!

60. Volodia has stuffed all the pieces of paper in his mouth. He is chewing them with difficulty.

61. And just now he notices the instructor looking at him with surprise.

62. Volodia is about to choke.

63. The instructor beckons him with a finger.

64. Volodia goes up. His mouth is stuffed with paper.

65. The whole group of friends laugh so hard that they are almost crying.

AND VOLODIA DID AFTER ALL BECOME A SCRAPER-LOADER OPERATOR

66. Volodia IS skillfully operating a scraper-loader.

67. On a mound nearby stands the whole group of young scraper-loader operators.

68. Flowers are presented to the instructor.

69. A little farther off, in the shade under a lilac bush in blossom, lies the huge dog. The little dog Belka with a bow on her neck is curled up between his paws.

(Krivoi Rog Sortie)

11 A Crazy Locomotive

(Comic event, 1932)

The railway depots were thoroughly run down after two wars[1] and the attendant destruction. The maintenance of locomotives was poorly organized.

A. Medvedkin

1. Everything begins with a kiss

3 LOCOMOTIVES! **[intertitle]**

2. Another kiss

3 LOCOMOTIVES!

3. And another excited kiss

HURRAH! 3 MORE REPAIRED LOCOMOTIVES IN EXCESS OF THE MAINTENANCE PLAN!

4. A locomotive is shining like a birthday boy. Ten workmen equipped with rags are putting a shine on its tired body.

5. A puff of black smoke bursts from its stack. From under its wheels comes steam.

6. Its wheels spin. It's as if the birthday locomotive were dancing.

7. It is next to a triumphal platform, made of hastily knocked-together planks.

8. Workers in front of the tribunal are applauding.

9. On the tribunal the overseer begins a speech.

10. The birthday locomotive performs a little dance.

11. The supervisor distributes presents to the shock-workers.

12. A samovar to one.

13. A samovar to another.

14. And a samovar to the train driver Maslatsov[2].

15. The driver is led in triumph to the locomotive. He is holding his samovar on his head.

16. He clambers onto the steps,

17. Handshakes,

18. Wishes for a safe journey.

19. The samovar is put into his hands.

20. The locomotive slowly moves off.

21. Hurrah! Caps are tossed in the air.

22. On the tribunal the supervisor is still praising the shock-workers.

23. The locomotive is already far away.

24. People still wave their hands and handkerchiefs at it.

25. The locomotive is far away. And suddenly, like a young, mischievous colt, it stops, it is enveloped in steam, and it moves backward . . .

26. Panic on the tribunal. All the shock-workers quietly disappear.

27. Except for the portly Overseer, who gets stuck as he is climbing down from the tribunal.

28. Without reaching the ground, his feet remain suspended in the air.

29. The locomotive is away in the steppe. Suddenly it jolts to a stop and is shrouded in steam. The engineer Maslatsov hastens down from the locomotive with an oil can.

30. He makes haste to lubricate the moving parts.

31. At the tribunal the Overseer has again gathered the workmen.

SLIPSHOD WORKMEN!

the Overseer says reproachfully.

32. The men guiltily raise their hands

WE DISPATCHED A MALFUNCTIONING
LOCOMOTIVE ON A TRIP!

33. He is taking back the samovars from the workmen:

GIVE BACK THE SAMOVAR!

34. He takes a samovar from a second workman—

YOU TOO GIVE IT BACK!

35. Angrily he demands of a third one—

YOU, TOO!

36. The locomotive is standing in the steppe as if it were dead.

37. Maslatsov unscrews the lid of the oil can: the can is empty.

38. He does not see the locomotive quietly moving away.

39. The locomotive is accelerating.

40. The locomotive has gone off.

41. Maslatsov runs after it.

42. The locomotive is going faster and faster. It goes round a bend and disappears.

43. Maslatsov is now far behind and hurries to the bend . . .

44. On the tribunal the Overseer has again assembled the workmen. He is instructing them:

IT'S NOT ENOUGH TO OVERFULFILL THE PLAN
YOU'VE GOT TO OVERFULFILL IT WELL

45. And the final shot. The locomotive is slowly creeping along the tracks.

46. The engineer is sitting by a window. He blows on some tea in a dish and drinks it.

47. And he waves a whip like a coachman:

48. Because the locomotive is being pulled to the depot for repairs by a team of six oxen.

49. Maslatsov has harnessed them in the same way as for a cart and set them walking between the tracks to the depot. There has to be a way of getting there! . . .

12 "The Unholy Force"[1]

(Satiric comedy, 1966)

[Preface]

Our quarrel with religion here usually focuses on minor matters and not on basic philosophical principles of Christianity such as the doctrines of the immortal soul and eternal bliss. And yet in the writings of the church fathers there is nothing more naive—and therefore vulnerable—than the ideas about Paradise and Hell. Despite their obvious absurdity, these "doctrines" keep the minds of millions of peoples in thrall, while old, moldering icons migrate freely into new, brightly lit homes. I hardly need mention villages—when the door of an izba is opened to let in the bright light of the present, it will still happen that a weary, oft-defeated god in one of the front corners shoots its fire at it . . . Let us give this god an opportunity to speak about the basic dogmas of Christianity! Let the ancient icons come to life and the Kingdom of Heaven become a reality with all of its sanctimoniousness![2]

And let Man, for whom WORK is the chief meaning and greatest joy of his life, take the measure of the dreary idleness of the Kingdom of Heaven and the Fiery Furnace, in which the righteous and the sinners alike are condemned to millions of years of doing nothing!

The author did not fabricate the theme of this satire: it is based on an old tale from Onega about the soldier Kuroptev.

> Come unto me, all ye who labor and are heavy laden, and I will give you rest!
>
> Christ

A soldier, released from service, is on the open road.

Coming to an ancient chapel at a crossroads, he stops. He kneels before an icon old as Russia itself, and prays to the Almighty: "Lord! I have served my tsar and country faithfully and honestly for twenty-five years. For the glory of Mother RAHSSIA I've endured Turks beating me and wounding me. I'm on the open road, going I know not where! I have no wife, no mother! No land, no birthright! No farm buildings, nothing to call my own! Defend me, save me, have mercy on me!"

"You are a righteous man, Kuroptev!" says the Almighty from the icon.

(Our very own Russian God-the-Father, snub-nosed and kind, in peasant homespun and wearing bast shoes; a good, wise, and simple god, just and all-merciful)

"You are a righteous man, Kuroptev!"

"And who are you?" cries the soldier.

"I am your Lord God!"

"You don't say so?!"

"God's truth! And your prayer has been heard today. Do you want to go to Heaven?"

Kuroptev is confounded.

"But is that the regular track for men from the ranks?" he asks in disbelief.

"Why not?" The Almighty shrugs his shoulders.

Kuroptev is confounded.

"Lord, but I stink of tobacco and drink!" the soldier honestly warns him. "And Lord, I'm the biggest curser the regiment has ever seen. And when it comes to women and sex, God, I've sinned—I can hardly deny it—more than most."

"Nonsense!" says the kind God. "Nobody on earth is holier than a soldier. A soldier is the first holy martyr! Anyway I don't know what to do with you. Here on the strength of our acquaintance is a note that will admit you directly into the Kingdom of Heaven without standing in line!"

With these words the Almighty puts on a pair of round, grandfather specs, pushes aside his halo, which is in his way, and sucking on a pencil, laboriously writes something down in a crooked scrawl on a piece of paper (our God is not highly lettered) . . .

Stone walls defend the gardens of Paradise from the earthly vale. The walls are studded with sharp pieces of glass and rusty nails of forged iron, for the laceration of sinners: for indeed these shameless, sly people will strive, at any cost, to rip off any little parcel of heavenly bliss! And so, as in a good Russian prison, guard towers rise at the corners of the fortress walls, with vigilant archangels in them.

The soldier stops before the iron gates of Paradise and hearkens . . . All is in order! The bosom of Abraham, the Kingdom of Heaven! . . . From somewhere nearby, on the other side of the walls, a monotonous hosanna pours forth like viscous tar. The soldier removes his cap, frenziedly crosses himself, reaches for his order paper, and knocks at the gates.

The peephole opens with a clatter and Saint Peter, Christ's keeper of the keys, sticks out his nose.

"What do you want, soldier?"

"Holy Apostle Peter! Private Kuroptev, of the Prince Wirtemberg 118th Kaksholm Regiment, is here for a term of heavenly bliss!"

"Am I supposed to admit you?" yawns the sleepy apostle.

"Yes, indeed! Here is a note from the Almighty: *To be registered for all forms of heavenly pleasure!*"

The heavy gates open with a screech. The gloomy apostle lets the soldier into the Kingdom of Heaven, slides back the hundred-pound bolt and, with a rasp, fastens shut the solid prison lock.

In Paradise there are strange, paradisian apple trees bearing golden fruit.

Undreamt-of flowers bloom in Paradise.

Everything is as on our grandfathers' icons—including the birds of Paradise, Sirin and Alkonost, with women's faces.

The saints and holy fathers are singing. Their black faces are authentic, from ancient Russian icon-cases.

They are standing in thick, thousand-faced throngs on the paradisian meadows, on Mount Sinai, on Mount Golgotha, along the Jordan, under the walls of Jerusalem, and in the celestial pavilions of Zion.

They form a vast multitude. And the entire innumerable assembly is chanting, "Hosanna."

Long, thin, bearded, crushingly dreary, they stand stretching forth their hands and drawling out a monotonous "A-a-a-a-a-a-h!" without fervor. It is as if a humming of mosquitoes was hanging over Paradise.

The soldier has seen changes, but as for this one here—why, holy mother!

He looks, a sinful stranger, at the wonders of Paradise—golden apple trees; fleet-winged archangels; flying archistrategoi with generals' medals; dry, jaundiced, holy women-martyrs.

What is a soldier to do when he has been ordered by God himself to experience eternal bliss? Why, he has to be blissful!

Kuroptev sorts out his ammunition and then takes a place among the groaning throng of saints. Raising his arms, he tries to look despondent and meekly drawls out: “A-a-a-a-ah!”

The soldier’s voice is not celestial; it is hoarse and not at all pious! The others shush him and hiss and wave at him, and a jaundiced old woman, a holy martyr, pokes him with her crutch.

The soldier has to beat a retreat.

He plucks a golden apple of Paradise, frenziedly crosses himself, wipes it on his sleeve—gives God thanks—and tries to take a bite. . . .

Something is wrong! The apple is pure gold.

Kuroptev has broken his teeth on it. He carefully hangs it back up in the tree.

The flowers blooming in the paradisial meadows are ones that a happy man could only dream of.

The soldier takes off his backpack and shoes, neatly hangs up his foot wrappings to dry on a celestial cloud, lies down in the flowers, and looks around . . .

In the paradisial pavilions nearby, Saint Mary of Egypt is enjoying the feeling of bliss. She is swarthy and slim like the wife of his worship, the staff commander Zhukov. With surprise she looks the soldier Kuroptev up and down.

Giving her a wink, the sinful soldier invites her to lie with him.

She blushes, sticks her tongue out at the tempter, turns her back to him, and takes a few steps, swaying her curvaceous body so temptingly that the sinner almost chokes. Keeping his eyes on this alluring queen, he reaches for his pouch, takes out his fat-bowled pipe, packs it with tobacco, strikes a spark with his flint, and draws on the pipe with pleasure.

The smoke of the Morshansk shag mixes with the divine incense, throwing the whole throng of saints into a state of confusion.

All at once the paradisial singing breaks off, and the saints turn on Kuroptev.

They surround the soldier, stir up an angry commotion, grab his pipe, and force him to retreat. He beats an inglorious escape from the field of battle, perhaps for the first time ever.

The saints are again standing in thousand-faced throngs, as on the icons, and wailing, on and on and on.

“Well, if that isn’t our village priest Evlampi!” exclaims the soldier, looking at an old, dry, red-haired man. “Is that you, Father Evlampi?”

"Myself!" responds Evlampi.

"Are you blissful?"

"Oh, yes, I am blissful," sighs the dispirited, dried-up priest, who is sick with boredom. "I'm all prayed out—what else is there to do? All my innards are dried up. I had brains and a heart, but now they're all dried up and withered like a kippered carp's."

"Is it because of the meager diet or worry?" asks the soldier.

"The diet's not too bad. And how can the righteous have worries?" asks the priest, trying to make sense of his infirmities. "But it is tedious!"

"Like a liturgical service?" the soldier suggests.

"A liturgical service is good because it is soon over!" the priest admonishes him. "Whereas here the years drag on, and you have to go on droning, and not see the world! . . ."

"A-a-a-a-ah!" he despondently whines, raising his arms up high, and then he looks round like a thief and in a low voice confides his terrible secret to the soldier: "The church fathers did not really explain what eternal bliss is . . . Basically it is . . . an everlasting church service! Had I known this, Kuroptev," he says tearfully, "I surely would not have brought our Korezhino peasants to Paradise."

"Did you really bring them?" cries the soldier.

"Well—I did, unworthy priest that I am!" sobs Evlampi.

Upon catching the suspicious gaze of the archangels on patrol, the priest hastily and fearfully whines, "A-a-a-a-ah!" . . . Once the danger is past, he says to the soldier, "I was strict with them. And they believed. Then once they had had a taste of bliss, they broke four of my ribs and, you can see, pulled out my beard! Oh, the lectures the accursed ones gave me! If I were to tell all! . . . A-a-a-a-ah!"

The Korezhino peasants are powerful, hairy, long-limbed men with homespun pants, and thin bast shoes when they are not barefoot.

In the Kingdom of Heaven they stick together in a bunch, looking angry and suspicious. Sinful and filled with longing for the earthly vale, they gather beneath the prison wall in a secluded part of the heavenly pavilions, away from the flocks of the righteous and the archangels and the stupefying piety.

Here they suffered together as one people, all, the ragamuffin children, the nasty old women, the lusty young women. Somehow the peasant women had contrived to bring a cow with them (as in the Russian saying "Let a peasant woman into Paradise, and she will bring a cow!").

The peasants exclaim: "This can't be our Kuroptev! Is that you, the soldier Kuroptev?"

"Indeed it is," the soldier raises his cap to them. "I am here to experience eternal bliss according to instructions from on high. What is it you are digging here?"

The peasants shush him with their hands. "Quiet. The priest is nearby! There will be big trouble if he hears!"

"Why are you digging a hole?" the soldier persists.

"It is a tunnel!" the peasants confess, as they look around fearfully. "We are digging under the wall of Paradise to freedom!" . . .

"Are things bad for you here?"

"Stop talking soldier! . . . Or we will kill you! . . . There's no comfort here!"

"To escape from Paradise—that is our hope!"

"Phew! . . . The priest! . . . Evlampi is coming! . . . Look blissful!"

With a hissing, angry whisper, they start moving and press together in a thick line in order to hide the tunnel underneath the wall of Paradise from the priest . . .

They raise their arms in a depiction of bliss, just like the godlies, and chant the jarring, irritating A-a-a-a-ah! . . .

Hairy, sinful, nasty, they pour all the bitterness of the peasants' unhappy lot into their dissonant hosanna.

In tears the priest Evlampi casts himself down on his knees before them: "Peasants, forgive me! For God's sake forgive me! I didn't lead you to the right place! I didn't look for truth in the right place!" . . .

"Forgiveness comes from God, Father! You weren't evil but unthinking!"

"How can we blame a fool?! . . . God will give you forgiveness!" mutter the peasants, in whose pure hearts there was as much goodness and readiness to forgive as sorrow and tears.

They carefully raise the dried-up old man from the flower-covered ground of Paradise:

"Don't let this destroy you, Father! We loved you and love you even now. It doesn't mean anything if we settled scores on your ribs and pulled out your beard!"

"It means nothing," the peasants amicably say. "Things are bad for us in the Kingdom of Heaven, but it's no bed of roses for you either! . . . We are bound by the same rope!"

"But the hour of deliverance is at hand: we will save ourselves and deliver you, priest, from the bosom of Abraham. Look—here is a tunnel leading to freedom."

The priest's fright is beyond description. "Sacrilege!" he yells. "Accursed people! Anathema! In the name of the living God, I conjure you to listen to me!" . . .

"Hurry up, Father!" the peasants roar and threaten. "Hurry up! We haven't a moment to lose! There are archangels all about! Quickly, Father!"

"Orthodox people!" Evlampi sobs in deep sorrow. "Mankind is a vast multitude before the throne of the Almighty, having many faces, speaking many tongues. But never in the ages of ages have mad men run away from the bosom of Abraham and escaped from the Kingdom of Heaven as if 'twas a prison. Are you an unholy force?"

"Stop it, priest! We are Russians! From Korezhino!" the peasants roar. "No one tells us where to go."

"Farewell, priest! You'd better keep quiet, or . . . Come on, Korezhino men! God bless us! God be with us!"

They are rushing into the tunnel when someone calls out in warning: "Careful! That witch, Saint Tattletale, again!"

"Careful!

The Korezhino villagers instantly stand like a thick throng of saints, raise up their arms and chaotically and hypocritically chant a dissonant hosanna. Wailing "A-a-a-a-h!" they completely hide the tunnel burrowing under the wall of Paradise. The poor priest cannot decide what to do: betray his already long-suffering flock or protect the rebels.

The soldier gives him an eloquent kick, and the priest, though he hesitates and looks back, joins the Korezhino villagers. But how much pain it costs him!

Saint Tattletale, an odious hag with a crutch and a lopsided halo, is a recognized holy martyr: more than two hundred years ago, in the province of Arkhangelsk, she endured torments on earth for being an insufferable meddler and gossip. "I see! I see it all! You are attempting to escape from Paradise. I'll go and tell the Lord! He'll show you how to escape from eternal bliss!"

Suddenly the soldier makes the sign of the cross for protection, easily parts the wall of nasty, hairy peasants, and pushes Saint Tattletale toward the hole they have excavated.

She begins to shriek, but he gives her a kick and easily shoves her into the hole.

"Come on, men of Korezhino, let's go. God be with us!"

The peasants rush into the tunnel groaning, cursing, and praying: "In the name of the Father and the Son! Damn, . . . your mother! Holy Virgin! Let's go! Come on! Leave your cow! . . . What the Devil! . . . Lord Jesus!" . . .

Like an explosion a bunch of them burst forth from the earth on the other side of the walls of Paradise.

"Glory be to God! Glory be to God! Glory!"

Rumpled but happy, they set Saint Tattletale on her feet and decide to keep tight hold of the tricky witch.

In Paradise only the priest remains by the breach. Father Evlampi's agitated soul is torn: whether to escape with the sinners to joyful freedom, or to stay in the exhausting prison of eternal bliss. To escape—he climbs into the breach. And to stay—he climbs back out of the hole and stretches out his arms and chants, "Hosanna." His torments are interrupted by two Korezhino peasants who have come back for him. They punch him and drag him off to the beckoning earthly vale.

"You'll be lost without us, you evil spirit, you long-haired water dog."

"Come on, bad as you are, you are our peasant priest, our own blood."

Both contempt for a traitor and warm pity for a perishing man are interwoven in a strange bundle of feelings. The Russian soul is incomprehensibly broad!

In agitation the righteous surround the throne of the Almighty.

The archangels, seraphim, cherubim, the lower ranks of angels, the martyrs, the just—all, are distressed:

"Lord! Look how your peasants have distinguished themselves!"

"They have escaped from eternal bliss! From the Kingdom of Heaven!"

"Through a tunnel under the wall of Paradise—out to freedom!"

"Lord, they are now free. Why are we less deserving?"

"It is an injury to the assembly of saints and to your own name."

God's anger is aroused. He raises his hand:

"Bring back the cloddish clowns! Fetch them! Restore them to the bosom of Abraham!"

The heavens are riven by thunder and lightning.

A storm strikes the world.

A shower of golden apples rattles down from the heavenly apple trees onto the flowers and the silken grasses.

A black cloud gathers over the escaping peasants. Something flashes in it and crashes down.

A strange whirlwind catches up the louts as if they were a pile of autumn leaves, sweeping them into the air.

Underwear, bark shoes, unkempt heads, the bewildered woman with the cow—all fly past.

The whirlwind from Heaven quickly tosses the Korezhino peasants back into Paradise, over the prison walls spiked with rusty nails and glass shards.

Only Saint Tattletale and Father Evlampi are left on the other side of the wall, forgotten in the hurly-burly, at liberty.

The saint is frightened to death. She shrieks so dreadfully that a shining cloud of angels appears, they lift her on their wings, and convey her to the place of eternal bliss, inside the fortress walls of the Kingdom of Heaven.

As for the red-haired priest, he joyfully makes the sign of the cross, seeing that he has been forgotten in the bedlam. Scarcely believing in his salvation, he looks back like a thief, takes one step, and then a second one, and then gathering up his paradisian tunic in his hands, tears away from the Kingdom of Heaven so fast that everything round him seems to swim before his eyes.

He runs like a convict who is suddenly and intoxicatingly free. His heart is bursting with joy, and his old legs are charged with inhuman strength . . .

When Father Evlampi hears the whistles of archangels far off in the distance, he starts to choke out of despair, presses his hands to his heart, and runs even faster.

The man is running from cold, boring immortality into the hot, sinful world, with all of its nasty torments, tears, pain, and sinful joys.

But the whistles keep coming closer . . .

The fleet-winged archangels appear . . .

Like a wolf tracked by dogs, the priest fights them off with his hands and feet; he bites; he howls and spits; he grasps a thorn bush by the roots, then he grasps some rocks, and then the rusty nails on the prison-camp walls of the Kingdom of Heaven.

Feathers fly from the gentle angels. A whole cloud of white feathers shrouds the battleground.

Radiant seraphim and cherubim are lying like lifeless corpses on the ground.

The feeble little priest is fighting to the death, defending his blessed freedom. This is his last chance! "Death rather than a liturgy without end!"

But the forces are too unequal! The priest is lifted up into the air and thrown over the wall of Paradise . . .

He is tossed onto a flowering meadow, and landing at the feet of the Korezhino rebels, he bursts into tears.

The merciful parishioners lift up their crying shepherd, shake the dust out of his clothes, and replace his halo, which has gotten crumpled in the fight.

In excruciating torment, Priest Evlampi stretches out his hands, and sobbing, chants a heartrending, tragic hosanna: "A-a-a-a-a-ah!"

Out of fellow feeling with their shepherd, and perhaps in protest, the peasants follow his example. They stretch out their arms and in all sorts of discordant voices give vent to furious scolding and threats, and no hallelujahs. The righteous recoil.

The assembly of holy inhabitants of Heaven is still in turmoil before the throne of the Almighty.

"Lord, Lord! Why are you punishing the righteous?"

"Why have you taken the rabble into the bosom of Abraham?"

"The Kingdom of Heaven will reek with the sour smell of sheep pelts and foot wrappings!"

"Lord! They are rabble. They are bound to stink even when they are right before your throne!"

"Master! Wreak havoc on them with burning sulfur as in Sodom and Gomorrah!"

The whole woodcut-picture world dreamt up by the church fathers seems to have suddenly realized that this awful proximity is unfitting and dangerous. The assembly of the righteous in their entirety fall down on their knees and implore the creator to deliver them from the unclean flock.

But God, our kind Russian God, is just. Without a second thought he takes the peasants under his protection. "You spiteful creatures!" he says in anger. "Is there is no limit to the evil that fills you. No sinner gets to be born but you oppress him 'til his dying breath, crush him, beat him with rods all in my name. You are bigots! Gendarmes! Always plotting to seize, break, and flog. You Pharisees, I will overwhelm you with thunder!"

"Don't be mistaken, Lord! There are thousands of us!" mutter the righteous.

"Quiet!" thunders the angry Almighty. "There are thousands of you, and of the peasants—thousands upon thousands! They are like the grains of sand on the bottom of the sea. And was it not I who said to them: "Come to me all ye who labor, and I will comfort you?" Now they did come to the Kingdom of Heaven. And here they felt uncomfortable with you, you spiteful creatures. They dug a tunnel under the wall of Paradise. They escaped. They escaped from eternal bliss. For the earthly vale! And yet they are peasants. God's children—that's who they are!"

The kind Russian God is thoroughly upset and wipes away a tear.

The righteous, now quiet, ask: "What shall we do, Lord? We are your slaves—we are ready to carry them in our arms."

"Go to these little ones," God orders. "Ask them what they need, and I will give it them!"

"What do you want, sinners?" the righteous ask the peasants. "What do you need? Say, and the All-Merciful will give it to you."

The somber, hairy rabble are silent. Nasty flashes of anger and rebellion smolder in their piercing eyes. They stand as a dense flock under the protection of the archangels. Frightened, the righteous keep their distance; the throngs of the godly swarm over the slopes of the valleys of Paradise.

Into the gold-leaf world like that of the Suzdal icon-daubsters,[3] there enters the alien herd of angry, disheveled peasants, reeking of tobacco, wine, and profanity.

The godlies are silent. The rabble, too, are silent.

But Saint Tattletale threatens the odious newcomers with her crutch and whispers to the righteous: "They have their priest, the red-haired man. He persuaded them to come to Paradise. It's him you should ask!"

"Sinners, who is it brought you to the Kingdom of Heaven?" sternly inquires a solemn saint. "Let that man stand before the court of the most holy!"

The peasants stir and rustle, and from deep inside their midst they thrust out the shaggy red-haired priest Evlampi.

"Was it you, priest, who brought the louts to the throne of the Almighty?"

"I did, unworthy priest that I am," sniffles the priest.

"Tell us what you promised them."

"Eternal bliss!" confesses the priest in a trembling voice.

"Did you tell the sinners what that was?"

"If only I knew, country fool that I am!" Evlampi opens his hands. "What this eternal bliss is I still don't understand. I brought the peasants here just in case!"

"How dared you do so?" shout the righteous.

Evlampi prostrates himself at the feet of the assembled saints: "Punish me, most reverend ones! I accept a martyr's crown. These peasants' unhappy lot is a bad one—worse even than your Paradise. They have been thrashed and starved; their masters have gambled them away at cards or traded them for dogs. Look at them!"

The men of Korezhino form a wall. Their thin, bony bodies glow through their tattered homespun clothes. They wear copper crosses dangling on thin cords.

In the tinselly paradisian world, the hairy, fierce peasants look like the offspring of Hell.

"Punish me, you holinesses!" shrieks the priest. "I did not understand the peasant soul: I brought them to Paradise, and they got me by the beard! I'll accept any punishment!"

"Expel him! Expel him from Paradise! Out!" roar the righteous. A mirage of the freedom he longs for again rises before the little, red-haired priest. He starts to choke with happiness.

He hurriedly crosses himself for protection, and gathers up his paradisian tunic and starts running.

But the peasants utter a menacing roar and manage to catch him by the hem of his sacred robe.

The priest howls, bites, shouts.

"Heavenly powers! Expel me!" come the desperate pleas of Father Evlampi from somewhere deep inside the jumble of peasants.

The two worlds are silently facing each other, when, all of a sudden, the heavenly thunder rolls, and the snub-nosed Russian God appears in a blinding flash of lightning.

The heavenly powers intone, "Hosanna."

The peasants crash down onto their knees and knock their foreheads on the ground.

"Rise up!" commands God the Father.

The frightened rabble jump onto their feet with such alacrity that they raise a wind.

Uncertain what to do, the perplexed Almighty scratches his bald spot and then suddenly remembers: "Where is that soldier, the no-good Kuroptev?"

The soldier takes three impeccably precise steps out of the peasant herd, salutes, and reports: "Private of the Prince Wirtemberg 118th Kaksholm Regiment, awaiting your orders" . . .

"You are part of the rebellion, are you, you no-good soldier?" asks God.

"That is correct, Lord!"

"Are you satisfied with eternal bliss?"

"In no way!" the soldier truthfully raps out. "A soldier must not lie!"

God is angered: "What is it you want? I took a personal liking to you, and I gave you a note to get you into Paradise without standing in line. I set you up in Paradise on the basis of our acquaintance . . . And you—why, this is disgusting!"

"I object," ventures the soldier. "I object in accordance with army regulations!"

"He objects! He has an objection!" God is sincerely distressed. "Fool! What do your regulations mean to me when I am the Almighty?"

"Regulations are regulations!" the soldier sternly admonishes him. "How can you violate them? Lord, even if you are thrice Almighty, these are ARMY RULES! There is no escaping them, since they lay down a soldier's right, in case of oppression, to address an objection to those in command."

"Hum!" The Almighty scratches the back of his skull. "So even I cannot violate the regulations?"

"No way, Lord! No way. That's it. They are regulations."

"Well, since you have the very God pinned to the wall, soldier, tell me what is your objection? Who is it that oppresses you?"

"My objection, Lord," manfully declares the soldier, "is that for a soldier eternal happiness is like having too tight a boot on a march. As any soldier will tell you, there are four necessary things besides prayer!"

"Name them, soldier, and in my mercy I will grant you everything."

Kuroptev bends his fingers: "A pot of cabbage soup and buckwheat, in accordance with garrison rations; next—a pipe of tobacco; next—a cup of vodka; next, well, a woman of some kind. That's basic, isn't it?"

At these words Saint Mary of Egypt casts a sizzling glance at the sinful soldier and, blushing, sways her curvaceous figure, moving the bearded saints to rumble in protest. The kind God suppresses a smirk and winks at the soldier:

"See? The entire assembly of saints is opposed to your sinful claims! Put yourself in my position: what shall I do with you?"

"Lord!" says the soldier, bitterly. "I've been beaten by the Turks. I have rheumatism in my legs. There's a lead bullet in my ribs. Old age and death await me. What kind of bliss is it you reserve as a personal favor for men from the St. George Cavalry? An unending church service? What's the good in that? Or was the heretic Terenti right when he said there was no eternal bliss, but only fog and delusion?"

The whole assembly of saints explodes with fury. They threaten the soldier, and one of the godly, raging like a sergeant, stamps his foot and orders: "Fetch the heretic here!"

The peasants stir and move about. In their fury they come to a decision:

"We will not give him up! You are not going to have him! He is our only scholar! Our one clear mind! You're not going to see Terenti!"

"Holy saints!" Priest Evlampi implores. "Don't ask for the heretic Terenti! Let the foul-smelling mouth of the atheist remain sealed before the Almighty!"

"An atheist? In the Kingdom of Heaven?!" groan the saints.

"Fetch him! Fetch the heretic here!"

"No! We will not give him up! You can cut us into pieces—but we will not give him up!"

This is now an open rebellion.

"Lord, crush these bandits!" cry the saints.

And straightaway lightning flashes and thunder rolls.

The herd of clodhoppers is flung down onto the ground, and Terenti is driven out before the assembly of saints, thanks to the miraculous power of the Almighty.

Terenti is a large-headed, powerful giant of a man, somewhat reminiscent of that other veteran of excommunication, Leo Tolstoi.

Quiet descends.

"Is your name Terenti?" a righteous sergeant begins the interrogation.

"My name is Terenti!" declares the giant man in a deep, quiet bass voice.

"Heretic, do you believe in the Almighty?"

"I believe in almighty Man and in his magic hands!" the heretic says with assurance. "The peasant is made for his hands. With his hands he can perform miracles: weave cloth, build palaces, cast cannons, and above all plow and sow. A peasant *is* hands. Hands *are* peasants. Or alternatively, you can raise your hands toward the mountain and sing hallelujahs. Once you are in the Kingdom of Heaven, what can you do? Where can a peasant escape from the hallelujahs? . . . But eternal bliss cannot be that. You can sing "Hallelujah" once, and you can sing it twice. But a peasant has to plow, since he is made for his almighty hands. Isn't that where bliss is? You can't knead dough with prayer."

"Smash him, Almighty One!" The entire assembly of saints crash down onto their knees and offer up a fervent prayer to the throne of the Almighty:

"Kill the false Wise Man, oh Sovereign Lord!"

"Rip out his sacrilegious tongue!"

"Crush the blasphemer!"

The nastiest of the righteous tear golden apples off the paradisiacal apple trees and hurl them like stones at the heretic.

This would be the end of him, except that God, the just and merciful, prevents the murder: "Stop, you Pharisees! you spiteful creatures! Leave alone the peasants who are coming unto me. For in the Scriptures it is said: 'Blessed are the pure in heart, for they shall see God!' Come to me, Terenti, servant of God. Tell me, the living God, whether you believe in eternal bliss."

The eyes of the whole assembly of saints, of all the peasants, and of God himself are fastened on the heretic with the large head.

Leaning on a cane, he thinks for everybody, and then, quietly says, as if continuing his thoughts aloud:

"There is no eternal bliss. And no immortality for man! What purpose could immortality serve? To sing "Hallelujah" eternally? To glorify you? What's that to you if you are almighty? Where's the joy in that? And why glorify you? Because of our vale of trouble? The dog's life we lead? The sickness and hunger? The landlords who squeeze three lives out of us? Lord Almighty, look at your peasants: their souls are black with grief, and their bliss is a trifling matter. A greedy man looks for it in roast mutton; a soldier—in a pipe of tobacco; and a girl—in a kind lad. But the young grow old, the tobacco gets smoked up, and only bones remain of the mutton. Do you want us to pay, Lord, for this trifle with eternal glorifying? Do you really need our bitter hosanna, our boring hallelujah? Can't you do without? Well if not, come on, peasants, we'll sing our rusty prayer to the Almighty!"

And the thin, somber louts somberly sing:

> Our Father, which art in Heaven.
> Hallowed be Thy name.
> Thy kingdom come.
> Give us this day our daily bread . . .

The sorrow of a tormented people so pervades their rough prayer that the old Russian God's eyes water, and he starts sobbing.

"What shall I do with you now, clodhoppers? How shall I proceed? Doesn't the world depend on you? What is your lot to be? What am I to do with you now?"

The heretic Terenti kneels before the living God and bows down to the ground, and says:

"Lord! Put us on a heavenly isle far away from your throne! There our stinking feet-wrappings will not offend you, and there will be less temptation for the virtuous. And Almighty, command us to enjoy bliss in the way our pure peasant heart dictates!"

"So be it!" God declares. "Let my peasants have the Lesser Celestial Isle! Let there be no interference with their sorrow-free life! And let the clodhoppers enjoy bliss as they know how!"

"But we should place a century of archangels above them!" stammer the righteous.

The Almighty pishes at them so forcefully that the whole assembly of saints hastily sing a hosanna to him.

Flocks of the righteous descend to the shores of the lake in order to see the louts crossing over to the Lesser Celestial Isle.

The soldier thrusts himself into the throng of holy worthies in order to "ravish" black-eyed Mary of Egypt and take her to the isle.

All the heavenly armies descend on the shameless assailant in order to defend their pure turtledove.

But for a Russian soldier what are the heavenly hosts? Together with Suvorov he once stormed impregnable Izmail,[4] and now he again acts quickly and boldly.

The pure turtledove, Saint Mary, knowing where her happiness lies, bravely fights off the bearded old men and archangels.

"Squeeze the life out of 'em, Vania! Beat 'em to the last breath!" she exclaims, egging on the soldier.

The whole heavenly throng is powerless in face of this attack.

Saint Tattletale bursts forth from a cloud before the seat of the Almighty: "Lord, Lord! This soldier has ravished Saint Mary!"

Kind God merely shrugs: "Isn't that what a soldier's for, to keep things lively."

"Lord! Lord!" cries Saint Tattletale. "Today it's Saint Mary he's ravishing; tomorrow it'll be me, a virgin. What is all this? Intercede and spare me!"

Scratching himself in irritation, God sternly says: "No such danger threatens you, miserable wretch. Go and sin not!"

Joyfully crossing themselves, the peasants advance in a solid phalanx into the water in order to cross over to the isle given them by God.

At first they are in up to their knees, then to their chests, then their necks, until finally they are swimming.

Their shaggy heads and unkempt beards form a terrible many-eyed mass of fur, which amazes the godlies, and it swiftly moves away from the shore toward the isle.

The air of Paradise grows cleaner.

Now there is nothing to disturb the sanctimony and utter tedium of the Kingdom of Heaven.

The archangels dig a tunnel under the wall of Paradise.

The cherubim collect an amazing heap of rubbish in a paradisial meadow—the miserable underwear, bast shoes with holes in them, clay pots, and all the clutter that over the ages has accompanied the peasant from the cradle to the churchyard.

On the isle the peasants breathe a sigh of relief.

Soldier Kuroptev lights a fire, dries some birch leaves, stuffs a nose-warmer pipe with them, stretches out, and laughs out loud for joy:

"Tobacco and a tavern—you don't need any other bliss."

The peasants lay out their underwear and foot wrappings to dry. They look around and think about how to begin the sorrow-free life given to them by God:

"First of all we'll build a bathhouse. See here, birch branches for bath whips!"

"Unless we have a steam bath there will be no Saturday."

"And without a steam bath and a woman—no Paradise."

"First of all, we have to dig up the roots and plow the land!"

"All this land going to waste—how exciting!"

The peasants' pent-up desire to plow acts like a charm. It excites them all. The Korezhino peasants raise a clamor and a hullabaloo.

"Dig up the roots! Look at the plow land!"

"Black earth—we can sow corn!"

"What yields there'll be! Twen-ty-fold!"

"Why sow corn when this bowl of land is crying out for flax?"

"Oats! Only oats!"

"But these are paradisiacal apple trees here! What oats, accursed men?" sighs Priest Evlampi.

"So what if these are paradisiacal apple trees?" object the peasants. "What do they yield? It's a no-good tree! We can't sink our teeth into the apples!"

"Just try biting them—they're gold!"

"Not plowing will mean starvation for us. The salt of life is all in the earth! That's where bliss is! Let's get started, men of Korezhino. Begin!"

They uproot the apple trees.

"Orthodox people!" howls Priest Evlampi. "What are you doing to Paradise? Don't you fear God?"

The peasants are seized by doubt. They address the heretic: "Terenti! Tell us what to do. After all this is Paradise."

"What is Paradise?" the heretic speculates. "Paradise is joy of the spirit. Your joy lies in plowing—and so, plow! What kind of Paradise has inedible apples? Spit on them! We'll leave this one grove for its beauty, and all the rest we will pull up and plow under!"

"We need to plow," the peasants agree. "We peasants are in a fix if we don't plow."

"Accursed people!" the priest interjects. "I will curse you at the seven ecumenical councils!"[5]

The soldier cocks a snook at him, and Evlampi stops.

The peasants—the whole flock of them—quickly cross themselves, as is proper before any great deed, to signify "May we be equal to the task!"

They spit on their hands, tighten their belts, and shake the apple trees.

The heavy, golden apples shower down on their backs. All together the shaggy flock throw themselves on the enormous paradisiacal apple trees and pull them up by the roots.

The peasants are excited.

Some handle the plow merrily. Others have set up a harrow.

Ten of the shaggy louts grab the reins of the horse belonging to Saint George the Conqueror. Praying, sighing, crying, the peasants jostle the saint:

"For the love of Christ forgive us, Saint George!"

"Forgive the accursed peasants! Heavy labor is our lot!"

"A peasant is in a bind without a horse."

"A peasant without a nag is no better than a chimney without a stove."

"Forgive the accursed ones, Saint George the Victorious!"

Saint George is all confused:

"How am I going to account for this to the Almighty? The horse is registered as mine. The records say it's mine."

"That's no problem!" the peasants reassure him. "We'll correct the receipt! We've wiquisitioned the horse—that's all! You're not to blame."

The louts lead off the horse, and harness it to the plow before the jostled saint can blink an eye . . .

. . . Saint Tattletale is scurrying along the shore and examining the isle.

She has sniffed trouble: there are lively construction noises, screeches, and rumblings.

The nasty old woman is distressed. This servant of God experienced her greatest bliss in Paradise only when the peasants arrived. Intrigue and tittle-tattle have made her appreciate the pointlessness of the wailing chants and a conflict-free life.

And so the noxious gossip finds her separation from the peasants an irreparable loss. With nowhere to direct her disgusting proclivities, she is feeling glum. And maybe she is feeling restless because of the happiness that has become the lot of Saint Mary of Egypt.

Upon hearing the sound of axes, Saint Tattletale whimpers and scurries along the shore like a dog cast off by its master. She climbs up trees to see the isle, and fearfully ventures into the water. Finally curiosity overcomes her fear, and the old hag rushes into the lake. She swims, sticking her sharp nose forward doggy-fashion, with her bothersome halo moved back on her neck. This is an incredible feat for she does not know how to swim!—and her eyes are transfixed with terror. Right in front of the isle she sinks, blowing bubbles.

The two angels on duty hiss: "Where the devil are you going, wretch? What has driven you into this lake?"

"Curiosity," admits the wretch, crying and spitting out water. "Don't condemn me. I am a woman!" And like a bloodhound she runs toward the peasant camp.

"A-ah, a-ah, a-ah!" A moan of complaint runs through the Kingdom of Heaven

The peasants have uprooted two dozen or so paradisiacal apple trees and are plowing the cleared land. "Git, Gray, git!"

The plow of Breast-Feeding Mother Russia has climbed high up into Heaven, and is laying furrow after furrow across the paradisian wasteland.

After the plow comes the harrow.

And after the harrow comes a man casting seed out of a woven basket. The Kingdom of Heaven has a changed look now—it is just like our own province of Penza.

"Fight back, holy saints! Fight back!" shrieks Saint Tattletale, running out along the shore of the lake. "They are plowing! I swear to God, the accursed ones are plowing! Strike me down if I lie! Plowing! Fight, saints!"

A hosanna breaks off in the Kingdom of Heaven and goes silent.

A throng of saints rushes to the shore.

"Fight back! They are plowing! They are plowing up Paradise!" To the accompaniment of the wild shrieks of the hag the whole thousand-faced righteous throng swims toward the isle.

Only their bright halos and scrappy beards stick out over the glossy lake.

They quickly reach the shore of the Lesser Celestial Isle.

Wet, and jaundiced from the eternal liturgical service, they look with horror upon the unruliness of the Korezhino peasantry.

The happy peasants have found true bliss.

"They are ploughing! harrowing! sowing! Building a bathhouse!"

"Miserable louts, what are you doing?"

"What are you doing to Paradise?"

"Clodhoppers, do you know what's going to happen to you because of this?"

"Look at what you have done!"

"Your Honors!" cry the peasants, conciliatory and embarrassed. "What's there to do if we don't plow? For us 'twould be a calamity."

"And you have horses that are serving no purpose!"

"The black earth of Paradise is wasted for no cause or reason."

"Fool around today, fool around tomorrow, and soon you will lose your shirt."

"You can't celebrate a mass forever! Amen is no substitute for a dough starter."

"Say your prayers, but add flour to the dough starter!"

"How could things be otherwise? Git, Gray. Git!"

"They've wiquisitioned George the Conqueror's horse," shrieks Saint Tattletale. "How is it going to be for George without a horse, for George unhorsed? Did you think about this, clodhoppers?"

"And how is a horseless peasant going to manage without a horse? Did you think about this, wretch?"

"Whoa! Gray!!"

The axes are merrily ringing in the pavilions of Heaven. The peasants are shaping logs.

"And what are you building here?" groan the righteous ones.

"A bathhouse!" merrily answer the men of Korezhino.

"What kind of Saturday will there be if there is no bathhouse? Can Paradise stand firm if it has no bathhouse or birch-wood whips? No, never!"

"A steam bath purges evil much more thoroughly than all your praying does! Can't you see? Come on, give us a hand!"

"But is a bathhouse allowed in Paradise?" babbles one of the godlies.

"It is allowed for sinners, but we are listed among the righteous."

"Here, move it!"

"Why are you just standing by, righteous fathers? Why are you just staring? Can't you see, it's hard for us. Let's move it! All together!"

And the godlies put their shoulders to the heavy logs, timidly at first and then with growing strength and enthusiasm.

Saint Joseph spits on his palms and takes up the ax once again: for he was once a carpenter, before being relegated to the ranks of the venerables.

Saint Tattletale runs to the shore as fast as she can. She pants and triumphantly commands: "Archangels! Convey me to the throne of the Almighty! I shall tell all to the Lord! May my eyes burst if he does not cast the people out!"

The archangels grab hold of the noxious old woman and convey her through the air!

"Lord! Lord!" the holy martyr wails. "See how your peasants of Korezhino have distinguished themselves. They are plowing! Look: they are planting seeds in the Kingdom of Heaven! May I collapse here on the spot if it's not true that the clodhoppers are plowing. I have seen it myself!"

The Almighty has been trying to snooze on a soft cloud, and now, like an autumn fly, the old woman is disturbing his rest.

"Plowing?" placidly inquires God without looking.

"If that's not enough to disturb you—they are plowing and sowing!"

"Are they crying or rejoicing?" The Almighty yawns.

"Lord, how they are rejoicing, the accursed ones! They have knocked together a bathhouse."

"A bathhouse?" The Almighty rises.

"A bathhouse!" shrieks the saint. "If not, may my tongue wither! —A bathhouse!"

"A steam bath?" Old God is getting interested; he scratches his long-unwashed body.

"Of course!" Saint Tattletale chokes. "It's all because of that soldier! The things I know about him—I can swear to them on a cross!"

"And bath whips?" God interrupts her.

"Yes, bath whips!" hisses the old woman. "Before my eyes the shameless peasants stripped twelve paradisiacal birch trees. Then I saw them take off their pants."

"You saw everything?" God asks caustically.

"Everything! May I be consumed in flames if I didn't!"

"Good," says God.

"What's good?" groans the holy martyr.

"The bathhouse, and the steam, and the bath whips. The smell of birch. Listen, you miserable wretch," the Almighty pronounces. "Go and find out about the bathhouse. What kind of steam does it have? Smoky or not smoky? Go to the head of the line and wash all the nastiness out of you, then report back to me!"

The old Russian God rubs himself with enjoyment. "Let them heat it up! It's been a long time since *we*'ve been to the bathhouse."

"Lord! Lord! But how can I—a virgin—" the holy martyr preciously and peevishly sniffles.

"Go and sin not!" the Almighty sternly admonishes her.

The archangels on duty lift the crying virgin up into the air and carry her off . . .

Meanwhile the peasants are in full swing.

Axes are ringing, and saws humming. Somewhere in the pavilions of Heaven an old Saratov accordion with bells is playing.

New throngs of godlies keep swimming over to the isle.

They look at the soldier in silence, with fear and curiosity, as he paces out a paradisian meadow, drives in stakes with the butt of his ax, stretches a thin cord between them, and does some calculations.

"Soldier Kuroptev, what else have you thought up?" the godlies fearfully ask.

"I am building a tavern," replies the soldier, without interrupting his work, "with a wine cellar. For drinks on the premises and to take out. Korneev beers, and also Gorshanov and Gold Label. Crayfish to accompany the beer, and tidbits and salt-fish! . . . A German musical organ. Here, grandfather, grab hold!"

And he shoves a rope into the hand of a dried-up martyr.

What can the terrified saint do but help the sinful soldier to measure out the foundation for the drinking establishment.

"He's putting up a tavern!" the worthies flutter.

"Crayfish and beer. Lord, what a temptation!"

"Hey, have you gone mad, soldier Kuroptev, building a tavern in the Kingdom of Heaven?" indignantly cry the righteous ones.

The soldier suddenly grows angry: "Who are these idle chatterboxes? Is this Paradise or the Alexandrovsky Central Prison for convicts? If a prison, then say so, and let soldier Kuroptev be damned. And if it is Paradise, then don't stand in my way! Don't step on the feet of a simple man. Don't take away my salt-fish. A soldier on holiday is just another unfortunate peasant wetting his throat. What? Can't you speak, your reverence?"

The soldier advances; the saints fall back. "I am an infantryman of the Prince Wirtemberg 118th Kaksholm Regiment! What is it I am supposed to do if I am bound to the chorus of saints in order to suffer bliss?"

"Sing 'Hallelujah!' . . . Pray! . . . Glorify the Maker!" timid voices are heard.

"Hallelujah?" the soldier is indignant. "For how many years?"

"A thousand! . . . Forever! . . . In the ages of ages! . . . A million years!"

"And is that all there is to bliss?" the soldier asks, surprised.

"How can you escape it? Where can you run away?"

"What is your idea of bliss?" the saints ask.

"Like this," says the soldier as he continues taking measurements. "Here's where we'll set up the drinking establishment; we'll put in separate tables, special rooms. You can wash down your hallelujah with intoxicating home brew or vodka.—Maybe then even thousands of years won't be tedious! If we're going to have bliss, let's have true bliss!"

. . . Things are going hummingly!

Happy, well-steamed peasants come tumbling out of the new bathhouse.

Red, sweating, covered with bits and pieces from the birch whips, which have been worn down to the handles, they stagger blissfully off to the celestial pavilions in the shade of the paradisiacal apple trees.

The peasants carefully lead Saint Tattletale by the hand out of the steam bath and past the now-quiet throng of saints.

The old woman has washed all the nastiness out of her and is surprisingly transformed. She has twisted a wet towel about her head, and for the first time in her life a kind smile appears on her face, which has turned wine-colored with the steam.

She is happy.

"Was the steam bath good?" some saints in the throng inquire of her.

"True bliss. There, only there, in the bathhouse! What bliss!" The saint, languidly rolling her eyes, collapses on the shoulder of the sinful, bearded blacksmith of Korezhino.

And with a moan the throng of long-unwashed saints rush to the bathhouse.

"Stand in line please. Your Honors, in line!"

"I was in line!"

"No, Father, you were not."

"I was saving this place for Panteleimon the Healer."

"And that's not all. After him comes Ivan the Warrior and then Simon on the Pillar.[6] And then me . . ."

"Father, no trespassing! After Simon on the Pillar comes Epifani Without a Rib, then Cyril and Methodius,[7] then myself—"

"But Father, how did you get here?"

"I was here!"

"No, you weren't! No, No, No!"

Each of them is carrying a bundle and a bath whip. The queue of saints, counting one-and-a-half thousand halos, wind in a serpentine course up Mount Sinai and lose themselves far away in wreathing clouds, which might have escaped from an icon by a mischievous icon-daubster of the Suzdal school.

New throngs of holy worthies keep crossing to the enchanted isle of the peasant paradise.

This paradise is a special one!

The enduring happiness of sinful man is found in labor. Only in labor does man infallibly find eternal bliss.

Only in labor can man achieve true immortality, to which the astonishing, age-old monuments produced by the genius of man are testament.

The paradise thought up by do-nothings and populated with do-nothings, whose only bliss lies in prayer and glorification, is something different . . .

The peasants of Korezhino have brought to the Lesser Celestial Isle their naive conceptions of bliss, which greatly amaze the holy saints.

The peasants are mowing the meadows of Paradise with fervor.

They sharpen their scythes,

rake the hay into stacks.

And the godlies timidly help them.

Potters are making wonderful jugs out of ordinary clay on an ordinary wheel. Suddenly one of the bearded godlies is shoved forward out of the throng of curious worthies . . .

He resists and draws back in fear. But finally curiosity wins out: he sits at the wheel and under his hands there grows an object of wet clay that makes the whole assembly of saints shake with laughter.

Some of the venerables go to the blacksmith. They look around in embarrassment, cross themselves for protection, pick up a heavy hammer, and start to forge some iron.

They enthusiastically learn how to make bast shoes, and impatiently grab from one another the simple tool (a kind of awl) that is used in plaiting bast.

One valorous saint strives to knead dough, and gets so entangled in the sticky stuff that the assembled saints laugh till tears come to their eyes.

It seems that a fresh breeze has brought a wave of human joy to the lifeless kingdom of shadows!

An old-time popular song comes whistling out of an old Viennese barrel organ:

> Matshish is a dance,
> That sizzles and burns.
> From the country of valor true
> A Spaniard brought it here.

A roughly made, fun-fair merry-go-round turns to the nasal music of the barrel organ.

The hairy, still somber peasants sit on the wooden horses, lions, and fabulous birds . . . In their grief-filled, tragic life, there was simply no conception of bliss. But here, on the orders of God himself, the whole flock of them has entered onto the road of bliss and accepted God's commands as their destiny:

They enjoy bliss artlessly, as their pure hearts direct them; their faces are serious and calm.

The wooden carousel amazes the godlies, just as the first airplane or satellite amazed mankind.

The whole assembly surrounds it, without daring to partake of the tempting, sinful joy.

From their ranks they shove out first one elder, then another, trying to get them to jump onto a wooden horse and gallop round and round to the nasal music of the barrel organ . . .

Two sallow-faced, desperate martyrs come forward.

Nudging one another, they make a very tiny sign of the cross, straighten their halos, gather up their heavenly tunics, and jump onto two wooden swans.

And God's world goes spinning round the desperate elders!

Their faces glow with happiness. Their green biliousness is all gone.

"Shame! . . . Sin! . . . Temptation!" . . . shrieks Saint Tattletale, who has suddenly come to her senses. "I denounce you, shameless men! Servants of Beelzebub! You will burn in the fiery Gehenna, where there will be a wailing and gnashing of teeth!"

Shrieking, she wields her staff and knocks the heroic martyrs who have succumbed to temptation off the merry-go-round; and they penitently bow their heads.

The odious old woman could have kept on reviling the unworthy 'til evening, but suddenly the saucy soldier grabs hold of the holy martyr as he whirls past and seats her next to him on his wooden horse.

Screeching and sputtering, Saint Tattletale spins round with all the others . . .

And then once again an expression of true bliss appears on her face.

"The temptation! The sin!" she croaks shamefacedly, abandoning herself more and more to a joy that is beyond words. "What sin! what sweet sin! . . . Oh . . . !" When the soldier mischievously and unexpectedly casts her down at the feet of the two valiant martyrs she had abused, her head continues its wonderful spinning; she half closes her eyes, still in the grip of dazzling sensations, and in a paroxysm of desire says: "Oooh, what sweet sin.! . . . What temptation! Ah!"

An elder sternly knocks her on the halo with his staff. The old woman comes to her senses. She sticks her tongue out at the ruffians and jumps with unexpected sprightliness onto one of the wooden horses on the merry-go-round . . .

And again a dazzling paradise spins before her eyes. "Temptation! . . . What sweet, divine sin!" . . .

In the new tavern the still-somber peasants of Korezhino find bliss in home brew.

The barrel organ continues to screech the same old Matshish dance.

Uncertain whether to go in, Saint Mary of Egypt grabs hold of the soldier by a button, and tenderly sings in tune with the music:

> I know your desire,
> the object of your concern.
> You need a shot of vodka,
> And a piece of herring!

The peasants are finding bliss in Russian home brew and beer.

Their mustaches and beards are spattered with foam. But there is no wild orgy in this paradisial drinking establishment. The hairy louts, the trusting Russian peasants, treat their bliss "seriously," spiritually; they are grateful for the gift from the magnanimous Russian God.

Here there are no godlies.

The godlies are fearfully observing the sweet sin from afar, from the celestial pavilions, where they lick their lips in envy and discontent!

"What's all this? Some get to drink wine, while others have to say Mass!"

Protest grows in the godly throng:

"This won't do!"

"No, this won't do! That's for sure!"

"We won't allow it!" roars the whole godly throng.

"We stand and stand, and deny ourselves" . . .

"No rest, no joy, no glimmer of light!"

"And look, would you believe it—true bliss! Beer and a steam bath!"

"No, this won't do! We won't agree to it!"

The whole assembly of saints is in a wild rage.

"I am in charge!" suddenly declares Saint Sebastian. "Who is in favor of getting this rabble to build us eight taverns and a merry-go-round?"

"And a bathhouse as well!"

". . . and a newspaper, *The Evening Paradise*!"

"And some days off!"

"—and, moreover, six hours a day without hosannas!"

"We are voting!" shouts Saint Sebastian. "All those in favor of the reforms—raise your hand!"

As if by command, the entire multitudinous throng cross themselves and raise their hands.

"Let us go to the Almighty."

"Let him give his blessing to the real beatitudes!"

And they all rush away from the Lesser Isle.

. . . Except for the four most intrepid saints, who do not expect God to give his approval and who go off into the private rooms of the tavern. Looking round like thieves, they carefully make small signs of the cross over the goblets and the bread, toss the spirits into their mouths, and then follow up with prayers and more signs of the cross instead of pickles.

Isn't it the same here, on our sinful Earth?—where saintly teetotalers call upon alcoholics to abstain, while they hide in closets in order to drink something that is certainly not holy water!

Only Saint Tattletale is in a drunken fog. Staggering about, she pipes in a thin voice:

I was young and in a garden house
At a party.
And I was drinking from a pail . . .

"Blacksmith! Take me, a virgin, and marry me," she whispers to a dark, bearded peasant with the face of a brigand, and sits in his lap. "It is for you I have preserved my virginity 190 years."

"You are all lies, wretch!" the somber smith says, removing her from his lap.

Setting straight her crooked halo, the old woman shrieks: "Me? A liar? May I sink through the ground if I am!" . . .

And she sinks through the ground. A hole is formed at the spot at which she was standing.

From the hole comes a drawn-out, tedious hosanna, like a cold gust from an icehouse.

The entire assembly of the righteous has gathered before the throne of the Almighty. Everyone is speaking. All are flapping their arms in agitation.

Nobody is listening. The archangel on duty frantically rings a bell, to no avail.

The noise grows. Chagrined, the Almighty hurls thunder and lightning at the unruly.

At once the righteous come to their senses and promptly intone a melancholy-sounding "A-a-a-a-a-a-a-a-a-a-ah."

The All-Merciful stops them, and a dead silence descends. He says: "Let the wisest among you say what has happened to my paradise."

An emaciated godly falls down on his knees before God, sorrowfully sobbing: "Lord, Lord! Why did you send a great temptation to us, your slaves? To whom did you open the gates of Paradise? You gave away the bosom of Abraham to the sinful rabble. And they are plowing and singing, and building and singing. They are drinking beer with fiendish joy. You also gave them a bathhouse and a merry-go-round, and labor, and taverns! What have you given to us, the righteous, to enjoy forever and ever? We are all standing in one heavenly assembly and joylessly whining, like mangy puppies."

The old Russian God is deeply troubled. "What do you want, holy fathers and godly ones?" asks the Almighty, scratching his bald spot. "Ask, and I will give it you!"

The righteous exclaim: "Lord! Lord! Either expel the clodhopping louts from the Kingdom of Heaven, or don't discriminate in any way between them and the assembly of your holy godlies!"

"Or give us our own tavern!" one bold godly in the throng whispers a timid desire before nimbly slipping behind his bearded comrades.

It is as if he had tossed a bomb. The godly assembly explodes with sinful dreams: ". . . and a bathhouse with whips . . . and a merry-go-round . . . Twin Label beer . . . and the *Evening Paradise* newspaper!"

And all of the thousands upon thousands are shouting. Everyone is waving his hands. From the depths of the hearts desiccated by hosannas bursts forth a howl of joy, until the Almighty restores quiet by means of thunder and lightning.

In anger God descends from his cloud onto the Lesser Celestial Isle.

He hurls thunder and lightning at the peasants' self-made paradise.

He wrecks the merry-go-round and shatters the bathhouse, tavern, and organ . . .

He transforms the nurturing plow into a crooked tree,
gives the horse back to Saint George the Victorious,
converts the carpenters' axes and planes into sandstone.

The potters' wheels shatter, and the pots burst like soap bubbles . . . A storm roars over the Lesser Celestial Isle.

In a flash the peasants are gathered into a herd and driven to face the Almighty.

"I admitted you, louts, to Paradise on the strength of my own liking for you," angrily says God, "and you clodhoppers are leading the righteous into temptation! If you wish to remain, you shall enjoy the same bliss as the godly ones. If not, then you may plunge down to all the devils! The air will be purer without you."

"What is your Paradise for?" somberly roar the peasants.

"Is idleness supposed to be bliss?"

"Without swinging of axes or playing with scythes! Why did you do this to us?"

"Let's settle accounts!" The peasants are in a white heat. "This is not for us! Your Paradise does not suit us! Give us exit papers."

"Silence!" thunders God. "Bring the soldier forth."

In conformity with all the rules of military protocol, the soldier takes four steps forward, brings his foot down with a crash, and, saluting, hand beneath his visor, says: "Private Kuroptev, Prince Wirtemberg 118th Kaksholm Regiment, at your orders."

Testily God says: "Soldier, it is true to say that on the strength of our acquaintance I assigned you to my throne, ahead of the whole queue. And you, you Akhlamon [lord of a fool's paradise], what have you done with the Celestial Isle? Scoundrel, what is the mess you've created? Why have you upset the whole assembly of the righteous?"

Offended, the soldier responds: "Lord, I told you I drank and swore, and that regarding womankind I could give no guarantees. What complaints can you have against me, a sinner?"

"All that's left is to consign you to Hell along with all the clodhoppers!"

"When may I have the travel documents?" gloomily says the soldier.

"In that place they take everyone and his brother without papers!" thunders God, very angry.

Thunder and lightning . . .

Black clouds . . .

Whirlwinds . . .

Threadbare underpants, worn-out shoes, and the unkempt heads of peasants flash by inside a cloud . . .

The saucy soldier flies past, holding the comely holy martyr Saint Mary of Egypt . . .

The heretic Terenti flies past, then the pregnant peasant-woman from Korezhino with a cow . . .

Only the priest Evlampi is stopped and returned to the throne in accordance with orders from the Almighty.

Two archangels tear him away from the herd, set him down on the soil of Paradise, and escort him . . .

He resists mightily . . . He desperately strives for freedom! The grief-maddened, red-haired, little priest kicks against the ground and bites an archangel's finger.

A knee kick in his rear end targets him:

"You called yourself godly. And so be blissful!"

In the Kingdom of Heaven dispiriting sanctimony again reigns, after the disruption by the Korezhino peasants.

It is as if Paradise were dying away. To the monotonous humming of the righteous, the Almighty snoozes in his habitual fashion on a light cloud.

"A-a-a-a-a-a-ah!" tediously drawl out the godlies.

"A-a-a-a-ah!" heartrendingly sobs Father Evlampi. And in this cry there is so much grief that the godlies subdue him with blows.

"A-a-a-ah," the throngs of the righteous drawl on. Raising their desiccated arms toward the mount, they sway as if asleep or dead.

The tarnished world of the Suzdal icon-daubsters might as well never have existed. The solemn countenances of the righteous have turned black with tedium; they are covered with dust, and bear no resemblance to living ones.

Only the priest Evlampi, deeply unhappy, sheds bitter tears for his forever foregone freedom.

With a screeching the Korezhino peasants fly through the air until, all together, they drop down into a deep gorge.

For a while, long legs with bast shoes, and arms, and beards and pants are seen sticking out of the earth, motionless.

Then, all of a sudden, all this strange mess stirs, revives, and buzzes.

The unharmed peasants crawl out of the earth. The whole bunch of them shake themselves and, relieved, they laugh aloud:

"Thank 'od!" . . .

"We almost got assigned to the body of saints! As if we needed it!"

The whole troop laughs coarsely and joyously. "Barely got away with our feet . . ."

"And as for that bliss! . . . And the lousy tobacco!" . . .

"What are we going to do now, peasants?" asks the soldier, covering his plump woman friend with his jacket.

"First of all," says, the smith, black as a beetle, spitting out some earth, "we need to give our accursed priest a quick lesson, so that in future the long-haired devil will know where it is we'd like to go!"

"Aha, he's got his comeuppance!" the peasants laugh. "The archangels have set him up for life . . ."

"Took him off, forever and ever! . . . The priest ran out of luck!"

"Lord! . . . If you're unlucky, even the heavenly paradise turns out to be a prison camp."

"Peasants, there's no way out," sighs the soldier. "Let's be on our way to Absolute Hell. If we must go, then we must go!"

And the peasants of Korezhino gloomily wander off to meet their unhappy fate.

. . . Here it is—Hell!

"This is it! . . . Lord! . . . What horrors!"

At the bottom of the gorge is the entrance to the Fiery Furnace.

All around are burrows gnawed out by devils.

Hellish fire pours forth from all the slits.

The poisonous vapors fill a sinner's soul with terror.

"Remove all crosses!" orders Private Kuroptev.

The subdued peasants, ready to endure any tortures, hurriedly cross themselves and remove their cords with copper crosses, and give them to the soldier.

He hangs them on a crooked, dry branch and glances at the fiery hatchway.

The subdued peasants bunch up behind one another.

They are terrified.

Flashes of red, hellish fire are reflected on their distraught faces. Blue smoke eats away at their eyes.

"Well then . . . let's go, peasants!" sighs the soldier.

"If we must, so be it."

Private Kuroptev takes three steps back, makes a tiny, tiny sign of the cross, takes a leap, and plunges in headfirst.

Behind him the desperate Russian peasants make tiny signs of the cross and hurl themselves into the furnace . . .

It is as if they had never existed!

There is only the wind agitating the crosses hanging on cords.

And three old crows who caw forebodingly as they rise into the air and fly away from the horrible place.

In contrast with the deathliness of Paradise, Hell is filled with the bustle and turbulence of life.

Devils are tormenting the sinners.

They place firewood beneath Hell's cauldrons.

They scurry and screech and fan the flames of Hell.

They pursue their clients with red-hot irons.

Inside the fiery wall, the Prince of Darkness himself, Beelzebub, oversees trials and the administration of justice.

Satan is fed up with his hard life. He is concentrating on a chess game with a green devil, and does not look at his clients.

The devils have marshaled the newly arrived sinners in a huge queue before him, and they thrust them out one by one to behold the greatest devil of all.

His justice is quick.

"Glutton!" is the recommendation of the devils regarding the next man in line.

"Feed him till he bursts! Next!"

"Bribe taker!"

"Brand him! Next!"

"Huckster and cheat!"

"Into the cauldron."

"Monk and sensualist!"

"The cauldron!"

"Landowner!

"The cauldron!"

"Chatterbox!"

"Make him lick a hot frying pan."

"A peasant, a muzhik."

"To the bathhouse. Next."

"Extortioner!"

"The cauldron!"

"Police captain!"

"Boil him in oil!"

"A peasant!"

"Bathhouse! Next!"

"The soldier Kuroptev. And with him 108 peasants and a virgin—the soldier's mistress!"

"Set aside the mistress. Cast the soldier and the peasants to the devils!"

"How so, cast us to the devils?" shout the Korezhino men. "According to what judicial principle?"

"We've been thrown out of Paradise; we're being chased out of the Infernal Abyss; our master drove us off the Earth. Where is there supposed to be justice? Where's a peasant supposed to go? Did you think about this?"

"Cast them to the devils!" angrily says the Prince of Darkness, interrupting his game of chess. "Next!"

The devils fill their lungs with air and in consort blow it out onto the peasants.

In the Infernal Abyss a dust storm swirls. Before the men of Korezhino realize it, the unclean force has expelled the whole hairy horde of them out from the devils' realm and into a ravine.

The devils quickly batten down the heavy hatch of Hell.

A bunch of them hold onto the bolt from below in order to prevent the peasants from sliding it open . . .

Bewildered and singed with hellfire, the peasants wander away from the Infernal Abyss.

They wander in a dense herd, and the autumn wind tears at their unkempt hair.

When they emerge from the devils' ravine, Private Kuroptev stops them.

"Where shall we go?" . . .

"It seems there's nowhere to go" . . .

"But it's also impossible not to keep going!" . . .

"Go where? Where is there a place for us? There's no Heaven or Hell or Earth for us" . . . the people cry.

"Maybe we should hang in the air?"

While the perplexed men are tossing ideas about, the soldier goes back to the closed hatchway of the Infernal Abyss and examines it on all sides . . .

He places his ear against it and listens to the devils' shrieks.

The men call, "Well, soldier, shall we conquer Hell's gates?"

Kuroptev lights up a cigarette and, lost in thought, says: "Izmail[8] conquered a fortress, and, God knows, it was high . . . But here we have no room for maneuver!"

He stamps out the cigarette. "Men of Korezhino, pray!" comes the unexpected command.

The peasants cross themselves, angrily and all together, and whisper prayers with the ferocity of a storm in a forest in fall.

"Charge!" cries the soldier, as in a battle.

"Charge! We'll conquer the gates of Hell!"

And the whole troop of peasants rush upon the hatchway of the Infernal Abyss.

A bunch of devils down below blocks them and struggles against the accursed force.

But the peasants continue to press on . . . There's nowhere they can go to. Singed, black, lit by the baleful fires of Hell, the whole mass of peasants attacks.

Smoke! Flames! Horror!

The devils groan, cry, shriek, and finally cannot resist.

They scatter away, shrieking.

The nasty clodhoppers have vanquished Hell's gates.

Furious and desperate, they rush into the fire with stones and cudgels in their hands . . .

They wreck the devils' establishment . . .

They overturn the cauldrons with sinners in them . . .

They hurl red-hot frying pans at the heads of the terrified masters and sinners.

In deepest Hell they make such a hell that the devils feel sick . . .

The smith, black as a beetle, grabs the very Prince of Darkness by the throat.

"Let me in, and everyone who is here."

"We've nowhere to go. Let us in."

"If not, we'll make such a mess you won't sort things out for a hundred years."

"We'll wreck all your devilish kingdom, strangle the devils, and as for you, serpent, we'll sell you to a tavern keeper for drink."

"Don't imagine we are meek. Everything has made us furious!"

"We are Russians!"

Beelzebub angrily blows a foul odor at them, and the peasants appear to yield.

The Prince of Darkness asks: "Is there at least one rational man with whom I can speak?"

"Yes. Terenti, the heretic."

"Bring forth your heretic."

Terenti steps forward. He bows.

The Prince of Darkness asks him: "Are you possessed, or what? You burst into a functioning enterprise, overturn the equipment, upset cauldrons with clients in them, frighten the personnel, disrupt the daily work charts. What is this? Do you want to leave the world with no Infernal Abyss? To bring back universal chaos? Have you thought about that?"

"And where are we supposed to go? Have you thought about that?"

"Why don't you live in your village?"

"Live in it, yourself!" roars the smith.

"As things are, it's warm enough for me here."

"You reptile, we'll make things really hot for you."

Beelzebub exhales onto the dispersing peasants, and they appear to choke.

He orders Terenti: "Heretic, you do the talking!"

A giant of a man roars: "What is there to say? Things are unbearable in the village. The masters, landlords, and gentlefolk do with us as they please. They whip us, but that's the least of it. They sell us like firewood. They gamble us away at cards. They barter us for dogs!" . . .

"Worst of all is the hunger! Children die. For the women it is a disaster."

"Don't chase us away, Your Dark Excellency!"

"Be like a real father to us."

"Please, have mercy on us! Father! Don't chase us away!"

"It doesn't matter who we pray to; it's all the same. You are our God!"

They fall on their knees before Satan. "Be our own father. One way or another we'll settle with you. We'll have a place to rest our head."

"Of course, it'll be hot, but we're used to anything" . . .

The whole troop roars: "That's nothing to us! We'll bear it. All we need is a corner of our own! We don't need much."

Beelzebub exhales, and the peasants stop speaking.

Feeling sorry for the boors, Satan asks: "And why don't you go to God in Heaven?"

"But that's where we've come from!" says Terenti, the heretic. "The Kingdom of Heaven does not suit us! That's the situation."

Satan is truly surprised. "Doesn't suit you?"

The peasants roar out all together: "Not at all! We tormented God till we wore him out and led the saints into temptation, and as for ourselves we were overwhelmed with gloom. We were expelled from the Kingdom of Heaven. That's the situation."

Beelzebub is troubled. "How can this be? You poor people, you have so much to endure on Earth. You receive so many knocks."

He even bursts into tears.

"The hairs of my pelt stand on end when I look at you. Where is the truth?"

Satan is crying. The inescapability and depth of the peasants' grief have suddenly penetrated even to the Devil's heart through the matting of fur that has grown over it.

"How heavy your souls are! . . . So benighted! . . . So full of sorrow! . . . Why don't you choke, you poor wretches?!"

"Don't cry, Evil One, don't fret! . . . We can endure everything, Your Most Infernal Excellency. And thanks for your tears!"

"You are the first to take pity on us."

"Even though you are the Devil!"

"Drink a little vodka. Don't cry, brother!" the Korezhino men say in a warm murmur.

"Well who is Paradise for if not for you?" says the Prince of Darkness, now quieter, sniveling.

"That paradise is not suitable," the heretic dejectedly shrugs his shoulders. "We tried it this way and that; it just doesn't work for us . . . It was thought up by useless people, and useless people settled there. Whereas, we, Your Most Infernal Excellency, are working people, the same as bees. Assign us to your enterprise, and we will boil the cauldrons, carry firewood, and see that the pans are red-hot. We'll forge all kinds of forks for the devils, hooks and hammers . . . We'll feed the fires and rake out the ashes. Our hands can do everything!"

"As we see it, not working is the pits, and you have a lot to do here. Your devils are run off their feet."

"You should give us, say, a peasant's nook in the infernal regions, so we can open a pottery."

"We're great potters!" the peasants all chant.

"We made pots for all of Iarsolav province! . . . Our pots have gone as far as the town of Orenburg" . . .

"And even to Saratov!"

"The kilns in Hell are just the thing."

"The very best! . . . Great kilns! In these furnaces, hey, we can make anything! . . . And for us Hell's clays couldn't be better."

"The clays here are magic! What more do we need?"

The peasants get carried away. "Just understand, we'd have covered all Russia with good ringing pottery!"

"Well clodhoppers, what shall I do with you?" the kind Prince of Darkness wavers.

"Keep us, Your Dark Excellency!"

"You can always expel us!" says the heretic Terenti, and bows.

The heartsick Prince of Darkness gives in to the peasants. "Well, we'll have it your way. Stand by the kettles, clodhoppers, climb down into the shafts, make torture instruments in the smithy . . . I entrust to you the newly deceased landlords, merchants, and village policemen! . . . To the devil with you!"

The peasants jump to their feet, and what starts up now makes the devils feel sick again.

At first everything is as well as can be.

The homeless peasants suddenly feel they have settled in a warm place.

This is happiness! They have hungered for work and are as if welded to Hell's huge workshops.

They carry wood, . . . heat up the cauldrons, . . . fan the fires, . . . heat the frying pans, . . . pour molten metal . . .

They hammer out bars of metal in order to forge pincers, hooks, and torture instruments for the devils . . .

They play cards with merry devils . . .

The grief-darkened souls lose to the mischievous devils but they do not mind . . .

On the whole, the devils turn out to be a perfectly decent and jolly bunch . . . The peasants enjoy smoking coarse tobacco with them in the furnace rooms,

Drinking Hell's rough vodka in the devils' saloon,

Fooling around near the furnaces,

Joining in mockery around the boiling cauldrons with sinners in them . . .

But the peasants' greatest joy is work!

They work selflessly!

The potters' wheels whirr. Amid the flashes of Hell's fires forty potters happily turn Hell's clays into forty splendid pots, jars, and crocks.

Others take the earthenware and prepare it for firing.

A third group do the firing.

When the ringing, blue-glazed pots are removed from the kilns, they are so pretty that the sinners in the cauldrons on top of the furnaces forget the torments of Hell for a moment and take an interest in this new industrial enterprise.

"Clodhoppers, what have you started now?" exclaim the demons.

"Making pots and vessels!"

"What for?"

"No man can last a day without a pot," declare the potters without interrupting their work. "How can you drink water or make cabbage soup or kasha without a pot?"

"You can't cook kasha in your hand. And your furnaces are burning for nothing. Without pots a man is lost."

The devils are amazed. "But what's that to you clodhoppers, since you been given permanent residence here in the Infernal Abyss?"

A potter catches the inquisitive devil by a paw, thrusts a finger at his forehead, and instructs him: "The reason a peasant has hands is so he can make any useful thing with them."

"Consign us to the bottom of the sea—we'll find work there!"

"Drive us inside a giant rock—we'll make ourselves known there too!"

"That's why we are peasants. Sit down, we'll instruct you!"

The devils joyfully rush to the potters' wheels.

And soon the Infernal Abyss is turned into a huge rumbling factory, in which a potter can scarcely be distinguished from a devil, and a devil from a smith, and where the chief clients, the sinners, prove to be the chief obstruction.

But the peasants begin to pull the sinners out of the cauldrons and set them up with hammers and files.

The peasants put all the passion of their famished souls into furious work.

Wiping off their sweat as they pause for a quick drink of cold kvass, they joyfully exclaim:

"Now this is bliss!"

"What more do you need?"

"There, lean hard, evil one . . . That's it."

"Good! . . . It's so good!"

"*This* is the righteous life!"

But Hell is hell—an establishment in which sinful human souls are subjected to hellish torments.

The cruelty of the Infernal Abyss is eternal and infinite.

Soon the peasants start feeling unwell. "Look what's going on!" the troubled soldier says to Terenti, the heretic. "Sinners are boiled in cauldrons and lacerated with hooks for all eternity—and all for a pip-squeak sin. Maybe a hundred years ago he shortchanged a neighbor two kopeks, or stole an old horse collar from a priest back in the time of the Green King, or sinned with a nun one night in May. Is it worth roasting a man in a pan for something so trivial—even for a day or two? For a hundred or two hundred years? For eternity? Forever! A million years! What kind of measure is this? Who made it into a law?"

"Let us suppose God made the law," answers Terenti, the heretic, as if thinking aloud. "But why then is he called perfectly good and all-merciful? And why is he almighty if he brings forth villains and shameless cheats? It's better not to create a scoundrel if you are almighty, and not to shove him into a cauldron for a thousand years for a stolen kopek if you are all-merciful. So it turns out you are neither the one nor the other! That's the fact. You weren't thought up right."

"Where's the truth? And whom are we serving here?" says the soldier.

"This is not the right work for us," agrees the blacksmith, lighting up his pipe. "We'd be better off dragging out a thrice-cursed mass in Paradise for a thousand years."

. . . The Russian peasant kept a pure, warm heart throughout his dark, joyless life in a vale of bitter tears, and it remained unsullied by selfishness or baseness. His heart is still big and beautiful.

And so the peasants of Korezhino are unable to reconcile themselves to the cruel injustice of Hell, even if their situation here—cozy and free of sorrow—felt like home.

It all began with the gypsy.

"Damn you for being so eager, idiots!" says a sinful gypsy to the peasants, as he sticks his head out of a cauldron. "At least the devils spare the firewood, while you clodhoppers go at it as hard as you can."

"Stop sinning, you! What a temper! What are you doing penance for?"

"I'm a horse thief!" groans the gypsy.

"A horse thief, ah-ha? Build up the fire!" The peasants are all agitated. "Men of Korezhino, there's a horse thief here! We need more firewood."

"Vavilo! Get moving! A horse thief has been found!"

"Your Honors!" cries the sinful gypsy, leaning out of the cauldron. "Have a conscience! All I took was three old nags, and for that the devils will boil me in cauldrons for 325 years! A hundred years and more for one nag—where do these prices come from? . . . I was a thief because I was hungry! Tell me, how are you going to feed little gypsies?"

"Well, now, you've really got into it deep, gypsy!" . . .

The peasants start wondering: "Maybe it makes no sense."

"And I'm not the only one, Your Honors!" sorrowfully exclaims the horse thief. "Here next to me is an old woman who's being boiled for four hundred years . . . Filateva, look up! Tell these kind people why you've been cast into the Fiery Furnace."

An old, ancient woman sticks her head out of a cauldron. "I ate forbidden foods during Lent," she mumbles. "Licking sour cream, and sometimes chewing lard—that is my whole sin."

"And how many years have you been boiling in a cauldron, granny?"

"After licking a hot frying pan for a hundred years, I've spent two hundred more being boiled in cauldrons."

"That a lot for some sour cream. It passes belief!" the peasants are in an uproar.

"My case is nothing. We have a young one, here," the old woman says. "Frosska, come on, show your face to the people."

A young woman who has been boiled in the cauldrons bursts into tears.

"What did they get you for, woman?"

"I was made to marry an old man, and I ran straight from the wedding to a young one. The old man salivated and was repulsive."

"And you did the right thing! The right thing, woman!"

"How long have you been suffering for this sin, maiden?"

"Five hundred and twenty years and three months!"

"So that's the situation!" say the peasants.

"It would have been better to love the old man," someone says.

"You don't understand," Saint Mary of Egypt says. "For love, real love, a woman will do anything."

She gives the sinner Frosska a jug of cold water, and adds: "They've been boiling you, a sinner, for five hundred years, and as for me, a saint, I've run away from the Kingdom of Heaven for the sake of love."

"What shall we do, peasants?"

"Put out the fires! Overturn the cauldrons!"

"Wait a minute," the soldier stops the peasants. "You can overturn one cauldron—but there are thousands of them here! . . ."

"Peasants, you should start with the devils. At any rate you could tear off the devils' heads," says a black-bearded giant, popping out of a cauldron.

"And who are you?"

"Stenka Razin! And this is Emelian Pugachev, the peasant tsar!"[9]

"And what did they get you for?"

"For peasants' justice! For choking landlords!"

"God, what is all this about?" sigh the peasants.

"Brother peasant, let me finish smoking," Stenka Razin says, inhaling, and adds, "Three hundred years without a smoke is real hell."

"And who's in those big cauldrons?" the peasants ask him.

"All Tartars, Mohammedans, . . ."

"Many?"

"Every last one!"

"All of them? How is that possible?" the peasants ask, amazed.

"This is the situation," answers Stenka. "Even if you are the holiest of men but your mother is a Tartar, it will follow that your god is Allah and Mohammed—your prophet. And even though you didn't chose them yourself, you cannot escape the Infernal Abyss."

"The children too?"

"Where else are they to go?" asks Stenka.

"But are they guilty?!" the people shout.

"Oh, you miserable clodhoppers," Stenka howls. "Why did you choose to work in the ovens, and assist the devils?"

"Let's go to Satan!" roar the peasants. "But where is the truth?"

Beelzebub is poised over his chessboard, fighting off an attack by the queen, when the hairy peasant troop appears before him. "What more do you want?" bellows the Prince of Darkness as he prepares to move a piece.

"Your Infernal Excellency," says the soldier, "there is no truth in your establishment, only evil. We do not agree to subordinate ourselves to the devils. Our peasant conscience does not allow us to act as executioners."

"I'm not the one who invented Hell," he says in a conciliatory tone, as he moves his knight. "The cunning fathers of the church thought up Hell in order to hoodwink us fools and keep us in submission. I am just a salaried employee; I do not have the right to close down the establishment and I cannot help you in any way . . . Check to the king! . . . I, too, was thought up only in order to engender fear. Check to the king!"

"So what are we to do? What a situation!"

"That's for you to say, Your Honors," laughs Beelzebub. And the devils howl, giggle, and whistle.

The peasants are downcast.

"What a calamity!"

"A calamity!" sighs the heretic Terenti. "We are in a real bind now, peasants!"

"We're trapped: in Paradise we were nearly enlisted with the saints, and in Hell we've turned ourselves into destroyers of souls."

"Think, Private Kuroptev! Think in what way we can save our peasant conscience."

Kuroptev resolutely butts out his cigar, stands, and says: "We are going to pray!"

"Oh, Lord! . . . Is the peasants' misfortune a pit without bottom?"

"We are going to pray!" repeats the soldier and paces about in the Infernal Abyss.

He marks out a small space, just as he once did in Paradise. He paces it, drives in pegs with the butt end of an ax, and runs a rope around the pegs with the assistance of juvenile demons.

The devils ask: "What have you thought up now?"

"I am building a cathedral!" declares the soldier. "A shrine in honor of the Shroud of the Most Holy Mother of God!"

"In honor of the Mother of God? In Hell?" gasp the unclean spirits.

"Have you gone mad? In Heaven you opened a tavern, and in Hell you want to build a church? What will happen to the Infernal Abyss?" shriek the devils.

"That's your affair," snaps the soldier. "We can't do without a church."

He stretches the ropes, hammers in the pegs with the butt end of his ax, and mutters: "With you devils around we turn into beasts. Our minds don't grasp what it is you are doing to the sinners! If we don't watch it, matted pelts will grow over our hearts."

"Without a church we are in a quandary!" the peasants agree. "A clear peasant conscience is our only wealth. If you take that away, what's left? And here there's nothing but cauldrons and bestial deeds."

"In our stupidity we stoked the furnaces."

"Now we'll have to spend a hundred years repenting for these sins. Not having a church is a disaster for us. We shall send for Father Evlampi and his incense burner."

The devils shriek: "A priest? . . . And an incense burner?"

"We'll put things in order here," the angry peasants say in a threatening voice to the devils.

They shove aside some demons who are heating up some frying pans for sinners.

The soldier threateningly inquires: "Which devil got you to heat the pans?"

"We're doing it for sinners, so that they lick them."

"And have you tried to fry pancakes in them?"

"We haven't tried that," admit the demons. "Were pans invented for pancakes?"

"Yes, indeed, you fiends!"

The peasants fidget. "Let's have some batter with yeast and some fat. Where is the fat? A smaller fire! Is it sizzling?—that's what a pancake's for—it's got to sizzle!"

Smoke! The smell of burning! Ten pans turn out ten pancakes at the same time.

Every sinner gets one pancake . . .

Every devil gets two pancakes . . .

The soldier is a renowned pancake maker; he's nimble.

As he puts batter in a sizzling pan he says: "If you've got a hot frying pan, why lick it? Fry pancakes instead."

The peasants are looking into a boiling cauldron at the same time as they give the furnace-stoking devils some intensive instruction: "If you've got a boiling cauldron, what do you put in it?"

"Sinners!" the artless demons answer in chorus like schoolboys.

Kuroptev bursts out: "Fools. The devils are obsessed with sinners."

The unclean spirits are at a loss. "What are you going to do if you have a boiling cauldron?"

"Throw in balls of dough made with pork fat, you foul thing! Or dumplings stuffed with fruit!" roars the smith.

"Or else dumplings stuffed with meat!"

Now the devils have clearly understood. They are furious and scream: "Do you think this is a market? The gourmet section? . . . And that you are going to have pancakes, a cathedral, and a village priest with an incense burner?"

"We won't allow the Infernal Abyss to be defiled. It is our Kingdom!"

"OURS! . . . YOU clodhoppers get out!"

"Where are we supposed to go?" says the soldier, shaking with rage, as he grasps a bespectacled devil by the throat.

The peasants echo: "Where are you chasing us to?"

"Beyond the far mountains!" yell the furious devils.

Here the peasants' patience finally breaks.

They angrily cross themselves and hurl themselves at the devils.

The devils immediately blow up a whirlwind, and it blows the peasants down. The dust of centuries blinds them. And the foul stench overwhelms them.

There is no limit to their rage.

They grab hold of the gaunt devils, and knock their foreheads together. They coil their tails, tie the devils up in pairs, and toss them into the furnaces. They make the sign of the cross over them.

"In the name of the Father and the Son—"

"—And the Holy Ghost!"

"Amen! Amen, foul thing! Amen!"

"Beat the devils! Crush the evil ones!"

The battle rages. Dust, yells, and punches!

"All blow together!" shriek the devils. "Blow!" They all blow, and a new whirlwind knocks down the peasants.

"Fight!" shout the peasants. "Put out the fires! Overturn the cauldrons!"

"Overturn them! Ready, steady, go!" The peasants tip over the cauldrons containing sinners.

They extinguish the furnaces. They throw the red-hot infernal frying pans at the devils' heads.

The vanquished and frightened demons all run in a bunch to Beelzebub, who has just exchanged a rook for a queen, but is uncertain whether his move was the right one.

"Oh, Greatest One!" shout the two hundred voices of the two hundred devils. "Why did you let in the rabble? They're building a cathedral for you. In honor of the Mother of God! Here in Hell! They've sent for a priest with an incense burner. They've opened a factory and are making pots. They are boiling dumplings in the cauldrons. They've made the sign of the cross over us! They're nailing us down with amens!"

They are screeching so wildly that Satan understands nothing. With difficulty he turns away from the chessboard and with one exhalation silences them:

"Speak!" he orders a crooked, decrepit devil with a broken horn and a torn ear.

"The peasants are destroying the Infernal Abyss! They are smashing our institution—" is all the decrepit devil manages to get out when—

There is a great rumble, and the chessboard flies up in the air.

Dust . . . Fire . . . Screeching . . . Fighting . . .

God the Father is listening with delight to the tedious chanting of an assembly of black-faced, utterly boring old men and women. In all the many thousands of years he has not tired of them. He is undiscriminating in his pleasures and amazingly vain!

Of all the living vices in the Universe vanity is the most ridiculous. A sense of superiority or greatness can give rise to a nagging itch, as if something was scratching you on the inside of your rib cage. Praise of any kind, however feeble, takes away this feeling and makes you feel better. But as soon as the hallelujah-singers pause—the itching resumes. It is the same as for an inveterate smoker when he comes to the end of a smoke.

Our old Russian God was incurably sick with vanity.

. . . Just now he is listening with pleasure to a heartrending duet by two antiquated godlies who are tone-deaf. The poison of vanity has dulled his kind heart.

Suddenly, from a cloud at his feet, emerges the head of the Prince of Darkness, Beelzebub, who has escaped from the blows of the peasants.

"Why did you send the peasants to me?"

"Where was I to put them?" the Almighty asks, slyly squinting.

"They have overturned my cauldrons with sinners in them, they are building a cathedral, and they have opened a pottery factory. They will destroy the Infernal Abyss!"

"That's better. Here they plowed over the whole Celestial Isle, and set up a tavern and even a merry-go-round!"

"What are you proposing to do?" asks Satan.

"How should I know?" says God angrily. "They are an unholy force! What can I do with them?"

"You are God. You hold the cards."

"And you are the Devil. You too have cards in your hand. Think. And leave me to my concert!"

"While you are listening to your soloists, cauldrons are being overturned in my establishment," Satan angrily reminds him.

"That's your business!" snaps God.

"We are two ends of one stick," Beelzebub reminds him. "Can Heaven exist without Hell? If they finish off the devils what will happen to you?"

"Of course it is a disaster for me if there are no devils," God agrees. "We are bound by the same rope . . . Go, Satan, go in peace, Satan! . . . Don't disrupt my concert . . . I will punish them!"

God is punishing the insubordinate peasants.

A cloud of poisonous yellow smoke bursts from the Infernal Abyss and carries the peasants up over the Earth . . .

The peasants seem to be suspended in fixed, extremely awkward positions:

some are hanging head down . . .

some are suspended upright . . .

others with limbs wide apart . . .

some with bent legs . . .

others hang any how . . .

the pregnant woman with her cow . . .

and the soldier with his lover.

They are suspended high above the ancient Vladimir Highway.

They hang for a long time and talk to one another apprehensively.

"Think, Terenti, what shall we do?"

"What will be will be . . . We are not meant to have another place in God's world . . . And so we must remain suspended."

The peasants groan, the whole troop of them.

"The only thing we can do," says Terenti, "is to ask Private Kuroptev to go to our God. Let God look at what is happening to the peasants."

"It is past comprehension!"

Go, soldier! Let the Almighty defend us and have mercy on us!"

"I can do that," says Kuroptev. He buttons up his uniform, straightens his cap, and prepares to throw himself from the blue abyss down to Earth.

At the last minute he is overcome with doubt:

"But what can I ask of our God? On Earth there is nowhere for us: the master flogs us to death. Heaven does not suit us. Hell—suits us still less. Say, what can I ask?"

"It seems there is nothing to ask," hums and haws Terenti. "We've been hung out, and so we must hang!"

. . . And so the unholy force remains suspended in winds and storms, waiting for the Last Judgment.

Through the whistling fall winds, many people in the Vladimir area that year heard the peasants' voices, thick with rye bread, praying:

> Our Father, which art in Heaven!
> Hallowed be Thy name. Thy kingdom come.
> Thy will be done, on Earth as it is in Heaven.
> Give us this day our daily bread . . .

The wind tousles their hair.

The slanting autumn rain penetrates them to the bone . . .

"No, it's not yet the Last Judgment!"

And the soldier Kuroptev can stand it no longer.

He tears himself away from the suspended herd, and jumps likes a parachutist from the blue sky down to Earth.

By the road stands the same old chapel.

Here once upon a time God gave the soldier an entry slip for the Kingdom of Heaven. In the chapel still hangs the ancient icon with the dark face of our Russian God.

The soldier falls on his knees before the Almighty and delivers a passionate prayer.

"Lord and Heavenly King! It was absolutely wrong to create the peasants! . . . But since you made that mistake, Lord, and since you did fashion the stinking louts—do assign them somewhere. Set them up somehow, even if their discomforts remain. The people of Korezhino cannot remain suspended in the air. *That* passes comprehension."

"You blockheads, you are like a bone stuck in my throat," God says in anger. "All people behave like people. Everyone is set up—some in Paradise, some on Earth, and the worst ones in Hell. It is only you accursed ones, who are disrupting the order of the Universe."

Unexpectedly, God sobs.

"But you are peasants, God's own children! Soldier, ask anything of me, and I will give it you in my mercy."

"Lord!" Kuroptev exclaims in despair. "What can I ask of you? You yourself can see, Master, we can go neither backward nor forward nor up nor down. Look all round . . ."

"Well, take this." God pronounces. "Go, soldier, to your peasants. Take one another by the hand, stay in a tight pack, and in my mercy I will perform a miracle. I will cast you, blockheads, two hundred years into the past or two hundred years into the future."

"Going back would be bad," says the soldier. "In the old days they flogged us much worse . . . Send us into the future, Almighty!"

"Peace be with you, soldier! Let it be as you say."

. . . As soon as the peasants suspended in the air are gathered in a tight bunch, there is a clap of thunder and flashes of lightning. An invisible force lifts the peasant troop off and carries them through space and time.

Through day and night, storms and bad weather, the woodlands of the taiga, mountains and deserts, through years and decades, the tightly knit bunch of Korezhino peasants flies, screeching.

. . . They readily overtake a dozen nuclear-powered ocean liners, and . . . drop down into a vast field of fabulously rich corn.

The battle to gather in the harvest is on. Extraordinary combine-harvesters move like ships. Thousands of vehicles and machines raise clouds of dust along the roads. A helicopter hovers in the sky. And nearby an unseen monster—a train—rumbles across a bridge.

The eyes of the peasants show fear.

"What next? Tell us Terenti."

"Tell us! What do you think?"

"I think they will take us to the police," says Terence. "And then they will lock us up . . ."

"Where?"

"In jail! Peasants, you must deny everything. We know nothing. We've seen nothing. We are from the other world!"

Fear shows in the peasants' eyes. "We are from the other world!"

And all around, everything is rumbling and rattling, and clouds of dust are thrown up, as in a war.

And just as in a war, one of the trucks gets bogged down in a low, muddy spot nearby the peasants. The wheels spin, and the engine races. The eyes of the suffering driver see the peasant troop.

"Come on, hurry up! What are you waiting for?"

"We are from the other world," the peasants timidly explain. "We are here on an unrelated matter."

"Hurry up, hurry!" shouts the driver. "We'll sort things out afterward."

And the peasants come running. They move the truck out of the bog as if it was a toy, and put it on the road.

"Get in!"

The peasants are flustered. "We're here for an unrelated matter. We are from Korezhino."

"We have no passports because we are from the other world."

The driver gets angry. "So what's the problem. I tell you, Get in. Stop wasting time!"

The driver whisks them across the steppe to the grain elevator. The fresh wind strokes and tousles their beards and unkempt hair, puffs up their homespun shirts, and makes it difficult for them to breathe.

And all around the battle for the grain harvest is rumbling and roaring . . .

"Stop! Stop, I say! . . . Get out!" The brigade leader, standing by the elevator and exhausted after nights without sleeping, gets them down from the truck.

"Your Honor . . . We are from the other world!"

"Come over here. Quick! Distribute the shovels."

"Your Honor, regarding the passports, please sort things out, for God's sake! . . . Sort things out, Your Honor."

"Dear fellows!" the brigade leader almost cries. "When? When can we sort things out? Look at the cloud creeping up. It's going to drop rain on the wheat . . . Hurry up. Let's go to the fourth stack. Run! Follow me!"

He runs with his shovel to the fourth stack.

Behind him the peasant troop come running with their shovels, as if on the attack.

The black cloud creeps across the sky.

Over the great Siberian land the battle for the harvest rages.

The peasants of Korezhino, too, have found their own place in this battle.

They rush to complete the job before the rain. They shovel a huge mountain of wheat and cover it with canvas—the fourth stack . . .

The fact that they come from the other world is of no account. Our kind of people always sort things out!

The peasants' gloomy misfortune is long gone. Even tales about it are heard less and less often!

(dated 1936–73)

1966 conclusion:

God is punishing the insubordinate peasants.

A cloud of poisonous yellow smoke bursts from the Infernal Abyss and carries the peasants up over the Earth . . .

The peasants seem to be suspended in fixed, extremely awkward positions:

some are hanging head down . . .

others with limbs wide apart . . .

some with bent legs . . .

others hang any how . . .

the pregnant woman with her cow . . .

and the soldier with his lover.

They are suspended high above the ancient Vladimir Highway.

They hang for a long time and speak to one another apprehensively.

"Think, Terenti, what shall we do?"

"What will be will be . . . We are not meant to have another place in God's world . . . And so we must remain suspended."

"Oh Lord! . . . For a long time?"

"A long time! . . . Until the Last Judgment!"

"And will it ever take place, this Last Judgment?"

"Maybe yes, and maybe no! . . . Who knows!"

"And in the meantime we're to continue to hang?!"

"Where can we complain?"

"Lord, Lord! . . . Where does our lot lie?"

And so they, the unholy force, continue to hang, buffeted by winds and storms, while they await the Last Judgment, . . .

Through the whistling fall winds, many people in the Vladimir area that year heard the peasants' voices, thick with rye bread, praying:

Our Father, which art in Heaven!
Hallowed be Thy name. Thy kingdom come.
Thy will be done, on Earth as it is in Heaven.
Give us this day our daily bread . . .

The wind tousles their hair.

The slanting autumn rain penetrates them to the bone . . .

"Well, look what our prayers have brought down on us!" says someone speaking with a frightened voice. "Here comes the police captain!"

"All right, peasants, stand fast! This is worse than Hell! . . ."

"Is this the Last Judgment, Vania?" Saint Mary of Egypt fearfully asks the soldier.

"No, this is not yet the Last Judgment!"

Dashing along the Vladimir road comes a jaunty, mustachioed police captain. 'Whoa!!" . . .

The coachman reins in the horses when they are underneath the peasants.

The policeman jumps out of the carriage, cranes his head back, grows furious when he identifies the Korezhino rebels, and roars:

"What are you up to? . . . Rebelling? And leaving the landlord to swell up from hunger and die! . . . the fields are unplowed and unseeded, and you, what are you doing, eh? . . . What are you up to, idlers? I'll get you! . . . I want one Cossack company, right now!"

A Cossack company appears . . .

"Now is this the Last Judgment, Vania?" fearfully whispers Saint Mary of Egypt to the soldier Kuroptev.

"No, not yet! . . . Fear not, Masha!"

Horsemen with forelocks and shaved heads catch the peasants with lassos and bring them all down to earth.

Only the soldier and his lover escape. The dashing Cossacks of the Don could not get him with their lassos . . .

The captured peasants are driven into a herd, surrounded by escorts, and driven along the Vladimir Highway, the Road of Russian Suffering . . .

Clouds are driven by the wind. The day seems to be dying . . .

An autumnal drizzle begins. It covers the black earth and the wet highway with a gray shroud.

And it looks as though the herd of Korezhino rebels, under the escort of forelocked horsemen, has dissolved into this shroud.

By the road the same ancient chapel still stands. Here, once upon a time, the soldier Kuroptev obtained from God himself—on the basis of their acquaintance—an admission pass to the Kingdom of Heaven.

Now he has returned here with his Mashenka.

He places his sweetheart on the grass, covers her with a new soldier's coat, gently strokes her hair, sits down, and, taking his time, starts rolling a cigar . . .

In the chapel there is still the same ancient icon with the dark face of the bearded God . . .

And God is moved when he sees the faithful love of the soldier, his tender care for the woman, whom he, the soldier, had torn free from the assembly of saints, from under the nose of the vigilant archangels and the whole of the heavenly militant host.

"You are a just man, Kuroptev!" God cannot help exclaiming. "I bless your love!"

"What does your blessing amount to?" the soldier skeptically says, shrugging his shoulders. "It's meaningless!"

"But I am God!" the Almighty says indignantly. "I am judge for all eternity! . . . How dare you not recognize me? . . . For you, you, know, I . . ."

While shouting, he almost topples out of the icon, and his old tin halo falls with a clatter onto the floor of the chapel."

The soldier gives him back his halo and smirks:

"What can you do with me?"

"Send you . . . to the Fiery Furnace."

"Been there!" . . .

"Send you . . . to Paradise!"

"Been there!" . . .

"I'll . . . suspend you in the air!"

"Done that!" . . .

"I'll hurl thunderbolts!"

"We've had thunderbolts!" . . .

"I b-beg you!" says God, suddenly bursting into tears. "Stop being rude! . . . Whatever the truth about me may be, I am worshipped . . . Don't be rude: I was thought up this way, to be almighty! . . . I can do nothing about it!" . . .

"Say so then, that you can do nothing!"

"I can do nothing!" says God, and droops.

"Oh, Vania, look!" says Mary of Egypt. "Why has the sky turned red over there?"

Dawn blazes over the Vladimir Highway.

"Here, now, is the Last Judgment!" says the soldier, rising. "It's time to go, Masha!"

And they vanish.

The old God has almost climbed out of the icon in order to look at the dawn.

Some people were running away from it.

His pants falling down, Tsar Nicholas II is in headlong flight.

"What's going on?" shouts God, on the point of tumbling out of the icon.

"The Last Judgment!" sobs one of the anointed, who then escapes.

The Supreme Commander[10] is fleeing.

"Stop! Who are you?"

"Kerensky, the Supreme Commander!"

"What's going on?"

"The Last Judgment!"

"And who are the judges?" cries God. "Who are the judges?"

But the "Supreme Commander" has no time for God.

"Comrades, comrades!" he shouts, as he runs off. "That's not the way to do it!"

Kerensky vanishes, too.

Gathered up in a ball, merchants, rich men, factory owners, and other abusers of the people roll past . . .

A red whirlwind sweeps them away like autumn leaves . . .

The workers brigades begin their difficult march.

In their hands they hold rifles. In their ranks we see the Korezhino peasants.

Some are still in sackcloth, while others are in singed soldiers' smocks and coats.

Facing them are Cossack companies, pale officers, and cannons.

The cannons fire at the workers brigades.

One cannon blast, another one, and a third . . .

The third blast happens to hit the chapel . . .

Perplexedly the Almighty gathers up his knocked-off halo and stands, not knowing what more to do . . .

With difficulty the old Russian God squeezes into the entrance of a peasant hut . . . Here he is squeezed! . . . On his right is Gagarin, and on the left, Tereshkova, and below, the heavenly brothers Nikolaev and Popovich.[11]

And it is not clear for whom the icon lamp is lit—whether for the cosmonauts, or for the Jesus Ascending Into Heaven on the old icon . . .

Outside the window there are explosions! . . .

Outside the window a gigantic new building is going up. Explosions are blasting mountains into the air. Huge rocks are flying.

13 "Gogol"

(1941)[1]

Tale, as told by a Moscow police sergeant

If you happen to be in Moscow, do drop in to see us in Division 24 in the Arbat. There you'll meet Fedoseev, who got the story straight from Larikov. And why would Larikov tell a falsehood after being stationed on Arbat Square for sixteen years? Considering, too, he doesn't drink even on his own name day, and never once lied from the day he was born.

And anyway, Citizen, sir, why are you bothered over whether or not this is a true story? It's not you I was telling it to, but rather this citizen here, a woman from Rostov, who does indeed believe me, as you can tell from the look in her eyes!

Come, Madam Citizen, it will be better if we go somewhere else! . . . With some people it's useless! . . . Their big-city manners and sour look can poison the atmosphere for a whole week even in a vacation resort! Both at work and on the beach, the same oppressive thought buoys them up: "I am better than anyone else! And more intelligent! . . ." A man of this kind takes this thought with him to the theater, the steam bath, and to bed! He'll die without having noticed all the good and real people he has elbowed aside!

Come over here, Madam Citizen! . . . I don't like that sort of people! Let them blow themselves up with a sense of their self-importance. Let their itching sense of superiority consume them!

In any case, the future doesn't belong to them, and so why shouldn't you and I take a walk down to the beach?

. . . All the same, the story the police sergeant told here is a strange one! If you do in fact come to Moscow, don't go to Division 24 in the Arbat and don't look for Fedoseev. Fedoseev must have lied when he repeated Larikov's tale, and I don't trust Larikov any more than I trust that sergeant! For that matter, there's no way even I could reconstruct what happened without some inventions of my own.

When the dawn blazes over the Kremlin in July, a short period of silence descends on Moscow.

The clatter of the streetcars and trucks suddenly seems to break off, the streets grow empty, for a moment the town seems to fall asleep.

In the morning twilight the town squares slumber, the streets are silent, the boulevards are asleep.

High up on his pedestal, Gogol's bronze statue silently perches and listens to the stillness.

An aged caretaker comes out with his broom and lazily passes it to and fro over the dusty ground at the foot of the monument. A pink puff of dust coils up like incense, slowly and gently in the still air.

Then, suddenly . . .

Suddenly, Gogol slowly rises up on his pedestal, lazily stretches his limbs, and says in a soft, Ukrainian, tenor voice:

"Oh, God! . . . Sitting here is so boring!"

The old man is stupefied. He stops sweeping and fearfully looks asquint at the monument. With shaking hands he reaches for a birch-wood snuffbox, but as soon as he gathers a pinch of snuff to shove into his wide nostrils, Gogol politely bows and gently says:

"May I ask you for a favor, sir? It's been a long time since I have had some Kremenchuk tobacco!"

With chattering teeth, the old man holds up the snuffbox to Gogol.

"No, dear sir! . . . ," exclaims Gogol. "Please don't go to any trouble. It will be better if I climb down to the ground."

He puts himself in a position to climb down.

At this point, the terrified old man lays the snuffbox on the ground, grabs his broom, and, shaking with fear, runs away.

The bronze Gogol climbs down from the pedestal . . .

. . . For sixteen and a half years, policeman Larikov had been stationed at Arbat Square. His shifts on duty had always been uneventful. But now Larikov looks in the direction of Gogol Boulevard and starts to feel strange:

The bronze Gogol flourishes his cloak and jumps from the pedestal onto the ground.

The policeman blows his whistle in a panic and runs toward the boulevard.

Nikolai Vasilevich Gogol sits down on the steps of his monument, stuffs his nose with a good pinch of snuff, and—oh, with what delight!—he sneezes . . .

Panting in agitation and with an awkward salute, police officer Larikov nervously babbles:

"Come on, enough of this! Please go back to where you belong, Nikolai Vasilevich! Otherwise, we'll be in a mess."

Gogol grows angry:

"What nonsense! . . . Sir, you wouldn't last three days on that rock, while I have been stuck on it for fifty years[2] without moving the least little bit! . . ."

"Order, please!" Larikov passionately pleads. "I love you, Nikolai Vasilevich! I've read *Taras Bulba* three times. And *Mirgorod* and *Dead Souls*. I rate *The Inspector General* higher than Shakespeare! . . . But please, let's get back in position."

"No, No!" Gogol angrily says. "Dear sir, there's no way you will persuade me to do so . . . I won't climb up there . . . I've done my stint there!"

"Why, Nikolai Vasilevich," Larikov says, almost crying, "I've an unblemished record of sixteen-years service in the police! I've been awarded a trip to the resort at Gagry in recognition of my being the best Stakhanovite Worker[3] in Division 24! . . . Nikolai Vasilevich, please understand!"

"Sir!" Gogol begs. "Allow me to wander about for just one day! . . ."

"I cannot allow it, no, I cannot!" Larikov says feelingly. "What would this mean? We are in close contention with Division 18, and Vasichkin himself will start giggling! . . . And indeed, why shouldn't he giggle if Division 24 allows Gogol to be taken away from the boulevard! . . . Get back up, please! . . . Stop your disruption of order! . . ."

"No, no, I don't want to," insists Gogol.

Larikov grows angry:

"I am an elderly man! My son is a lieutenant in the air force who was awarded a star in the battles against the Fascists. As a father I have no right to bring shame on the head of a man who has a medal! . . . Come on, please stop, or I will phone the division, and then things will take a turn for the worse! . . ."

"Well, let them take a turn for the worse, but I am not climbing up there!" sighs Gogol.

The discomfited police officer runs off to phone the division.

Moscow is still asleep. The chimes on the Spaskaia Tower ring four times.

An empty doorway to a club, with a rather tattered sign:

Today in the club the young playwright
Serafim Kotenkov will give a reading of his new play "The School of Humility"

In the lobby of the club an exhausted young man is reading the conclusion of the play:

"The Stakhanovite men shake hands with the Stakhanovite women. A loud 'Hurrah!' Curtain. The End! . . ."

His words resonate in a completely empty hall.

A red-haired youth, the one, lone listener, is humbly sitting off to one side.

"Where is everybody?" the dramatist babbles, suddenly noticing the empty hall.

"You read the whole night long, and the people left a long time ago in order to sleep!" meekly says the youth.

Serafim Kotenkov feels sad:

"Thirty plays, thirty failures! . . . One can't look to one's contemporaries for understanding. Pushkin had to pass through this! . . . But just as Pushkin devotees appeared, so Serafim Kotenkov will have his Kotenkov devotees! . . . And maybe the best of my plays, 'The School of Humility,' will shine like a star! . . . Your interest in my play, young man, serves as a pledge of success for me! For you stayed, didn't you?"

"You were sitting on top of my cap the whole night long!" the youth awkwardly confesses, and blushes.

Surprised, Kotenkov extracts the crumpled cap from underneath him. The youth grabs it and rushes for the exit.

Distraught, Kotenkov trudges along the boulevard.

Gogol rises to meet him and says, "Dear sir, I call on you to help me!"

"Gogol!" exclaims Kotenkov. "Aleksandr Sergeevich[4] Gogol! . . ."

"Excuse me," Gogol corrects him, "I was always called Nikolai Vasilevich! . . . but that is of no importance! . . . Whoever you are, sir, I beg you to take my place on this pedestal for just one day! . . . I implore you!"

Kotenkov reaches for his glasses. He puts them on and methodically sizes up the pedestal, then says:

"Well, to be truthful I have no right to refuse your request! Shakespeare had *Hamlet*, you had *The Inspector General*, and I have 'The School of Humility.' Aren't these the best theatrical works that the creative genius of man has produced? . . . Help me up!"

Gogol readily lifts the vainglorious youth onto the pedestal. He tosses him his bronze cloak and hurries down the steps to Arbat Square.

Almost at once, a shiny, new ZIS limousine runs into him.

Its fender noisily scrapes the bronze metal. The car sharply brakes. A girl jumps out of the chauffeur's compartment and angrily turns on Gogol:

"What are you doing, eh? . . . You are a monument, and you want to throw yourself under the wheels of a car? What if you'd smashed my radiator?"

"Excuse me, madam, in truth I am not to blame!" Gogol nervously says. "Your extraordinary tarantass[5] was galloping along without horses, and to be honest, this is something I am not used to, miss! . . ."

"Madam, or milady!" says the girl, making fun of him and laughing! "All right, then! . . . I am in a big hurry, and have no time for surprises! . . . Sit down, Nikolai Vasilevich, in this 'tarantass'! . . . And I will take you for a ride! . . ."

Gogol climbs into the car. The door closes, and the ZIS smoothly moves away.

Putting on Gogol's cloak, Kotenkov arranges himself as comfortably as possible on the pedestal, inclines his head in imitation of Gogol, and strange as it may be, begins to look like Gogol.

When the agitated police officer Larikov runs up to the monument, after raising a huge alarm in the police station, he doesn't notice the substitution: Gogol is in his usual spot, immobile and silent in the usual manner. The police officer has a feverish fit:

"Now then!" he wails in his fright. "Why have you returned to your place, Nikolai Vasilevich?! . . . I have given the alarm; the Comrade Superintendent is on his way to sort things out! . . . I won't be believed! . . . They'll think I am crazy! . . . Please, come down to earth! . . . Please, let's do climb down! . . ."

Alas, Gogol is silent! As if it wasn't him that had been so eager to get off the pedestal. And when the superintendent accompanied by two policemen leaps out of a car, Larikov knows he will not be believed.

"Comrade Superintendent of Division 24," he moans, almost losing consciousness, "do with me what you want, but he really did jump down to the ground! . . . I can swear to this, Comrade Superintendent! . . . I can fetch Vasichkin from Division 18 to make sure he won't dare to laugh at our division because of a false alarm! . . ."

To the superintendent it is obvious that the good police officer Larikov has lost his mind.

"I don't yet know, Comrade Larikov, what we shall do with you!" he angrily says. "For Vasichkin it will of course be very funny when he snatches the first place for us with the help of the writer Gogol! . . . As for you, I should send you to the Kanatchikova clinic[6] for lunatics! . . ."

"That's what I need, Comrade Superintendent!" sighs Larikov. "I shall be happy if the clinic finds me insane so that Vasichkin doesn't dare to chalk up a false alarm in order to defeat us! . . . Nikolai Vasilevich! you are an unrelenting prankster! When you were alive, you thought of fiendish inventions, which still make people's eyes pop out today, and just now you've played a trick on an old man! . . ."

Here Gogol's substitute Serafim Kotenkov suddenly sneezes.

The policemen rush to the monument.

Kotenkov meets their inquisitive gaze with haughty indifference.

"Comrade Superintendent!" anxiously whispers Larikov. "Allow me to report that this is not Gogol! . . . Nikolai Vasilevich's nose looks like a nose, but what we have here is not a nose, but, excuse me, some sort of a button!"

The policemen and Kotenkov take each other's measure with their eyes, until at last the young dramaturgist is embarrassed and starts to climb down from the pedestal.

"Sit!" imperiously commands the superintendent, pinning him in his position. "Who are you and how did you get here?"

"I am Serafim Kotenkov," the youth guiltily answers. "You see, the thing is I wrote a play 'The School of Humility' . . . Well then . . . It's Gogol himself who installed me here. He asked me to sit here for twenty-four hours until he returned . . . But I'd better come down!"

"Sit!" sternly commands the superintendent. "You'll have to remain sitting until we find the statue. You, Larikov, stay here and do everything possible to prevent any kind of damaging scandal! . . . No one on the boulevard must notice this strange substitution! . . . As for you, Citizen Kotenkov, I urgently request you to forget that you are still a living man, or else your longing for immortality will have unpleasant consequences! . . ."

Kotenkov cringes. He wants to protest, but yields.

"I will say just one thing, Citizen: the results of the competition with Division 18 are of concern to us. May the holy powers of a scrambled egg preserve you if you mess up our records! . . . Don't you dare to breathe!"

And what about Gogol?

Somewhere far away from Moscow a shiny ZIS car stops on a paved road.

Nikolai Vasilevich Gogol emerges from the car and excitedly says:

"Madam! . . . I lack the words to describe what I have seen! . . . My God! . . . Not even a century has gone by, but how Russia has been transformed! . . . Not one of my contemporaries was able to sketch a picture of the magnificent life that you, our happy descendants, enjoy! . . . What will things look like in fifty years, or a hundred? . . . Where does this movement end? . . . I thank you, madam, I thank you! . . ."

Gogol bows down low and follows the speeding car with his gaze for a long time.

The day turns out to be a hot one.

On days like this we have lots of people out on the boulevard.

There are nannies and infants, the always-in-a-rush Muscovites, people here on assignment, and some last relics of the Russian Empire—the eternal old women and their dogs with variegated coats of hair, as well as assorted visiting folk.

Serafim Kotenkov is suffering on the pedestal, in continual fear of exposure and the scandal that would ensue.

Meanwhile, police officer Larikov is pouring gobs of sweat. He selflessly spares the youth countless dangers . . .

First, there are two boys with upturned faces who are looking with surprise at the snub-nosed fellow who has taken the place of Gogol. Larikov has to distract them by showing them his prize watch.

Next comes a solid citizen from the category of visitors. He starts reading the inscriptions on the pedestal. The only thing Larikov can think up is to ask him for a cigarette.

Then an old lady with a dog suddenly pulls out a pair of old-fashioned glasses, obviously intending to study the expression of the great writer. Larikov carefully provokes the old lady's dog, which starts hysterically barking and drags its mistress off in pursuit of the trickster . . .

Each new danger throws Serafim Kotenkov into a fit of shivers. At moments he despairs and is on the point of running away, but each time the implacable police officer Larikov threatens him with his finger and hisses:

"Stay sitting! . . ."

Yes, dear Comrade! You are sitting at home and reading these lines, and the distress of the unhappy youth may seem trivial and unimportant to you. But imagine just for a minute that you have no table or lamp beside you, and no sweet wife, and that at your feet you have a noisy, crowded Moscow boulevard, while you are sitting on a pedestal and shamelessly impersonating a great writer, and that people seen from above look short, nasty, and dangerous, because you are afraid of the painful moment when they will find you out and expose you, and laugh at you without mercy till tears come to their eyes, all because of your stupid vanity . . .

Accordingly, if you are ever consumed by a longing for immortal fame and things are not moving as fast as you would like, you must never forget Kotenkov's bitter experience and always remember that the best and universal attribute of a great man is modesty.

Let us pity Serafim Kotenkov, the author of thirty unsuccessful plays, and let's dispense with judging him harshly if only because he now faces a catastrophe . . .

The catastrophe comes in the form of Vasichkin, that is to say, the man before whom quakes a whole Moscow police division, starting with the superintendent.

This is hardly surprising! This Vasichkin is short, unsophisticated, and unprepossessing. Little, piercing eyes flicker in his pockmarked peasant face. His uniform fits him like a sack, and under his arm he holds a worn cardboard folder.

Vasichkin's folder has an awful power because he is the recognized record-keeper for the competition, and nobody is better than him in digging out almost invisible defects and deeply buried merits in the difficult work of a policeman.

He rises up before the monument as if out of the ground, and Larikov turns pale, understanding at once that all is lost.

"Comrade Vasichkin! . . . Comrade Vasichkin!" he stammers, shaking his tormenter's arm and trying to divert his attention from the monument.

But to draw Vasichkin away is not possible.

He easily frees himself from Larikov, goes up to the monument, and fixes his piercing little eyes on the face of the confounded Kotenkov, and venomously asks:

"Are you sitting?"

"Yes, sitting!" moans the young man.

"Well, Brother Larikov, have they made off with a whole statue of yours?" asks Vasichkin, with a poisonous smirk. "Today they have made off with Gogol, tomorrow they will make off with a pharmacy . . . Who is it was supposed to be on duty?"

Larikov starts to feel queasy.

He blinks rapidly and repeatedly, chokes, and bursts into tears.

A dusty cart-track gets lost in vast expanses of golden wheat.

Nikolai Vasilevich is standing in the road and is looking spellbound up at the sky, where a silver plane is sailing into the distance.

An open Gazik all-terrain vehicle is kicking up a cloud of dust on the cart-track.

"Hey there, friend!" a fat man shouts from the vehicle to Gogol. "If you need a ride to the fair at Sorochinsk,[7] take a seat. We'll drive you! . . ."

"I thank you!" gladly answers Gogol. "I will go to the fair at Sorochinsk with the greatest pleasure!"

He sits next to the driver, and the vehicle travels between high walls of wheat.

Behind Gogol's back, two crafty, fat men bouncing up and down on the seats are engaged in animated conversation:

"You've got wonderful wheat, Ivan Ivanovich! . . . Yes, masses of it. What grain! . . . More like peas! navy beans! walnuts rather than wheat grains! . . ."

"I thank you for your kind words, Ivan Nikiforovich!"[8]

"Would you let us have two tons of it, Ivan Ivanovich?"

"Why not, Ivan Nikiforovich? We'll give you the wheat, and you give us the stallion."

"What the devil, Ivan Ivanovich! How can you ask for the stallion? . . ."

"What do you mean, 'What the devil?' Besides the wheat I'll give you the fat pig . . ."

"You and your fat pig can go and get lost! . . . The kolkhoz is worth millions, and our president is another Pliushkin![9] . . ."

"And you, Ivan Nikiforovich, aren't you a millionaire? . . . You should be ashamed of holding on to that stallion! . . . You have five of them! . . . There'll be no wheat for you!"

"And no stallion for you! . . . You can go and kiss your pig, Ivan Ivanovich! I don't want to know you! . . . At the district meeting I'll say things about your kolkhoz . . ."

"And what is it you will say about our kolkhoz, Ivan Nikiforovich?"

"Aha! Confound you! Ivan Ivanovich!"

And I say: "Confound you, Ivan Nikiforovich! You are a nasty man! . . ."

They spit, sulk, and turn away from one another.

But suddenly Ivan Ivanovich discovers that the passenger sitting next to the driver is made of bronze.

He looks closely at the back of the passenger's head and is surprised: indeed, it is made of bronze.

He flicks his fingers on the sleeve of Gogol's frock coat: it rings like metal.

"Eh, friend!" whispers Ivan Nikiforovich in surprise, and nudges his neighbor with his elbow.

Once again he flicks his fingers on the bronze: it rings!

"What devilry!" whispers Ivan Nikiforovich and gives Ivan Ivanovich a frightened glance.

"Hey, dear fellow," shouts Ivan Ivanovich, grabbing hold of Gogol's sleeve, "you are not real! . . . Say, who are you? Why do you ring like a bell?"

"Who has dispatched you here?"

Turning toward them, Gogol gently says:

"I venture to assure you, kind sirs, that I am no less surprised than you to find myself meeting literary personages imagined by me in a very different time . . . And you may believe me, kind sirs, that the pleasing vitality of your characters is bound to flatter the vanity of a humble author . . ."

"Who are you?" shouts Ivan Nikiforovich, who understands nothing of what the writer has said.

"Allow me to introduce myself. I am Gogol, Nikolai Vasilevich Gogol! . . ."

The fat men jump up in the car:

"How can you be . . . Gogol?" shouts Ivan Ivanovich.

"Why are you . . . Gogol?" exclaims Ivan Nikiforovich.

"Well, that's the way it is . . . Gogol!" sighs Nikolai Vasilevich. "I look like a monument, but if you look more closely I am not a monument at all!"

"A monument?" joyfully shouts Ivan Nikiforovich. "Well then we will set you up in the town square!"

"The devil knows what you are saying, Ivan Nikiforovich!" protests the writer. "You have erected a monument to Taras Shevchenko!"[10]

"Shevchenko is Shevchenko, while Gogol is Gogol! . . . Please don't object, Ivan Ivanovich, it is essential for us to have another monument! . . ."

"You want to have two monuments, while there is not even one monument in our famous kolkhoz, which is named after Comrade Budenny![11] . . . Have you seen such a thing, Ivan Nikiforovich? . . ."

"Aha! . . . So you are giving me the finger, Ivan Ivanovich?"

"No, not the finger, but the V sign! . . ."

"It's all the same, Ivan Ivanovich, whether it's a finger or a V sign. After this I cannot go to the market with you! I'll have to go back on foot, so that I can prepare a report for the District Committee . . ."

Ivan Ivanovich runs after Ivan Nikiforovich.

"What kind of a report?"

"This kind: that you took two of my foremen. And now you want to take Gogol!"

"And why did we set up a projection system for you when we brought you a sound film?"

"That involved a film, but this is a monument to Gogol! . . . We are the most important kolkhoz!"

"Whatever your wishes, Ivan Ivanovich, I will install Gogol in our kolkhoz!"

"You lie! . . . The Gogol monument shall stand in our kolkhoz, and you and I, Ivan Nikiforovich, will jointly choose the place where it will stand! . . ."

"We shall have the monument!"

"No, we shall!"

"We shall!"

"No, we shall!"

Gogol smirks as he follows them with his eyes, and walks away, sighing:

"Good luck to you, Ivan Ivanovich! . . . And to you, Ivan Nikiforovich! And why did I create you?"

The blue sky suddenly hums with a loud, droning sound.

Two blunt-nosed red birds fly toward one another, and in the heavens there begins a show that Gogol could never have imagined.

The astonished Nikolai Vasilevich sits down on an old birch stump, and cannot detach his eyes from a strange duel of extraordinary airplanes.

They pursue each other, fall, slide, rise up with a roar, only to hurl themselves down almost to the ground.

But Gogol's attention is drawn by an even-more-amazing spectacle. From a dark forest a cloud of airplanes rises up with a roar. And it's as if they are peppering the sky: thousands of dots tear away from them and hurl downward.

And suddenly the immense sky blossoms with thousands of different flowers.

Nikolai Vasilevich even stands up because the spectacle of the airborne operation is so amazing.

It would seem that there could be nothing more remarkable. However, the ground beneath Gogol suddenly shakes and rises up in the air along with the birch stump.

The snouts of menacing machines are seen from below.

They flash fire and roar with such strength that Nikolai Vasilevich reels, and he rushes away.

He heads for a copse of young birch trees standing nearby on the bank of a river.

And as if to finish off amazing this man of bronze totally and for all time, the woods suddenly roar, stir, and sway; little birch trees fall down; and a hundred extraordinary rapid tanks rush forward.

Like fleas they jump over a trench, go down to the water, and swim, like a flock of geese . . .

"Comrade Lieutenant-General, a bronze man has been arrested on the training grounds of the regiment entrusted to me. He persists in saying that he is the writer Gogol. The arrestee is here, with me."

"Bring him in!" orders the Lieutenant-General.

And Gogol is led into the tent of the general.

"It's all your fault, Ivan Nikiforovich!" says the fat man almost in tears to his friend, as he gets into the car. "Drive on! . . . You wanted two monuments, and he slipped away."

"Look, stop your lamentations, Ivan Ivanovich! . . ."

"It's always the same with you! . . . You make a hopeless mess, and then you want to calm me down . . . And he was made of bronze!"

"Stop your lamentations, Ivan Ivanovich! . . . Take my stallion: our kolkhoz won't be the poorer for it."

"Why? Do you imagine that our kolkhoz will be the poorer if we let you have some wheat? . . . Take three tons of it, and the big pig, and on top of that the Rambouillet ram! Blast you! . . ."

"I won't take your Rambouillet . . . Later you will say we did you a favor."

"You are so quarrelsome, by gad!"

"You are the quarrelsome one, Ivan Ivanovich! . . . The devil knows what kind of a man you are!"

"What do you mean, the devil only knows?"

"Well, it's obvious! . . . I've been observing you for thirty years, and I can see that you are truly an unbearable man!"

"How dare you say such things?"

"Because I do! . . ."

Gogol is sitting in the general's tent.

The Lieutenant-General says to him:

"You must understand, Nikolai Vasilevich, it is an awkward situation . . . The center of the capital . . . An unoccupied monument . . . In truth, you ought to return to your place! . . . You can give a performance at our amateurs' night, and then I will give you an airplane, and you will be in Moscow before dawn! . . ."

"All right, then!" sighs Nikolai Vasilevich. "But, God! . . . I'd like to live with you! . . ."

A new dawn is blazing above the old Kremlin.

Once again the streets are empty and silent.

Once more the old caretaker emerges from the gates with a broom and a dustpan.

As usual, he stuffs a good pinch of tobacco up his nose, and he is just about to sneeze in the empty street, when he sees Gogol coming toward him.

The old man reels and leans against a wall, his knees give way, and he gently slides down onto the pavement, still clutching the broom.

On top of the pedestal the sleeping Kotenkov is blissfully snoring.

On the boulevard Vasichkin is walking away from the monument. The police officer Larikov catches up with him:

"Comrade Vasichkin, be a father to me! . . ." he beseeches. "Wait one hour! . . . It is quite a business, isn't it? I implore you, Vasichkin! . . . Gogol isn't the kind of man who would deceive a policeman! . . . You'll see, he will return!"

At this time Gogol is already standing at the base of the monument.

Joyfully sobbing, Kotenkov hurries to climb down. He is afraid of falling, and gropes with his feet for a perch. With a nervous stammer he says:

"Eh, Nikolai Vasilevich! . . . This immortality is not worth a damn! . . . I nearly died of fright! . . . Climb up quickly! And here this Vasichkin is sticking his nose in! . . . It's terrible!"

Climbing into his place, Gogol excitedly says:

"Go to Sorochinsk! . . . You must go to Sorochinsk, my friend! . . . You will see things there that you could never imagine! . . . What devil draws you to this hateful rock? . . . The important thing is to live! . . . Do go to Sorochinsk! . . ."

"No, I want my mommy!" mutters the youth, as he runs off.

Upon seeing the youth escape, Larikov whistles in a panic, and he and Vasichkin pursue him.

As they run past the monument, they suddenly see that Gogol is back in position.

Gogol is in his place. All traces of life have disappeared from his bronze face, and it exudes the usual sad pensiveness.

Joyfully saluting him, the policeman Larikov pronounces with a trembling voice:

"I thank you, Nikolai Vasilevich! . . . I told him you would return! Each of us has his own place assigned to him: your place, you great joker, is to be on a pedestal, and mine is to stand in a town square, but both of us will serve as worthy ornaments of the beautiful capital!"

The contented Larikov marches away, without even looking at Vasichkin.

8.1.41

Moscow

Satire—a Militant Art

14 The Elation of Fighting[1]

(ca. 1985)

With the advent of Soviet power, which was without precedent, filmmakers were faced with distinctive new challenges. Political film superseded the impoverished "art of illusion."[2] It led to powerful, far-reaching artistic experiments involving the Five-Year Plans and the life of the people.[3]

When I turned to filmmaking, I was fortunate to have acquired some very relevant experience as a political worker in the Red Army. My little stage company for soldiers, and the things I did in it, had served as an invaluable laboratory for comedy, satire, and experiments with the grotesque.

Those were happy days, when you could come to a new juncture and take any artistic path you wished. My experience emboldened me to go down the road of satire, which I had explored . . .

"There's elation in fighting!" This became my motto. I lived my life in a state of military preparedness. During the whole sixty years of my life in film, I tackled all sorts of things, from primitive newsreels and satirical "pamphlets" to big satirical comedies, as in *Happiness* and "The Unholy Force."

I cannot say that I have been spoiled by artistic success. My path was a thorny one. There were many mistakes. There was vexatious interference, with any miscalculation becoming a pretext for major trouble. And even a major success was generally passed over as an accident.

I will devote a few words to this subject.

My arrival in film was met with general hostility.

At the time I presented my first satirical comedies[4] to my colleagues for consideration, Anatoli Lunacharsky[5] gave a speech in which he said:

> These comedies have given rise to sentiments of uneasiness and spite, and this points to a familiar and ugly truth: film workers are not necessarily filled with comradely feelings toward one another.
>
> Political accusations are being dumped on Comrade Medvedkin. In actual fact the aim of his comedies is splendid, and their feelings

> are utterly pure and Communistic. . . . We shall prove ourselves horrible managers of our affairs if we drive such an original artist off the open highway and force him into a cranny somewhere. If we are going to "work over" every pioneer in this way because of his mistakes, then everyone will be afraid of originality—and that will be the end of creativity. If this comes about we ought to be scattered in the wind, for this sort of attitude is a dead end for art.[6]

These words were spoken almost sixty years ago.

And strange to say: Anatoli Lunacharsky spoke like a prophet foreseeing my road to Calvary. I suffer from an enduring, bitter sense of injustice, in spite of some great victories I have celebrated.

My best film, *Happiness*, was scarcely shown to Soviet spectators. Every single copy of the film,[7] including the negative, was stripped. Not a single kind word—nor a word of condemnation—was published about the film in our press. Only one voice spoke out in this deafening silence, Sergei Eisenstein's. He was shaken by *Happiness*. He spoke about it in lectures at VGIK and wrote an excited review at the same time.[8] It was published only thirty-five years later, with the caveat "Part of the text is missing."

Here we make a further caveat: what follows are only some excerpts from the review.

> Just now—today—I have seen our laughter on the screen. And for the second time in just five days I am driven to exclaim with enthusiasm over yet another achievement of our cinema.
>
> Today I saw Mededkin's comedy, *Happiness*, and to use the common expression, I cannot remain silent.
>
> Today I saw how a Bolshevik laughs.
>
> One may begin a comedy with the declaration that Chaplin has no part in it. And it will indeed turn out that Chaplin has no part in it.[9]
>
> But one may also make a comedy without thinking about Charlie, and it will turn out that he is in it.
>
> Not Chaplin himself, nor something borrowed from him. But Chaplin as an indication of magnitude, as a basis for reference, as something profoundly specific.
>
> Chaplin "in a new quality."

It was only thirty-five years later [i.e., after the making of the film] that some progressive filmmakers led by Chris Marker dug up an accidentally preserved copy of *Happiness* in Brussels,[10] and organized an extraordinarily triumphant premiere for the film in Paris. They sent me a packet of enthusiastic reviews from newspapers of all different political leanings, and the film made its way to the leading television stations on every continent.

In spite of this, I failed in my attempts to show *Happiness* on screens here at home, even in film retrospectives. This helped me to appreciate the perspicacity of Lunacharsky, who at the very beginning understood my thorny road to Calvary in the pathways of satirical film.

Everything that happened with *Happiness* had also occurred with the Kino-Train. GUK [the Main Directorate of Film] openly opposed the creation of a traveling kino-factory that was meant to serve as a weapon for the First Five-Year Plan. We were helped only by the intervention of higher authorities.[11] But even after this the persons heading GUK blocked the publication of every single positive assessment by journalists who had formed a high opinion of our work on the front lines of the First Five-Year Plan.

Accordingly, during the whole year of work of the Kino-Train not a single line was written, even about our real achievements. Surely it is not true that GUK was justified in regarding our Kino-Train as a costly adventure.

Here are some documents and some testimonies.

In Paris Chris Marker shows, along with *Happiness*, his documentary *The Train Rolls On*,[12] showing it, moreover, in commercial distribution. In Paris, Argentina, and Mexico books have been published about the train. Articles have been published in different countries and in different languages. And as I have already said, the train has paved the way for the creation of independent studios and groups working with genres and forms of film they have borrowed from us, from a country far removed from the capitalist order of society.

I paid a high price to defend my right to make satire, and I could report to Lunacharsky that the attempt to "hole me up" did not succeed, in spite of the many enemies and the waste of my productive time, which I think adds up to several decades.

I needed to remain in a fit condition to work. And so in the breaks between battles, during the tiresome days of unnecessary holdups, I did not stop working: "A minimum of one line a day!" The scripts I wrote in those days had no chance of being made into films. (Some of them[13] are included in this book.)

Today, whatever my artistic fate, I want to remain faithful to the tested motto There's Elation in Fighting! I have survived trials that might have broken me or tied me. My backbone is still strong and unbent, and with my experience I am ready for new battles.

15 Satire

An Assailant's Weapon

(ca. 1966)

Our cinema, while still in its youth, was caught up in the extraordinary upheavals of the First Five-Year Plan.[1] The whole frame of our life was shattered when our enormous country took its first steps down the uncharted paths of Socialism. My first films were made for uneasy people.

The kolkhozes were just being born. Peasants were taking their own horses to communal stables; this was a momentous event. The kulaks were waging a last battle against the new order. Surviving NEPmen,[2] priests, and remnants of the White Guards still clung to a hope of taking Russia back to the nineteenth century. It was as if this vast country was in turmoil. The trains were packed to overflowing—with the builders of Turksib, Magnitka, DneproGES;[3] with kulaks on the run; with mobilized Communists.

The days were grim, the nights anxious! . . . while in the evenings (as if nothing had changed in the world) the flat shadows of "heroes" flitted across the screens of movie theaters, infecting the revolutionary spirit of the people with domestic dramas and the venom of tawdry happiness . . .

I came to film from the Red Army without any intention of getting caught up in this kind of "art." I came with people of a like mind and commitment, determined to overthrow it, force it into open battle, and drive it off the screen in order to replace it with a real revolutionary art of film!

Now this may seem comic and pretentious, but in those days we rushed into the fight, naively believing that with one "winder" we could knock the living breath out of the bourgeois "art of illusion"[4] . . .

It turned out then that I knew what to do in film and how to do it. Today, too, every beginner in film knows that he is the one who holds God by his beard!

We had started up a quite interesting soldiers' theater for pantomime and grotesque skits in the army toward the end of the Civil War.[5] Its lifeblood was drawn from satirical clowning, folk wood-block prints, homegrown operettas, comic gags. The soldiers wrote everything themselves, rejecting all work with "regular" plays. Once we got beyond the soldiers' humorous tales, we developed a taste for big, incisive subjects. For instance, there was a satirical improvisation, *The Meeting of Horses*, with a Chairman, a Secretary, and a Reader of a Report, who were all Horses. A bucket substituted for a water pitcher on the lectern. From time to time, the Report Reader lowered his carefully made cardboard head into the bucket (the only costumes were horse heads and felt cloaks). Amid quips and gags and wonderful variety-show pieces, the horses "launched proceedings" against the 31st Cavalry Regiment and certain individual comrades. The horses recalled their bitter experiences, such as being beaten on the neck, deprived of food, and shameful neglect. The "heroes" were named. Interludes were performed (one horseman spends the night with his girlfriend, leaving his horse to spend the night exposed to the wind).

The characters in our operettas and vaudeville skits included God-the-Father, a Master Showman, General Kolchak,[6] Old Calamity, Saint Nicholas the Miracle Worker, and an array of quite amazing comic figures . . .

To speak about them is not my concern here. I will simply note that in 1930, when I took up the fight, I had clearly defined for myself what it was I was going to set against the bourgeois "film of illusion."

My first one-reel comic satires produced a big social scandal. The organs of the GPU[7] received letters calling for investigations into the filmmaker who was responsible for them and the persons who had promoted and approved defamatory satire in films. The newspaper *Kino* encapsulated the heated fights over the first satires in boldfaced headlines at the top of a page: "**Kino or Medvedkino**."

This might well have been the end of our campaign had Anatoli Lunacharsky[8] not suddenly given us some unexpected help. Concerned by some disturbing signals from ARRK [the Association of Revolutionary Workers of Cinematography], he addressed them on the subject of Soviet satire and offered a critique examining some errors we had made. Using his authority, Lunacharsky supported our explorations and insisted we be given more normal, lenient conditions to undertake them.

Although we had suffered a fair amount in the ARRK discussions (and in those years people fought without fear of giving offense and without sideward glances at the authorities), we determinedly held our ground. I set forth our artistic platform in an article, "We Will Not Yield Our Position" (*Proletarskoe kino*, 1931, No. 9, 16–19).

Thirty-five years later, I am happy to recall my artistic principles and to lay them forth in the polemical form I used in that programmatic article, to which I am still happy to subscribe my name today.

This is the basic principle I formulated at that time:

> Our aim is to arm Soviet film with a totally new genre—political satire. This task is a particularly difficult one, as we have to feel our way, with absolutely no models to follow in foreign or Soviet film (p. 16).

The time was 1931. New problems were continually arising for the country; there was an upsurge of unexpected difficulties. We badly wanted to find our place in the unprecedented battles! But we felt we were without weapons. I wrote (p. 17):

> In matters concerning industrial and fiscal planning, credits, quality of production, transactions in kolkhozes—all the contentious areas of the Five-Year Plan, our great silent film[9] turns into a stammerer, a stutterer, an inarticulate mumbler, and always misses the mark.
>
> Soviet film needs a year and a half if faced with a task such as mobilizing the attention of the masses to, say, the construction of the Magnitka steel mill. To actually build and start up the mill, the working class needs only one year.

Hence, we came to the decision to make short satiric comedies on urgent topical questions.

One-reel films! Trenchant, gripping films! Quickly made, they would be spliced onto action movies like a burr on a dog's tail, and travel through all the film-distribution networks! Perhaps the big dog of a film would be forgotten. But our burr of a film had to get stuck in a spectator's heart, make it chafe, and stay there for years!

Of course the idea of a cavalryman attack on the old "film of illusion" could catch fire only among fearless, young fighters, who did not understand all the difficulties of the project. But who is not audacious in his youth! As a basis for our experiments, moreover, we had made some pretty good calculations and thought out our methods of work. As we said in our article (p. 18):

> What does it mean to make a one-reel film? It means to find completely new laws of structure, quite different from the dramatic laws of full-length films. The film will consist of just a hundred shots and will take twelve to fourteen minutes to screen. Within these limitations, we need to acquaint the viewer with the theme and situation, lay out and develop the plot, and find a resolution of it.

To make the challenge even more difficult, we were trying to make problem-films rather than anecdotal ones, squeezing big, focused, fundamental questions into the tight space of one film reel.[10]

This tied us to a decisive economy and transformation of material, with the reworking of a political thesis as a proverb, aphorism, or fable.

> The mottoes we work with are: No unnecessary episodes in a script. No unnecessary shots in an episode. No unnecessary objects in a shot. (p. 18)

These resolutions were not mere paper declarations. There were many miscalculations, false moves, and lapses, but our group of enthusiasts determinedly translated our artistic platform into film.

I have always been lucky in my encounters with talented people.

Bold lads came to my help in casting down the "laws of the film of illusion"; they believed, like me, that the time of upheavals for the movie screen had arrived.

An actor from Vsevolod Meyerhold's theater, Volodia Maslatsov, came from the leftmost flank of this "leftist" theater, and with his training as an "eccentric actor" was in full possession of the qualities needed for the highly "stylized" genre of our first comedies.[11]

Fearlessness distinguished the young assistants Mikhail Afonin (subsequently a prominent international journalist) and Grisha Serpukhovitin.

The taciturn, unbelievably punctilious Garri Piotrovsky joined the group later. His pedantic calculations were very important for us in the heated atmosphere of our impetuous experiments!

P. A. Zinoviev played the part of the Fool, Ivan Ivanovich Duren [8]. He also did an excellent job as the principal character, Khmyr, in the full-length satirical comedy *Happiness*.

. . . Our first three comedies, *A Little Log*, *Stop Thief!*, and *Fruit and Vegetables*,[12] were excellently received by viewers even if the unfamiliar genre somewhat baffled them. But their responses pointed in the right direction! At any screening one could hear people saying: "A machine purchased abroad has been left outdoors in a yard in the wet for a whole year, yet it had been paid for in gold!" "Our cabbages are rotten! Who is to blame?—Nobody knows!" "A house was built, and nobody can live in it! Let the director say why!"

These were the reactions we wanted. It was to get them that we made our satires, condemned ourselves to fiendish torment, and suffered the abuse and mockery of the arrogant devotees of the old film of illusion.

In an analysis of our first films Anatoli Lunacharsky asked: "What are the main features of these things? First of all, they publicize issues and they have a focus. The scripts are modeled on fables. The story is expressed in images; the entire exposition in images has one definite goal—to make the meaning of the fable clear. The author does not hide that he is indeed elucidating a fable, and that an image serves as an argument in the demonstration of the meaning of the fable, from which further conclusions arise of their own accord. Shall we accept such a method? We will, of course . . . We can vividly depict the incongruities of our life, in order to generate laughter and to have the viewers conclude: this we must fight, this we must put an end to! These little scripts work on this principle . . ." (A. Lunacharsky, "Kinematograficheskaia komediia i satira," *Proletarskoe kino*, 1931, No. 9, 4–15, 14).

What were our miscalculations?

There were painfully many: at first, not surprisingly, we had difficulty escaping the characteristic trivia of a feuilleton in our endeavors to develop our own language of grand, deep satire for the screen . . .

The author was in an awkward position tantamount to a double bind. The viewer could not be amused too much: "Laughter induces good humor and takes away anger about vice!" This could lead to attempts to provoke anger and shame at outrages instead of laughter.

The main difficulty, however, lay elsewhere; it was of a fundamental political character. The beginning of our work came in difficult years. Every defect of the young, not yet solidly established society gave the still-uncrushed enemy a weapon against the progress of Socialism.

What could we do since the basis of our satire (as of all satire) had to be a far-reaching discussion of vices?

These were some of the topics of our satiric comedies:

A seven-floor building is under construction.[13] A brick topples down from a great height onto a shoemaker below, hits him on the head, and—disintegrates into dust! As if nothing was wrong, the shoemaker picks up a fragment of the brick from the ground, crumbles it in his hand like a piece of earth, and turning to the viewer, says:

THIS CAN'T BE A BRICK, CAN IT?

This satiric "poster" took up six meters of film.

. . . A Chase:

STOP HIM!

A furious crowd is running down a street. They want to catch and destroy a pitiful man wearing a white apron . . .

STOP HIM! . . . HE'S ONE OF THE WORKERS FROM THE BUILDING!

Another seven meters of film.

In an office somewhere workers are looking for a lost document.[14] They search and search in cupboards, desks, and on shelves. A flurry of papers in the office:

WHAT ARE YOU LOOKING FOR?
THE ARCHITECTURAL PLANS AND CALCULATIONS!

Now a sea of papers is in turmoil. The workers plunge and swim as they search. The office cupboards are floating. The desks rock on the waves . . .

A storm! . . . A Commission of the RKI [the Workers and Peasants Inspectorate] arrives, standing on an overturned cupboard and rocking on the waves of paper.

WHERE IS YOUR CONSTRUCTION PLAN?

—the Inspectorate demands of Ivan Ivanovich Duren as he emerges from a dive.

OH, I DON'T THINK THERE WAS ANY!

—the soaking-wet Duren recollects, and then drowns . . .

"What kind of a country is this," Anatoli Lunacharsky indignantly asked, "where fools constantly scramble to the top and wreck things? . . . When a whole detachment of the militia arrives to arrest a pig in a play,[15] I assure you that one does not have to be a big enemy of ours to say, 'So these are their administrators, these are the new Ugrium Burcheevs!'[16] . . . One might say, the devil knows what this is, a counterrevolutionary had to have written it! In actual fact the problem lies with the BLUNTNESS OF THE AIM" (p. 15).

In those years the question as to the targets satire could take aim at was of critical importance. We could not, we were told, take aim at an enemy if it meant harming our own side . . .

But nobody could say how not to harm.

For instance the theater critic Blium came out with a whole theory based on the principle that satire was incompatible with dictatorship of the proletariat.[17]

Nusinov, a member of the Communist Academy, asserted that a sense of humor was alien to the proletariat.

The art scholar Shchukailo gave us the most trouble. Amassing accusations against us, he demanded that, in addition to, and right next to, the factory with no toilets built by Ivan Ivanovich Duren, we show at least one of the 518 "shock-construction" projects of the First Five -Year Plan.

Many critics decided that satire was the weapon of a suppressed class, and therefore a revolutionary artist could not fight with the existing order, unless he was a counterrevolutionary artist. Consequently, it was wrong to dabble in satire . . .

Not everything was clear even for Anatoli Lunacharsky. We ceaselessly defended our position from every possible platform, challenging his main claim:

> Each artist who uses laughter against some of our internal targets must always remember the absolute rule never to produce a satire without contrasting that which is mocked with our great, healthy principles. (Lunacharsky, p. 9)

Many years were to go by before art experts decided that, in Soviet satire, the vividly expressed author's position—his angry castigation of vices—was the very positive factor[18] that contrasted with the satiric depiction of particular aspects of our life.

Unfortunately, many in those years did not understand this, and nothing prevented our opponents from thundering against any satirist, and demanding that he be held responsible for unsettling the foundations of society and for counterrevolution.

All the same, the theorists who quarreled with us openly and for their own reasons, on open platforms and in newspaper columns, were not the most dangerous ones.

What was frightening was the invisible, petty, mediocre enemy who shook hands with you, and gave you a Judas kiss, and then delivered blows paralyzing all your efforts. Devotees of the bourgeois "art of illusion," casual fellow travelers, rivals who were not established, and established fools of all kinds—the "heroes" of our satires, these operated surreptitiously, in concert and with assurance. Documents from those years preserve evidence of this uneven fight.

To explain my complex artistic fate, I must dispense with modesty and cite some documents that perhaps set too high a value on my efforts but that call things by their names.

The chairman of the discussion at ARRK,[19] V. A. Sutyrin, said in his speech there:

> In conclusion I will say a few words about the appeal for calm that came from the lips of one of the speakers today. I have said that there are reasons for this appeal. An intolerable atmosphere surrounding Medvedkin is being created through the efforts of some people.
>
> . . . There have been rumors that either Medvedkin has been detained by the GPU as a saboteur and counterrevolutionary or that he is about to be arrested. . . . There have been base aspersions that go beyond even the bounds of demagogic criticism of his pictures . . .
>
> It is clear that enemy hands are involved in this. For Medvedkin is a young Soviet director and, moreover, a Communist. The bourgeois portion of the film-workers cadres legitimately see him as their enemy. For them he is, moreover, a talented and dangerous enemy. ("O sovetskoi satire," *Proletarskoe kino*, 1931, Nos. 10–11, 14)

Anatoli Lunacharsky had to speak about the same thing in his speech:

> These comedies have given rise to sentiments of uneasiness and spite . . .[20]

[*In Medvedkin's typescript this passage follows, which he later crossed out*]

When I go over in my mind everything that followed, I am inclined to say that this appeal [by Lunacharsky] was like a voice crying out in the desert.

Regardless, our diminished group decided that we would stick to our positions and intensify our search for incisive political genres able to measure up to the exigencies of the tumultuous events during the First Five-Year Plan. This led to the Kino-Train, a film studio on wheels, which we set up in three railway passenger cars.

Today we shoot—tomorrow we screen! without accompanying music. We were going to put up on the screen critically urgent film documents exposing various crimes—botched work, outrageous practices, disruptions of plans—and persons who were a disgrace—truants, drunkards, the everlasting tribe of fools . . .

We were going to shoot not just your factory, but scandalous practices at your neighbor's factory, which involved you either as a participant or as an unconcerned observer. Without hesitation, we were going to haul up on the screen not just your close acquaintances, but the bungled . . . [*The crossed-out fragment ends here. NL*]

16 Bronze Monuments

The play *The General Meeting of Horses*[1] led me to the exploration of great satirical works. And although my investigations suffered because I was only half-educated, I never forgot the great Russian satirists even in the most difficult times on the front lines in my youth. Because of them, I remained faithful to satirical genres. Throughout my artistic life I have drawn on the immortal creative work of Saltykov-Shchedrin, Gogol, Nekrasov, Pushkin, and Chekhov.

The "bronze" forebears of Russian satire are immortal because each of them had the boldness and temerity to go beyond the barriers of everyday naturalism and to find an immortal image of Truth beyond the mendacious limitations of pallid ordinary thought.

When I gave up my books for a soldier's uniform, I still didn't know very much about them.

Many years layer, I discovered the names of Rabelais, Swift, and Molière. With the help of these giants I remained faithful throughout my artistic life in the Red Army and in film to the constant, well-tested motto Satire Is An Assailant's Weapon.

Gogol taught me a lot. How much true poetry there is in his "Christmas Eve"!

The devil steals the moon from the winter sky. A witch flies out of a chimney on a broom. The blacksmith saddles the devil and flies on him to the Empress in St. Petersburg to get hold of her slippers . . .

What a bold imagination!—all resting on the unassailable Truth of the life of the people and on living images of simple people!

I desperately aspired to master the bright poetic gift of creation for my theater for the heroic soldiers of the 31st Cavalry Regiment of the Red Army.

Or take the following astounding satire by Saltykov-Shchedrin. In the tale "The Wild Landlord" the master suffers from the smell of peasants. "Lord!" he cries, " I am very pleased with everything you give me and reward me with. Only one thing is unbearable for my heart—the strong smell of peasants. Take these stinking boors away from me!" His prayer goes up to god. A whirlwind forms on the floor where his serfs were threshing his wheat. Peasants' bast shoes and pants, and chaff, flash past in the whirlwind. When the whirlwind dies down, no peasants are left. Too late the landlord comes to his senses. Without the peasants, he has lost the foundation of his life; he is in danger of dying. He cannot harness a horse, make cabbage soup, or pick an apple. The artistic form and philosophic depth of this tale fueled my explorations, and I found a whole collection of satires in Saltykov-Shchedrin!

How can one overlook the tale "The Watchful Eye"? In a faraway kingdom in a faraway land lived a public prosecutor. He had two eyes: a drowsy one and a wakeful one. With the drowsy eye he saw nothing at all, while with the wakeful eye he saw only unimportant things. The metaphor of this tale retains its philosophic relevance today.

In my youth I already understood that behind the vivid images of folktales one could feel the great sadness that characterized Old Russia, with its boundless expanses that were left for Nekrasov's peasants to tread in their bast shoes in their quest for "a Russia in which life is free and easy and joyful."[2]

17 Springboards

(ca. 1985)

Before beginning a film, I always reach for my card file, in which I keep all sorts of things: incisive popular proverbs; epigrams; sketches of fantastic tales; witticisms; priceless words and lively images born in the people's love of comic play.—In short, everything that can serve as a good springboard for thought and help me to avoid compromises. This card file is like a living flower: I provide it with life-renewing pellets and new finds, and discard anything old and moribund.

From the card file:

A hyena who is going to eat her cub imagines it smells like a goat.

As soon as grass grows, a donkey is there to eat it.

The higher a monkey climbs, the better we see his ass.

Their conscience did not suffer; they had none.

Taking an ax to a murderer is like giving a murderer an ax, but in reverse. [The Russian contains an untranslatable play on the words *otpor* and *topor*. *NL*]

They buried him in the planet Earth, but he was just a soldier . . .

Said by the physicist Ralph Lapp: This crusader sits in the last car of the train with his eyes looking back.

Ralph Lapp: Not even the most brilliant minds of our time know where science is taking us.

The American historian Clinton Rossiter: It is our misfortune that we don't have our own Marx.

An imaginary TV newscast: The First Exhibition of Vices and Virtues has opened. The names of some of the pavilions in it are The Mechanization of Truthfulness; Cobbled Solutions; Apathetic Men; Half Truths; Outsiders . . .

Pleasurable mutual back-scratching.

Once there was a very kind wolf. He tried to become an herbivore, and almost died of hunger.

There is the truth of the Wolf and the truth of the Rabbit.

Cecil Rhodes: Love thy neighbor as thyself, plus another 5%. ["Pure philanthropy is very well in its way but philanthropy plus five percent is a good deal better."]

A heart attack is not the worst misfortune. The worst is when your heart is overgrown with coarse hair and has turned into a brick. That's when you are finished.

Onward to the 19th century!

Stop the Earth! I want to get off!

Cain, where is your brother Abel? Lord, I am not my brother's keeper!

An evil dictator gave a written order saying STAY OR FLAY.[1] It was hard to make sense of the dictator's handwriting. Nobody was willing to risk asking questions. What to do? It seemed flaying was the safer course.

He wanted to shear, but came back shorn.

An unripe watermelon story: it may be pretty, but wait till it's ripe.

Providing for yourself may amount to burning yourself up.

Stop a chatterer or he'll make a tree shrivel.

Don't confuse a "beaut" with the beautiful.

I do not cease to wonder at the miraculous power of popular proverbs. How much strength must be encapsulated in one word in order for the wisdom of one sentence to live on for centuries and get passed from generation to generation as part of our national patrimony. I know of no better springboard for creation. Here are several Russian proverbs in which I found the subject of a comedy or an image or an unexpectedly relevant situation or a summing-up of a character.

From the card file:

If you have bile in your mouth, everything is bitter.

Only a crab is made beautiful by fatality.

The master is no better than a boil: he pops up anywhere he wants.

Evil does not lie still—it's off roaming, or comes crashing down, or rains on your shoulders.

Even a bishop will steal if he's hungry.

Your tongue won't help you to weave a pair of bast shoes.

There's no luck to be had anywhere for our Ivan.

For whomso I serve I dance.

What clever people! They hatched a chick from a baked egg!

They sold a beaver, which turned out to be a pig.
He's two feet taller than a scoundrel.
A horse fought with a wolf. A tail and a mane are all that remain.
Don't undo stitches unless you know how to sew.
He's a talker, but he's also a taker.
A man who has everything thinks he doesn't have enough.
You'll have to wait for as long as it takes apples to grow on a willow tree.
He is the kind of thief who can make off with your horse from right under you.
The devil puts a spoonful of honey in another man's wife.
A thin beard is no misfortune if you have a circular mustache.
You can't manufacture a hat out of a thank-you.

The two great writers Mikhail Saltykov-Shchedrin and Nikolai Nekrasov breathed the air of popular wisdom. Everything I have done in film has left a trace, however small, of their civic-mindedness and faithfulness to the cause of the people.

My best script, "The Unholy Force," ripened for years under the influence of Nekrasov's immortal poem "Who Can Be Happy in Russia?"[2] And correspondingly, my passionate attachment to the proverbs of the Russian people grew. Here are a few verses from that poem:

[*about the ax*]
It kept on bowing its whole life long,
but it was never kind.

[*about the saw*]
A peasant's fare is a fine one.
An iron saw gnaws forever,
While he doesn't get to eat.

Shadows, dark shadows!
Who can outrun you, who escape you?
No one can catch you, dark shadows,
No one embrace you!

Travelers, no need to ask
The soldiers and beggars you pass
If their life is easy or hard.
The soldier's razor is no better than an awl,

And the only heat he gets comes from smoke.
What happiness is there in that?

The great Russian satirist Mikhail Saltykov-Shchedrin overwhelmed me with his mastery of matchless searing hyperbole. This is what he saw in the history leading to the formation of the great Russian state:[3]

"It all began when the Volga was kneaded with flour; then a calf was dragged to the bathhouse; porridge was boiled in a bag; a goat was enveloped in risen dough; a pig was substituted for the beaver that was paid for, and a dog was killed instead of a wolf; bast shoes were lost, then searched for in different yards, and seven shoes were found instead of six; a crab was greeted with the ringing of bells in a tower; . . . a stockade was caulked up with pancakes; a devil was sent off to the army; . . . the heavens were propped up with stakes. And finally everyone was exhausted and stopped to see what would come of all this" . . .[4]

For me the influence of these two giants of nineteenth-century Russian literature was unsurpassed. It was clearly under their influence that I found a character such as Khmyr, who decided to die, in consequence of which orders were given to "whip him till he was half-dead yet still alive!" Or the firemen, who take so long to arrive at a fire that everything is burned down, and who then spend half an hour looking in the charred remains for an ember to light their cigarettes . . .

Satire is the instrument of an assailant; it is a dangerous and thankless affair: a wish to "kill the mocker" can be aroused in firemen, or government ministers, writers, and physicists. I wouldn't be surprised if after the publication of this book, people of a different mind will want to hold me in a death grip. And it will be a shame. I can present them with my excuses, and for consolation go back to the proverb

If You Have Bile in Your Mouth, Everything Is Bitter.

Contex-tualizations

18 Eisenstein on Medvedkin's Chaplinesque Genius

Eisenstein's 1935 review[1] of the film *Happiness* offers the major contemporary assessment of Medvedkin's originality and his comic and satiric genius. It was Jay Leyda's intention to use this article as an introduction to the Medvedkin book, with the incorporation of relevant excerpts from Eisenstein's lectures to his film students. The Russian word used for the film in the title and body of the article was Medvedkin's original one, *Stiazhateli*, an archaic and unusual word denoting men and women possessed of greed for property and acquisition. It is difficult to translate this in a single word. Jay called the film *Snatchers* in his major book on Soviet cinema. Here I have given the title of the film as *Happiness*—the name by which the film became generally known, while I have translated *stiazhateli* as applied to characters in the film with variations on "predators" and "property holders," depending on the context. Several excerpts from the lectures that explicate points in the article are appended to this translation. At the time Jay Leyda and Medvedkin planned the book, the viewing of *Happiness* had been largely restricted to festivals and special screenings (both in the West and in the Soviet Union). Fortunately, the film is now much more readily available and is a major part of Medvedkin's accessible artistic legacy. It has been released on DVD by Icarus (together with Chris Marker's *The Last Bolshevik*) and by Hperkino (with a very important accompanying commentary by Nikolai Izvolov); versions of varying quality have also been uploaded to the Internet. Eisenstein's article is of course best read in conjunction with a viewing of the film. *NL*

Eisenstein, "[*Happiness*]"

Just now—today—I have seen our laughter on the screen. And for the second time in just five days I am driven to exclaim with enthusiasm over yet another achievement of our cinema.[2]

Today I saw Mededkin's comedy, *Happiness*, and to use the common expression, I cannot remain silent.

Today I saw how a Bolshevik laughs.

One may begin a comedy with the declaration that Chaplin has no part in it. And it will indeed turn out that Chaplin has no part in it.[3]

But one may also make a comedy without thinking about Charlie, and it will turn out that he is in it.

Not Chaplin himself, or something borrowed from him. But Chaplin as an indication of magnitude, as a basis for reference, as something profoundly specific.

Chaplin "in a new quality."

This is what I felt today when I was watching Medvedkin's *Happiness*.

It is easy to praise *Chapaev*[4] at the height of the storm of enthusiasm stirred up by this remarkable film.

It is more difficult to write about what I saw in the small screening room, where I was sitting between the nervous filmmaker and two friends[5] who had dropped in.

It is all the more necessary to speak up about this film as a remarkable one, and about its maker as one marked by a particularly interesting individuality. [See Lecture Excerpts A below.]

And about the genre of the film as one that opens up and establishes a distinctive conception of film comedy.

It is difficult to avoid laughing at Khmyr in the scene where he is snipping off ears of rye.[6] But he is not simply a crank or an idiot—this is the "idiotism of rural life"[7] from which we have emerged, to which there is no going back. The one that looks a hundred times more idiotic when it is located in the era of kolkhozes and combine harvesters.

It is difficult to avoid laughing at Chaplin.

Here I want to express my enthusiasm about Medvedkin for developing the wonderful things he gives us—on an equivalent level and with an equivalent understanding.

A gag by Chaplin is alogical in individual terms.

A gag by Medvedkin is alogical in social terms.

Chaplin is always going away. Chaplin always goes off into the distance. A Chaplin film takes Chaplin away. There is no extricating himself. One leg goes here, the other one there. There is no drive to unity.

The bringing in to the collective: Khmyr begins where Chaplin ends. He is apart, alone, far off. And Khmyr is brought in: his wife; the political-section head; the whole situation. And Chaplin-as-Khmyr comes in from all those faraway places to which Khmyr-as-Chaplin goes off at the end of all his films.

That's the way it is. And here is another contrast for you.

Khmyr is given a rifle. Khmyr stands guard over the kolkhoz barn. The barn is supported on pilings. The kulak riffraff[8] are scheming to get hold of the barn. A kulak releases a goat into Khmyr's vegetable patch. From the mound from which he is guarding the barn Khmyr tosses stones to drive the goat away. Khmyr has a stronger interest in his own good than in the good [of society]. His back is turned to the barn. The kulaks creep under the barn. They stand up and lift the barn off its pedestals. The barn is supported on the feet of the kulaks and priests and their underlings. And not just standing, it is moving. And not just moving, but running. Khmyr has driven away the goat and turns back around. The barn on piles is not there. The barn is running across the field on the feet of the kulaks. Khmyr runs after the barn, and so begins a series of new adventures.

A house taken off its footings is an old device in the world repertory of gags. The best "Western" example is once again a house in Chaplin, in *The Gold Rush*.

A storm envelops the little log cabin in which Chaplin is spending the winter with another gold-digger, the Giant. Just at this moment the Giant sees Chaplin as a chicken (this is shown) and wants to slit his throat. There is a long business with gusts of wind knocking the opponents together. Finally, the storm grabs hold of the hut, and the hut slides away. It is suspended on the edge of a precipice, and rocks up and down with the movement of the men inside. The hut is like a ship deck. It slides and rocks, etc.

And again: it's funny in both places. But there the fight is between two men. Whereas here the fight is internal, the struggle of a former "possessor of property" with today's guardian of collective property. In Chaplin the gag is a simple one, deeply rooted in the class situation. It is a concrete expression of a metaphor from Bruegel about the eating of small fish by big ones. When this gag becomes a signifier for expressing the Socialist view of property, "possession" is what wins out [at first]. But this is not the end. Another scene overlies this one, correlating with a scene [in Chaplin's *The Pilgrim*] where a philanthropic sheriff releases a convict on the other side of a frontier. [See Lecture Excerpts B below.]

The villainy of the kulaks increases in intensity. Now instead of the goat and the barn, it is the stables, into which a kulak drives the kolkhoz horses, intending to burn them up, and Khmyr's hut, which the kulak sets on fire to stop Khmyr from interfering with his attempt to burn down the stables.

And this is a brilliant scene: two fires and two conflagrations. Khmyr's own hut is in flames. And the fire in the kolkhoz stables is blazing. Medvedkin is wonderful here: his Khmyr runs from one fire to the other—comically!—and does not know which one to tackle.

Finally, he runs over to the kolkhoz property—and saves the horses and equipment from the conflagration.

He has been flinging himself from left to right. An inner conflict. The two fires: "possession" vs. the sacredness of kolkhoz property. And a comic and exceptionally brilliant resolution. The only one I know equal to it is a scene in a Fatty Arbuckle comedy (which was screened in Moscow). Fatty is the hero, and he saves the heroine. But the villains have hidden themselves left and right in the hut in which the heroine is tied up. Fatty comes in through the door. He looks right—a bandit is standing there; he looks left—another bandit is standing there. He looks at his hands—a double-barreled gun is lying in them. He rests the double-barreled gun on his knees. He yanks the barrels apart, one to the right, the other to the left. He pulls the trigger. Two shots go off at once, right and left. Both villains fall down dead, one right, one left.

Two brilliant scenes, outwardly similar. But in significance and in basic nature a chasm of understanding separates the two.

You laugh at Fatty. He is indisputably wonderful. But with Medvedkin you don't simply laugh. Your laughter with the former is uncomfortable, while your laughter with the other is accompanied by a wonderful uplifting sensation.

These are just elements, fragments. It is only an illustration, drawing on Medvedkin, of my main thesis.

Namely: a comparison of mature masterly achievements coming from different [social] classes provides specific correlative material for examining the relationship between them . . . [here part of the text is missing].

We have a superb piece.

We also have a wonderful master.

Who has a truly original, mature individuality.

The first point we commented on is the fundamental one.

Not a transference or appropriation of a gag. Not a pilfering from the American bags of tricks.

But a true assimilation and resignification.

A solution of what is most important. Not the gag as such. Not a gag for the sake of a gag. But a search to find that for which the gag can be a sign.[9]

What intellectual and ideological content can be expressed through comic interpretation of an *apparently* traditional gag?

Fig. 8. Still from *Happiness*. The hapless peasant Khmyr, the central character of the film, is seized by a troop of soldiers, all with identical faces, when he attempts to make away with himself.

I have worked on this quite a bit myself. In my artistic "stores" there are several pieces that can rival Medvedkin's.

Sometimes I watch a joyless film, and I feel very downhearted. Was I wrong to put aside my comic work without completing it?[10] Today I feel at peace and happy. Happy with the happiness you can only feel in a country in which greed for possessions can only be the object of laughter. Happy that Medvedkin has solved the problem of our sense of humor just as I would have done had I shot and made the film myself!

Any claims about sidetracking, etc., are pathetic.

In conclusion, I need to share my sincere enthusiasm about yet another scene: Saltykov- Shchedrin in Medvedkin.[11]

An ancien-régime scene.

You madly applauded the "psychic attack."[12] Can you imagine a comical analog to this scene?

Medevdekin has done this.

Khmyr turns his back on possessions.

Enough! Possessions have led nowhere. For every man with a plow, there were seven with a spoon. However much he gathered, he was regularly fleeced.

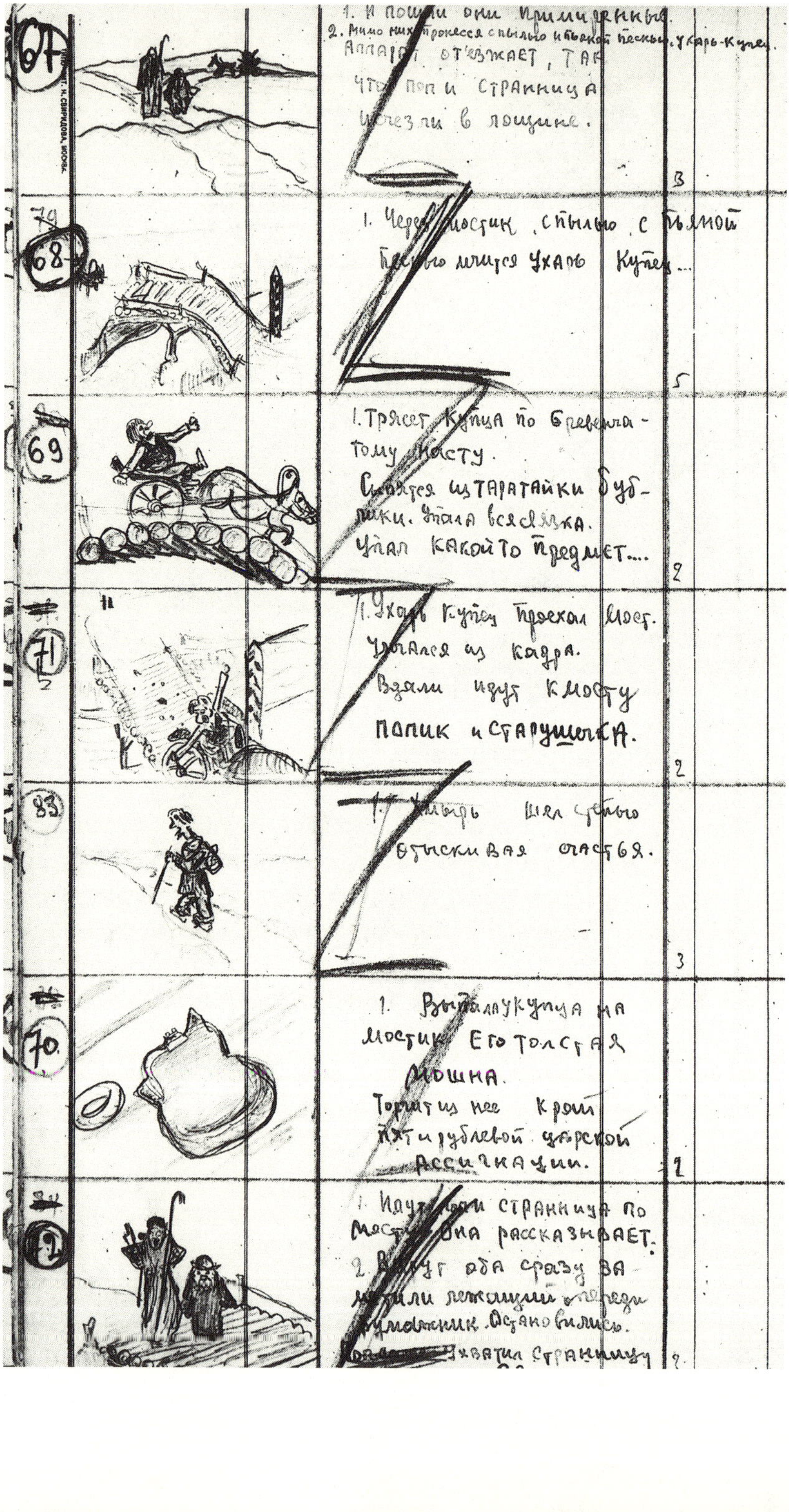
67
1. И пошли они примиренные.
2. Мимо них пронесся с пылью и пьяной песнью Ухарь-Купец.
Аппарат отъезжает, так что поп и странница исчезли в лощине.
3
68
1. Через мостик, с пылью, с пьяной песнью мчится Ухарь Купец...
5
69
1. Трясет купца по бревенчатому мосту.
Сыпятся из таратайки бублики. Упала вся связка.
Упал какой-то предмет....
2
71
1. Ухарь купец проехал мост. Умчался из кадра.
Взяли идут к мосту попик и старушонка.
2
83
1. Хмырь шел степью отыскивая счастья.
3
70.
1. Выпала у купца на мостик его толстая мошна.
Торчит из нее край пятирублевой царской ассигнации.
1
1. Идут поп и странница по мостику. Она рассказывает.
2. Вдруг оба сразу заметили лежащий впереди бумажник. Остановились.
Ухватил странницу
2.

Khmyr decides to try dying. Khmyr planes some boards and knocks together a coffin.

All-round panic. Who will there be left to exploit for the kulak, the village priest, the powers-that-be?

A priest comes running. He threatens Khmyr with the Scriptures. Khmyr continues knocking togther the coffin, and tests it for size. The policeman shouts at him. Khmyr makes some adjustments to the coffin. A Metropolitan Bishop runs up with the village priest. A view of the hillock. A view of the village. Some geese fly away. A carriage is rushing up. Senators, civil servants, police chiefs, and district officers. And hussars, hussars, more hussars. Everything is on the move—to stop the peasant from dying.

Khmyr chews his last piece of bread and gloomily looks at the coffin. From behind the hillock come row upon row of troops: dark, with rifles, marching with a frightening, strictly measured pace, tsarist troops. All to stop Khmyr from dying. The troops draw near. Black like Kappel's soldiers. Machinelike, like them. Nearer. Wonderfully grotesque: the troops are in masks. Everyone with the same face. Mustachioed, with yawning mouths. This synthetic image of the old army makes the flesh creep. This is the best bit. Here Medvedkin rises to a true grotesque level. Here, underneath the craziness and absurdity of the cardboard mug faces, repeated over and over in the troops, we see the deadening face of the regime. This is Shchedrin.

They don't let Khmyr die. They let him live. They leave the deed only half-done. They whip him till he is half-dead for his attempt to die of his own volition. And Medvedkin achieves an effect worthy of Goya in his ending of this part, with groups of soldiers in cardboard masks bashing out a

Fig. 9. (*opposite*) Frame sketches for *Happiness*. An example of the detailed drawings Medvedkin made before shooting his films: (67) the two [the priest and the pilgrim woman] are walking after making peace with each other; a fine fellow of a merchant dashes past them, raising a cloud of dust; the camera pulls back, and the priest and the pilgrim woman disappear in a depression in the road; (68) the dashing merchant rushes over the bridge in a cloud of dust and with a drunken song; (69) the merchant rattles over the logs of the bridge; sheets of paper are scattered from his carriage; a bundle falls out, and also one particular object; (71) the dashing merchant has crossed over the bridge and galloped out of the frame; in the distance the little priest and the old woman are walking toward the bridge; (83) Khmyr is walking in the steppe in search of happiness; (70) the merchant's fat pouch has fallen on the bridge; the edge of a tsarist five-ruble bill is sticking out of it; (72) the priest and the pilgrim woman are walking across the bridge; she is talking; suddenly they both see the pouch lying ahead of them; they both stop; . . . [illegible] takes hold of the pilgrim woman.

melody on an accordion and groups of soldiers in cardboard masks dragging poor Khmyr off in order to execute his punishment.

Lecture Excerpts A. On Medvedkin's originality and the risks of misunderstanding he runs. (Lecture No. 12, 22 November 1934, for fourth-year film-direction students in the Film School VGIK)

. . . You have here the attributes of an absolutely wonderful comedic genre, totally different, absolutely original, and extremely interesting. How the picture will be received, how assessed, what will be said about it—I don't know. I am not sure a commission of the Central Committee has looked at it yet.

. . . The film comes out of a true culture. Each successive shot is worked out through and through. . . . When I showed sketches of the shots in my first lecture, the view through [the focal point of] the camera did not appear. Each of the planes of a shot is comic. Here there is some real thinking and a very distinctive individual approach.

. . . In the film there is something authentic, a film director with his own individuality. And not just that: he is a master with his own genre, his own style, and a set of conventions to which he sticks. The man never slips up; there is not a single fault in the film. It is a wonderful sensation when you feel that something is definitely, really, there.

Lecture Excerpts B. The frontier gag in Chaplin's *Pilgrim* and Medvedkin's Socialist reinterpretation of it. (Lecture No. 16, 13 December 1934, for fourth-year film-direction students in the Film School VGIK)

. . . The hero is a former convict, but he is honest. The church's collection box has disappeared. He finds it and returns it. There is a duality: on the one hand, he is a former convict; on the other, an honest man. The sheriff who is supposed to take him to prison is overcome with magnanimous feelings. The sheriff takes him to the Mexican border, to allow him to escape abroad. But Chaplin misunderstands the situation. Then the sheriff notices a flower growing on the other side of the border and sends him to pick it. Chaplin picks it. Meanwhile the sheriff tries to ride away. But Chaplin runs after him. Finally, the sheriff more or less kicks him over to the other side, but once more he comes back. I don't remember the last shot, but I think he is walking along the border. His feet straddle the border and he walks off into the distance, straddling this line.

. . . A kulak drives the horses into the stable and sets fire to it. Khmyr looks at this matter differently. He wants to put out the fire. Then the kulak runs over to Khmyr's house and sets fire to it. Khmyr runs hither and thither, not knowing which fire to extinguish. This is the same construction as when Chaplin vacillates between two sides of the frontier. What is taken is not the gag, but the basic principle, the struggle between two motives. His house burns down, and he saves the horses. But the moment when he is running between the two conflagrations is one of the best places in the comedy.

19 Film Comedy and Satire

Anatoli Lunacharsky

(Excerpt from a speech to ARRK,[1] 1931, on a sheet in Medvedkin's personal archive)

Political accusations are being dumped on Comrade Medvedkin. In actual fact the aim of his comedies is splendid, and their feelings are utterly pure and Communistic. . . . We shall prove ourselves horrible managers of our affairs if we drive such an original artist off the open highway and force him into a cranny somewhere. If we are going to "work over" every pioneer in this way because of his mistakes, then everyone will be afraid of originality—and that will be the end of creativity. If this comes about we ought to be scattered in the wind, for this sort of attitude is a dead end for art. . . . Film comedy and satire are an infinitely rich and productive field, but it has been disgustingly poorly developed, and needs our special attention.

From *Lunacharskii I kino* (Moscow: Iskusstvo, 1965), 211–12.[2]

Medvedkin's copy of this excerpt is followed by this undated note:

The comedy *Happiness* was released three years[3] after Lunacharsky's speech. His appeal "not to force the artist into a cranny" was not heard.

20 Alexander Medvedkin and the Traditions of Russian Film

Notes about an Evolving Poetics

NIKOLAI IZVOLOV

Medvedkin is one of world cinema's truly original auteurs. His poetics have not so far received special attention investigating (1) the connections underlying his various, apparently disparate artistic discoveries, and (2) the semantic interdependences of these discoveries. This preliminary study aims to set forth some guidelines for such an inquiry.

In 1926, as a young worker in PUR (the Political Directorate of the Workers and Peasants Red Army), Alexander Medvedkin had his first real encounter with film. This was a time of very rapid creative growth in Soviet cinema. One after another, films that were to become classics of Soviet and world cinema were being released (or were in production). Film theory was being investigated, with the *Poetics of Film*, written in 1926 and published in early 1927,[1] as a brilliant example of a collective endeavor. Theory and practice were thoroughly interwoven at this time: almost all the young directors—whether they had made a film or were just in the stage of planning one—sought to interpret their work (or projected work).

The intense experience people were living of history in the making seemed to crush any possibility of rational analysis. The artistic legacy from these times is permeated by a sense of a need to triumph over a chaotic, provisional history, which had not crystallized into a well-ordered system. Almost nobody was studying the history of film as such, the more so as this was understood as referring to the young filmmakers' own experience, which of course was of recent origin. The first part of B. S. Likhachev's *Film in Russia*: *Materials for the History of Russian Film*, going up to 1913, was the only study of the kind, and it proved to be quite irrelevant to the concerns of people when it came out in 1927.

Medvedkin had not previously been concerned with the history or theory of film. He had a supervisory position at Gosvoenkino (the State Military Film Organization, a production company attached to the army), where he was assigned the tasks of preparing a report on ways in which cinema could serve the needs of the active-duty army, and of developing organizational structures for the rapid mobilization of the film industry in a wartime situation. His main duties involved production and the economics of production.[2] He was acquainted with the [military] conflicts that interfered with film distribution in different republics and prevented the widest possible dissemination of films. He was also familiar with many other aspects of the disorganization of the film industry. As a military man, he found all this a source of considerable aggravation. In considering whether film production in the state it was at the end of the 1920s would be able to deal with a wartime situation, he came to a categorical grim conclusion:

> "War will risk bringing about the liquidation of the Soviet film industry. War will entail a multitude of disasters. Many of them are INEVITABLE and can be predicted, because they directly and logically follow from the sum total of the 'natural' characteristics of our cinema. . . . NO VESTIGES of the historical lesson delivered to Russian film manufacturers in 1914 remain to us. . . . The films we now discourage and have little use for are the very ones that matter—newsreels, shorts, animation films with a political message. . . . We must remember that the Russian manufacturers in 1914 could rapidly switch to wartime production not just because they were flexible, but also because the films they had been throwing into the market IN PEACETIME were exclusively shorts, which they could make in a matter of days, Since we now need on average of four to five months to make a film, the position we shall have to start from is one of an absolute lack of preparation for wartime agitational work" (quoted from a typescript in Medvedkin's personal archive).

One point is immediately striking—Medvedkin, who in age and spirit was close to the avant-garde directors of Soviet film—looks back to early Russian film in order to find a way of ending the "lack of organizational direction." This is unparalleled in his time and generation, and many succeeding generations of filmmakers. The papers in Medvedkin's archive contain a four-page draft of a larger study focusing on the set of problems identified in the above quotation. These pages (sheets nos. 43–46) give a more specific analysis of the newsreel output of the Skobelev Committee in World War I.[3] Our contemporary film scholars have not given this newsreel production the assessment it deserves. It is the more remarkable that, in 1927, a man who had only recently come to filmmaking was giving a detailed examination of the production and distribution work conducted by the Military Film Department of the Skobelev Committee, and its achievements and shortcomings.

Medvdekin was especially interested in requests coming from a specific audience he knew well, namely, soldiers, and also in the relationship of a filmed man to a film [with him in it] and of a viewer to film in critical wartime situations. He writes:

> Session leaders who had conducted screenings under different conditions and with different military units generally came to the same conclusion: Soldiers gave their preference to military newsreels and to comedies. When newsreels about the life of the Western Allied troops were screened, the viewers from the trenches remarked on thousands of details that normally escaped notice (equipment, arms, ordinary objects, and so on).

Comedy was evidently liked inasmuch as it gave a strong stimulus "to forget oneself" and "to relax in healthy laughter" (sheet no. 43 in Medvedkin's archive). Furthermore: "The Skobolev Committee sent cameramen to all the military front lines. Enduring all the hardships of life on the front lines, they worked under fire from the enemy, and produced a number of exemplary newsreels (*The Fall of Peremyshel, The Conquest of Ervezerum, The Siege of Lvov,* and so on)" (sheet no. 45). Nonetheless: "It is true that the difficult life of the army was left to continue free from the influence of film, and that film practice continued down its own road, which took it far away from the exhausted army" (sheet no. 43).

The soldiers' response to film held true for all of them without exception, in spite of the fact that they were an audience comprising different social origins, education, age, and personal predilections. What drew this heterogeneous mass together was the fact that they were all in the same situation, which was a very different one from their familiar, normal situation.

In consequence, a [production] field is formed with the following components:

> Comedy. Politics. Newsreels (filmed in conditions that the viewer understands but that differ from habitual ones). Various combinations of these. Short films and shots of maximum effectiveness.

Accordingly, a film becomes a semantic node for a network of social, psychological, and economic linkages with the external world. The aura of these external relationships does not exist without the films, just as a film does not exist without the aura of these relationships.

This is the second striking thing about Medvedkin: namely, before he even made a film, he had laid down a system of interconnected conditions that was to be characteristic of the poetics and language of his future films.

Medvedkin had a strong sense of the important role played by the very rapid contact with viewers in early films and especially in early newsreels. (It is relevant to note that in the late 1920s Lev Kuleshov,[4] who had begun his work as a filmmaker before the Revolution, surfaced as another initiator and promoter of rapidly made films. In the credits of his film *The Breakthrough* he proudly proclaimed, "The film and the script were completed by the Mezhrabpomfilm Studio in shock-work time: 48 hours.") In the first two decades of the twentieth century the language of film was not conceptualized as something standing apart from the actual conditions of film practice, whereas in the 1920s this took place almost simultaneously in several countries. There were, however, certain manifestations [of language] in early film, even if they were not theorized. Just as an alphabet comes before grammar, so the language of early film, which developed in a natural way, had a characteristic function of communication, in the way that all natural languages do, calling for immediate contact between the communicating parties. This function was not part of the concerns of filmmakers in the 1920s, since their foremost preoccupation was with the metadescriptive function of film, so that film language began to interact with the material of film rather than with the viewer. Early films may be regarded as missives sent to a universal addressee without worries over grammatical correctness, whereas classical examples of film from the 1920s are a system of grammatical rules, which do not always make a point of providing examples on the basis of which the rules are set forth. However, taken to an extreme, a principle can turn into its opposite. At the end of the 1920s, Eisenstein, who was one of the most radical reformers of film language, formulated the theory of "intellectual film," according to which *The General Line*[5] was supposed to be "an experiment understood by millions."

The dominance of the function of communication explains why early film practice was many times more efficacious than the social-activist film practice in the first decade of Soviet Russia. The following example from newsreel films of the 1910s is typical: on the day the tsar's family entered Moscow at 4:00 p.m. for the celebration of the three-hundredth anniversary of the Romanov dynasty, Pathé News made a film that was screened in movie theaters at 7:30 p.m. the same evening. The most quickly made film of the Soviet period, about the May Day celebrations in 1918, did not beat this record; it was screened at approximately the same time, but the shooting had begun in the morning.

In 1927 Medvedkin made his first experiments in film direction. What is immediately striking is the absence of any traces of a teacher's influence or of imitation—which might be forgiven in a beginner—and also the absence of struggle with existing norms and traditions. He is an innovator, not an archaist.[6] At the same time, rather than reject the old culture, he pursues aspects of it that had never received wide circulation. His study of the Skobolev Committee had not been in vain.

The film *On Patrol*[7] presumed the active participation of the viewer during the screening. It had four parts: "The Mysterious Hillock," "The Missing Patrol," "Messing Up," and "The Enemy." In each of these a problem was presented—of increasing difficulty from part to part—and a solution. Short intermissions were scheduled so that the viewers could compare their own solutions with the author's. As Medvedkin recalled, the viewers' involvement was excited to the fullest extent.

A more-or-less common ground in films of the 1920s was the idea of overcoming the passivity of the viewer. The basic assumption was the coparticipation of the viewer, rather than the entertainment of the viewer. Eisenstein's theory of intellectual film, which was mostly formulated in 1928, assumed that the structure of the film corresponded to the perception of the viewer, which certain archetypal laws of thought structured in the viewing process. But even though this theory was subsequently developed into a fundamental investigation of the nature of the film image, it did not lead to a practical result that was as effective as Medvedkin's *On Patrol*. It may be noted that Eisenstein's experiment in staging the play *Gas Masks* inside a factory[8] was not met with any special understanding by the factory workers, who were busy with their own work.

In contrast, Medvedkin programmed into the structure of the screening the viewer's own reflections on a subject that directly concerned him. In this way Medvedkin solved the problem of how to activate a receptive mind with the rough elegance of a man cutting through a Gordian knot.

It is likely that the structure of this unique experiment was not repeated before TV serials of the "You Be the Detective" type appeared. But even in these we do not find as complicated a symbiosis of life and art. The film *Look after Your Health*, about hygiene for a Red Army soldier, was supposed to be a straightforward tool of instruction. The subtitle *A Poster-Manual*, however, plays on distinct shades of meaning of the words: a poster is something you can always look at, whereas a manual is something you can put in your pocket. This does not apply to a film, which you cannot always look at again, while the information from the screen is usually deposited only in the passive memory. Here Medvedkin destroys the principle of the poster structure, which combines bare information and rectilinear clarity. He departs from a linear exposition of medical recommendations, and breaks the material of the film into several pieces, into which he introduces a half-comic individual who is afraid of water, while a part of the informational material travels through the film from episode to episode in various reminiscences and reminders. The episodes sometimes take the form of sophisticated miniature novels. A title appears: "Illnesses have torn thousands of the best fighters from the active ranks of the Red Army." And then appears a shot of a detachment of marching soldiers. A series of fade-outs follows, with shots showing fewer and fewer soldiers; the formation is broken; men are limping; they prop themselves up on their rifles; isolated ones are left behind in ditches and thickets; and then the last living one stumbles up to a spreading tree and sits down beneath it . . . and there is a fadeout to a grave marked by a traditional cross. The title at the beginning could have been included with equal success in a sequence with a sanitary inspection, or with a garrison commander giving a routine order, or an epic story. The series of fade-outs is a direct allusion to early cinema, while the eternal cross in place of the expected red star severs this episode from any specific historical time. This shot with a cross appears again in a bathhouse episode as a warning, after the title "Not everyone knows how to wash himself in a bathhouse." This highly ironic juxtaposition is also a reminder of the cruel conditions of life during the Civil War. A shot of a cat washing itself suddenly stops in a freeze-frame showing the cat with its jaws agape at the sight of the man who is afraid of water. A sequence from an actual newsreel made during the Civil War flashes past showing soldiers picking lice out of their shirts, then lice are shown in a close-up racing from outside the frame onto some beautiful gray cloth.

The extremely serious material of the film is continually viewed with an ironic attitude. Accordingly, the film is open to different interpretations by a mixed audience of soldiers. "Eccentrism"—a characteristic of the whole spirit of Soviet film in the 1920s—in Medvedkin is rather different from that of Eisenstein in his early work or that of the FEKS[9] directors.

The film [*Look after Your Health*] can be seen as a complex formation with several independent structures inserted into one another. The elements of these structures, from different times, are intended to interact with one another through an almost magical repetitiveness (several decades before the "distance montage" of Peleshian!), but they also form local connections with the peripheral elements of other systems. The expansion and compression of this semantic accordion make the film a sort of incantation that acts on both conscious and subconscious levels: "Don't be afraid of water . . . Beware of infecting your eyes with dirty hands . . . Water is the best defense against dirt . . . Don't be afraid of water . . . Water fortifies the skin . . . Water prevents colds . . ."

A cycle of magical formulas and rhetorical figures of film-speech later serves as the supporting structure of the film *Miracle Worker* (1937).

The intonations in a Russian epic *bylina*—whose function in folklore has analogues with the ritual structures in old Russian literature, with the rhetoric in sermons, and with the repetitions in solemn oaths—become a pattern for the meaning of the entire material of the film—in the responses of secondary characters and in the widely ramifying dialogues, and the organization of the narrative structure and space.

"In four years no one has overtaken us . . . For four years the first place in the district has been ours . . . Eight kolkhozes were in competition, but the first place was always ours . . ." This is the language that Medvedkin's kolkhoz workers of the 1930s speak. There is one incantation in the film that is not buried in the forms of Soviet reality and that can serve as a classical example of the vitality of the pagan tradition, whose old magical formulas naturally absorbed new material involved with the canonical saints of the church. They bring together the Isle of Buian with a "pharaoh containing twelve deaths"; the Saints Frol and Lavr (protectors of cattle) with Vlas (the god Veles), their unbaptized forerunner; the Lord's thunder with earthly illnesses—with the same appeals for them to go away, the thunder into water, and the illnesses into a mountain.[10]

What is, moreover, very unusual for the tradition of apotheotic endings in Soviet cinema of the 1930s is a return to the ancient injunction against pronouncing the word "God." The finale is the most "laconic" of all the sequences in the story. The heroine goes off to the capital. The address is simply MOSCOW, THE KREMLIN . . . And HIMSELF, whose name pronounced with fear and trembling is the archlogical last term of this triad, makes a flashing appearance in a newsreel sequence that emerges from the incantatory pattern of the whole structure of the film and leaves a Voice that mercifully grants the heroine permission to shed tears before the assembled people. And to whom is it that this powerful choir of ancient voices from a multitude of cultural traditions is addressed? To the main personage in the film—the girl, Zinka, who was able to get the cow named Witch to yield the milk she had been holding back.

The last film Medvedkin made for Gosvoenkino was *Torpedoes*, a one-reel instructional film. Even in this very simple case the director remained faithful to his principle of breaking causal sequences: first comes an explosion at sea, then its cause—a torpedo, and then an explanation of its mechanism with a gradual presentation of its parts and components.

In 1930–31 Medvedkin filmed his five famous short comedies—*The Log*, *Stop Thief!*, *Fruit and Vegetables*, *A Cock and Bull Story*, and *Hey Fool, What a Fool You Are!*[11] The basic commitments remained the same: fast work; low cost (versus cinematic quality); satire; short footage. For the first time elements are introduced to destroy a sense of everyday reality: masks and props. These lend themselves, moreover, to metaphorical readings, as with the copper foreheads fastened with tightly fitting screws to the blockheads' skulls; the bureaucrats floundering in a sea of papers on their desks; the dauntless sailor and Civil War hero patiently queuing on Golgotha as he waits his turn for vegetables, with a flashback to the same sailor in an open field facing a stage-prop cannon. Likewise in the moving episode with a grave [in *Look after Your Health*], Medvedkin destroyed any notion of real time by means of a series of fade-outs. (The absence of real time is one of the most significant features in Russian religious writing and Russian chronicles, as well as in the tradition of icon painting.) Medvedkin achieves a specific "agitational" effect, and proceeds with the same deliberation to destroy the representation of the real world of objects in film, along with the space in which this world is located. The apotheosis of Medvedkin's fantastic vision is attained a few years later in the episode in *Happiness* where Khmyr imagines what he would do if he were tsar: he is placed within the three-dimensional *reverse*-perspective space of Russian icons. Nothing of this sort can be found in world cinema before or after Medvedkin's film. This might have been the path taken by early Russian cinema if a fully conscious search for the linguistic possibilities of film had begun twenty years earlier. It is Medvedkin's achievement that he was the only one of the pleiad of young reformers of film language to draw on the traditions of religious and folk culture in order to transform the characteristic practices of early Russian film.

In 1931 he organized his Kino-Train. Here his idea of the interpenetration of life and art took a unique form.

This train became one of the first legends in film history. It had, moreover, certain historical associations that the young Medvedkin was very aware of. The cars making up the Kino-Train had been built in 1916, and Medvedkin was inspired by others in planning the transformation of these cars and drew on their experimentation. In his archive he carefully preserved an album published in 1912 with the title *Basic Principles of Construction and a Primer for Railroad Work*. In it there is a vivid juxtaposition of carefully drawn drafts with wood-block prints of peasant workers on the railroads.

In early film practice there were experiments with the use of trains in order to deliver hot news items. Georges Sadoul has described the special train that the British Gaumont Studio hired and equipped with a laboratory in order to film the coronation of the Prince of Wales in Carnarvon Castle in 1910. The film was screened in London six hours after the coronation, and several hours later in Paris.[12] But neither this example nor the examples of other studios with news compilations edited while being distributed can bear comparison with the Kino-Train: it was an efficiently operating factory that traveled out to people, like a mountain coming to Mohammed; it was a machine that took on the functions of a man who makes films that actively engage people in a dialogue. Its films directly addressed specific viewers and were about these viewers, but avoided giving a mirror reflection of their lives in the way that early newsreel films did. (These newsreels gave a mirror reflection inasmuch as their time scheme was immediate in their focus and provided the conditions necessary for viewers to communicate with themselves, so that it made sense for people to go to a screening singly, individually. Accordingly, it was no accident that Pathé News was first known in Russia under the name "Mirror of the World.") The Kino-Train films were a preparation for life: they inserted themselves into a causal chain of real events and became real events themselves. New film genres were born: the letter-film, the summons-film, the lecture-film, the prosecutorial-film, the accountability-film. The spectator of the Kino-Train films was different from that of the official newsreels of the time: the screenings were not conducted in anonymity. The potential object of the camera was also a potential viewer who would know when and where he was seeing himself and what role he was playing. The titles of the films showed the authors of the film, and along with the Kino-Train [team] and a local coauthor of the news the films might also be signed by the actor-viewers. There was no anonymity in (1) the events, (2) the people, and (3) the screening.

For the first time, the screen was discovered as a transformer of life rather than a mirror of life. At the screenings, a viewer's interest in himself gave rise to a strange alienation effect: likewise a person, who hears his own voice every day, is surprised by the sound of his voice on a tape recorder, or who is used to seeing himself in a mirror, scarcely recognizes himself on-screen.

About the Kino-Train almost nothing was written. The strange combination of the official status of the film factory and the semiofficial silence of the press made it a forerunner of all the contemporary forms of underground and avant-garde film. Medvedkin's Kino-Train films and his other films, all focused into themselves—for their time—the multiplicity of relations between things in the external world. And because of the different points in space and time these things occupied, the films became nodes of semantic organization, serving to connect past and future.

This is a general attribute of cinema, one that makes it particularly germane to our interests as human beings. We look with considerable amazement at a newsreel made in 1912 that features a man who participated in the Patriotic War of 1812,[13] who had been born in the eighteenth century.

What is at play here is no doubt a metaphysical law of succession. When Medvedkin was writing his scripts in the cramped Kino-Train compartment on leftover sheets of paper from the old Ermoliev Studio,[14] bearing his own telegraphic address SLONFILM, he could scarcely have known that his experiment would be attempted again, forty years later, by the SLON group in Besançon.

Like medieval annalists, film scholars spent many years copying one another's texts about the Kino-Train. And in this way they fostered the belief of readers—and maybe also their own belief—that Medvedkin's films were a part of living history and were an active presence for the filmgoing public. Certain scrupulous people sought to correct that impression by claiming that none of the footage had been preserved. But, as it turned out, all parties were wrong. Nobody had seen the films for fifty years, and yet, as has recently been revealed, some of the films did survive in an excellent state of preservation.[15] Thus a very persistent film legend has suddenly acquired a material reality. This is a story very much in the spirit of Medvedkin's own film stories. And it is likely that there are more such stories to come. Medvedkin is not simply an exemplary classic, but a legendary classic. And therefore he may be "discovered" many times, each time with a transformation of the supposedly definitive picture. And what is wonderful is that the "factualization" of the legend does not diminish this film director's legendary status, but rather serves to confirm it. And this progression will no doubt continue. This applies to further discoveries coming from the archives (the more likely to occur, the less there is a basis for them). It also applies to the investigation of whole fields of the director's activity that are not obvious and have unfortunately remained outside the scope of this article. For instance, few people know of Medvedkin's activities as a playwright or as a scriptwriter for productions by other people (yet he is as original a scriptwriter as he is a director). The subject of Medvedkin and animation film warrants special attention in light of the surviving sets of photographs from the Kino-Train animation films and in light of *First Aid*, an animation film that was "shelved" immediately upon completion [see G. N. Borodin's article in *Kinovedcheskie zapiski* 49 (2000)]. Finally, it would be worth investigating Medvedkin's influence on the aesthetics of Soviet color film; one of the climactic episodes in *Happiness*, Khmyr's dream, made the first use of color in the Mosfilm Studio.[16]

The legend of Medvedkin and his film work is enmeshed in a web of fruitful connections with the outside world. This legend has a capability for self-renewal, yielding new mysteries and similarly surprising discoveries. It thrives, it grows.

CVs and Addenda

21 First "Autobiography"

A Bolshevik's CV

(1946)

The Russian terms *biografiia* or *avtobiografiia* are frequently used for what we would call a curriculum vita, or CV. Mdvedkin's "Autobiographies" are really expanded CVs. Jay Leyda was worried that the "Autobiography" Medvedkin proposed to include in the book might lead to problems of space. In fact, it is likely that Medvedkin had nothing more in mind than something like these expanded CVs, one written in 1946, the other in 1980 and updated in 1984. The earlier one, written at a time of renewed repression, focuses on his political activity as a loyal Communist and avoids any mention of the difficulties he encountered as an artist. It was probably written in response to the political campaign promoting the role of positive heroes in film and the other arts and further restricting the role and presence of negative heroes. Medvedkin alludes to this campaign in his entry for 1946–48 in the second "Autobiography" [22]. *NL*

"Autobiography" (1946)
Member of the All-Union Communist Party (of Bolsheviks),[1]
A. I. Medvedkin, film director

I was born in the town of Penza in 1900. My father was a railway foreman.

Until 1919 I studied, first, at a church-run parish school; then, at a junior secondary institution; last, I completed the third-year program of a technical institute.

In May 1919 I organized a volunteer detachment of students from the technical institute and went to the front lines in the south. I worked as a senior foreman of the 12th Army fieldworks near Tsaritsyn.[2]

July 1919: With my echelon I was taken prisoner by rebel Cossacks led by General Mamontov near the station of Arched on the South-Eastern Railway.

In September detachments from the 1st Cavalry liberated me.

October 1919–June 1920: soldier and squadron clerk in the 31st Cavalry Regiment of the 6th Caucasian Division of the 1st Cavalry.

June 1920–Jan. 1921: adjutant in the same regiment.

Jan. 1921–March 1923: chief secretary of the Party Bureau and club director in the same regiment.

March 1923–Feb. 1924: section head of the Political Directorate of the 6th Caucasian Regiment.

Feb. 1924–June 1925: senior instructor in the Political Directorate on the Western Front (PUZAP) and then in the Western Military Region (PUZVO).[3]

June 1925–May 1927: senior instructor for the Main Political Directorate of the Workers and Peasants Red Army (GLAVPURKKA).

May 1927: transferred to the GLAVPURKKA reserves, and then released to the inactive reserves in connection with my move to the State Military Film Organization (Gosvoenkino), where the first military-instruction films in our country were made.

September 1929: appointed as film director at Soiuzkino.[4] Made a series of short films: *A Little Log*, *Stop Thief!*, *Fruit and Vegetables*, *A Cock and Bull Story*, and *Hey Fool, What a Fool You Are!*

August 1931: I organized a "traveling studio"—the Kino-Train. At several large factories and kolkhozes and along the railway lines I made and released a series of short films focusing on production breakdowns. About twenty films in all.

May 1933: returned to the film studio Mosfilm in the capacity of film director. I made several feature films: *Happiness*, *Miracle Worker*, *Blossoming Youth*, *We Await Your Return and Victory*.

November 1941: appointed deputy director of the Baku Studio, following the reorganization of film production into different national centers.[5]

September 1943: appointed military film team director first on the Western Front and then on the Third Belarusian Front, where I worked till the end of the war, directing the filming of military operations of Red Army units and releasing the following film news-journals for screening throughout the Soviet Union: *Minsk Is Ours*, *Vilnius*, *East Prussia* (two installments), and *Königsberg*.

With the backing of the now-deceased A. S. Shcherbakov, I organized two experienced teams of cameramen—thirty-two men in all—drawn from the ranks of military scouts. On my initiative special film equipment was constructed for them.[6]

For my successful direction of the cameramen on the battlefield and for bravery, I was awarded the Order of the Red Banner and the Order of the Great Patriotic War, Second Class.

May 1945: designated as the director and producer of a big feature film about the revival of the destroyed economy—*Liberated Earth*. The film received a good assessment and was accepted by the Ministry of Cinematography, and is due to be shown on screens in Moscow and in the provinces.

May 1946: designated as director and producer of a feature film based on a poem by Tvardovsky—*Vasili Terkin*.

Member of the All-Union Communist Party (Bolshevik)[7] since 1920. Frequent member of the Party Bureau and Party committees. Director of the Agitational Collective of the Frunze District Committee. Was mobilized for kulak liquidations and grain procurements.[8] At the present time, I have been elected to serve as a member of the Party Bureau and as First Deputy Secretary of the Mosfilm Party Organization.[9]

I have not allowed any deviations from the Party general line and have not belonged to any oppositional groups.

Member of the All-Union Communist Party (Bolshevik),
and film director,
A. Medvedkin
24.5.46

22 Second "Autobiography"

A Filmmaker's CV

(1980, 1984)

The "Autobiography" given here is a compilation of two overlapping résumés with this title: a longer one running to 1980, and a shorter one running to 1984. The shorter one contains details omitted in the longer one, and is clearer for work in the later years. Passages taken from the shorter one are enclosed in square brackets. This autobiographical summary is a testimonial to Medvedkin's many unrealized projects and noteworthy for its listing of the many obstructions he encountered from the highest authorities. *NL*

[Born in 1900 into the family of a railway foreman.

Member of the Communist Party of the Soviet Union from 1920.

1920–21—participant in the Civil War. Combatant, clerk, adjutant of the 31st Cavalry Regiment of the 6th Caucasian Division of the 1st Cavalry Army.

1921–27—political worker for the Red Army of Workers and Peasants (RKKA): director of the regiment club. Section head of the Political Directorate of the 6th Caucasian Division. Instructor for the Political Administration of the Western Front; senior instructor for the Main Political Directorate of the Workers and Peasants Red Army (GLAVPURKKA).]

1927

Transferred from GLAVPURKKA to Gosvoenkino (the State Military Film Organization). Films:

1. *Torpedo*—instructional, 2 reels;
2. *Hygiene for a Red Army Soldier*—military instruction, 2 reels;
3. *On Patrol*—my first experimental film, in four reels, with four solutions for a challenging tactical exercise involving a group of military scouts in a tight spot. The screenings of the film were interrupted in order to give viewers a chance to find a way out of the state

of play. Then, following an on-screen discussion, one of the correct solutions was given. The film enjoyed great success with Red Army soldiers and with youths.[1]

1928-29

Directorial assistant to N. P. Okhlopkov for the experimental film *Way of the Enthusiasts*—a story about the October Revolution focusing on a peasant soldier's fate, told in conformity with heroic [narrative] conventions.

Following stormy discussions, the film was not released.[2]

1930-31

First satiric comedies:[3]

A Little Log—mocks people who are so apathetic that they fail to fix appalling situations; one reel;

Stop Thief!—everybody is enthusiastic to catch a petty thief, but lets a big one go unnoticed; one reel;

Fruit and Vegetables—a satire on submissive attitudes to bureaucrats: three train-car loads of potatoes have been delivered. A queue of five hundred people stand and wait in torment for two whole days. But three bureaucrats with copper foreheads tacked on with screws are intractable; one reel;

A Cock and Bull Story—some incompetent masons build a no-good building, which is collapsing, and a cobbler in this building makes lousy shoes, which fall apart . . . Everybody is unhappy, and everybody is shouting; two reels;

Hey Fool, What a Fool You Are!—an idiot in the top ranks of the bureaucracy builds a big factory without making any cost estimates or drawings. When he is punished and sent to a kolkhoz to dig wells, he gets bogged down in cost estimates and drawings. Everything he does is miscued: his "introduction" of Socialism to the kolkhoz, his introduction of accounting procedures, and so on; four reels.

For these experiments in comedy I suffered considerably. At a critical juncture, I was saved by Anatoli Lunacharsky, who gave strong support to my experiments in a special speech on film satire delivered before ARRK (the Association of Revolutionary Workers of Cinematography), calling for me to be given the necessary conditions to continue my bold explorations in the field of satire.[4]

1932

Headed the group behind the initiative to establish a traveling film studio—the Kino-Train. Accomplished the big task of procuring the equipment for the train.

294 days of "sorties" for this new experimental enterprise. Served simultaneously as head of the Kino-Train, chief editor, representative of the Main Repertory Committee, and principal film director.[5] Made the following films as director:

A Socialist Calling to Account by the Blacksmiths of Mine No. 3—a trenchant critical exposé in film of the terrible quality of the ore carts produced by the Krivoi Rog factory. By means of this film the blacksmiths successfully insisted on a restructuring of the manufacturing process

Counter-Claim—the Krivoi Rog factory acknowledges the blacksmiths' claims, improves the construction of the carts, and puts forward counter-claims demanding an end to poor handling of machinery, technical ignorance, and mess ups and sloppy performance—with the most salient facts recorded on film. The agit-educators from the Kino-Train worked for two months with this film in all the Ore Administrations of Krivoi Rog; two reels

Kino-Gazette No. 2—newsreel exposés of problems with the unloading of ore from Krivoi Rog;

Kino-Gazette No. 3—the same;

About Love—the first comedy of the Kino-Train. The jolly escapades of a country fellow, which end with his becoming the best machine operator in the mine;[6] two reels;

The Hole—"feuilleton" documenting a whole series of losses during the harvest, featuring the actor V. Maslatsov;[7] one reel;

Tit—"eccentric" comedy about a freeloader on a kolkhoz ("Tit, go and thresh wheat"—"Can't, I've got the stomachache");[8]

Kino-Gazette No. 17—critical pieces exposing harvesting losses in the Ukraine;

Pitfalls—army comedy, shot during maneuvers, about a soldier with his wits about him; two reels;

Steel—film about problems in the smelting of high-grade steel in the Donbas; two reels;

A Vacant Place—satirical piece documenting a breakdown in the training of machine operators in the Donbas mines; one reel.

1934

Happiness—satirical comedy using material from Russian folklore. A peasant spends his whole life striving to find happiness. Khmyr's ideal is the secure realm of a kulak.[9] Nothing turns out right for him, and when real happiness arrives in the form of a prosperous kolkhoz, he fails to understand it, and this leads to a series of tragicomic escapades.

This film, my best one, was suppressed by Shumiatsky[10] and the official and private advisers behind him.

After the war the film unexpectedly received a second life in the West. It was shown in Sweden, Belgium, Yugoslavia, Poland, the Federal Republic of Germany, the German Democratic Republic, and other countries.

The film is silent and was not provided with a soundtrack here because it did not get recognition. Some progressive filmmakers gave it a soundtrack in the Federal Republic of Germany and showed the film on television in Cologne.

1935

I worked on the script "The Unholy Force"[11] and prepared to film it. It was a film about the tragic fate of the Russian peasantry. The script was a further development of the genre of satire I had explored in *Happiness*.

The top film-workers in Mosfilm gave the script a high appraisal, and it was approved for production; actors were chosen, costumes made, drawings for sets completed . . .

The film was stopped by Shumiatsky on the eve of the scheduled beginning of shooting.

I was refused any explanation for the decision in spite of all my efforts to obtain one. At the same time, callous suggestions were circulated as to the total uselessness of my artistic explorations in the genre of satiric comedy in *Happiness*.

Twenty-eight years later Mosfilm appropriated the script "The Unholy Force" to the director A. Saltykov.

1936

I wrote the script for and made—

Miracle Worker. The film was shot on the shores of the Oka River. The chief heroine, Zinka, is a kolkhoz girl who turns into an outstanding milkmaid after a series of merry adventures.

The film was successful, but the genre of realistic comedy was not close to my heart (particularly in the wake of the "Unholy Force" disaster). I regard *Miracle Worker* as a kind of "forced landing."[12]

1937

"A Big Heart"—script for an "eccentric" comedy written together with G. Iagdfeld. The subject of the comedy was the growth of a Pioneer troop-leader.[13]

The script was not approved for production, although it had been given a high assessment.

1937 was a difficult year. Shumiatsky exiled me to Kiev, where I wrote a script—"Wide Open Fields," together with E. Pomeshchikov. The script was approved by the Kiev Studio.

For reasons related to the removal of Shumiatsky I refused to make a film in Kiev and returned to Moscow.

1938

Jolly Moscow[14]—comedy based on the general reconstruction of Moscow. With the help of Muscovite architects, I attempted to show on-screen the future new district of Cheremushki in the southwest part of Moscow.[15]

The film was shelved, although no reasons were given for this.

1939

Physical Culture Parade on Red Square—a documentary. Three reels.

"A Soldier and an Officer"—script for a comedy showing the disintegration of the Poland of landed gentry. Not produced.

1940

"Russian Folk Song"—script. Not authorized for production. And besides, war broke out.

"A Bright, Happy Lot"—script of a satirical comedy. An attempt to return to the genre of *Happiness*. Bolshakov[16] rejected it without examining it.

1941

We Await Your Return and Victory!—the first military concert film. Codirected by Ilia Trauberg and released in July 1941.

1942

"A Dead Head"—script of a satirical comedy ridiculing Fascism and Hitler's Wehrmacht. The script was approved by my superiors. In my experience as author, I consider "Dead Head" to be one of my best scripts. Moreover, it was right on target.

Bolshakov crassly forbade it, declared that I would be restricted to administrative work, and appointed me deputy director of the studio in Baku.

"Sonabol's Pain"—script of a military and patriotic comedy based on Azerbaijani folklore, written together with Imrazh Kasumov. Not produced.

1943-44

During the war I was director of frontline film crews, first on the Western Front and later on the Third Belarusian Front (Smolensk, Vitebsk, Minsk, Vilnius, Königsberg).

On top of my regular work as overseer of the filming of military operations, I organized an experimental detachment of thirty-two "sergeant-cameramen," constructed special narrow-gauge-film cameras, ran an accelerated training course, and dispatched all thirty-two cameramen into the field in the last month of the war.[17] They successfully made films recording the war in East Prussia. Their work became part of the film journalism of the last phase of the war.

1945

—At the end of the war, I left the front. My work was recognized with high awards—the Order of the Red Banner and the Order of the Great Patriotic War. At the insistence of Bolshakov, I took on an accident-prone film: namely,

Liberated Land—an artistic film depicting the return of kolkhoz farmers to their homes in the Kuban after Hitler's forces had been driven out.

The film was prone to accidents: shot footage was thrown out in its entirety. I wrote a new script. I began work in June at the demand of the Minister, and submitted it to the Grand Artistic Council of the Ministry in December.

The film was accepted with an appraisal of excellence.

1946-48

The difficult years of "low film production."[18] I was given no films. The only solution I could see to avoid becoming completely disqualified was to keep up my training by writing scripts "for myself" . . .

Without paying much attention to the demands of the leadership, I worked on my scripts every single day. I submitted each of them for approval for production. Each one was rejected, sometimes indignantly; and I would begin writing a new script. All of these fruits of my "Sisyphean labors" are preserved in my archive, and I am conceited enough to believe that numbers of them could still be made into films.

"In Kaluga Region"—an "eccentric" comedy: a soldier returns from the front to marry a girl he has met by mail. After a series of amusing adventures, he marries the niece of the woman he had fallen in love with through the exchange of letters . . .

"In Kaluga Region"—after the first script was "hacked to pieces" by the Minister (who relied on K. S. Kuzakov[19]), I wrote a new script with the same title for a lyrical comedy with a subtle psychological pattern showing how a widow and a soldier left alone after the war find great happiness after great emotional turmoil.

"Mischievous Novellas"—an attempt to return to the genre of the first satirical comedies. Here are the subjects of some of them:

"Gogol"[20]—a statue of Gogol comes to life and has various nighttime adventures in the streets of Moscow in the spirit of the demonic tales "Christmas Eve" and "Viy."

"Vovka's Upbringing"—seven nannies turn a child into a monster by feeding him quantities of porridge beyond all reasonable measure . . .

"The Bashful Bribe-Taker"—a red-haired regional administrator goes red in the face as he is leading a cow away from a kolkhoz . . .

"Trash"—a piece making fun of a toady who almost dies of fear when he makes the mistake of taking the hunting boots of his new boss . . .

"The Witch"—a girl who is sweet and charming when two lads get acquainted with her turns out to be a real Fury when she is at work in a snack bar called The Dream . . .

"Beauty"—a well-fed girl, big as a horse, sprawled out on a sofa, is reading a book. Meanwhile, her old mother washes the floor in the same room, and moves furniture about, including the sofa with the girl on it. The girl allows herself to complain that her mother fails to wash the corners.

What book was the girl reading?—*How the Steel Was Tempered*.[21]

In the same vein—"A Master Tale-Spinner of Colorful Deeds," "Black Cats," "How a Pine Tree Was Edited," and others.

Later some of the novellas were brought together in a script for a full-length comedy—

"The Jubilee of Our Severian." This script is preserved in my archive.

"All for You" and "The Love of Evil"—two scripts for satirical comedies about the adventures of Serafim Angelov, a perfunctory kolkhoz worker who is a petty speculator and loafer, and an unreformed individualist. He winds up in tragicomic situations, with the kolkhoz growing and becoming richer, while he cannot make ends meet . . .

"Song about the Future"—script for a large "eccentric" comedy, a fantasy tale about the bright future world and two petty, greedy graspers transferred to it straight from one of our markets today. Out of habit, they grab hold of anything that is left lying around, but it turns out that there is no point in doing this in the new world. And this drives the two graspers mad . . .

1948–49

In my capacity as Secretary of the Party Organization of Mosfilm, I wrote a sixteen-page statement to the Central Committee of the All-Union Communist Party about the tragic consequences for Soviet filmmakers arising from the "low-production" regime.

The Minister[22] gladly granted my request to be transferred to documentary work. He even entrusted me with the making of a film called—

Renewal of the Earth—about the big Communist construction projects, the forest zones, climate change, etc.

All I needed to do was to arrange my transfer from Mosfilm and set off into the field. But the Minister betrayed me and removed me from the picture. I tried to get him to see me: he did not receive me and gave me no explanation . . . And indeed, what could he have said to me?

I. P. Kolpan, who took my place, did not even think it necessary to meet with me: he took over the assignment without saying anything, although he could see the position I had been put in.

Having no way out, I was compelled to agree to take on the role of Roman Grigoriev's codirector for the film—

Glory to Labor—this was a film about the heroic feat of the Soviet people in fulfilling the Fourth Five-Year Plan ahead of schedule.[23]

Swallowing my disappointment, I worked with Roman Grigoriev on an equal footing. We made a successful film, and it got the Stalin Prize. The prize was received by Grigoriev. At the last moment (when the editorial offices of newspapers already had snapshots), the Minister removed me from the list of names. I was not a recipient of the prize. The Minister declined to give an explanation.

1950

Soviet Tuva. I was given this film only after a large number of directors of newsreels had turned it down in view of the catastrophic poverty of this Republic. In those years the studio made a series of documentary films about the Republics of the Soviet Union that openly glossed over the real situation, giving a not-very-truthful picture of the happy and prosperous life of the people. In Tuva there was nothing to gloss over: there was not one factory, no railway line, no steamboats on the river, and not one least-bit successful kolkhoz. The Arats, steppe shepherds, led difficult, poverty-stricken lives. Soon, help would come in the form of tractors, brigades of builders, engineers, and doctors—that would wake up and improve this distant border area. But all this was not there to show on-screen.

I discarded the stereotypical model for films about the Republics,[24] and based my approach on the idea that Socialism, everywhere, provides a release of tremendous joy and an inspiration for popular initiative.

In the composition of the film, the poverty of the country served the overall purpose, and episodes showing the first tractor, the first combine-harvester, and the first doctor to arrive in a village stood out for their unusualness. The film got an excellent reception from the Tuva District Party Committee, and the artistic collective of the studio had a high opinion of it.

Bolshakov shelved the film for the simple reason that it did not correspond to the rigid stereotype that was accepted for films about the Republics. In order to show my total artistic incompetence he dispatched a new film team to Tuva, giving them the task of showing "a blossoming Tuva," in accordance with the accepted stereotype, featuring industrial achievements, agricultural abundance, a flourishing culture, horse races, and so on.

This was a difficult time. My task was given to the film director G. M. Bobrov. Apparently he was in no position to refuse the unpleasant assignment, but not surprisingly he was unable to make a documentary film about a flourishing Tuva: the film he made could not be released, and Bolshakov's attempt to finish me off failed.

But my life became very difficult. Openly and in my presence, the Minister gave a stern warning to the studio director N. A. Kastelin that he would be severely punished if he failed to keep a stranglehold on me.

This was a direct order to give me no work.

And so I started to get no work. I managed to get an assignment for one issue of the *News of the Day*[25] at the cost of accepting to be basically released from my functions as president of the professional association of the studio.

1952–53

I released one issue of the *News of the Day* film series. The times were grim. The studio was run by a group of predatory "artistic operators," who hated me fiercely. These were the people who had cast Dziga Vertov out into the street. And I am convinced that many of the cruel actions Bolshakov took against me were a direct result of their nasty intrigues, although they always had a pleasant smile for me.

It has taken me fifteen years to bring myself to write about these difficult times in this document relating to my biography.[26] I had to write about it. Soon I will die, and film historians often treat Truth like a wire that can be bent every which way, an example of which is provided by their shifting attitude toward Dziga Vertov.

1954

First Spring

A film about the first "virgin lands," made together with I. Poselsky on the basis of a script by A. Mariamov.

The film got a good appraisal, and it has a place in the archive of best documentary films. It is a romantic and enthusiastic tale contrasting stereotypical, officious combatants with ordinary, interesting Soviet people, who have their own feelings and joys, and who go off to settle the virgin lands.

1955-56

Restless Spring—a film comedy made by me in the Alma-Ata Film Studio, devoted to the same subject, about young people in virgin lands.[27] Like my earlier realistic comedies, *Miracle Worker* and *New Moscow*, it is not one of my great artistic achievements,[28] although it was well received by viewers.

1957

Thoughts of Happiness—a big documentary film about the striking Socialist transformations of Soviet Kazakhstan.

The film received a good appraisal: the government awarded me the Order of the Badge of Honor.

1958-59

I returned from Alma-Ata to Moscow, to the Central Studio of Documentary Film. I made several film-gazettes in the *News of the Day* and the *Moscow Chronicle* series, and my first documentary lampoon, namely—

Alert! Rockets on the Rhine!—the script was cowritten by the journalist N. Polianov. The film raises the alarm about the growing militarism and revanchism of West Germany. The film was given a good appraisal.

1960

Together with the journalist B. Leontiev I wrote the script for, and filmed—

Reason against Madness—documents from the two world wars and reportage about feverish preparations for a third world war, and about the Cold War and the struggles of the Soviet people for peace and disarmament.

The film got an excellent assessment.

1961-62

The Law of Ignobility—a documentary lampoon on the collapse of the colonial system in Africa, the machinations of the neocolonial powers, and the success of national liberation movements.

The film got an excellent assessment.

1963

Morning in the Republic of Ghana—film-tale about achievements during the first years of independence in Ghana. The film got an excellent reception from viewers.

1964

One More Monument—film-lampoon on Salazar for erecting a monument to himself in Mozambique, an absurdity at a time when the peoples of Angola and Mozambique were fighting against the Portuguese colonizers.

1964-65

A Break-and-Entry Friendship—film lampooning the power and weakness of American imperialism, its methods, cruelty, and crazy warmongering.[29]

1966

Our Friend Sun Yat-Sen—a film about the great Chinese democrat and his role in the revolutionary movement in China. The film took aim at Mao Tse-Tung.[30]

1967

The Shadow of the Corporal—a lampoon on the rise of neo-Nazism in West Germany, the danger of a new world war, the rise of revanchism, and the aggressive policy of the West German government.

A special prize for the best film against Nazism was awarded to it at the International Festival in Leipzig.

1968

Sclerosis of the Conscience—a lampoon on the moral degradation of the capitalist world, the collapse of Christian civilization, the increasing amorality and the danger of a new world war. The film is a response to the events[31] in Czechoslovakia: it poses the question, What is democracy without Communists?

The film received an excellent assessment.

[1969

Letter to a Chinese Friend—a film about Maoism and the desecration of the friendship of two peoples.

1971

Night over China—a film about Mao Tse-Tung's destruction of the Chinese Communist Party.

Peace in Vietnam!—the failure of the American imperialist aggression.

1972

Disturbing Chronicle—a big documentary film about the danger of a biological catastrophe in consequence of the destruction of nature and the catastrophic disruption of the environment.

1975

Truth and Untruth—a film pamphlet about the falsification of history by Maoists, who assert that they drove out the Japanese occupiers, as if the Soviet Union played no part in this . . .]

1975

Beware! Maoism! . . . Grimaces from the Cultural Revolution.

[1976

Pekin—A Threat to Mankind—a film about Mao's heirs, their hostility to the Soviet Union, and their determined pursuit of global supremacy.]

1979

Madness!—the aggressive strategy of American imperialism. The arms race.

1984
Alert! [The Reagan administration's pursuit of military supremacy, the development of nuclear conflict, the establishment of American dominance in the world.]

[Social Contributions
Member of the Party Bureaus and committees of many Party organizations in the Red Army and in film studios. Twice elected as Secretary of the Party Bureau of the Mosfilm Studio. Served in this studio as president of the artistic division and as agitational propagandist.

In the Central Studio of Documentary Film: elected several times as member of the Party Bureau. President of the Studio Committee, agitational propagandist, etc.

Jury President of the International Moscow Festival (for documentary film) in 1971 and 1973. Jury member at two Leipzig festivals and at the festival in Lille.

Graduate of the Evening University of Marxist-Leninism (1949).

Honors and Awards
Meritorious Artist of the Russian SFSR (1965); People's Artist of the Russian SFSR (1969); People's Artist of the USSR (1979); Laureate of the Government Prize of the USSR (1974).

Awards: two Orders of Lenin; the Order of the October Revolution; the Order of the Red Banner; the Order of the Great Patriotic War, Second Class and First Class; the Order of Merit; the Medal for Distinction on the Battlefield.]

23 Marina Goldovskaia, Interviews with Medvedkin[1]

(Excerpts, 1988)

1. The "difficult" year—1937[2] (pp. 11–15)

"Gosvoenkino,[3] where I was working, was making a movie about the ballerina Ksheshinskaia, the mistress of Nicholas II, a big feature film. But I hadn't come to film in order to adapt myself to that morass and live in it, but instead to pull things apart. And so I was bad.

"But this cost me some big efforts. In particular, this was 1937, you know—a difficult year. I was summoned at night by the Minister, the president of GUK, the Main Directorate of Film. 'Boris Zakharovich[4] asks you to come at once.' It was nighttime, between midnight and 1:00 a.m. A car came for me.

"I arrived at Gnezdikovsky Passage, where Goskino has its headquarters now. I was told to familiarize myself with a script. 'What for?' The answer: 'Read it. Your advice is needed because you have worked on the theme of peasant life.'[5] I looked at it, and said it wasn't a script yet, but it could be made into one, there was something to build on. 'Good. Go to Kiev, and make the film. Introduce yourself to the studio director, Comrade Arelovich.' I thought, 'Fine, we are already acquainted'; but instead I said, 'No, I am not going anywhere.'

" 'What do you mean: Not going anywhere?'

" 'Boris Zakharovich, I won't go anywhere.' To be brief, the matter was settled at an upper level. I was summoned to Comrade Shutko, a man who could get things done, an Old Bolshevik and a very interesting man. He said to me: 'Why are you making trouble? Why won't you go to Kiev to make a film? They need film directors. Their [production] plan is in jeopardy, and we have a duty to help their national[6] film production.'

"My answer was 'I won't go because I have been singled out and not given an apartment. Everybody has got one, but not me. I take it as a sign that I am out of favor; I have come here, but I am not needed. That's why I won't go. That's all.'

" 'Why didn't they give you an apartment? That's not possible.' Me: 'This is why. The boss, Boris Shumiatsky—he's at work, in his office.

Phone him.' Comrade Shutko, a very decent man, good, an Old Bolshevik, phoned Shumiatsky and said: 'Give him an apartment. Do so within two days, without argument.' He hung up. And the next day I was summoned to GUK, and the deputy in charge of household matters was sent for. There was some whispering, and then I was installed right here, where we are, in this very building,[7] which was not yet full, in this apartment, which was still vacant. The key was given to me as had been specified in the Central Committee,[8] and I was told to get to Kiev within two days.

"And of course, since the key had been given to me, I left it with my wife, Vera, and set off for Kiev.

"I arrived in Kiev, expecting to be met by Arelovich, the director of the VUVKU studio,[9] but instead of him, there was someone else. He said: 'We'll not go to the studio, but to the Directorate.' At VUVKU I was immediately taken to the president of the National Directorate, Comrade Tkach.

"I asked Tkach why Arelovich hadn't met me. He said that Arelovich had been arrested; he was in prison and no longer to be had. I thought there was nothing for me to do, since my agreement was with Arelovich. Tkach said, 'Well, we have just received a telegram from Boris Shumiatsky, a telegram has come saying that notwithstanding Arelovich you are to make a film here.'

"I dragged my feet and tried to avoid this directive. But nothing worked. Then I specified that I had to divide up the assignment. I would write a script, and if the script was successful, then—good. And if it wasn't, we would discuss separately the question of my participation in the making of the film.

"Two or three days after I began work, all kinds of difficulties arose. In particular, there was an article in the newspaper *Kommunist* saying that I, Pyriev, and Ekk were three directors from Moscow and that we were taking the place that belonged to national [Ukrainian] film directors. And that we made films that were a slander on Soviet reality.

"Using this newspaper, I sent a cable to Moscow, to GUK, to say that I considered myself free, since I could not make a film in these conditions.

"Back came a cable saying: 'I forbid you to leave. Wait for my deputy Usievich.'

"Usievich arrived, and asked: 'Why are you rebelling? What's wrong with you? You know that things don't work out well for you.' But what was I supposed to so. I was well known in the Ukrainian Central Committee because my main work with the Kino-Train was in the Ukraine, during the harvests, in the Donbas, etc. The Kino-Train did tremendous work there. In fact, it saved from failure a lot of enterprises, kolkhozes, coal mines, ore extraction processes, and more. The attitude toward me in the Central Committee was a fairly understanding one.

"Nonetheless, the refusal to let me go back to Moscow was categorical. I had to finish a script. This gave me a real stimulus to finish everything as quickly and as well as possible.

"I made a script for Ivan Pyriev. He had made the film *The Rich Bride*. And I wrote a script called 'Three Tank Men.' The script met with approval. The directors of the studio liked it, the artistic committee, and the director. And this opened up a possibility for my going to Moscow. They tried to prevent this, but I defended myself, saying that I had to go, that I had fulfilled the conditions agreed upon at the start of the work, that the theme and material of the script were serious.

"In Moscow I was met by the director of my film team, with whom I had made two or three films. And he said, 'Dear Sasha, there is a story that Boris Shumiatsky is gone, that he has been removed from his post.'

" 'Removed, or something more?'

" 'Removed, I do not, not . . .' But for me this was enough. I was so happy. You understand—the apartment key and my family. There was the script that Pyriev had received well. He reworked it, and asked me to be the coauthor. But I was so happy and had such plans that I turned down the proposal to be the coauthor."

[In another version of his return to Moscow, given in the same interview, Medvedkin says: "When I returned to Moscow I was met by the director of my team, and he very joyfully told me that Shumiatsky had been removed and arrested. For me this was a matter for great joy."]

2. *Happiness* as an animation film? (pp. 15–16)

"*Happiness* is another thing I did against the wishes of the leadership. I could not get permission to make it because it was decided in the Main Directorate of Film that *Happiness* was an animation film. It was suited for animation, and not for real cinematography with actors.

". . . The Main Directorate of Film did not believe in a "real" treatment, and therefore decided that Medvedkin had to film two or three episodes as trial shots, to find out whether this genre was suitable for an acted film, and not just for animation film.[. . .]

"I went along with this because there was no alternative. We constructed a set for the very first episode, where Khmyr and his wife, Anna, peer through a slit-hole to look at their neighbor who is eating dumplings as if he were Gogol's Patsiuk.[10] The dumplings flop down into the sour cream and then fly straight into his mouth. Each successive dumpling does the same thing. He sits and empties the bowl of dumplings. On the other side of the fence are hungry, indigent peasants, and they sit and just salivate. Then there was the second episode . . . [pause]

"I did it. I got a message from the Main Directorate that they had decided that the film would work, and that I was given permission to carry on: Let him go ahead.

"I believe things worked out because some real Bolsheviks, real people, saw my ordeals with my films, and how difficult my relations with the authorities were, and they made it possible for me to make *Happiness*. And so I made it."

3. The silence surrounding *Happiness* (pp. 18–19)

Question: "Why wasn't *Happiness* accepted at the time?"

"It was not accepted because that was the situation in Soviet film. Film was like a stepmother to me. That was the situation not only with *Happiness* but also with the Kino-Train. It took me half a year to free up the train cars and get permission to organize the train. It proved itself, but even today there are difficulties."

"Why?"

"Because I am not very—"

"Opportunistic?"

"No, not 'opportunistic.'"

"Conformist?"

"Something like that. *Happiness* did not get a single review. Except from Sergei Eisenstein.[11] Not one. That is to say, not a single newspaper took the risk of praising it or championing it. It was shown for two or three days in movie theaters that were not of the first rank. And then it was totally withdrawn. It disappeared, and later I was told . . . [pause]

"The worst weapon in film is silence. When people are silent. You've made a film, and it's as if nobody has noticed. You organize a Kino-Train, and, so to say, nobody ever, ever writes about it, until afterward, when Chris Marker makes a two-reel documentary called *The Train Rolls On* (1973).[12]

"And again, nothing was said a third time, when I was head of a front-line film crew, and I thought up another, equally complicated operation, with sergeants serving as cameramen.[13] [. . .]

"This was the third instance. And finally there is a book, *Chroniclers of Our Time*, a book about documentary filmmakers, compiled by Prozhiko and Firsova, with Lebedev and Makhnach as reviewers.[14] All of them are comrades whom I respect, and with whom I go back some years. But in this book, which comes after *Happiness*, and after the cameramen-soldiers, and after the Kino-Train, there is not a single word about me or the train.

"As I've said, I don't need fame, but I do want truth. If in the conditions of *glasnost*, people are resorting to games of this sort, I don't need their friendship."

4. Peasant origins (p. 6)

"I was born in a peasant family. True, my father was a railway foreman, and my grandfather built one of the first railway lines in central Russia—in the province of Penza. From childhood I loved railways. I have always respected them and been interested in them."

5. Childhood labor in a church choir (p. 52)

"It was in a church choir that my working or laboring life began, and I was paid thirty kopeks a month. I was an altar boy, and sang at vespers and the communion service. I was eight or nine years old."[15]

6. Satire as a suicidal path (pp. 28–29)

"I did not have one single follower. Not because my path was defective or my creative standards were too high, but because my path was suicidal. It was the path of a man who was being killed. 'They' killed me with the Kino-Train, 'they' killed me with the cameramen-soldiers, with "The Unholy Force," and with *Happiness*.

"Everywhere film was like a stepmother in the way it treated me, even though my whole life was spent in film and in artistic investigations. I haven't told you about my searches for all sorts of comic devices, nor about my concern and my attempts to organize our amateur movement, our new, young, 'lesser' cinema and to make it into a poetic cinema."

7. The peasant question in the Kino-Train films and in *Happiness* (pp. 17–18)

"The Kino-Train did its work in the Ukraine, where we filmed the harvest and the gathering in of the crop, and the work of the kolkhozes [collective farms]. The kolkhozes were young, they were just beginning to develop. In the kolkhozes I found people who were not happy that they had given their horses to [communal] stables, and that the conditions in the first years . . . the existence of the kolkhozes was very difficult. There was no experience, no technical knowledge.

"Horses often keeled over.

[pause]

". . . [A man] who did not live with the good of the kolkhoz in mind, but dreamed of his own horse, and barn, and a good harvest and grain, and so on. Such a man was a poor devil, without a heart, who did not do any work himself, and interfered with the others. You understand? This was a characteristic phenomenon of the just-born kolkhozes. I understood that something had to be done; maybe I needed to make a film about happiness, about the way such a man looked for happiness, the way a peasant looked for happiness. Yes. But happiness didn't come to him. He was driven to the point where he wanted to die.

"This was the foundation on which the film was constructed. But there was a positive ending; Anna, his wife, was a shock-worker, and she received a [good share of the] harvest, while he was an asocial peasant, without a firm belief in the kolkhoz, and remained quite uninvolved. It ends with the kulaks recruiting him. But in this situation, he gets in the way of the kulaks, he is fairly clearheaded, and interferes with the kulaks when they are going to burn down the stable with the horses in it at the time the sowing is about to begin.

[pause]

"You might want to hold the author guilty in this matter. But thirty-five years later the film has been seen in big countries and in big theaters."

8. Maxim Gorky's support for "The Unholy Force" (pp. 30–32)

"Every fight has an ending. That was the case with 'The Unholy Force.'

I tried to drive this film past one authority, then another, and then a third, all without result. To rid myself from my oppressive feelings of disaffection and break with my dreams and thoughts about the shooting of 'The Unholy Force' I sent the script to Maxim Gorky. At that time, he was ill and lived in the Crimea, in a villa. It was an act of despair. And unexpectedly I received a letter saying that Gorky remembered me and was not opposed to meeting with me as long as I could travel there, since he was ill and busy writing a book.

"Of course, I at once dropped everything and went. I was not admitted to see him straightaway. He already had . . . he was very ill. He was finishing his book *The Life of Klim Samgin*.[16] There were doctors, nurses, secretaries. People spoke in hushed voices in the hallway, while he sat in his office and wrote.

"When they learned that I had come to see him, they were horrified: 'Have you gone mad? Why have you come?' I answered that I had come after receiving a letter from him. 'But Aleksei Maksimovich[17] is finishing a book, and he is in such a state that there is no point in thinking about this matter.' To which I said, 'Comrades, or rather you, Comrade Secretary, the letter I received bears your signature. Truly.' In short, I had no alternative; I had to hold my ground, and I did.

"And so this comrade, the secretary, went to Gorky. And *he* said: 'Let him come in. Where is he? Has he arrived? Well then, he must see me.'

"So I went in to Gorky. He was sitting, and continually smoking. He'd finish a cigarette, toss it away while it was still burning, and light another. And at the same time he was writing. When I came in, he put his pen down. 'Well,' he said, 'what's going on? I've read your script. It is on the same level as *Happiness*.' And he had liked *Happiness* a great deal, and shown it to Romain Rolland, and someone else, it doesn't matter who. Romain Rolland approved of it, and he had also read the script, 'The Unholy Force.'[18]

"Gorky said that I had not succeeded in doing everything as I wanted, but that I was on the right road. 'You are faithful to the peasant question, and that is right, that is the right way. Keep to it, and make, so to say, a real film. Judging from *Happiness*, I believe that you can do it.'

"Since the script was like *Happiness*, he approved of it. And so I said almost nothing, and just listened and focused on remembering. He said, 'I met with some film workers not long ago, and I didn't like the meeting at all. I didn't like it because writers are being driven out of film work, and makeshift, improvised scripts are left, because many directors are unable to produce anything better. As for me, I am going to Moscow in the near future, in June, and I will try to meet with the people I need. And I will also try to help you. I have made a note of it, don't worry.'

"And so I got up, said good-bye, and left. And he went to Moscow, and there he died.[19] That is the story of my meeting with Maxim Gorky."

24 The Suppression of *Happiness*

A. Note by Medvedkin dated 4 March 1988[1]

The fate of *Happiness* was uncommon. After a few days in distribution, the film disappeared from the screen. The press "unanimously" ignored the release of the comedy, although my success was sufficiently obvious that, with it for inspiration, I firmly resolved to devote the rest of my artistic life to the development of the film genre I had discovered.

In keeping with this resolution, I began writing a new script in 1936.

Thus a new work, "The Unholy Force," came into being.

This time I spared neither time nor effort in the attempt to show on-screen, with all possible satiric force, the tragedy of the Russian peasantry under serfdom.

All fifty years of my artistic life have been devoted to attempts to beat a path for this kind of film. And all authorities and levels of authority have raised fundamental objections to it.

In the thirties Gorky tried to help me;[2] he held the comedy *Happiness* in high esteem. And in recent years the great master of film, Sergei Bondarchuk, has devoted considerable efforts toward making the new film possible.

Now it seems the administrators in charge of film do not object to the making of "The Unholy Force," but I am more than eighty-eight years old.

This is the paradox! I never ceased to work on comedies during all these years, but, bitterly, I call this a time of "forced imprisonment." All the attempts to destroy my passion for satire and get me to satisfy myself with ordinary film comedies—which are fundamentally alien to me—failed and still fail to release in me the kind of fire I felt for *Happiness* and "The Unholy Force." This is true even though these film comedies were generally warmly received by spectators. And I include here the lyrical comedy *Miracle Worker*, which found great success when it was shown in Paris.

I want to explain the basis of my fascination with *Happiness*.[3]

B. From Filmed Interviews with Marina Goldovskaia (p. 27)[4]

An artist's full maturity is between the ages of thirty-five and fifty. Basically I lost the years starting when I was thirty-five and ending in my fifties, when I could have made five films, at least five, like *Happiness*. I was filled with strength, filled with inspiration.

25 Color Film in *Happiness*

The film scholar and Medvedkin expert Nikolai Izvolov was told by Medvedkin that there was a color sequence in *Happiness*. Izvolov has found further confirmation for this in an advertisement in the newspaper *Kino* announcing the pending completion of *Happiness* and its release in Moscow movie theaters. It includes the words:

> **The film contains episodes with COLOR FILM**
> **(Khmyr's dream of a happy life).**

These episodes—evidently shot with a two-color process—do not survive in the one existing positive copy of the film, from which a new negative was struck.[1] *NL*

Remembrance and Revival

26 The Kino-Train Filmography

TRANSLATED BY JAY LEYDA

Jay attached great importance to Medvedkin's "Filmography" recording the collective film work of the Kino-Train crew. He translated it himself, and used it as part of his dossier demonstrating the importance of a book devoted to the revolutionary achievements of Alexander Medvedkin.[1]

The first year of work of the Kino-Train from 25 January 1932 to 15 January 1933[2]

SORTIE 1: TRANSPORTATION (Dnepropetrovsk Railway Station)
25 January–21 March 1932

The launching operation; tests of equipment and materials; putting the laboratory process in order; first experimental films; investigation of methods of mass-agitational work; first experiments with screening a film *on the same day it was shot*.

Assistance to railway workers in solving problems attached to the unexpected increase of freight traffic over the fall and winter.

1. *Kino-Gazette* No. 1 (318 m) Made to acquaint railway workers with the work of the Kino-Train.
2. *Axle Box* (287 m) The axle box of a loaded boxcar, the source of frequent accidents; film shows an expert oiler.
3. *Kino-Gazette* No. 2 (280 m) Special edition showing faults in the freight-loading section of a large metallurgical plant.
4. *Kino-Gazette* No. 3 (146 m) Celebration of Red Army Day at Dnepropetrovsk. Film shown on the same day it was filmed.
5. *On the Way* (590 m) Snow blocks railway lines. The film appeals to all to clear the tracks; it shows the example set by the best workers.
6. *Kino-Gazette* No. 4 (275 m) Topics focusing on a station depot.

7. *Satirical Adventures of a Camel in the Railway Car Maintenance Section of Dnepropetrovsk* (383 m)
8. *Kino-Gazette* No. 5 (291 m) Topics focusing on work on the railway lines.
9. *The Terms of a Socialist Competition: The Railway-Car Team versus the Locomotive Team in the Dnepropetrovsk Depot* (350 m)

Total: 9 films—2,925 m

SORTIE 2: KRIVOI ROG 4 April–30 May 1932

In the spring of 1932 the mining of iron ore in the Krivoi Rog Basin was lagging, creating serious problems for the main metal factories in the south. The Kino-Train was sent to this district on the recommendation of , People's Commissar for Heavy Industry Sergo Ordzhonikidze.

At the station of Vechernii Kut:

1. *Kino-Gazette* No. 6 (280 m)
2. *Kino-Gazette* No. 7 (104 m) Two films on the daily life of the iron-miners.
3. *Forward to New Technology!* (350 m) Film on the successes and faults of the mining district's reconstruction.
4. *A Socialist Calling to Account: From the Mine-3 Blacksmiths to the Central Krivoi Rog Workshops* (184 m) The film was written by the blacksmiths who had proposed the theme. Poor construction of the carts transporting the ore had caused huge losses and retarded the work. After projecting the film at the factory, management was compelled to hasten construction of the containers.
5. *Counter-Claim: From the Krivoi Rog Workshop Men to the Miners of the October Mine Organization* (275 m) Having accepted the challenge of the blacksmiths, the factory workers are shown presenting counter-claims demanding an end to the wrong attitude toward equipment. The workers call for training workers cadres, taking care of the equipment, and penalizing poor workers, who are also shown in this film.
6. *No Avoidance of Personal Responsibility* (335 m) About the attitude to be adopted vis-à-vis the new techniques; and personal responsibility vis-à-vis each machine. The film depicts damage done to the new technology.
7. *For the Brigade* (337 m) With the example of two mines, the film demonstrates the superiority of the new organization of labor, fol-

lowing the principle of independent brigades. Critical material is included.

8. *Kino-Gazette* No. 8 (157 m) How technical training was mishandled in one mine; how the same work was well organized in an adjoining mine.
9. *Kino-Gazette* No. 9 (287 m)
10. *Kino-Gazette* No. 10 (112 m)
11. *Kino-Gazette* No. 11 (275 m)
12. *Kino-Gazette* No. 12 (215 m) Criticisms on disorganization in the extraction of minerals; aspects of the miners' daily lives.
13. *The Need for a Mastery of Machinery* (254 m) The Komsomol youth's mastery of new machinery and their responsible attitude toward new techniques. Positive and negative examples.
14. *A Socialist Assessment of the All-Ukrainian Ore-Mining Conference*. The discussions of miners with engineers about acute problems in improving the output of mines and about technical reequipment.
15. *Kino-Gazette* No. 13 (178 m) On shortcomings in transport.
16. *About Love*[3] (500 m) First of the eccentric comedies made on the Kino-Train; this shows the adventures of a young miner and his girlfriend.
17. *Join the Battle for Technology* (300 m) The miners of the Red Guard Mine initiate Socialist competition in the implementation of new technology.
18. *How Goes It, Comrade Miner?* (500 m) Sharp criticism of a bad canteen for miners compared with the excellent canteen at a neighboring mine.
19. *A Film-Letter* (355 m) Sharp contrast of the life in two dormitories, one of them inhospitable, the other clean and excellent, with an enthusiastic leader.
20. *The Jackhammer* (618 m) An instructional film on its mechanism and how the best miner in Krivoi Rog looked after it and used it.
21. *Film Report of the Kino-Train to the Miners*, on its work for the past two months (300 m) The journey to Krivoi Rog produced the richest of harvests; the train helped in the reconstruction of the district's work; the train's collective was awarded the "Red Flag of Honor"; the best brigades competed to be designated as a "Kino-Train Brigade."

Total: 21 films—6,320 m

SORTIE 3: COLLECTIVE FARMING (Ukraine, Crimea) 8 July–19 August 1932
Excursion to help the collective farmers at harvesttime. Young collectives, not yet strong, had difficulty testing new forms in organization of the harvest. Communicating through film the experience of the vanguard farms and the leading brigades alongside those that were lagging was of great importance in strengthening the collective farms.

1. *Veitlus* (395 m) Film on the work organization of the best kolkhoz in one region of the Ukraine.
2. *Kino-Gazette* No. 14 (333 m) Various observations on shortcomings in the gathering of the harvest, the loss of grain, the experience of the best brigade.
3. *The Hole* (335 m) Film-feuilleton on the losses in the "grain-chain" at harvesttime, when between the field and the barn there was a loss of nearly one-third of the harvested wheat.
4. *Kino-Gazette* No. 15 (238 m) Concerning the best avant-garde farmers at the moment of harvest.
5. *For the Assembly Line* (300 m)[4] A film to prove the advantages of a new organization of work based on a system of "links." The story of the best work of the best team.
6. *Sheaving the Wheat!* (308 m) Propaganda film for the best method of binding wheat into sheaves, to avoid loss; comparing the best kolkhoz workers with the laggards.
7. *Tit* (670 m) The second "eccentric" comedy by the train: about a lazy kolkhoz-member; based on the Russian proverb

   Tit! Time to do some threshing!
   I've got the stomachache!
   Tit, time to eat kasha!
   Where is my big spoon?

   The result was a comic hit when shown in all subsequent journeys.
8. *Pioneers, Hurry to the Fields!* (285 m) On their way to fields already harvested, a team of Young Pioneers collects mounds of wheat ears. On the screen, the Pioneers call to the schoolchildren of the Ukraine to go into the fields to glean wheat lost during the harvest. The appeal was heard in many regions of the Ukraine.
9. *Kino-Gazette* No. 16 (185 m)
10. *Kino-Gazette* No. 17 (255 m)

11. *Kino-Gazette* No. 18 (295 m)

    Challenging subjects on deficiencies in the work of harvesting, portraits of the best kolkhozians, kino-feuilletons on the organization of work, etc.

Total: 11 films—3,659 m

SORTIE NO. 4: RED ARMY MANEUVERS (based at Vinnitsa)

1–10. Films on military subjects, tied to the progress of the maneuvers.

11. *Absorbing* Problems (720 m) A test by screen of the soldiers' intelligence. The posing of problems (sending out a patrol, the scouts find themselves in a catastrophic situation). The film is halted at the most critical moment: during an open discussion, the audience proposes various solutions, after which the screen shows variations on the correct solution of the problem.
12. Pitfalls (755 m) The third eccentric comedy: adventures of a somewhat simpleminded soldier.

Total: 12 films—5,385 m

SORTIE NO. 5 (Dneprostroi) 5-11 October 1932

The Opening of DneproGES (400 m) The film was completed on the day of the inauguration and was screened at the banquet. That evening it was shown to the metalworkers of the Petrovskii Factory, singing "The Internationale." The next day it was shown in Moscow and Kiev. This was an unusual procedure; the film created a sensation (television was still in the future).

SORTIE NO. 6 (Donbas) 20 October 1932-15 January 1933

In the fierce battles for the First Five-Year Plan, the main goals were bread, coal, and metal. Our journey to the Donbas was the longest and most significant.

COAL

1. *The Conveyor Belt* (550 m) Showing the production success of the winning shock-worker miner, Diky, the first to work with shifting the conveyor in the mine, greatly increasing the yield.
2. *Pickax Heroes* (550 m) Story of the innovative miner Nikita Izotov.
3. *The "Komsomol" Mine Calls!* (400 m) An appeal for Socialist emulation of the method of identifying the mineral strata, which had made it possible for the "Komsomol" mine to double its output.

4. *Circumstances beyond Our Control* (550 m) Grave problems of the foreman's role.
5. *A Vacant Place* (550 m) Satirical reportage. Comic and satirical story ridiculing the errors in preparing cadres for one mine.
6. *The Jackhammer* Five looped animated instructional films, explaining the operating principles of the mechanisms of the jackhammer. Three-meter-long animation films were pasted into a loop, so that they could be continuously projected while a lecturer explained the mechanisms.

   The jackhammer had just been introduced to the mines of the Donbas. Thousands of miners had to learn to use them. One hundred fifty copies of the looped films were printed, and were successfully used in the training of cadres.
7. *The Coal Cutter* Five looped animated films, following the principle of the jackhammer animations.

METAL

8. *Pushkin's Secret* (600 m) How the Makeeva blast-furnace workers won the contest; we show their secrets and their portraits.
9. *How to Train a Worker* (400 m) A brigade of elederly steelworkers who sponsor young workers.
10. *The Problem of Holes* (500 m) Indictment brought against the steel-mill workers who allowed damage to a Martin furnace. (The workers allowed steel to escape from the furnace, resulting in the formation of a "sow.")
11. *Steel* (550 m) A critical film on the making of special steels: why are there so many mishaps?
12. *Gas Generator* (550 m) Steps taken to improve the gas in Martin furnaces; the film promotes precision work as against approximation.
13. *The First Soviet Rolling-Mill* (250 m)
14. *Blast Furnaces* Five looped animated films for instruction about tall furnaces and the production of iron.
15. *Letter from a Kolkhoz Worker* (315 m) A letter addressed to steelworkers complaining of sabotage by kulaks. Our film-investigation was filmed in accordance with the letter. The saboteurs were prosecuted.
16. *Adventures of the Camel on the Railway Tracks* Animated-film comedy about confusion in the transport workshop of a metallurgical plant.

Total: 16 films—5,830 m

During the Kino-Train's first year, from 25 January 1932 to 15 January 1933, we made 70 films, using 24,565 meters of usable footage. The political workers of the train made daily use of these, in lagging sectors of production in factories, collective farms, and construction sites. In the DonBas alone, at the thirty-nine mines visited by the Kino-Train, the results were

i. sixty-seven screenings and technical discussions;
ii. the establishment of thirty-five courses, groups, and technical schools;
iii. the establishment of thirteen technical centers;
iv. the dismissal and prosecution of forty-eight incompetent workers;
v. the reorganization of the work of eighteen canteens.

Signed: A. Medvedkin
Former Head of the Kino-Train

27 Surviving Kino-Train Films

Prefatory note by Medvedkin: In December 1987 the VGIK student Nikolai A. Izvolov searched the State Film Archive (Krasnogorsk) and found eight one-reel films from the Kino-Train, made by us during its first trip in the Ukraine.

Signed: The Former Head of the Kino-Train,
A. Medvedkin, January 1988

1. *Let's Organize Production Links.*[1] During the gathering of the harvest, a linking of responsibilities proved to be the best form of organization for kolkhozes, which are not yet solidly established. The one-reel film contrasted the experience of lagging kolkhozes with that of the leading ones.
2. *"Veitlus."* The president of a Lithuanian kolkhoz, a born organizer, shows how he organizes labor. (A one-reel film.) His kolkhoz is the best one in the Crimean oblast.
3. *Kino-Gazette* No. 4.[2] A critical examination of the lack of resourcefulness, responsibility, and discipline in the harvesting. The experience of the best brigades and production links. One-reel film.
4. *Letter to the Donbas Kolkhoz Workers.* A summons to join in the fight for the grain harvest. The discovery of three kulak cells, and the trial. One-reel.
5. *How Goes It, Comrade Miner?* The "October" Ore Administration of the Krivoi Rog Basin. The semicollapsed state of the shafts. The causes: the turnover of workers; the cheats and thieves in the new kitchen factory; the dirt and drunkenness in the dormitories. In contrast with these outrages, the "Red Guard" Ore Mine was presented. Here the food was good and the living conditions were clean, and the plan quotas were met better than elsewhere.
6. *The Reconstruction of the Krivoi Rog Basin.* Technical advances displace the antiquated wheelbarrow. Scrapers; mine carts; motors; jackhammers. The chief obstacle—a hostile disposition toward

mechanization. Bosses who are not held accountable. Drunken disorder.

7. *Forward to New Technology!* The struggle for mechanization. The lack of accountability of bosses. Bureaucratization. One reel.
8. *The Opening of DneproGES*. The celebration of the start-up. The speeches of S. Ordzhonikidze and M. I. Kalinin. The screening of the film at the banquet on the same day it was shot.

In an e-mail dated 24 July 2015, Izvolov says that these films are all located in the Russian State Archive of Documentary Film in Krasnogorsk. He adds that one more film, *A Vacant Place*, directed by Medvedkin, has recently been found by Petr Bagrov.

28 History of *The Alexander Medvedkin Reader*

NIKITA LARY

Jay Leyda's last major project was a book devoted to Medvedkin: "It was to rescue a great talent from oblivion that began this project, and I see that part of my task is to hold us together to carry out this rescue. How Chris Marker will find his place editorially is another part of this task. He has already done more than anyone else to bring the films and principles of Medvedkin to European and American notice. One of my big hopes for the book is that it will bring more than one of Medvedkin's films outside his native country. This is part of my A.I.M. (Medvedkin's initials)."[1] The greater part of Medvedkin's work had been lost (the ephemeral Kino-Train films), suppressed (*Happiness*), or prevented (the "Unholy Force" film). The book Jay envisaged would record Medvedkin's work as that of an original, experimental filmmaker and a satirist who remained a committed Bolshevik.

Medvedkin participated in the making of the book as the principal author and compiler; it was to be *his* book. Jay's initial collaborator was Michael Heim, who met with Medvedkin in Moscow and collected archival materials from him; he was the likely translator. In 1984, when other projects had a more urgent claim on Michael Heim's time, Jay—a colleague at York University—asked me to join the editorial team and take over as translator. I met with Medvedkin four times in 1984 and 1985, and again in 1988, discussed the book with him and his concerns about it, and collected more of his writings. I began translating them. Jay saw first drafts of the translations of the greater part of the contents of the book and made corrections in them. However, my progress was slow; I had not finished the translations at the time of Jay's death in 1988. His role in the completion of the project he had defined in this way: "Besides giving more shape to the translations, I see that the fitting together of the scripts and autobiographical fragments may be my main function."[2] Following his death, I set aside my work on the book until a time when I would be free to devote myself wholeheartedly to it.

It had been Jay's hope that Chris Marker would participate "editorially," although his role remained undefined. He expressed this wish to Marker in letters, and also asked Medvedkin to write to him with the same request: "I hope you will write to Chris. He imagines that his presence among the three editors will damage the project. I think he is wrong, or possibly exaggerating the difficulties of his position. I want his collaboration as much as you do. Please tell him" (letter dated 11 September 1981). Marker feared that his participation might be an obstacle to approval of the project. In his article reprinted in this compilation ("The Last Bolshevik" [29]), he speaks of his work in forming "Medvedkin Groups" in France, and says: "A rumor started to grow—about a long-forgotten Russian director who had done strange things under Stalin. . . . I kept Medvedkin informed, but, to be frank, I was slightly apprehensive about the response in the U.S.S.R.: a nation doesn't obligatorily appreciate that its rebuked artists are rediscovered abroad."

Jay continued to write to him about the book's contents. Marker apparently planned to contribute an article to it. The independent filmmaker Matt Peterson, who met with him in 2008 and 2009, said that Marker believed the book would include "a sort of festschrift, with essays, articles, testimonies on the man and his work from colleagues, filmmakers, critics, scholars, etc., of which Marker was only one."[3] After Medvedkin's death in Febuary 1989, Marker saw that the best contribution he could make to Medvedkin's legacy was as a filmmaker.[4] He subsequently gathered filmed interviews in Russia with people closely associated with Medvedkin and edited them into a film, *The Last Bolshevik* (1992); it is a distinctive Festschrift in film. With the collapse of Communism in Russia the previous year, the French title of the film, *Le tombeau d'Alexandre*, carries a particular resonance. The ideology that enclosed Medvedkin while he lived was dying. The film about Alexander Medvedkin is also a meditation on the end of a dream. The article Marker wrote after the making of the film is obviously not the article he would have written before Medvedkin and Leyda died; it is nonetheless republished here.

Leyda and Medvedkin were in substantial agreement about the contents of the book. Both wanted an account of the Kino-Train work; the short satirical scripts; and the scripts of *Happiness* and *Miracle Worker*. Leyda was probably the one to ask for the *Miracle Worker* script (Medvedkin felt it was a compromise, a comedy rather than a satire). Neither of them mentioned *New Moscow*, which Medvedkin regarded as another comedy. Leyda would have liked to have the original shooting scripts: Medvedkin preferred to write "literary scenarios." In a letter he said: "I have completely reworked the script of *Happiness* frame by frame. This was necessary. Now the script reads as a FULL-FLEDGED literary work."[5] Both men wanted to include the script for Medvedkin's major unmade film, "The Unholy Force." The many postwar years devoted to make-do documentary films would be passed over. In a letter to Marker, Jay said: "We both are as uneager as you are for an anti-climax of the post-war compilation films."

Medvedkin would have liked to include materials relating to the reception of *Happiness* in France when it was screened there by Chris Marker and to the revival of the Kino-Train experiment by two groups of workers in that country in 1968. And he proposed to write an autobiography. (Jay felt that there was not room for both proposed inclusions.) Medvedkin also wanted to write a special article explaining why he became a satirist: "It seems to me that the success of the book wholly depends on a precise and truthful answer to this question. . . . The mode of attack in each of my works is organically connected with the titanic efforts of the Russian people to overcome everything that prevents a victory over material and spiritual poverty, and the construction of a new, unprecedented world."[6] Medvedkin feared that his book might be unacceptable because of his attacks on Western militarism in his recent documentary films (about which, in fact, little was known abroad). He also fretted that after the book was published, the satires would be turned against themselves: "It would be distressing if the satirical themes and motifs of my films were used by the dregs of mankind, who hate us, as material for defaming our heroic reality. In my view we must keep in mind the possibility of such a reaction."[7] He knew from his own experience that satire was a double-edged sword.

When Jay saw all the material sent by Medvedkin, he realized that the book was basically written. The material included some new pieces on satire and revisions of pieces Medvedkin had in his archive. Everything was covered: his experimental work in film on the Kino-Train and in the Second World War, and earlier in theater during the Civil War; the scripts; and the explanation of the fundamental importance of satire in his work. Jay wrote to me: "The best news is that he need not face a great writing job—he has already done his book. If he wants to polish the scenarios (you have the short ones) or extend the three pieces of prose (I sent you the one that we need), that's good—and easily accomplished."[8] In affirmation of Medvedkin's position as author, he stated: "Medvedkin's authoritative text comes from his own archive."[9] The editors were to refrain from criticism and analysis. In an undated letter to the French film critic Marcel Martin, Jay exclaimed:

> Rejoice, Marcel! Medvedkin is at last to have a book of his own—something to replace the lost and unrealized films, plus scripts of the few triumphs he had realized.
>
> Introduction, of course, by Eisentein.
>
> If you have any suggestions or discoveries, please let me know. This has to be THE Medvedkin book.

When I returned to the book with an editor's eye, it was apparent that the translations could be improved; I worked on this and on finding the best way to sort out and fit the different pieces together. It was also apparent that some light footnoting and commentary were needed to help the reader who was not a specialist or who was not going to read the book the whole way through. I could see that Eisenstein's review of *Happiness* could not stand as an introduction to the whole book. No doubt, Jay could have presented it in a way to fulfill this purpose. I wrote a preface. An article by the leading Russian scholar of Medvedkin, Nikolai Izvolov, was added to the contents [20]; its inclusion had been approved by Jay.

In the final discussions about the book with the University of Chicago Press, the situation had changed in one important way. The inclusion of the scripts for *Happiness* and *Miracle Worker* could present international copyright problems that had not earlier been a concern. However, the former of these films was now available on DVD, whereas before it was not readily available. Both films could also be viewed on the Internet. Eisenstein's review of *Happiness* can therefore be read in conjunction with a viewing of the film. And the book can remain true to its original purpose of focusing on and rescuing the many forgotten, lost, and suppressed parts of Medvedkin's considerable achievement. It can lay claim to be "THE Medvedkin book." Some aspects of Jay's conception can only be guessed at. Among the notes he left for this book is this tantalizing one: "Medvedkin's use of folklore as basic language for his satirical films and scripts is what sets him alongside Mark Twain." Unfortunately, this hint remained undeveloped.

29 The Last Bolshevik: Reminiscences of Alexander Ivanovich[1]

CHRIS MARKER

It all began in Brussels' Film Library ("Cinematheque Royale") when my friend Jacques Ledoux, the flamboyant conservator, received a package of brand-new prints from Moscow. In it, classics like Eisenstein, connoisseurs' choices like Barnet, and one totally unknown: *Schastie (Happiness)* by A. I. Medvedkin. Ledoux hadn't ordered it, he didn't even know the man's name. Apparently, one hidden hand had thrown that bottle into the sea of Cinemathèques, hoping for a welcoming creek.

I happened to see *Schastie* almost at once. Ledoux invited me often to watch his new discoveries. Both of us were flabbergasted, as were to be all who would discover the film after us, by its unique mixture of humor, lyricism, and cinematographic mastery. Plus the mystery of the date: 1934—and yet a silent picture. Plus the fact that flim and filmmaker were completely forgotten by the historians of Soviet Cinema, starting with our respected Sadoul. Only in Jay Leyda's monumental *KINO: A History of the Russian and Soviet Film* did I find one page—only to arouse my curiosity even more. It mentioned, besides *Schastie* and another feature film, an incredible experiment in the Thirties: a *Kinopoezd*, a film-train, carrying cameras, lab, editing tables, screening material and even actors, to produce the first rail-movies, films made on the spot, in collaboration with the local people (workers in factories, peasants in *kolkhozs*), shot in one day, processed during the night, edited the following day, and screened in front of the very people who had participated in its making. Contrary to the agitprop trains, which carried official propaganda from the studios to the people, here the people were their own studio. At the very moment bureaucracy was spreading all over, a film unit could go and produce uncensored material throughout the country. And it lasted one year (1932)! Curtain.

Act two: The Leipzig Festival, 1967. Jay Leyda is there.[2] I haven't seen him for a while (he doesn't know anything about my daydreaming around his page) and the first thing he says is, "There is one man in the Soviet delegation you absolutely must meet: Alexander Medvedkin." He could as well have said, "Sergei Mikhailovich"—for me, there wasn't the slightest doubt that Medvedkin was dead. (Later on, Medvedkin himself would be enchanted by the anecdote, he would roar to any benevolent ear, "And Chris said: That man couldn't be Medvedkin—he's dead!") Hence a double bewilderment: me, to be face-to-face with a man who ten minutes earlier belonged to the history of forgotten geniuses of the past: he, to listen to an unknown Frenchman who seemed to know more about his best film and his railway adventures than most of his countrymen. The commotion was resolved the Russian way, that is, with a considerable amount of vodka, amidst a cheering choir of dissident East Germans (Wolf Biermann was there) and outspoken Cubans (this was 1967, remember). At dawn, all of us were severely stoned, but for Alexander Ivanovich and Chris Krazykatovich it was the beginning of a friendship which would last until the death of the former, in 1989.

From that day on, I had the project of doing justice to Medvedkin's personality and works through a film. Needless to say, there were soberer days during the festival, and I learned a lot about *Schastie* (that it was banned for a while, distributed with difficulty, that S. M. Eisenstein came to the rescue), about the Train (that the actors embarked in the adventure belonged to the troupe of—guess who?—Meyerhold, that they made cartoons along the way, that they had prewritten titles to intercut in their on-the-spot inquiries, and that the most widely used was, "Comrades, this cannot last!"), and also about the origins of Alexander's passion for showbiz: during the Civil War, he was a horseman in Budenny's First Cavalry Army, and immediately created a 'Horse Theater,' a satirical performance where, between two battles, cavalrymen disguised as horses criticized the company's daily deeds. (Example: the horse of a womanizing commander complained loudly about having to stay out all night in the rain while the boss enjoyed himself. And the commander was in the audience! Shades of Isaac Babel.) Now Medvedkin was apparently confined to small documentaries, the type nobody else would care for —about China, for instance. And there was a wide "blank" in his biography, between the second film, *Chudesnitsa* [*Miracle Worker*], in 1936, and 1942, when, like others in the same category, he would be sent to the front. Leipzig was his first mission abroad.

These were the blossoming years of the political cinema in France. I derive a certain pride to be able to date the beginning of our film experiments with factory workers from 1967, not 1968. Medvedkin's anecdotes were so typical of the spirit we all wished to share, that very soon they became legendary among our little groups, and the *Groupe Medvedkine* arose quite naturally to christen the first one, in Besançon, during a long strike in December '67. A rumor started to grow—about a long-forgotten Russian director who had done strange things under Stalin. . . . I kept Medvedkin informed, but, to be frank, I was slightly apprehensive about the response in the U.S.S.R.: a nation doesn't obligatorily appreciate that its rebuked artists are rediscovered abroad.

Times were apparently ripe, however, for a happier ending. In a session of the Filmmakers Union in Moscow, Sergei Yutkevich himself invited his colleagues to applaud "our comrade Medvedkin, whose name has become the banner of the working class in France, fighting capitalism with the weapon of cinema." A clear overstatement, considering our small proletarian troop, which never exceeded twelve people, but a blessing for Alexander Ivanovich. It was for him the turn of the tide, suddenly he was remembered, honored, with all the material advantages that accompanied official favor in the U.S.S.R. The climax came when he was awarded a Lenin Prize (in '70, I think). The bottle tossed into the sea had been picked up, after all. But most important (for me, at least): Medvedkin was allowed to travel. With typical *muzhik* ingenuity, he persuaded the Documentary Studio that the source of stock shots for his next picture (on ecology) could only be found—in Paris. And so we saw ol' man Medvedkin among us, in 1971, ebullient and strong as the bear whose name his own contains (*medved*). With stolen film stock, borrowed editing table, friendly technicians and—last, not least—an Iranian cameraman, I managed to build up a short documentary called *Le Train en marche* (*The Train Rolls On*) in which, for the first time, Alexander Ivanovich told in his own words the whole story of the *Kinopoezd*. He had brought us the only remnants—in '71, that is—of the Train adventure: some twenty photographs, which I used gladly. But the film, moving as it is with that unique testimony (and which we used as an introduction to *Happiness*—for, taking advantage of our sudden honeymoon with Russian officialdom, we had obtained the distribution rights for France), remained for me a kind of trailer, the first draft of the real film I still longed to do—in an undefined future. So many things would have to change in the U.S.S.R. to make such a project possible.

Well, many things have changed. Medvedkin is dead, for one. Sad as it is, I dare say he died on time. I met him on my way back from Tbilisi in '88—both of us knew it was the last encounter—and he was beaming in the euphoria of pristine *perestroika*. "Telling the truth, asking people to participate, criticizing without fear, that's what we always wanted, that's what we tried to do in the days of the Train." He belonged to that rarest breed who had kept unspoiled the faith of his youth: the tragedy of all those bloodstained years was just the sort of trick History plays—but now the clouds had been wiped out, and *perestroika* was the way to achieve real, pure socialism. In a sense, he was *the last Bolshevik*. He played Mayakovsky's *Klop* (*The Bedbug*) in reverse: a genuine revolutionary artificially preserved to be shown "as it was" to an incredulous audience. One year more, and he would have watched the ruin of his hopes.

Another thing has changed: people talk. Many episodes of Medvedkin's life (and their social and political context) can be approached bluntly today, while not so long ago we had to satisfy ourselves with hints and hushes. Those six years of silence, for instance, at the peak of Stalin's reign before the war: he was very cagey about it, and I never wanted to use our friendship as a key to open doors he so clearly wanted to keep shut. In 1990 I found witnesses, starting with his daughter, who took care of him during the last years, after the death of his wife. It is at that point, brooding over that exemplary life span, that I started to conceive a new approach to this long-borne project: a *Citizen Kane*-like inquest whose purpose would be not so much to achieve a biography, however fascinating, but to draw the portrait of an era through the portrait of a man .

And finally, something exceptional happened: pieces of the Train film material were found. The discovery itself is part of the story, because it is after Medvedkin's new fame that a student of VGIK, Kolia Izvolov, decided to use his first professional years, not to start his own film career, but to dedicate himself to the research of these reputedly lost vestiges. They deliver only a partial view of the Train Saga, but nevertheless this is fresh material coming to us straight from 1932, never seen before, bringing traces of these years of collectivization which we knew only, cinematographically speaking, through the lyrical bias of *Old and New*, or the satirical treat of *Schastie*.

I am left with many questions concerning Medvedkin: as exceptional as his freedom of action was on the Train, how was his team perceived by the people at the bottom? Weren't they also, willy nilly, symbols of a hated central authority? Weren't they even manipulated by some, to hide the party line in a democratic shroud? When and how did he have to compromise? I grasp, around his trials, this typical Wellesian theme (from *Kane* to *Macbeth*): how far can one go along with Evil? All these questions, if they were only mine, would be futile, but I am sure they are shared by many who are not content with the present Manichaeism about Soviet history—as if between the Nomenklatura and the Dissidents, there were nothing but a shapeless crowd.

Fig. 10. Alexander Medvedkin and Chris Marker at the Moscow Film Festival in 1971.

In an interview by Pascal Aubier, at one moment Medvedkin turns to the camera and addresses me: "Chris, you lazy bastard, why don't you ever write to me, send me a letter, even that short . . ." and with two fingers he makes the gesture meaning "a little bit." I froze the image there, and blew it up until only the fingertips were visible, and said, "Dear Alexander Ivanovich, I couldn't tell you then all I wanted to. Now I can. And all I have to say about you and Russia will be much more than this little space embraces, but let's go . . ." That's my opening scene, and then follows the story of that time and of that man, the *Citizen Kane*-like inquest into the life of the Last Bolshevik whose Rosebud was a red flag.

ACKNOWLEDGMENTS

The book as conceived by Jay Leyda was above all Medvedkin's: *he* was the primary author, and *he* would be providing the principal texts for it from his personal archive. The book was to be the first major compilation of his writings in any language. The working title of the book, "The Bolshevik Satirist," sought to capture the ambiguity and paradox of Medvedkin's position in art and in life as both a committed Bolshevik and a searching satirist. The revolutionary—and simultaneously Bolshevik—nature of Medvedkin's practice was a second, related focus of the book, especially in the attention given to his Kino-Train work and to his attempts to change an audience's experience of viewing film and to make film a revolutionary instrument.

The compilation presented here is as much as possible the book Jay intended. I have benefited from the help and advice of several people who have been anxious to see the publication of a book preserving the memory of Medvedkin's achievement and originality. Generous scholarly assistance has been provided by Naum Kleiman and Nikolai Izvolov in Moscow and Robert Bird in Chicago. Susan Bielstien at the University of Chicago Press has been a wonderfully supportive editor; she understood the interest of Medvedkin's unorthodox film work and of Jay Leyda's contributions to scholarship. Her assistant James Toftness showed a welcome tact in the task I faced in transforming a sometimes refractory manuscript into a book; it was a pleasure to work with him. Marian Rogers, the copy editor assigned to the book by the press, was concerned to bring consistency of terminology and formatting to texts written over many years and for many different purposes; I am particularly grateful to her for the questions she raised challenging me to clarify the translation. I am responsible for the remaining inconsistencies and obscurities. I am grateful to Masha Bloshteyn, Pavel Erokhin, and Anna Makolkina in Toronto for suggesting corrections and improvements of the translations. Matt Peterson in New York provided much useful encouragement at a necessary time and sent me reports of his conversations with Chris Marker and transcripts of Marina Goldovskaia's filmed interviews with Medvedkin. I wish to remember

Bella Epshtein, who worked in the Foreign Section of the Union of Filmmakers in Moscow and who arranged the five meetings I had with Alexander Medvedkin in the last years of his life. I also wish to remember my mother, who introduced me to the work of translation; she was a Russian émigré, who later in life was haunted by childhood memories of the Civil War that followed the October Revolution and its aftermath; her experience was in many ways the obverse of Medvedkin's; she knew hunger and starvation, fear and terror; the men in her family disappeared—killed on the battlefield or executed.

My trips to the Soviet Union were subsidized by grants from the Social Sciences and Humanities Research Council of Canada and York University.

Nikita Lary

NOTES

PREFACE

1. Alexander Medvedkin, pers. comm. Unless other sources are specified, the quotes from Medvedkin in the preface are from notes I took during our conversations in May 1984, January 1985, and February 1988. The word *svoeobraznyi*, translated here as "unusual," could also be translated as "distinctive," or even "idiosyncratic."

2. Numbers in brackets refer to pieces selected for this compilation of Medvedkin's works and related materials.

3. This quotation and the next are from "Cavalry Days" [1].

4. The Kino-Train operated under the auspices of the Ministry of Heavy Industry, although it was formally part of the central agency for film production, Soiuzkino.

5. In the collection of the major documentary film archive at Krasnogorsk, thanks in particular to the investigations of Nikolai Izvolov. (See [20].)

6. *Kinovedcheskie zapiski* 61 (2002): 286.

7. According to R. Iurenev, *Aleksandr Medvedkin, Satirik* (Moscow, 1981), 65. He mentions other films from the vaults that were screened in this retrospective: Kozintsev and Trauberg's *New Babylon*, Ermler's *Fragment of an Empire*, and Kalatozov's *Salt of Svanetia*.

8. See Chris Marker's account in his article "The Last Bolshevik" [29]. The film has since become a mainstay of Soviet film retrospectives.

9. Medvedkin, "The Suppression of *Happiness*" [24]. In our conversations about this book Medvedkin made an exception for the 1957 comedy *Restless Spring*, saying he would have liked to have it sent abroad.

10. Medvedkin's first paid job was as a choirboy in a church. See Marina Goldovskaia, "Interviews with Medvedkin" [23], excerpt 5.

11. Nikolai Izvolov, *Kommentarii k fil'mu "Schast'e"* (Moscow: Hyperkino, 2012), 54.

1. CAVALRY DAYS

1. This piece focuses on Medvedkin's experiences in 1920–22. He said that he wrote it in 1948, when he had some spare time. In places in the text speaking of fifty years of persecution, Medvedkin must be referring either to his approximate age in 1948, or else to fifty years starting in 1922, in which case the text he provided for this book is a later revision of the one he wrote in 1948.

2. The anarchist Nestor Makhno was called "Father Makhno" by his devoted followers. Baron Wrangel was one of the leading White generals. The places mentioned are on the mainland at the base of the Crimean Peninsula, between the Dnepr River and the Black Sea and the Sea of Azov. Chongar inspired Medvedkin's choice of the name Chongara for his daughter.

3. The Commissar was the representative of the Party in the Army.

4. A reference to the Triple Entente—France, Great Britain, and Russia—which

fought Germany and its allies in World War I. Russia's participation in the Entente was ended by the October Revolution.

5. In Russian the omitted word that rhymes with the last syllable of the preceding line is the vulgar word for "prostitute."

6. A reference to Lord Curzon, who as British foreign secretary in 1919 proposed the Curzon Line, which was supposed to demarcate the boundary between Russia and Poland.

7. A *lubok* (pl. *lubki*) was a wood-block print or an engraving that combined images and text to tell stories about heroes, saints, animals, etc. The *lubki* enjoyed great popularity.

8. A *stanitsa*, a Cossack village, enjoyed its own political and military organization in pre-Revolutionary Russia.

9. Semen Budenny was commander of the 1st Cavalry Army, in which Medvedkin fought and worked (and about which he is writing here). Budenny was famous for his prowess with the cavalry sword. (In a conversation in 1984 about this compilation of his writings, Medvedkin spoke of Budenny as someone who later helped him in his time of difficulties. *NL*)

10. "Grotesque"—a term associated with Meyerhold's theater, with particular reference to its exaggerations of types and its juxtapositions of opposites, such as terror mixed with laughter.

11. "Blue Blouse" theater was a widespread form of agitprop in the twenties and early thirties in which actors dressed in the blue shirts and clothes of workmen dramatized workplace problems and larger political issues in performances combining theater, song and dance, and acrobatics.

12. The Archangel Michael in his capacity as Leader of the Heavenly Hosts (an example of Medvedkin's knowledge of the church's iconography and teachings).

13. Alexander Kerensky, head of the Provisional Government at the time it was overthrown by the Bolsheviks in the October Revolution of 1917.

14. Following the collapse of the Provisional Government, power passed to the Petrograd Soviet and to Soviets throughout the land, made up of representatives from the Social Revolutionary, Menshevik, and Bolshevik parties. Alexander Kolchak was a leading figure opposed to the Revolution; he assumed the title of Supreme Ruler of Russia, but in actual fact he only controlled parts of Siberia, and that only for a short period of time; and he failed to coordinate the White generals fighting against the Red Army. He was executed in 1920.

15. Political Commissar of the 1st Cavalry Army (and later a top Soviet official).

2. THE KINO-TRAIN: 294 DAYS ON WHEELS

1. Rich or relatively rich peasants, characterized here by opposition to the formation of collective farms and the attendant socialization of private property.

2. *Konkretnye nositeli zla*. A less rhetorically charged translation is "carriers of harm."

3. The youth division of the Communist Party, for people aged fourteen to twenty-eight.

4. The sovkhozes were state farms on large land tracts, allowing for the industrialization of agriculture.

5. The Five-Year Plans were directed at the rapid industrialization of the country and the transformation of agricultural production. They were associated with Stalin's establishment of central control. The First Five-Year Plan covered the years 1929–33; in 1932 it was proclaimed that the Plan had been fulfilled one year early.

6. In early discussions, film was promoted (and sometimes dismissively categorized) as an "art of illusion" (culminating in a "factory of dreams").

7. In conversation in 1984 Medvedkin stressed the difference between the Kino-Train and agit-trains, which had gramophones and singers with folk instruments. The latter had a prepared program, and did not directly deal with local life. The Kino-Train dealt with local issues. The Kino-Train counted on local people agreeing to participate in the films. It could do so because of people's eagerness to appear on-screen looking their best. Thus real-life "villains" willingly shaved and dressed up for screen roles in which they were exposed. *NL*

8. By the People's Commissar for Heavy Industry Sergo Ordzhonikidze.

9. In central Ukraine.

10. 30 Jan.–4 Feb. 1932.

11. Much-celebrated projects for steelmaking, hydroelectric-power generation, and heavy-machine production.

12. DonBas is shorthand for the basin of the Donets River, located in the Ukraine.

13. Presumably class war, besides the material shortages of every kind.

14. My translation of *massovik*. A mass agitator was entrusted with education and consciousness raising, focusing on specific workplace issues and a heightened political understanding. As Medvedkin makes clear in his discussion below, his agitators did not come with a ready-made understanding of all the issues, and enlisted the participation of workers in interpreting and generalizing the templates proposed in the films.

15. Kolkhozes, or collective farms, were a major focus of the Kino-Train's work (and are a major topic of this memoir). They were formed through the amalgamation of individual farms and the "socialization" of property, including livestock. Their formation was greatly accelerated under the First Five-Year Plan. They met with considerable resistance from peasants who did not want to give up their property, and faced internal problems of operation owing to kolkhoz members who exploited weaknesses in the Socialist organization of labor.

16. The Krivoi Rog Basin.

17. *Look What Love Did!* [10].

18. On this actor from Meyerhold's theater, see "Satire" [15], note 11.

19. An operetta or musical set in the Rockies and other Canadian locations, first performed on Broadway in 1924.

20. On Meyerhold's theater, see "Cavalry Days" [1], note 11; "Satire" [15], note 11.

21. The sovkhozes were much larger than the kolkhozes. The sovkhoz workers were more like industrial workers, receiving wages rather than the payments in cash and in kind (grain and other produce) given to kolkhoz members. The MTSes provided tractors and other farm machinery to the kolkhozes.

22. Presumably a reference to Lithuanian settlers who formed the kolkhoz.

23. Members of the Communist youth organization for boys and girls ten to fifteen years old.

24. *Tit* is script [9] in this compilation.

25. *Muzhik* was the common (often disparaging) term for "peasant" in pre-Revolutionary Russia.

26. In addition to "Satire" [15], note 11, see the description of Maslatsov's work in *The Hole* and in *Pitfalls* below, and the script *A Crazy Locomotive* [11], in which he had a major role.

27. In 1932.

28. See the discussion of this film in Nikolai Izvolov's article "Alexander Medvedkin and the Traditions of Russian Film [20].

29. Ivan Bolshakov.

30. Mikhail Kalinin, member of the Politburo, and the official head of state; Sergo Ordzhonikidze, also a member of the Politburo, and commissar for heavy industry.

31. Shoes made of linden bark or other plant fiber.

32. One pood is roughly equal to 36 lbs.

33. Jan Pilsudski was a younger brother of Jozef Pilsudski, the commander of the Polish army in the battle with the Soviet Union in 1919–21 and later a major player in the consolidation of Poland as an independent country. Jan Pilsudski was active in Polish politics.

34. The name for warrior heroes in medieval chronicles and legends.

35. The actual year was 1932.

36. The sorties led by Medvedkin ranged less widely; they were confined to the Ukraine.

37. It is more likely that the time Marker refers to is the period following the revolutionary demonstrations and expectations in France in May 1968 (vividly expressed in film in *Le vent d'est* (1970), made by the Dziga Vertov Group, comprising Jean-Luc Godard and Jean-Pierre Morin, in particular.

3. SOLDIERS SHOOTING FILMS

1. Known as the Eastern Front in histories of the Second World War written from the point of view of the Western Allied Powers. The defeat of the German forces at the Volga in the Battle of Stalingrad in January 1943 had marked a turning point in the war, following which the Red Army moved westward in fiercely fought battles that were part of a grand strategic scheme.

2. After the war Königsberg was made part of the Russian SFSR and renamed Kaliningrad. It is a territorial exclave of the current Russian Federation.

3. Here feet rather than the metric measure of length is used, presumably because of the markings on the cameras.

4. *A LITTLE LOG*

1. The four satirical film sketches shot in 1930 were all made for the newly formed central filmmaking organization Soiuzkino.

5. *STOP THIEF!*

1. Presumably kopeks rather than rubles.

6. *FRUIT AND VEGETABLES*

1. During the Civil War following the Revolution, Kolchak bore the title Supreme Ruler and Commander in Chief of All Russian Land and Sea Forces, until he was taken prisoner and executed in 1920.

2. A member of the Communist youth organization corresponding to the scouts.

7. *A COCK AND BULL STORY*

1. See "The Kino-Train: 294 Days on Wheels" [2], p. 28 and passim.

8. *HEY FOOL, WHAT A FOOL YOU ARE!*

1. At that time TsKK—the Central Control Commission of the Russian Communist Party (Bolshevik)—was engaged in the punishment of incompetents and reprobates and in the exposure of interlopers in the Party, and at times resorted to announcements in newspapers in order to seek them out. [Medvedkin's note]

The Fool's name, Ivan Ivanovich, is indicative of a typical, ordinary man, as John Smith is in English.

2. In those years economists of the Trotskyist school claimed that money was a remnant of capitalist society. They called for its immediate abolition and for the building of Socialism with clean hands, unsoiled by money! [Medvedkin's note]

9. *TIT*

1. A Kino-Train film made in 1932. In conversation in May 1984, Medvedkin said, "*Tit* is my most successful comedy," and then added, "most successful of all." *NL*

2. For 1929–33, declared fulfilled one year early, in 1932.

10. *LOOK WHAT LOVE DID!*

1. Another Kino-Train film. In this script Medvedkin directly introduces the name of the lead actor, Volodia (Vladimir) Maslatsov. (For more about him, "Satire" [15], note 11.)

11. *A CRAZY LOCOMOTIVE*

1. The First World War and the Civil War following the 1917 Revolution.

2. Again, Medvedkin's favorite actor, who played this role. See "Satire" [15], note 11.

12. "THE UNHOLY FORCE"

1. The first version of "The Unholy Force" script was written in 1935. It was Medvedkin's most ambitious exercise in the genre of satiric comedy. The making of the film was ordered stopped on the day before shooting was to begin. Medvedkin clung to a hope of completing the project for over forty years, and when he realized he no longer had the strength to undertake the work himself he was willing to entrust the film to other directors. During this time he subjected the script to multiple revisions. Jay Leyda selected this version of the script from the copies Medvedkin gave to him.

In this prefatory note, Medvedkin capitalizes the words "paradise," "hell," and "kingdom of heaven." For the most part, however, he follows Soviet convention and does not capitalize these terms or the word "God." The convention generally but not universally followed in this translation is to capitalize these words.

2. The film script has ambiguities that are forceful reminders that satire is a double-edged sword. It is a rejection of Christian doctrines written by a man who knows well the language of Russian Orthodox Church services and its enduring influence on the language and thought of the people. It is a celebration of sinful and rebellious man, who can find no happiness in the heavenly paradise, but who might also leave us with doubts as to whether he would accept any utopian order on earth.

3. The icons of the "primitive" Suzdal school had their own sophistication. Medvedkin's use of the rather dismissive term *bogomaz* is at odds with his generally favorable view of the work of the old icon painters.

4. A fortress on the Danube, an outpost of the Ottoman Empire, captured by the great general Suvorov in 1790.

5. According to Eastern Orthodox tradition, the doctrines and canons of the church were fully elaborated at seven ecumenical councils (the first in 325, and the last in 787). The Russian word for "council" is the same as for "cathedral" (*sobor*), and it is likely that the village priest, Evlampi, is confusing these two senses of the word.

6. Saint John the Warrior and Saint Simeon Stylites.

7. Epifani—Epiphanius; Cyril and Methodius—translators of the Scriptures and liturgical texts into Old Church Slavonic.

8. Possibly a reference to the warrior and ruler Ismail, who in the early sixteenth century established a kingdom in Azerbaijan and then extended it to Iran.

9. Leaders of peasant rebellions in the seventeenth and eighteenth centuries, respectively.

10. Kerensky, the leading politician in the Provisional Government set up after the February 1917 Revolution and prime minister from July of that year until the October Revolution.

11. Some of the first Soviet astronauts.

13. "GOGOL"

1. At the end of this piece, Medvdvedkin specifies the date as 8.1.41 (and gives Moscow as the place where he wrote it). Presumably this is 1 August 1941, after the start of the German attack on the Soviet Union, which led to the quick invasion of the Ukraine, where most of the last part of this piece is set.

2. In fact the monument was put up in 1909.

3. Someone who exceeded his work quotas many times over. Named after Aleksei Stakhanov, a coal miner who in 1935 mined fourteen times the quota for one shift.

4. Aleksandr Sergeevich was in fact the name and patronymic of the poet Pushkin.

5. An old-fashioned horse-drawn wooden carriage.

6. The Moscow Psychiatric Hospital No. 1.

7. The fair at Sorochinsk was an annual event and was also the title of a tale by Gogol.

8. These two characters are taken from Gogol's "Tale of How Ivan Ivanovich Quarreled with Ivan Nikiforovich."

9. A serf-owner in Gogol's *Dead Souls*, characterized by hoarding, meanness, and sloppy management of his estate.

10. Taras Shevchenko (1814–61) and Gogol (1809–52) were both born in the Ukraine. Shevchenko was a great advocate of the Ukrainian language as a literary medium, and Gogol, of Russian. Medvedkin is possibly suggesting that the same man would not want to commemorate both of these writers.

11. Semen Budenny, commander of the 1st Cavalry Army, in which Medvedkin fought. See "Cavalry Days" [1], note 9.

14. THE ELATION OF FIGHTING

1. The title is taken from a song inserted in Pushkin's little tragedy *Feast in a Time of Plague*. The song suggests that experiences of elation or ecstasy can also be had on stormy seas, in hurricanes, and during the plague.

2. See "The Kino-Train" [2], note 6.

3. Apart from a general reference here to the politically engaged filmmaking of Eisenstein, Dovzhenko, Pudovkin, Vertov, and others, there is a specific reference to Medvedkin's experiments with mobile film production and exhibition, which he describes in "The Kino-Train" [2].

4. See scripts [4], [5], [6], [7].

5. The Commissar of Enlightenment, in effect the minister responsible for culture and education.

6. Speech delivered to ARRK (the Association of Revolutionary Workers of Cinematography) in July 1931. Printed in "Kinematograficheskaia komediia i satira," *Proletarskoe kino*, 1931, No. 9, 4–15, 15. A slightly longer excerpt from this speech is included below in "Film Comedy and Satire" [19].

7. One copy fortunately did survive (but not a copy with the color sequence).

8. For the full review, see "Eisenstein on Medvedkin's Chaplinesque Genius" [18].

9. A dig at Grigori Aleksandov's *Jolly Fellows*.

10. The copy of the film Chris Marker saw in the Cinémathèque Royale de Belgique was probably part of an exchange with the Russian Film Archives (TsGALI). The film had been previously screened at the First Moscow International Film Festival in 1959 (according to statements by the Soviet film scholar Rostislav Iurenev). Thus a copy of the film had in fact survived in Russia.

11. The Central Committee of the Communist Party, with Ordzhonikidze, the Minister of Heavy Labor.

12. Marker's documentary, made in 1971, is about the Kino-Train experiment.

13. In particular, "The Unholy Force" [12].

15. SATIRE: AN ASSAILANT'S WEAPON

1. Beginning in 1928.

2. Entrepreneurs who prospered under the New Economic Policy, introduced by Lenin in 1921, which allowed for a limited reintroduction of private enterprise.

3. Three of the largest, much-celebrated industrial projects (a railway line linking central Asia and Siberia, a steel mill in the Urals, and the hydroelectric dam in the Ukraine that Medvedkin wrote about in "The Kino-Train" [2]).

4. See "The Kino-Train" [2], note 6.

5. An account of this experimental theater is given in "Cavalry Days" [1].

6. Leader of the White forces opposed to the Bolsheviks (with the titles of Supreme Ruler and Admiral). Captured and shot in 1920.

7. The acronym of the State Political Directorate, the secret police.

8. See "The Elation of Fighting" [14] and "Film Comedy and Satire" [19].

9. Soviet film was still essentially silent in 1931.

10. Nikolai Izvolov argues in his article in this book [20] that there is a pre-Revolutionary Russian tradition of filmmaking into which these films can be inscribed.

11. As an "eccentric" actor from Meyerhold's theater, Vladimir Maslatsov would have had training in pantomime, masks, and clowning, and in conventions for expressive action and movement rooted in acrobatics, gymnastics, and dance. Other aspects of Meyerhold's theater for which Medvedkin had an affinity were his experiments in breaking down the barrier between the stage and the audience and his use of circus and fairground attractions to restructure the space and time of the performance.

12. Scripts [4], [5], and [6].

13. *A Cock and Bull Story* [7].

14. *Hey Fool, What a Fool You Are!* [8].

15. See "Cavalry Days" [1].

16. Ugrium Burcheev—a tyrannical, arbitrary, and stupid governor in Saltykov-Shchedrin's 1870 novel, *The Story of a Town*.

17. A reference to Vladimir Blium's article "Vozroditsia li satira?" in *Literaturnaia gazeta*, 27 May 1929.

18. The room for this "positive factor" was further restricted during the institutionalization of Socialist Realist art, which came in the years following the controversies Medvedkin discusses here.

19. Referred to above, and also in "The Elation of Fighting" [14].

20. Here Medvedkin repeats the identical passage he selected for quotation in "The Elation of Fighting" [14] above, and accordingly it is omitted here.

16. BRONZE MONUMENTS

1. See "Cavalry Days" [1] and "Satire: An Assailant's Weapon" [15].

2. "Who Can Be Happy in Russia?"

17. SPRINGBOARDS

1. The Russian says literally: "FLAY AND APPROVE."

2. Composed in 1869–73, an epic poem about the attempt of seven peasants to find just one happy person in Russia.

3. From the novel *The Story of a Town* (the chapter "Roots of the Origins of the Fools-Town People").

4. See also "The Tale of How One Peasant Fed Two Generals." AM

18. EISENSTEIN ON MEDVEDKIN'S CHAPLINESQUE GENIUS

1. First published in 1968 in Sergei Eizenshtein, *Izbrannye proizvedeniia* (Moscow, 1964–71), 5:231–35.

2. According to an endnote in the collected edition of Eisenstein's writings, the other film was Ermler's *Peasants*.

3. Naum Kleiman says that this is a dig at Grigori Aleksandrov and his *Jolly Fellows* (also known as *Jazz Comedy*).

4. A film about a Red Army commander in the Civil War, made by the Vasiliev "brothers"' and released in 1934. Anecdotes about the hero quickly entered popular lore.

5. Alexander Dovzhenko and Eduard Tisse (according to lectures to his film students). In conversations with me in 1985, Medvedkin said that Dovzhenko was another strong admirer of the film and of "The Unholy Force."

6. With a huge pair of scissors.

7. A phrase in Marx and Engel's *Communist Manifesto*.

8. I.e., peasants opposed to collective ownership of property.

9. Eisenstein was writing before Chaplin made his more socialistic *Modern Times*, which came out in 1936 and for which Eisentein did not have to make allowance.

10. Eisenstein's major project for a comic film was "MMM," for which he wrote several scripts.

11. For Medvedkin's own enthusiasm about Saltykov-Shchedrin, see "Bronze Monuments" [16] and "Springboards" [17].

12. In the climactic scene in *Chapaev*, in which White Army soldiers under General Kappel advance on the hero, using shock-and-awe techniques.

19. FILM COMEDY AND SATIRE

1. Association of Workers of Revolutionary Cinematography.

2. Also published in Lunacharsky, "Kinematograficheskaia komediia i satira," *Proletarskoe kino*, 1931, No. 9, 4–15, 15. The greater part of the excerpt was also reproduced in "The Elation of Fighting" [14].

3. The actual release date was 1935.

20. ALEXANDER MEDVEDKIN AND THE TRADITIONS OF RUSSIAN FILM

1. With articles by the Formalists V. Shklovsky, Iu. Tynianov, and B. Eikhenbaum.

2. He also made his first films. See under the year 1927 in his "Second 'Autobiography'" [22].

3. A charitable organization for assistance to wounded soldiers, founded in 1904. It had an active film department.

4. One of the "Fathers" of Soviet film, best remembered for *The Extraordinary Adventures of Mr. West in the Land of the Bolsheviks* (1924) and *By the Law* (1926) and for his theoretical insights (the "Kuleshov effect") and writings. *The Breakthrough* was made in 1930.

5. Made in 1929; better known as *Old and New*.

6. A reference to a book by Tynianov, *Arkhaisty i novatory*, published in 1929.

7. Made in 1927.

8. A production of the Proletkult Theater in 1924.

9. FEKS—the "Factory" of the Eccentric Actor—was set up in 1921 by the directors Grigori Kozintsev and Leonid Trauberg in Leningrad.

10. The Isle of Buian was known in Slavic mythology (and Russian folklore and literature deriving from folklore) as the site of beneficent supernatural powers. The reference is to a scene in the film where the sorceress Uliana casts a spell in an attempt to get a cow to release her milk to the inept milker Varvara.

11. See the "Scripts" section of this book.

12. *Histoire générale du cinéma*, vol. 1 (Paris, 1946).

13. Russia's war against Napoleon's invading army.

14. The Ermoliev Studio was established in 1915, and existed until the nationalization of the film industry in 1919. Its logo was an elephant, and this elephant survives in the name Slonfilm (Elephantfilm) adopted by Medvedkin for his telegraphic address. In turn Marker took this name for the collective of filmmakers he formed with workers in Besançon in 1968.

15. See "Surviving Kino-Train Films" [27].

16. The sequence was probably shot with a two-color process. On the surviving copy of the film, from which the present copies and DVDs in circulation have been made, this sequence appears in black and white.

21. FIRST "AUTOBIOGRAPHY": A BOLSHEVIK'S CV

1. The name of the ruling Communist Party from 1925 to 1952, after which the parenthetic "of Bolsheviks" was dropped.

2. Renamed Stalingrad in 1925; now Volgograd.

3. The activities of the various Political Directorates referred to in this autobiographical summary included education and propaganda.

4. The main, central organization for film production, with a specially built film studio, completed in 1931 and subsequently called Mosfilm.

5. Owing to the war.

6. See "Soldiers Shooting Films" [3].

7. In actual fact the ruling Communist Party was called the All-Russian Communist Party (of Bolsheviks) between 1918 and 1925, before becoming the All-Union Communist Party (of Bolsheviks). The specification "of Bolsheviks" was a survivor from the split in the Russian Social Democratic Workers' Party between the Bolsheviks, led by Lenin, and the Mensheviks.

8. When? Possibly (?) an indication of some more direct action than he undertook in his Kino-Train films.

9. Medvedkin was twice ratified as Party secretary of Mosfilm, and seems to have satisfied the demands of both administrators and creative workers. He prided himself on his fairness in this role. In my first conversation with him in 1984, he said that he censured the director Ivan Pyriev for destroying part of a set constructed by Eisenstein because he needed the space for a set of his own. Moreover, in consequence, Pyriev was banned from the studio for one year. According to Naum Kleiman, the set in question

would have been the one for *Bezhin Meadov*, and the likely date was the end of 1936 or early 1937 (he could not, however, confirm Medvedkin's role in adjuducating this conflict).

22. SECOND "AUTOBIOGRAPHY": A FILMMAKER'S CV

1. A fuller account of this film is given in "The Kino-Train" [2].

2. This film has not survived. According to Jay Leyda (*Kino*, 3rd ed. [Princeton, NJ, 1983], 287), all Medvedkin's subsequent work "can be regarded as a continuation in that genre of satire and fantastic comedy."

3. Scripts [5], [6], [7], [8], and [9].

4. See "Satire" [15] and "Film Comedy and Satire" [15].

5. For Medvedkin's account of the Kino-Train, see [2].

6. *Look What Love Did!* [10].

7. See "Satire" [15], note 11.

8. Script [9].

9. A peasant characterized by a degree of material wealth, and later by opposition to the new kolkhozes, or collective farms.

10. From 1930 until his execution in 1938, Boris Shumiatsky, a Party operative, was the head of the country's film production, charged with major, often conflicting responsibilities: establishing central control over the studios and individualistic film directors; introducing planned industrial methods of film production in parallel with the industrialization of the economy under the Five-Year Plans; developing a cinema for the masses that was commercially successful; and, eventually, ensuring that films conformed to Stalin's chosen aesthetic doctrine of Socialist Realism, with its stress on positive heroes.

11. Script [12].

12. In conversations with me in 1985, Medvedkin said that he was being forced to make saccharine comedies with love triangles.

13. The Pioneers—the Communist organization corresponding to the Scouts in Western countries.

14. Finished and known as *New Moscow*.

15. For his relatively low opinion of this film, see the entry for 1955–56 below.

16. Ivan Bolshakov assumed control over the film industry in 1940, later holding the title of minister. He collaborated intimately with Stalin in deciding the fate (including the need for censorship) of each just-completed film at private screenings in the Kremlin.

17. The cameras were mounted on wooden stocks like those for guns. See "Soldiers Shooting Films" [3].

18. The low film production of these years was partly connected with the material shortages and difficulties following the war; more importantly, it was connected with a campaign stressing the need to portray positive characters and criticizing filmmakers for the use they had made of negative characters.

19. An official with major responsibilities in the field of propaganda and culture; later revealed to be the illegitimate son of Stalin.

20. The script with this name [13] is presumably an earlier version of the one described here.

21. A classic Socialist Realist novel by Nikolai Ostrovsky, first published serially in 1932 and 1934. The volume the girl is reading here would have been based on the 1936 edition, which more narrowly conformed to the now-codified Socialist Realist norms.

22. Still Bolshakov.

23. The Plan focusing on rebuilding the economy after the war (1946–50).

24. I.e., for the less-developed republics in the USSR.

25. A daily newsreel series.

26. This autobiographical summary, which runs to 1984, appears to have been revised and updated over several years. This comment evidently comes from an earlier version.

27. In conversation with me in 1984, he said that he would have liked to send this film abroad. *NL*

28. Emma Widdis devotes two chapters to the earlier "realistic comedies," making a strong case that in them comedy and outright satire subvert the idealist Soviet project. Widdis, *Alexander Medvedkin* (New York: Tauris, 2005).

29. Shown in English as *Forced Friendship*.

30. Presumably the motivation for making this film came from Mao's launching of the Cultural Revolution.

31. The Prague Spring.

23. MARINA GOLDOVSKAIA, INTERVIEWS WITH MEDVEDKIN

1. Marina Goldovskaia filmed a series of interviews with Medvedkin in 1988 with the intention of making a film about him. At this time, however, Medvedkin's health was failing, and Goldovskaia did not feel the interviews provided the material she needed to complete the film. She has kindly made the transcripts of the interviews available for this book. The excerpts are translated with light editing to eliminate some repetitions and incomplete phrases.

2. The peak year of the Great Terror. See also "Second 'Autobiography'" (1980, 1984) [22].

3. The State Military Film Organization.

4. Boris Zakharovich Shumiatsky, who had the principal responsibilities for film production.

5. Presumably in the suppressed film *Happiness* and the stopped film "The Unholy Force."

6. I.e., Ukrainian.

7. Marina Goldovskaia grew up in an apartment in the same building, in which Medvedkin still lived in 1988.

8. Kirill Shutko was a member of the Central Committee, in principle the ruling body of the Soviet Union. He had a particular interest in leftist film and art.

9. The All-Ukrainian Directorate of Film.

10. A sorcerer in Gogol's tale "Christmas Eve."

11. Published here [18]. The review was not in fact published until later, in the six-volume edition of Eisenstein's works.

12. Emma Widdis indicates that the silence was not total (*Alexander Medvedkin*, 33–34).

13. See "Soldiers Shooting Films" [3].

14. Published by Iskusstvo (Moscow) in 1987.

15. He had a good, powerful voice, and during his Kino-Train travels one group of villagers implored him to stay behind as their deacon. (From conversations with Medvedkin; *NL*)

16. In the event, Gorky did not get to finish this work, which had been conceived as a series of novels.

17. Gorky's name and patronymic.

18. In conversations with me in 1985, Medvedkin said that Gorky, who could see anything he wanted, had seen *Happiness* three or four times. He also said that the other person Gorky showed it to was André Gide. *NL*

19. In 1936.

24. THE SUPPRESSION OF *HAPPINESS*

1. A note at the top of the page indicates this was published in the French press, although it does not say where.

2. See Goldovskaia, "Interviews with Medvedkin" [23], excerpt 8.

3. The note breaks off here. The explanation is no doubt best laid out in his writings on satire ([14], [15]).

4. See Goldovskaia, "Interviews with Medvedkin" [23], note 1.

25. COLOR FILM IN *HAPPINESS*

1. In another respect, however, the filmmaking technique used in *Happiness* was out of date. In conversations in 1985 Medvedkin noted that it was the last silent film made in the Soviet Union, and that it was screened with a piano accompaniment. *NL*

26. THE KINO-TRAIN FILMOGRAPHY

1. Medvedkin's other film work is documented in his "Second 'Autobiography' " [22]. A formal filmography has been published in *Kinovedcheskie zapiski* 49 (2000): 86–115.

2. I have revised Jay Leyda's translation in light of the account of the films Medvedkin gives in "The Kino-Train" [2], and made some changes of film titles to ensure consistency of translation. In some cases Medvedkin appears to refer to the same film by different titles; I have kept the different titles in translation. *NL*

3. *Look What Love Did!* [10] in the "Scripts" section.

4. Translated as *Let's Organize Production Links* in "The Kino-Train" [2] and in "Surviving Kino-Train Films" [27].

27. SURVIVING KINO-TRAIN FILMS

1. Corresponds to *For the Assembly Line* in "The Kino-Train Filmography" [26].

2. Nikolai Izvolov has confirmed that the description of *Kino-Gazette* No. 4 Medvedkin gives here is wrong. The film is about locomotives and not about harvesting. Medvedkin did not view the rediscovered films, and his memory in this instance was faulty.

28. HISTORY OF *THE ALEXANDER MEDVEDKIN READER*

1. From the draft of a letter (undated, probably 1984) to Maud Wilcox, a book editor, who was interested in the book. The "us" in the letter refers to Medvedkin, Michael Heim (the designated translator), and Jay Leyda.

2. The same undated draft of a letter.

3. In an e-mail to me dated 1 August 2009. *NL*

4. In the same e-mail, Matt Peterson wrote: "He said contributing to Medvedkin's 'rediscovery' was his proudest achievement as a filmmaker."

5. Letter dated 17 January 1985.

6. Letter dated 12 February 1985.

7. Letter dated 17 January 1985.

8. Letter dated 21 April 1984.

9. In notes about the book left by Jay Leyda.

29. THE LAST BOLSHEVIK

1. *Cineaste* 33, no. 4 (Fall 2008): 17–18.

2. Just before he died in 1988, Jay Leyda was working on a monumental Medvedkin anthology, including his diary of the train, scripts from the movies, and lots of critical pieces. Then he passed away, and I never heard anything further about the project, as if it never existed. A true mystery. If anyone has any information about this, or knows the whereabouts of Leyda's Medvedkin materials, please contact me c/o *Cineaste*.

GLOSSARY

AGIT-TRAINS OR AGITPROP TRAINS. Trains that in the immediate post-Revolutionary years carried the message of Communism deep into the country by means of posters, leaflets, books, speakers, gramophones, theatrical pieces, and films. Their programs and materials were basically prepared in advance. Medvedkin saw the work of these trains as very different from that of his Kino-Train in 1932. The Kino-Train was charged with addressing workplace and production issues in specific locations. People directly involved in the predicaments participated in the making of films about the issues, and also in discussing the films and, ultimately, in the resolution of problems with the help of the films.

ARRK. Association of Revolutionary Workers of Cinematography (first called ARK—Association of Revolutionary Cinematography), 1924–35. The association was founded by leading directors, including Eisenstein, Pudovkin, and Kuleshov, with a view to mobilizing filmmakers as effective fighters for Communism.

"ART OF ILLUSION." In this translation a term used to describe the film tradition from which Medvedkin broke away. Medvedkin uses various terms, including "film of illusion" and sometimes simply "illusion" (Russ. *illiuzion*). Illusion was fundamental to film, which provided an illusion of movement in space and through time. Because of the possibilities of playing with space and time, altered, imagined, and fantastic movement of people and objects could be readily created. The affinity of film with dreams was recognized as part of its allure. The dynamics of illusion were readily extended into films with escapist sentimental plots with wide popular appeal. Films from abroad entrenched this dominant tradition. The challenge it posed to revolutionary Soviet filmmakers was to find whether film could be redirected so that it dealt with and participated in the construction of a new reality.

BOGATYR. A heroic figure or warrior in traditional tales and poems, and in particular in *byliny*.

BYLINA (pl. BYLINY). An epic poem or song from the folkloric tradition, featuring heroic fighters, and sometimes saints, giants, and monsters.

ECCENTRISM. Began as a movement in theater rejecting the naturalism that had come to dominate theater in the nineteenth century. It looked to older forms of popular theater including clowning, acrobatics, mime, and commedia dell'arte, in an attempt to break down the "fourth wall" that separated the actors from the audience in naturalistic theater (and confined theater to a specific kind of building). Some of the leading directors associated with these experiments were Meyerhold, Kozintsev and Trauberg (with FEKS, the Factory of the Eccentric Actor), and Eisenstein (in the Proletkult Theater). These experiments found further development in Soviet film in the mid- and late twenties. "Eccentric" actors were noted for their training in expressive movement, acrobatics, song, and dance and for their ability to perform theatrical acts or "attractions" with an immediate impact on spectators.

FELLOW TRAVELERS. Supporters of Communism who were not usually Party members. The term indicates their possible unreliability.

FIVE-YEAR PLANS. The Five-Year Plans were designed to implement the policy of rapid industrialization of the country, along with the transformation of agriculture, and were associated with the establishment of a centrally planned economy. In the agricultural sector, collective farming was the new basis for production; apart from anticipated economies of scale, it would allow for a readier diversion of resources to serve the needs of industrial workers and urban dwellers. The First Five-Year Plan covered the years 1929–33, and was declared fulfilled one year early.

GOSVOENKINO. The State Military Film Organization, a film production company attached to the army.

GPU. State Political Directorate. The name of the secret police in 1922–23, with Felix Dzerzhinsky as its head. It was charged with ensuring "socialist legality."

KOLKHOZ. The kolkhozes were farms formed through the amalgamation and collectivization of peasant holdings. The movement to form collective farms became official policy under the First Five-Year Plan (1929–33); collectivization was enforced, and was met with considerable resistance from peasants. Kolkhoz workers were paid in kind and in cash from the farm's production and earnings.

KOMSOMOL. The junior branch of the Communist Party, for persons aged from fourteen to twenty-eight.

KULAK. In general, a rich or relatively rich peasant. In Soviet discourse in the twenties and thirties a kulak typically opposed collectivization of his property and the formation of collective farms (going so far as to destroy his farm animals rather than hand them over to the collective). Khmyr, in Medvedkin's film *Happiness*, is a poor peasant who in the beginning aspired to enjoy the benefits of property in the same way as a kulak. Inside the collective he worked halfheartedly, until he witnessed the wanton destructiveness of kulaks.

LUBOK (pl. LUBKI). A traditional wood-block print or engraving, combining images and text, used to tell stories about heroes, saints, animals, etc.

MASS AGITATOR. A person entrusted with the education and consciousness raising of ordinary people, focusing on specific workplace issues and a heightened political understanding of the problems facing the country.

MTSes, or MACHINE-AND-TRACTOR STATIONS. Depots providing tractors and other machinery to kolkhozes, along with repair and maintenance services. The kolkhozes depended on them for equipment they could not have afforded.

NEP. The New Economic Policy (1921–28) reintroduced a limited form of capitalism designed to allow the economy to recover from the toll of war and revolution (World War I, the October Revolution, and the Civil War). Small entrepreneurs were allowed; confiscations of agricultural produce ceased. "NEPmen" was the designation for men who had conspicuously profited from the new policy.

OBLAST. A region, usually with a formal administrative significance.

OLD BOLSHEVIK. The name for a Communist who joined the Party before the October Revolution.

PIONEERS. Members of the Communist youth organization corresponding to the scouts, aged ten to fifteen.

POOD or PUD. A measure of weight equal to approximately 36 pounds.

PUR, PURKKA. Political Directorate of the Workers and Peasants Red Army. It was charged with political education of the soldiers in accordance with the Party line.

SHOCK-WORKERS. Workers dedicated to exceeding their production norms. *See* stakhanovite.

SOIUZKINO. The main, central organization for film production, established in 1930. It had a specially build film studio that was designed to rival Hollywood's facilities and was completed in 1931. The studio subsequently became Mosfilm.

SOVKHOZ. A form of large-scale collective farming introduced on state-held land (including confiscated estates). The sovkhozes were much larger than the kolkhozes and were meant to be models for the industrialization of agriculture. They employed landless rural workers, who were paid wages in the same way as industrial workers.

STAKHANOVITE. A worker who sought to emulate Alexei Stakhanov, a miner who supposedly extracted fourteen times his quota of coal in a single shift.

VERST. A Russian unit of length, slightly greater than one kilometer.

VGIK. The All-Union State Institute of Cinematography. It can claim to be the first and most important film school in the world. The pioneering Soviet filmmakers who taught there included Kuleshov, Dovzhenko, and Eisenstein. VGIK played a major role in the development of film in the USSR. Its current name is the All-Russian State University of Cinematography.

INDEX

Page numbers in italics refer to illustrations.